Strategic Choices for a Changing Health Care System

THE BAXTER HEALTH POLICY REVIEW
VOLUME II

Strategic Choices for a Changing Health Care System

Edited by
Stuart H. Altman
Uwe E. Reinhardt

Health Administration Press
Chicago, Illinois   1996

DEVELOPED UNDER THE AUSPICES
OF THE ASSOCIATION FOR HEALTH SERVICES RESEARCH

00 99 98 97 96   5 4 3 2 1

Library of Congress Cataloging-in-Publication Data

Strategic choices for a changing health care system / edited by Stuart H. Altman, Uwe E. Reinhardt.
    p. cm. — (The Baxter health policy review : v. 2)
    "Research synthesis developed under the auspices of the Foundation for Health Services Research."
    Includes bibliographical references (p.) and index.
    ISBN 1-56793-040-9 (alk. paper)
    1. Health care reform—United States. 2. Medical policy—United States. I. Altman, Stuart H. II. Reinhardt, Uwa E. III. Series.
RA395.A3S854 1996
362.1'0973—dc20   96-2630
                                                                                CIP

Health Administration Press
A division of the Foundation of the
   American College of Healthcare
   Executives
1 North Franklin Street
Suite 1700
Chicago, Illinois 60606
(312) 424-2800

The Foundation for Health
   Services Research
1130 Connecticut Avenue, NW
Suite 700
Washington, DC 20036
(202) 223-2477

Contents

Acknowledgments

Work on this book, *Strategic Choices for a Changing Health Care System,* encompassed an extraordinary time in our nation's health policy history, spanning in less than 24 months the heralded unveiling of the Clinton reform plan, its crashing defeat, and the rise of a whole new thinking about the organization and financing of health care. The past two years have been marked by major retrenchment in federal health spending, devolution of power from Washington to the states and the private sector, and the accelerated growth of market-based principles. Living through this remarkable, rapid cycle of events presented, on the one hand, a major challenge to all of us involved in the writing of this volume; but it also added a special energy and sense of purpose to produce one of the first books to help front-line decision makers understand the evolution and implications of the new structure of the health care enterprise.

The authors and other contributors to this book had large shoes to fill. *Improving Health Policy and Management: Nine Critical Research Issues for the 1990s,* the first volume of The Baxter Health Policy Series, sold over 4000 copies. The book was awarded the American College of Healthcare Executives' James A. Hamilton Book-of-the-Year Award and the *American Journal of Nursing*'s Book-of-the-Year Award.

This volume has benefited from the encouragement, time, and expertise of many people. First words of thanks must go to The Baxter Foundation, in Deerfield, Illinois, for their generous support of this volume. Pat Morgan, executive director at The Baxter Foundation, brought to this effort not only valuable guidance and encouragement but also the prescience to realize that the responsibility for health care change would fall increasingly on those working at the community level in a diversity of settings. It is to these actors and decision makers that the book is primarily directed. Over the years, both The Baxter Foundation and Pat Morgan have shown an admirable dedication and commitment to supporting projects designed to recognize the importance of health policy research in informing the national discourse on health care policies and programs.

We owe immeasurable thanks and gratitude to Alice Hersh, executive vice president and chief executive officer at the Association for Health Services Research (AHSR), for contributing so much to the vision of this project and for lending her extraordinary experience and expertise to many aspects of the book's development, content, and organization.

The editors are deeply indebted to Marion Ein Lewin, director of Health Policy Programs and Fellowships at the Institute of Medicine, National Academy of Sciences, who served as the project officer for this effort. It was Marion's thankless task to make a group of perennially distracted eagles fly in formation. Without her gentle but persistent prodding throughout this project, the book would not have come about. As a skilled and well-known writer in health policy, she made significant contributions to the task of editing the papers in this volume and, thereby, to the overall quality of the book.

Enormous gratitude goes to Linda Humphrey for her superb editing help throughout the project. We are willing to wager that Linda knows this manuscript almost by heart, having read the various chapters again and again as they continued to be revised here and there to reflect the latest turn of events in the national health care debate. Through it all she remained good-natured and always helpful.

We are most appreciative to Walter McNerney who served as the chair of the advisory committee for both of the Baxter volumes. Under his wise leadership, the committee identified the major focus of the book and the priority themes to be addressed. Sincere thanks and appreciation are also expressed to the entire advisory committee: Stuart Altman, Linda Bergthold, Helen Darling, Chip Kahn, Janet Kline, Bob Patricelli, Uwe Reinhardt, Diane Rowland, and Steve Shortell.

Special gratitude is extended to those who served as reviewers for each of the chapters in the book. Their helpful and insightful reviews and suggestions contributed significantly to the quality and relevance of the final product. We are indebted to Don Berwick, Helen Darling, Gerben DeJong, Lynn Etheredge, Pierre Galletti, Jeffrey Geller, David Helms, Michael Johns, Stan Jones, Janet Kline, Gerald Laubach, Lauren LeRoy, Kathy Lohr, Joe Onek, Mark Pauly, Howard

Rabinowitz, Diane Rowland, Gail Warden, Alan Weil, Burt Weisbrod, and Paul Willging.

We also want to express very special thanks to Linda Kirk Dinga, administrative officer at AHSR, for an outstanding job in coordinating the many critical details of this project with great expertise and effectiveness. We also want to express gratitude to Valerie Tate Jopeck, program associate at the Institute of Medicine, for her valuable assistance and gracious help.

Last, but not least, we wish to record our deep appreciation to Daphne Grew, Nancy Puckett, and Kathleen Malone Prantner at Health Administration Press for their expert guidance and support in coordinating the final production of this book.

Editors
Stuart Altman

Uwe Reinhardt

List of Figures

List of Tables

List of Acronyms and Abbreviations

AAHC	Association of Academic Health Centers
ACG	Ambulatory Care Group
AHCCCS	Arizona Health Care Cost Containment System
AHCPR	Agency for Health Care Policy and Research
AHPs	Accountable Health Plans
BHCAG	Business Health Care Action Group (Minnesota)
CABG	Coronary artery bypass graft
CalPERS	California Public Employee Retirement System
CBER	Center for Biologics Evaluation and Research
CBO	Congressional Budget Office
CDC	Centers for Disease Control and Prevention
CDER	Center for Drug Evaluation and Research
CDRH	Center for Devices and Radiological Health
CHPAs	Community Health Purchasing Alliances (Florida)
CNM	certified nurse midwife
COGME	Council on Graduate Medical Education
CON	certificate of need
CPI	consumer price index
CQI	Continuous Quality Improvement
DCGs	Diagnostic Cost Groups
DNR	Do Not Resuscitate
DoC	Department of Commerce

DRG	diagnosis-related group
DUR	drug utilization review
EAPs	Employee Assistance Plans
ELA	establishment license application
ERISA	Employee Retirement and Income Security Act
ESP	Economic Stabilization Program (1971)
ESRD	End-Stage Renal Disease
FDA	Food and Drug Administration
FD&C	Food, Drug and Cosmetic (Act of 1938)
FEHBP	Federal Employee Health Benefits Program
FFS	fee-for-service
GAO	General Accounting Office
GDP	gross domestic product
GHAA	Group Health Association of America
GMENAC	Graduate Medical Education National Advisory Committee
GPOs	group purchasing organizations
GPWWs	group practices without walls
HCFA	Health Care Financing Administration
HCTI	Health Care Technology Institute
HCUP	Health Care for the Uninsured Program (Robert Wood Johnson Foundation)
HEDIS	Health Plan Employer Data and Information Set
HI	Hospital Insurance (trust fund)
HIAA	Hospital Insurance Association of America
HIE	Health Insurance Experiment (RAND)
HIPC	Health Insurance Plan of California Health Insurance Purchasing Cooperative
HMO	Health Maintenance Organization
HSA	Health Security Act (Clinton administration)
ICD-9-CM	*International Classification of Diseases,* Ninth Revision, Clinical Modification
IDE	Investigational Drug Exemption
IDS	integrated delivery system
IMGs	international medical graduates

IND	Investigational New Drug (application for treatment program)
IOM	Institute of Medicine
IPAs	independent practice associations
IRS	Internal Revenue Service
ISNs	Integrated Service Networks
JCAH	Joint Commission for the Accreditation of Hospitals (pre-August 1987)
JCAHO	Joint Commission for the Accreditation of Healthcare Organizations
JTPA	Job Training Partnership Act
MBHC	Managed Behavioral Health Care
MEWAs	multiple-employer welfare arrangements
MFN	Most Favored Nation
MSAs	Medical Savings Accounts Metropolitan Statistical Areas
MSOs	management service organizations
NAIC	National Association of Insurance Commissioners
NCQA	National Committee on Quality Assurance
NCS	National Comorbidity Survey
NDA	new drug approval (application for)
NIH	National Institutes of Health
NPPs	nonphysician providers
OBRA	Omnibus Budget Reconciliation Act (of 1981, 1993)
ODS	Organized Delivery System
OECD	Organization for Economic Cooperation and Development
OIG	Office of the Inspector General (of U.S. Department of Health and Human Services)
OTA	(U.S. Congress) Office of Technology Assessment
PACS	Payment Amount for Capitated Systems
PBM	pharmacy benefits management (companies)
PCCM	primary care case management
PET	positron emission tomography
PHOs	physician-hospital organizations
PhRMA	Pharmaceutical Research and Manufacturers of America

PHS	Public Health Service
PLA	product license application
PMA	premarket approval (application for)
POS	point-of-service
PPRC	Physician Payment Review Commission
PPO	preferred provider organization
PPS	prospective payment system under Medicare
PSRO	Professional Standards Review Organization(s)
P&T	pharmacy and therapeutics
PTCA	percutaneous transluminal coronary angioplasty
QMB	Qualified Medicare Beneficiary (1989 program)
RBRVS	Resource Based Relative Value Scale
RWJF	Robert Wood Johnson Foundation
SIC	Standard Industry Classification
SMDA	Safe Medical Devices Act (of 1990)
SSA	Social Security Administration
SSDI	Social Security Disability Insurance
SSI	Supplemental Security Income under Social Security
TEFRA	Tax Equity and Fiscal Responsibility Act (of 1982)
TQM	Total Quality Management
USIMG	international medical graduates (U.S. citizens)

Introduction

Where Does Health Care Reform Go from Here? An Unchartered Odyssey

Stuart H. Altman
Uwe E. Reinhardt

When first drafts of the chapters in this volume were being written, the nation was still in the midst of a fierce debate over the reform of the health care system. The second drafts came in several months after the demise of government-led health care reform in the fall of 1994. Now, as the volume is being published, the Clinton health plan and the many alternatives before the Congress in 1994 are scenes from a seemingly distant past. Issues such as whether to mandate that all employers offer and pay for health insurance coverage for full-time workers, how to control total health care spending with some form of national health care budget, and whether to expand the benefits offered to Medicare and Medicaid recipients are never mentioned. If Martians visited Earth today and obtained their information only from the media, they would conclude that most Americans have secure health insurance and that only the Medicare and Medicaid programs have a problem with the cost of health care. The visitors would be completely unaware that over 41 million Americans remain uninsured, that their ranks are growing, and that the health care safety net that provides a form of catastrophic protection for all Americans may be in trouble.

In the aftermath of the health care reform wars of 1992–1994, it may be worth recalling what started these wars, why the United States chose not to move aggressively to solve its health care problems, what problems this lack of action left in its wake, and what future battles are brewing. A broad retrospective and overview is the purpose of this foreword.

The Road to Health Care Reform

In 1990, an international poll conducted jointly by Louis Harris and Associates and the Harvard School of Public Health yielded some startling findings, findings that were widely discussed in the media.[1] Large random samples of adults in ten nations were asked which of the following three statements most nearly described their view of their own nation's health care system:

1. On the whole, the health care system works pretty well, and only minor changes are necessary to make it work better.

2. There are some good things in our health care system, but fundamental changes are needed to make it work better.

3. Our health care system has so much wrong with it that we have to rebuild it completely.

Responses to this survey indicated that only about 10 percent of the American respondents felt in 1990 that the U.S. health care system worked pretty well and needed only minor changes. Close to 60 percent felt that fundamental changes in the system were needed, and 29 percent called for a complete rebuilding of the system. Even more startling was the finding that citizens in other nations, although not overwhelmingly happy with their health care systems, certainly gave them much higher marks.

It was survey results such as these that pushed candidate, and later president, Bill Clinton to rank the problems of the U.S. health care system among the most pressing in the nation. It was often said that Bill Clinton was prepared to "stake his presidency" on his ability to draft and pass meaningful reform and restructuring of the nation's health care system. Yet it all went for naught. Why?

Much has been written about the complexity of the Clinton plan; some have said that the Republicans decided not to compromise and instead turned the issue of health care against the president; others allege that small employers and the health insurance industry distorted the issues and sabotaged the plan.

But we need not look under these political rocks to understand why no form of comprehensive reform was passed. Another set of survey results published at about the same time resulted in some very different, though not contradictory, findings.

Americans were queried on their feelings about the health care they had *personally* received in recent years. Eighty-five to 90 percent of the respondents declared themselves either "very satisfied" or "somewhat satisfied" with their personal health care.[2] That sentiment was expressed uniformly across income classes and was independent of whether the respondent was privately insured or covered by Medicare or Medicaid. Even two-thirds of the respondents without any insurance coverage at all declared themselves either "very" or "somewhat" satisfied with the quality of the health care they personally had received.

Concern over cost

A sensible inference suggested by these seemingly contradictory findings is that Americans were not dissatisfied with their health care *delivery* system, nor even with their own, personal health *insurance* coverage. They were upset chiefly by the *cost* of their care. When considering "cost," Americans focus both on their own family's out-of-pocket cost and on the cost of the system as a whole. The growth in total system cost had been deplored in the media in terms of the ever growing percentage of U.S. gross domestic product (GDP) devoted to health care. As the authors of the opinion surveys concluded: "Americans are dissatisfied with the cost of their health care, but happy with the access and with the quality of the care they receive."[3] While the Clinton plan was designed to combat the cost growth problem, fear that such actions would erode the ability of most individuals currently insured to obtain care, or that the quality of the care received would be diminished, pushed many initial supporters of the plan to question its value.

Economists have never been able to determine just what percentage of GDP a nation should spend on health care or, for that matter, on any other good or service. But even if one cannot judge a particular level of spending as too high or too low, one certainly can say something about the sustainability of a long-term trend. By the late 1980s, it had become clear that the level at which American health care spending was projected was not sustainable. If the historical differential of 3 percentage points between the annual growth of health

care spending and the growth in the rest of the GDP continued unabated into the twenty-first century, the nation would be spending
over half of its GDP on health care by 2050.

Also, it had not gone unnoticed in policy circles and in the media
that no other industrialized nation spent anywhere close to as much
on health care as did the United States during the 1980s. By 1990, no
other nation spent more than 10 percent of its GDP on health care.
Furthermore, most other nations had been able to keep the ratio of
health care spending to total GDP at more or less the same level, without visible ill effects on their populations' overall health status.

Concern over quality

It is now well known that significant differences exist between the
amount of health care provided to similar population groups in different regions of the country. Studies by Wennberg and Freeman
showed that residents of Boston, Massachusetts were 2.3 times as
likely as residents of New Haven, Connecticut to undergo a carotid
endarterectomy, 1.75 times as likely to have a knee replacement, and
1.5 times as likely to have a hip replacement.[4] Looking at Medicare
and focusing on a selected number of diagnostic and surgical procedures, Holohan and coauthors[5] found substantial differences in the
use rate of such procedures across metropolitan statistical areas. Only
a small portion of these variations could be explained by factors such
as the age, sex, and morbidity of the Medicare population. The most
powerful factor behind the variances appeared to be the supply of
medical specialists in the different geographical areas.

The medical profession was unable to explain these variations of
medical practice patterns in terms of the health status of the populations or in terms of differences in medical outcomes. Although the
general public believed that the quality of American health care is
second to none in the world, the health services research community
and the policymakers it informs became convinced that the clinical
theories on which physicians developed their treatment strategies
were more brittle than had hitherto been supposed—that the quality
of American health care was not uniformly high and, most certainly,
that its cost-effectiveness was not ideal.

This development had two important consequences for advocates of health care reform. First, significant variations in the per capita use of health care, unrelated to differences in outcomes, under-

mined the traditional argument that reductions in health care spending would inevitably entail commensurate reductions in the quality of health care. It became clear that this argument could no longer be used to derail any serious attempt at cost containment. Second, the Clinton health care reformers used the data to help develop a cost-containment strategy centered on encouraging Americans to join "managed care" plans, with their promise of lowering and standardizing utilization rates across areas. This approach would be backed up by areawide budgeting systems tied to an overall national spending target.

In hindsight it is clear that the health care reformers missed the mark on what the American people would accept in the form of change, particularly change that was orchestrated by government. In reality, many of these changes were already occurring in the private sector, not mandated by laws or regulations but fueled, instead, by economic forces. As it turned out, these economic forces were much more powerful and enduring than any legislative proposals.

Concern over the insurance system

Concern over the cost and quality of health care were not the only source of widespread public dissatisfaction with the U.S. health care system. The structure of the nation's health insurance system was also viewed as having a number of serious shortcomings.

First, the system links health care coverage for most privately insured Americans to a particular job in a particular company. Coverage is lost if that job is lost. While Americans tended to give their insurance coverage relatively high marks, the prospect of job loss during the economic stagnation of the late 1980s created anxiety even among the insured. Americans, survey results suggested, yearned for insurance coverage that could be carried from job to job and that would continue to be available if they became unemployed.

Second, persons not covered by employment-based health insurance, or by Medicare and Medicaid, found it difficult and sometimes impossible to procure adequate insurance coverage on their own. Throughout the 1980s the number of Americans who, at any point in time, were without health insurance grew steadily, a trend that continues unabated to this day. By the late 1980s, the uninsured population numbered between 33 and 37 million. Although about half tended to remain uninsured for less than a year, millions found themselves permanently without coverage, either because they worked at low wages for small companies that did not provide health insurance, or because they were unemployed.

To be uninsured, of course, has never meant that one goes without health care. Although uninsured individuals and their family members usually go without the preventive and routine curative care that the well-insured take for granted, they are able to obtain needed care at times of acute illness. Thus, it can be said that the United States does have a form of universal *catastrophic* health insurance even for low-income uninsured Americans who are unable to pay for their care. The problem is that this tacit insurance system is awkwardly financed and widely viewed as unfair. From the viewpoint of providers, the cost of that "uncompensated" care has to be recovered from paying patients. Medicare and Medicaid pick up part of these costs in the form of "disproportionate share payments" and extra payments to certain institutions (e.g., teaching and rural hospitals). But much of the financial burden is passed on to private payers in the form of higher charges. In essence, a hidden national health insurance tax is levied on the insured public. These cost shifts have come to be increasingly resented by private insurance carriers and the employers who bear the costs. They argue that if American society wishes to give the poor access to subsidized health care, it should be paid for directly with honest and above-board taxation.

Added to the bill of the privately insured are the extra costs incurred by hospitals and other health care providers that accept Medicare and Medicaid payments below actual costs. Without delving into the issue of whether the government programs pay too little, or whether the costs incurred by the health care provider are too high, it is sufficient to recognize that such a shortfall exists and that it is paid for by private payers. The Prospective Payment Commission estimated that for hospital care alone these extra costs or hidden tax amounted to $26 billion in 1992.[6]

Another troublesome aspect of the U.S. insurance system is the practice of basing the premiums charged individuals or small employers on the health status of these individuals or small groups. It is a practice known in the trade as "experience rating" or "actuarially fair pricing." In the absence of a mandate on every household to obtain health insurance coverage, or on every insurance company to charge the same rate to all enrollees (community rating), an individual insurance company competing on price simply cannot avoid charging such actuarially fair premiums. Without the ability to experience rate, groups who are relatively healthy will seek coverage from other carriers, who will charge them less. The insurance company that charges the same to all comers will be left with the sickest members of the community. It would not take long, under such a situation, for the entire system to destabilize.

For many households, premiums that seem "fair" to economists and actuaries may represent a major financial burden. For chronically ill individuals, actuarially fair premiums may become prohibitive. Consequently, in the eyes of the public, actuarially fair premiums tend to be viewed as asocial. When the public thinks of the catch-all term "insurance reform," it invariably thinks of prohibiting the practice of linking premiums directly to the health status of the individual, or excluding coverage for preexisting medical conditions. The clamor for health insurance reform grew loud during the latter part of the 1980s and did not go unnoticed by politicians.

A final perceived shortcoming of the U.S. health insurance system is the large share of private insurance premiums that go to marketing, administration, and the profits of insurance carriers. In general, the larger the pool of "insured lives" for which a single policy is written, the lower the share of the premium absorbed by administration, marketing, and profits. It is simply a matter of economies of scale. Large public insurance programs such as Medicare and Medicaid typically devote over 96 percent of their funds to payment for health care. For private policies covering 10,000 or more insured lives, the ratio tends to be between 90 and 95 percent. But for policies sold to individuals or to small groups, diseconomies of scale and high marketing expenses drive the ratio down to about 65 to 70 percent.

The factors causing low payout ratios may be technically justified, but they are not appreciated by the general public, which tends to interpret them as price gouging by private insurers. Not surprisingly, the high administrative costs of private health insurers has become a focus of intense criticism by the media and by those wishing to turn health insurance into a form of public utility.

The Failure of Health Care Reform

It is worth reviewing the state of affairs in the U.S. health care system in the early 1990s to appreciate the then-growing clamor for a *fundamental* reform of the system. That clamor seems all but forgotten today and the nation seems to prefer, once again, the more traditional American approach to public policy: *incremental* reform.

✓In retrospect, it appears that when Americans called for "fundamental reform" of their health care system they did not have in mind more government regulation or any significant redistribution of income. And most importantly, they did not wish to pay for such reform with any reductions in access to, or quality of care. They simply wished those aspects of the system that they viewed as problems to work better. When those who opposed the Clinton plan argued that it would lead to substantial redistribution away from the middle class and that rationing of health care would be inevitable, the plan was dead.

As it turned out, however, the reform of U.S. health care did not die completely with the demise of the Clinton plan. While notions of universal coverage, global budgets, and insurance reform based on community rating collapsed with the Clinton plan, the drive toward restructuring the health care system through competition and capitated managed care is alive and well. Although these forces were given some momentum by the President's embrace of the idea, they began to develop in the late 1980s without government assistance, and continue to grow without direct government involvement. Many of the chapters in this book focus on various aspects of this restructuring.

The Future Without Universal Coverage

✓If one wished to use a broad brush in painting the evolution of the U.S. health care system during the past few decades, one could describe it as an ongoing three-way wrestling match over market power among providers of health care, the government, and employers as purchasers. Each combatant has claimed it has the best interests of the patient in mind.

Until the mid-1980s, the providers clearly dominated the match. They had full discretion over the definition of what constituted "quality" in health care. They also had an unusually high degree of discretion over the prices they could charge for health care services—certainly in comparison with providers of other goods and services or by international standards.

Sometime in the mid-1980s, however, market power started shifting to those who paid the bills: government and employers. The federal government introduced several new payment systems that combined a form of administered prices with a budget control system for major components of the Medicare program. In so doing, it slowed the growth of per capita spending under Medicare significantly below projections.[7] At the same time, the private sector embraced the concept of capitated managed care, gingerly at first, but with increasing enthusiasm. By the mid-1990s, market power in the health care system had shifted substantially from providers to payers. But what about the patient or consumer?

Consumer power?

Many believe that patients themselves, acting as their own agents, will never have sufficient knowledge or power to be an effective force in the market for health care services. According to this thinking, individual consumers, particularly when they are sick, are poorly equipped to bargain with physicians and hospitals over prices or to assess the clinical merits and quality of the treatments prescribed. Bargaining over prices and assuring the appropriateness of treatments, according to this thesis, should be delegated to some kind of intermediary. The intermediary would review and approve the basic qualifications and prices of plans permitted to offer their services. As such, the underlying construct of managed competition is for consumers to select a health plan from a menu of approved options.

When American households are asked to select among health plans, however, they should have available reliable and understandable information on the cost and the quality of the product, so that they can make informed choices. At the time of this writing, this kind of information is mostly not available. Choice among competing health plans is often an act of pure faith.

Under the Clinton plan, the information for proper consumer choice was to be gathered, audited, and structured by state-run Health Insurance Purchasing Cooperatives (HIPCs). For better or for worse, that new hybrid organization became the first victim of opposition to the President's plan. In its place, the market is now developing a highly pluralistic set of auditors, including corporate benefits managers, state health departments, the Medicare program for elderly persons enrolled in HMOs, and sundry other entities. With respect to private employers, particularly very large employers, promising headway is being made in the area of information gathering. Tools used to gather information include the National Committee for Quality Assurance's (NCQA's) "report cards," which are based on the Health Plan Employer Data and Information Set (HEDIS), and other quality measures such as health outcomes. States also have begun to build monitoring systems for their managed care plans, and Medicare is working to develop capabilities in this area as well. But much more remains to be done.

Some advocates of market-based reform strongly disagree that consumers even need such intermediaries. In particular, the proponents of medical savings accounts (MSAs) recoil at the idea of merely transferring market power in health care from providers of care to private health plans or intermediaries. They express concern that these intermediaries will become over-regulatory, which will prevent the market from operating effectively.

The central theme of these critics is that individual consumers are capable of choosing rationally among alternative insurance products and health plan options. They also believe that, even in times of illness, individual consumers will be able to ascertain the information necessary to monitor the quality and cost of their care. They argue that, in the past, the conventional, comprehensive insurance policy, with its low deductibles and coinsurance rates, did not provide patients with sufficiently strong financial incentives to act as prudent purchasers. Only under policies with high deductibles (e.g., $1,500 per individual or $3,000 per family) or high coinsurance would consumers have sufficient incentive to become prudent purchasers. This group advocates the development of catastrophic plans that will pay all expenses after an individual or family exceeds a predefined maximum out-of-pocket payment.

To induce consumers to shift from low- to high-end coverage, proponents of MSAs advocate the creation of government-supported tax-sheltered savings accounts into which households could make annual deposits out of pretax income. All health spending in a year up to a specified deductible would be made from that account. If spending was less than the amount in the MSA, the balance could be carried forward indefinitely or used to pay for other health-related expenditures. Costs incurred over and above the deductible would be paid for by the catastrophic policy.

The concept of MSAs as a way of empowering individuals in the health care marketplace is currently very popular in the political arena. An MSA option for Medicare beneficiaries is being seriously considered in the Congress as part of a major restructuring of that program. The MSA approach, however, raises a number of serious questions that reflect the challenges that must be faced as the United States moves to a more competitive, market-oriented system. Will consumers in fact have access to the information needed to make informed choices? What if they opt for the MSA option and then change their minds? Frequent switching could destabilize the system. Is choice in a competitive environment potentially unfavorable for less healthy individuals, those without adequate safeguards or subsidies? In a recent publication, the American Academy of Actuaries[8] concluded that MSAs would redistribute income from employees who tend to have relatively high health care bills to those who tend to have low health care bills. On average, about two-thirds of employees would gain financially, while about one-third would lose. The latter would almost certainly be the sickest employees in the cohort. The typical American worker has become accustomed to the notion that the cost of health care is fully socialized through group health policies. It remains to be seen whether the redistribution of the cost of illness from the healthy to the sick will meet with public approval.

The uninsured

If anything became clear at the end of the health care reform debate, it was that Americans—or at least their legislative representatives—now suffer from severe battle fatigue. It is unlikely, therefore, that any form of a comprehensive and universal health insurance plan will be considered for several years to come. Those who were the real losers in the battle, the uninsured, must continue to rely on the "free" care at public clinics or in hospital emergency rooms. The question is how this haphazardly financed system will survive in the new health care marketplace. If large private payers and government are successful in lowering their payments to the health care system, this will reduce the hidden subsidies that have financed this "uncompensated" care. Who then will support the health care safety net as the market makes the old Robin Hood system less feasible?

 The complete absence of this topic from media reports makes it appear that the social problem of the uninsured has gone away. The opposite is more nearly the case. Their numbers are growing, and the willingness and ability of doctors and hospitals to underwrite the cost of caring for them through the "cost shift" appears to be waning. Is there a new "white knight" waiting at the edge of the arena or will this nation return to the overcrowded and underfunded public hospital system of the 1950s?

At some point during this decade, probably after the presidential elections of 1996, the nation may be forced to revisit the problems of the uninsured. It could happen once the new, price-competitive health care market has flushed the issue more fully into the open. To be sure, even if some action is taken, the coverage to be extended to the poor is likely to be limited, with fewer amenities than those available to the insured. One must hope that the health care services available to them will be appropriate and consistent with up-to-date medical knowledge. Such a system probably will be financed more explicitly, with public funds, rather than through hidden cross-subsidies. But even this more limited outcome is far from certain.

This introductory essay has focused more on the potential dark side of the future, not because it will overwhelm the positive benefits of the new health care system, but because these issues may get lost in the excitement of the new world order. The chapters in this volume elaborate further on some of the themes raised here and illuminate the pragmatic issues and strategic choices that will have to be considered and addressed by today's leaders at this time of unprecedented change.

Notes

1. R. J. Blendon, R. Leitman, I. Morrison, and K. Donelan, "Satisfaction with Health Systems in Ten Nations," *Health Affairs* (Summer 1980): 187–92.
2. R. J. Blendon and J. N. Edwards, eds., *System in Crisis: The Case for Health Care Reform* (New York: Faulkner & Gray, 1991), ch. 4, pp. 75–102.
3. Blendon and Edwards 1991.
4. J. E. Wennberg, J. L. Freeman, and W. J. Culp, "Are Hospital Services Rationed in New Haven or Overutilized in Boston?" *Lancet* (1987): 1185–89.
5. J. Holohan, R. A. Berenson, and P. G. Kachavos, "Area Variations in Selected Medical Procedures," *Health Affairs* 9, no. 4 (Winter 1992): 165–75.
6. Prospective Payment Assessment Commission, *Report and Recommendations to the Congress* (Washington, DC: ProPAC, 1 March 1995), p. 5.
7. ProPAC 1995, Figure 1.4, p. 18.
8. American Academy of Actuaries, *Medical Savings Accounts: Cost Implications and Issues* (Public Policy Monograph No. 1, May 1995), ii.

1

Health Care Spending: Can the United States Control It?

Stuart H. Altman and Stanley S. Wallack

Abstract. Health care spending in the United States has continued to outpace the growth in national income and the growth in spending in other countries. And yet many Americans are without sufficient health care. Since the failure of national health care reform proposals put forward by the Clinton administration and others, the United States has had to look for other solutions to the problem of how to control spending in this sector. Can the new competitive approach of managed care succeed where other cost control measures of the past have failed?

This chapter begins with an examination of the problems facing health care today, outlines recent trends in health care spending, and details reasons why spending is rising so rapidly at this time. The historical context of health care reform proposals and government attempts to control spending are described next and the reasons why some of these plans made no progress are explained. The health care payment systems of other industrialized nations that have seen some success in controlling costs are analyzed. Comparison of these systems with proposed plans for reforming the U.S. system provide insights and lessons for the United States.

Finally, the chapter describes managed care and managed competition and makes the argument that managed care has the potential to respond to many of the health care spending problems facing the United States. However, more data on this subject are needed, and the authors call for a national monitoring entity to assess the progress of managed care in meeting the health care needs of the public.

Since the demise of national health care reform and its regulatory mechanisms for controlling health care expenditures, the United States has moved aggressively toward a competitive managed care system as its primary approach to control spending. This new focus is based as much on expectations of the positive benefits of a competitive system and the likely negative consequences of regulation as it is on the actual successes of managed care in controlling the total spending rate for the country, at least during the late 1980s and early 1990s. Recent times have seen much more promising evidence that this strategy will be successful.

There is little doubt that managed care can bring about needed improvements in the efficiency with which health care services are provided and that these efficiencies can have both clinical and financial benefits. But will this competitive approach convert these efficiencies into significantly lower prices to consumers on a long-term basis, as opposed to larger returns for managed care organizations? And how effective will the competitive system be in slowing the rate of innovation of new and expensive forms of medical treatment? Growth in health care spending has been driven by the collective impact of these three factors—inefficiencies in the provision of health care services, continued large returns to the providers of services, and the easy availability of money to support more and more new technologies and treatments. Whether or not the new competitive approach will overcome the latter two factors will largely determine whether managed competition can succeed where various other cost control techniques that have been tried in the past 25 years have failed. There *is* reason for hope.

The Problems

Third-party payment

Health care spending and its annual rate of growth have become a problem for every industrialized nation. But in no country has the problem reached the crisis level that it has in the United States. For all countries, regardless of whether they spend 8 percent or 14 percent of their national income on health care, "excessive" health spending is a unique problem. It is not comparable to other problems because health care is among the very few services for which a third party, not the consumer, pays for most services used. Whether payment is made by the government or by a private insurance company, individual patients pay a price far lower than the cost of the service, and, as a result they attempt to use almost unlimited amounts of care. Lack of budget pressure has also permitted the suppliers of health care, particularly in the United States, to produce services in a less than efficient manner.

As a result of these factors, every country has been forced to seek alternative methods to limit health care spending. The problems that flow from excessive spending on health care center on two issues: how to find the great sums of money necessary to pay for these services (identifying the non-health services that will suffer as a result) and how to distribute the burden of paying for these services appropriately among various population and income groups.

Many attempts to control health care spending have been undertaken in the United States since the late 1960s; however, except for a few instances and for brief periods, they have been unsuccessful. The same is not true for most European countries or for Canada. Why have these other countries succeeded in controlling total health care expenditures where the United States has failed? Is the price paid by these other countries—a less responsive health care system and more structural rigidities—a price the United States is willing to pay to reduce its growth rate in health care spending? Will future trends in spending replicate the experiences of the past? In particular, will the United States adopt a cost-containment strategy, and stay with it, even if such a strategy creates problems for politically powerful interest groups? This question is especially meaningful in light of the failure of the U.S. Congress to adopt any significant reform during the 1993–1994 sessions.

The market for health care services

When consumers speak of the "cost" of health care, they most often mean the "price" of health care. This could refer to the doctor's bill or the price of a prescription. Or, it could refer to the premiums employers pay for the health insurance of their employees. For the nation, concern about the "rising cost of health care" implies concern about the increase in total spending for health care. This includes both growth in prices charged per unit of service and increases in the volume of services used. Added together, these two factors generated a spending rate of $884 billion in 1993, which approached 14 percent of the United States' gross domestic product (GDP). This represents a major jump from 1970, when health care spending was $74 billion and consumed 7.7 percent of GDP.[1]

Prices charged by suppliers for a particular service, while often related to its costs, can vary substantially depending on the conditions of the market. For example, the price of a service is likely to be much closer to its cost in a highly regulated market or a highly competitive market. If, however, the market is characterized by restricted competition, a permanent gap may exist. In these instances, the demand for the services is less price sensitive and such a gap can generate what are called "monopoly profits."

Many believe that most health care services are produced and used in markets with limited competition and that extensive monopoly profits do exist. Thus, the prices charged will be permanently higher than the true economic costs of production. Also, the produced amount or availability of services is likely to be greater than in a competitive market because of the existence of third-party insurance. Under such circumstances, even if costs are reduced, prices can remain high. Only if a tight regulatory system is put in place, or if serious competition is created through changes in the market structure for providing services and health insurance, will prices be reduced for the ultimate consumer.

The possibility of continued monopoly profits is behind the concerns expressed by some about what is happening in the managed care market (where reductions in the utilization of health care services are not being translated into proportionate reductions in the premiums charged to consumers) or what might happen if extensive consolidation occurs in the availability of hospital and physician services. Those two trends—consolidation of those who provide health care services and the growing integration of insurers and providers of care—now dominate the health care system. Whether such trends negatively or positively influence the future cost of providing health care services and the prices consumers pay for these services will determine whether recent slowing in the growth of health care spending will be maintained and even improved or whether the nation will revert to the higher spending trends of the late 1980s.

No one questions the idea that lower long-term prices and lower spending growth can occur only if the market for producing health care services becomes more efficient. But an efficient market may not be enough. Serious competition must be maintained both within the delivery system and among alternative insurers and managed care plans. Only if such competition is maintained will consumers benefit from a more efficient health care system. If this does not in fact occur, health care spending trends will again accelerate, and it is possible that pressure will build for the United States to do as other countries have done—adopt some form of national spending limit for health care.

The changing nature of health care

Any attempt to control health care spending must deal with the changing characteristics of health care services and the growth in the magnitude of procedures used to treat an illness. If innovation is the driving force behind most of the new and expensive services added to the health care system in the past decade, then increased efficiency in a given service may produce only a short hiatus from continued expenditure growth.

Unprecedented technological innovation in the past quarter-century has fundamentally changed the practice of medicine and, while some of these changes have helped to reduce the cost of treatment, on net they have added substantially to total health care expenditures.[2,3] What is more, there are clear signs that future innovations will continue to require much in additional new expenditures.[4]

Unfortunately, it is difficult to disentangle increases in spending generated by inefficiencies (using too many tests or procedures or unnecessarily expensive procedures) from the additional spending that results from using new services that lead to better outcomes. The many and various forms of payment used for health care services compound this problem. Some pay based on the price of a unit of service (e.g., a day in the hospital), others pay based on the price of a total service (e.g., a total stay in the hospital), and still others pay based on the price of providing all of the care used by a person during a year (e.g., a capitated premium).

The result

As shown, total expenditures (*TE*) equal the prices charged per unit of service (*P*), multiplied by the volume of services (*Q*), plus the value of new services (or improved quality) generated by technological innovation (*T*).

$$TE = (P \times Q) + T$$

Changes in total expenditures can result from

1. Changes in *prices,* arising from changes in cost of production (the use of more efficient technologies) or changes in market conditions (more competition or greater monopoly control of production);

2. Changes in *quantity* of services consumed, resulting from changes in consumer demand or provider-produced usage;

3. Changes in the value of *technologically induced new services*, resulting from prior investments made by government or private efforts.

Trends in U.S. Health Care Spending

Increased spending

One of the key factors that led to the emergence of health care reform as a major domestic issue in the early 1990s was the projection by the Congressional Budget Office (CBO) that the increase in national health care expenditures as a share of GDP would be as large between 1990 and 2000 as that experienced between 1965 and 1991.[5] CBO predicted in 1992 that by the year 2000 health care spending would represent 18 percent of GDP. Similar projections motivated President Clinton to include a series of tough spending control mechanisms in his reform plan, including a backup system for national expenditure limit control. Because of a slowdown in spending in 1993 and 1994, these dire predictions are being modified. As of early 1995, it appeared that by the year 2000 spending could grow to about 16 percent of GDP. While this is a lower level than originally projected, health care will still continue to consume a larger and larger share of total national income.

Even after adjusting for growth in the consumer price index, the 1993 per capita spending is nearly three times the comparable 1970 expenditure level. In other words, if spending for medical care had risen at the same rate as the economy overall, per capita health care expenditures in 1993 would have been $1,667 lower or about half of the actual amount. This *difference* is more than the total per capita amount spent on education (public and private combined) in that same year.

The rate at which health care expenditures have grown in the past three decades far exceeds the overall growth of the economy (as measured by changes in the GDP). While the growth rate has varied year to year, owing in part to governmental and private sector attempts to control expenditures, growth in health care spending has been consistently higher than growth in the GDP. Between 1980 and 1993, national health care spending grew 3.5 times while the nation's

Figure 1.1 Factors Accounting for Growth in Personal Health
Expenditures, Calendar Year Periods 1960–1991

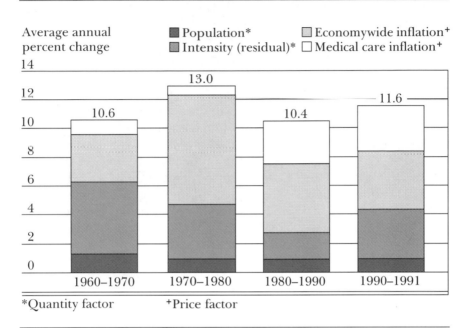

*Quantity factor.
*Price factor.
Source: S. Letsch, "National Health Care Spending in 1991," in *Debating
Health Care Reform: A Primer from Health Affairs,* ed. by J. Iglehart (Bethesda,
MD: Health Affairs, Project HOPE: 1993), 145–161. Based on data from
HCFA Office of the Actuary.

GDP grew 1.8 times. This resulted in a growth in health care from
9.3 percent to 13.9 percent of the nation's GDP.

Changes in national health care expenditures are due to variations in the quantity (volume or intensity) of services purchased and
the price of those services, and in the new and improved services
used. As shown in Figure 1.1, between 1970 and 1991, general price
inflation and additional medical price inflation were responsible for
the majority of the growth of personal health expenditures.[6] However, when general inflation and population growth are taken out of
the equation, increased use and intensity of services (both new and
old) accounted for most of the remaining growth (88 percent in the
1970s, 41 percent in the 1980s, and 55 percent from 1990 to 1991).

Unfortunately, most of the cost control mechanisms adopted by government and the private sectors in the 1970s and 1980s focused on controlling only one of the inflation factors at a time. The potential for success of a competitive system of capitated managed care plans is based on the ability of such a system to force limits on both the prices charged and the utilization of services.

International comparisons

The magnitude of the U.S. health care spending levels and their rates of increase are even more striking when compared with spending levels and trends in other industrialized countries. Not only does the United States spend more per capita on health care services than any other Organization for Economic Cooperation and Development (OECD) nation, but with a higher rate of increase, the difference has grown larger. At $3,094, 1992 per capita spending for health care in the United States was 2.25 times the OECD average of $1,374.[7] In 1980, the per capita spending comparison showed the United States at 1.85 times the OECD rate. Other industrialized countries have created national regulatory mechanisms to keep their health spending in line with their national income. No such national policy has been tried in the United States.

Questions about the value of U.S. expenditures are driven not only by the relatively high amounts spent, but by the comparatively poor results for the United States in terms of health status. Infant mortality in the United States at 9.1 deaths per 1,000 live births is substantially higher than in other industrialized nations.[8] Life expectancy at birth is at or near the bottom relative to these selected countries. While it is true that these broad measures are driven by more than just medical care, and that the benefits of the technologically advanced U.S. health care system are substantial in improving the quality of life for many patients, these arguments alone are not sufficient to justify either the magnitude of the spending growth trends or the poor health status outcomes.

Changes in consumer attitudes

The U.S. health care system is more accurately described as an illness care system. While most Americans value the availability of complex medical technologies, many are increasingly questioning the value of expensive, life-extending technologies. Many Americans believe that the emphasis on using technology to keep ill patients alive at all costs has been misplaced. Resources spent on high-technology interventions that provide limited payoffs could either be saved or diverted toward the greater availability of primary care. Such expenditures are even being questioned by the seriously ill who receive them. This is evident in the growing use of living wills and do not resuscitate (DNR) orders. The passage in Oregon of the "Right To Die" law reflects the willingness of at least some segments of society to focus on this issue.

Growing skepticism about the value the nation receives from the increasing portion of national income spent for medical services is also apparent in the strong and growing emphasis on provider accountability. Government and private payers alike are increasingly requiring proof from providers that the services they deliver are efficient and of high quality. Outcomes measurement in a variety of settings for a broad range of treatments is currently a primary management and research focus. Within the health care reform debate, both proposed new regulatory models and market-based models of delivery include extensive measurement techniques for assessing the quality of services provided.

Calls for improved quality measures and reporting on provider practices are also being driven by the dramatic rise in health care expenditures. The fact that the provider community is being held accountable for its performance, or at least to provide the necessary information to review its performance, is to a great extent due to a change in payer mix. The move away from individual out-of-pocket payments for medical services to a major purchasing role for government and private companies has consolidated the financial responsibilities these large payers carry and the clout with which they are able to negotiate with providers.

Changes in spending by sector

Although still the largest health provider sector, inpatient hospital care has seen the most dramatic reductions in spending in recent years (Table 1.1). In 1993, spending for inpatient hospital care accounted for 23.5 percent of all payments, a decline from a high of 29.1 percent in 1983.

Declines in hospitals' share of health care spending are due, in part, to technological developments that now allow formerly inpatient procedures to be performed outside the hospital, and also to an increased insistence by payers on the use of lower-intensity delivery settings. Even those patients who do enter the hospital have experienced

Table 1.1   National Health Care Spending by Sector, Selected Years

Sector	1965	1983	1991	1993
Hospitals	33.7%	41.0%	38.4%	36.9%
Inpatient*	19.2	29.1	23.8	23.5
Outpatient*	1.8	4.7	8.0	8.9
Other†	12.7	7.2	6.5	4.5
Nursing facilities	4.1	8.0	8.0	7.9
Home health agencies	0.1	0.8	1.3	2.4
Physicians	19.7	16.9	18.9	19.4
Other personal health care‡	27.9	21.0	21.3	22.0
Other spending§	14.4	12.2	12.2	11.5

*Includes patient care spending in community hospitals.

†Includes patient care spending in federal and noncommunity hospitals, and spending for nonpatient services in all hospitals.

‡Includes dental services, other professional services, drugs and other medical nondurables, vision products, and other medical durables.

§Includes research, construction, public health activity, administrative costs of health insurers, and net cost of insurance.

Sources: ProPAC, June 1994; Health Care Financing Administration, *Health Care Review,* Fall 1994.

dramatic reductions in the average length of stay. In 1979, the average patient stayed in the hospital for 7.1 days. By 1993, this average length of stay had fallen to 6.2 days. For patients over age 65, average length of stay dropped from 9.9 days in 1983 to 8.2 days in 1994.[9, 10]

To assist those patients who leave the hospital earlier, the nation's spending for home health care services increased from $4.9 billion in 1985 to $20.8 billion in 1993.[11] In total, spending by Medicare for nursing home care increased at an annual rate of 37.2 percent between 1987 and 1991 and 39.3 percent between 1991 and 1993 (Figure 1.2). The trend away from inpatient hospital services to care in other settings is likely to continue, due as much to patient preferences as payer cost concerns. Not all of the increases in home care services, however, reflect a shift away from more costly sites. Several studies have shown that many patients are now receiving services in the home that are not substitutes for other services, but instead are services for chronic as opposed to acute care needs.[12] This appears to be especially true for Medicare patients. These and other new services now being

Figure 1.2   Real Average Annual Growth Rates per Enrollee for
Selected Medicare Services 1987–1993

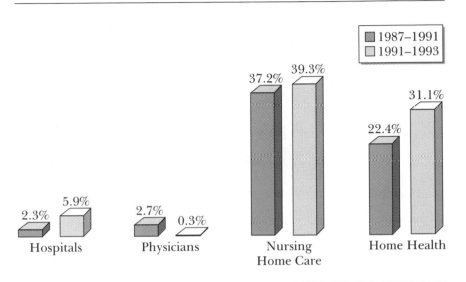

Note: "Hospitals" includes both inpatient and outpatient services.
Source: ProPAC 1994. © Stuart Altman, 1995.

provided have fueled much of the most recent growth rates in health care spending.

Why Is Spending Rising So Fast?

Demand: financing and payment

From World War II until the mid-1960s, expanding private employer-based health insurance coverage for workers and their dependents was a major force behind the rapid increase in spending for health care services. The number of persons with health insurance jumped dramatically after World War II. The passage of Medicare and Medicaid legislation in 1965 added third-party protection for an additional 50 million elderly and poor Americans. In 1965, out-of-pocket spending accounted for nearly half of all health care expenditures. By 1975, it had declined to 29 percent, and since that time has

Table 1.2   Payment Sources for National Health Care Expenditures as a Share of Total for Selected Years, 1960–1993

	1960	*1965*	*1970*	*1975*	*1980*	*1985*	*1990*	*1993*
Private								
Out-of-pocket	49.2%	45.7%	34.4%	29.0%	23.8%	22.3%	20.4%	17.8%
Health insurance	21.7	24.0	22.5	24.8	29.3	31.7	32.5	33.5
Other	4.6	5.5	5.9	4.8	4.8	4.6	4.6	4.8
Total*	75.5%	75.3%	62.8%	58.5%	58.0%	58.6%	57.6%	56.1%
Government								
State and local	10.7%	11.6%	23.9%	27.4%	28.8%	29.2%	29.3%	31.7%
Federal	13.8	13.2	13.3	14.1	13.3	12.1	13.1	12.1
Total*	24.5%	24.7%	37.2%	41.5%	42.0%	41.4%	42.4%	43.9%

*Totals have been rounded.

Sources: Congressional Budget Office, October 1992, based on data from Health Care Financing Administration; Health Care Financing Administration, *Health Care Review,* Fall 1994.

continued a steady but slower decline, to 17.8 percent in 1993 (Table 1.2, Figure 1.3).

Third-party financing breaks the direct connection between what consumers pay for health care services and what providers of such services receive. In a third-party financing system, a provider's willingness to deliver a service is determined not only by the level of payment but also by the type of reimbursement system used. For example, the extensive use of cost-based reimbursement by many Blue Cross plans and Medicare in the 1970s provided little incentive for hospitals to weigh the costs of a service against the benefits of that service. The introduction by Medicare in 1983 of the predetermined fixed diagnosis-related groups (DRG) payment system for hospital services changed these incentives somewhat, and the more extensive use of capitated payments by private payers in the late 1980s changed the incentives even more.

Rapid expansion of the third-party financing system substantially reduced the importance of consumer out-of-pocket payments. This change in financing did not simply shift the payment sources from consumers to third-party payers. More significantly, it substantially increased the ability of consumers to pay for more and better

Figure 1.3   Out-of-Pocket Payments as a Share of National Health
Expenditures, Calendar Years 1960–1993

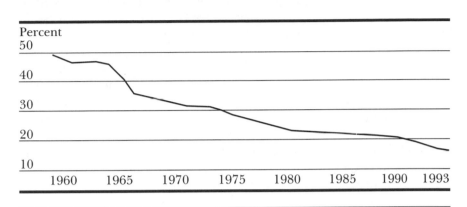

Source: Health Care Financing Administration, Office of the Actuary, 1993.

health care services. Faced with patients who had few financial constraints, providers could add new services and know that they would
be paid. Since most health care markets were dominated by providers,
payers were most often forced to accept the prices that their providers
set. Even the big government programs Medicare and Medicaid paid
hospitals based on *their* costs and physicians based on the fees *they*
charged.

The role of government did not stop with assisting the elderly
and poor to obtain health care services. Beginning in 1946 with the
Hill-Burton Hospital Construction Act and followed by several others
laws in the 1950s and 1960s, the ready availability of government
money encouraged rapid expansion in the number of hospital beds
throughout the country. This was followed in the late 1960s and early
1970s by federal funds earmarked to double the capacity of the
United States to train physicians and nurses. One distinct characteris-
tic of the health care industry is the response of available capacity and
services: it is not merely a passive response to demand by patients; it
also actively induces consumer demand for more health care services.

Serving as patient agents, physicians exert enormous influence
on patient demand. Under a fee-for-service payment system that paid
disproportionately higher rates for complex services, physicians had
strong incentives to provide more and more higher-cost medical

services. The increased supply of physicians, particularly those in highly specialized areas, rather than leading to lower fees as would have happened in most other markets, was accompanied by a significant growth in the use of physician services and a large increase in the rate of physician income, higher than the underlying inflation rate in the economy and the average growth in wages.

Advances in medical technology—including both new diagnostic and new treatment procedures—have also driven increases in demand for health care services and the resulting increases in health care spending. This growth has resulted, in part, from the ready availability of private and public financing systems that have paid for almost all diagnostic tests or procedures generally considered nonexperimental. Even procedures with few proven positive health benefits have been introduced and used by the health care community. The availability of these new medical technologies stimulates physician and consumer demands for more and different types of services. Third-party payers have been relatively powerless to deny coverage for these new techniques and procedures. In part, this powerlessness is due to insurance that guarantees payment for general types of coverage (e.g., hospital care), even if such services change dramatically and cost much more, and due to the lack of serious price competition for the purchase of health insurance coverage. Attempts to limit diffusion of certain very expensive technologies (discussed in the next section) have been largely unsuccessful. Therefore, many more "halfway technologies" or cost-increasing technologies have been developed than "complete technologies" or cost-reducing technologies.[13]

The dynamic interaction between health care supply and demand has become an important process in the development of the U.S. health care industry. Third-party financing encourages consumers to demand more and better services. The cost-based and fee-for-service financing system has provided an open-ended source of funds giving providers further incentives to provide increasingly more expensive services. Thus, the consequence of this dynamic process has been the persistent and rapid growth of health care spending. Without substantial changes in such a health care financing and payment system, this dynamic and interactive circle cannot be broken and health care spending growth will continue its current trend. Some believe that recent changes in the health care market have broken this chain, while others are less sure and question whether the long-term trend lines will truly be affected.

Government Attempts to Control National Health Care Spending

The 1970s and 1980s saw federal and state government develop a series of initiatives to control the rapid increase in health care spending. Such attempts focused on only a few segments of the health care delivery system or a limited number of third-party payers and, therefore, had minimal success in limiting growth in total spending. These initiatives focused on several aspects of health care, from controls on medical care prices to limits on questionable medical services to restrictions on the expansion of new capital formation. They began soon after the spending explosion generated by the passage of Medicare and Medicaid legislation in 1965.

Before turning to discussion of explicit cost control initiatives, it should be emphasized that not all government interventions are failures or have only negative results. In 1973, the federal government passed the Health Maintenance Organization Act, which both assisted new organizations to form capitated managed care plans and, more important, helped open up the employer market to capitated managed care plans by requiring most firms to offer them as an insurance option to their employees if a plan was available in the area. It is difficult to imagine what the managed care revolution of the 1990s would have looked like without this legislation.

Controls on medical prices

The first cost control effort by the federal government was made in conjunction with President Nixon's National Wage and Price Control Program (Economic Stabilization Program, ESP) in 1971. ESP was a broad-based system of wage and price controls designed to deal with general inflation that was perceived to stem from excessive increases in wages and other input costs. While controls on most of the economy were dropped by the end of the year, the special problems of health care inflation led a conservative administration to keep tight controls on the health care sector through 1974.

The ESP controls did generate a moderating influence on price increases for most medical services. Aggregate spending, however, continued to grow as quantities of services used and underlying costs, other than wages, increased. Once controls were lifted, inflation returned to its precontrol levels.[14]

As the first serious effort at controlling medical care inflation in the United States, ESP demonstrated that, while price increases can be limited for a short period of time, effective controls on total spending require much more extensive limits on the costs of production as well as on the quantity of services used. This lesson was to be repeated many times during the next two decades.

Controls on capital expenditures

Many analysts believe that any attempt to limit spending for medical care will ultimately fail unless serious restrictions are placed on spending for new capital formation, including the building of facilities and the creation and diffusion of technologies. All other industrialized countries do have such restrictions, and attempts have been made in the United States to implement such a system.

In 1974, the federal government created a nationwide health planning system and linked that system to a requirement that all new hospital expenditures of $150,000 or more were to receive approval by a state cost-containment agency. Failure to receive such a "certificate of need" would deny the facility payment from Medicare and Medicaid for the interest and depreciation of the expenditure. This law was known as the Health Planning and Resource Development Act of 1974.

Certificate-of-need (CON) programs were initially instituted by several states seeking to constrain the expansion of hospital and nursing home capacity. By 1980, this number expanded to include almost all states. In the early 1980s, the federal government moved away from its commitment to health care planning and eventually repealed the Health Planning and Resource Development Act in 1986. Between 1983 and 1988, 11 states followed the federal government and dropped their CON programs.[15]

Most of the empirical research on the effectiveness of the health planning and CON programs in the United States suggests that the programs experienced only limited success in controlling the expansion of hospital capacity and did little to control the diffusion of expensive new technologies.[16] One early study found that state CON programs had no effect on total capital spending but may have caused some hospitals to substitute equipment for beds.[17]

In the end, the ineffectiveness of these planning and capital control programs was to a great extent attributed to the absence of incentives for the local or state agencies to truly control such capital expansions. These agencies did not bear directly the financial burden of the extra spending that flowed from such expenditures. Without limits or budgets for total investments in each area or state, planning agencies did not have to make real choices. On the contrary, approval of projects often resulted in more services and more jobs for the community.

Medicare controls of the 1980s

Having failed to create an effective systemwide control program for all medical prices and capital formation in the 1970s, the federal government turned its attention in the 1980s to limiting the growth in what it paid for inpatient hospital services and physician care. In 1983, the Medicare prospective payment system (PPS) for hospital payment was introduced. PPS paid hospitals based on the complexity of the patients treated using DRGs. Several years later the government introduced a nationwide physician fee system using a Resource Based Relative Value Scale (RBRVS). Total payments for Medicare physician services were limited by linking these payments to a predetermined volume performance standard.

The DRG payment system was designed to provide incentives for hospitals to "look hard" at the number of hospital days and the cost of ancillary services for a given type of illness by establishing a preset amount for each patient regardless of days of care or services provided to that patient. This payment amount is based on the illness category (DRG) of the patient and the average cost of treating similar types of patients throughout the country. The system also adjusts for differences in wages in a given area and for whether the hospital trains graduate medical students or disproportionately serves low-income patients. Annual updates to the DRG payments also included an amount for major capital expansion and new technologies. Thus, the DRG system dealt with the three reasons for cost increases in hospital inpatient care: prices, volume, and technology. However, the DRG system affected only inpatient hospital care and only Medicare patients.

As a result, while the DRG system has been effective in controlling Medicare payments for inpatient care, it has had limited success in controlling total Medicare expenditures and the actual cost structure of hospitals.[18] Ample evidence shows that hospitals were successful in shifting the responsibility for paying some of these higher costs onto private patients. In 1992, it is estimated that private patients paid over $10 billion in extra payments to cover Medicare's lower payment.[19] This is not to say, however, that Medicare paid too little. Rather, it can be argued that hospitals did not control their costs adequately and that the private payment system was too compliant in its willingness to pay higher rates. All of this seems to be changing as more aggressive private managed care plans force hospitals to price their services more competitively and hospitals are keeping a much tighter limit on their costs.[20]

Since instituting the hospital payment DRG system, Medicare has turned its attention to physician services. A resource-based fee schedule has been developed to realign physician payments away from expensive procedures and toward medical evaluations. In addition, the physician program includes an overall limit on physician payments, which establishes payment restrictions for "excessive" increases in volume. With limited ability to influence directly the number and type of procedures used by Medicare beneficiaries, the federal government has focused on controlling the prices it pays per procedure and its total expenditure amount. If total physician expenditures exceed an established amount, future Medicare fee increases are reduced to keep within the budget established for the program.

The fundamental criticism of the RBRVS system is that, while it controls total Medicare spending for physician services in the aggregate, it does so by arbitrarily lowering the prices for all physician services provided under the program and for all physicians. It does not, however, provide much of an incentive for the individual physician to question the provision of a given service. On the contrary, by lowering the prices each physician receives per service, the system may be encouraging physicians to offer more services to compensate for lost revenues.

In effect, the federal government has relied on various forms of administered price systems to control expenditures and has done little to influence either the purchasing decisions of beneficiaries or the production decisions of providers. In contrast, the private sector exerts less control over what it pays per unit of service and instead relies much more heavily on trying to control utilization of services. Both systems have their pluses and minuses and their winners and losers. During the 1980s, it appeared that the administered pricing system of the government was more effective. It now appears that the rate of growth in per capita private spending for health care is growing less rapidly than the per capita growth rate for government spending (Figure 1.4). The success of the private sector seems to be

Figure 1.4   Real Change in Per Capita Medicare and Private
Health Insurance Expenditures 1979–1993

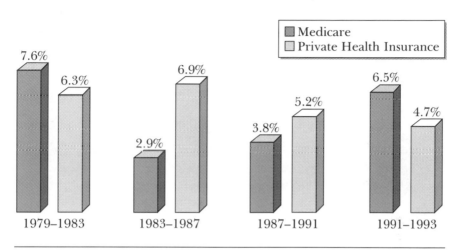

Source: ProPAC 1994.

related to the requirement that employees join and use a managed
care delivery option in which total expenditure (all services used and
prices paid) are controlled. Many states are now building on the private sector model and requiring all Medicaid recipients to join some
form of managed care. Pressure is building as well for Medicare to
become more aggressive in shifting beneficiaries into such programs.
But before Medicare can benefit from such a shift in the form of lower
spending rates, it will have to change the way it pays managed care
plans and it may have to make it more difficult for beneficiaries to
switch plans.

State efforts at innovative spending control programs

Often states have been ahead of the federal government in trying new
approaches to controlling health care spending. The prime motivation for these programs has been to slow the rapid rates of growth in
state Medicaid spending. But several states have gone beyond Medicaid to develop all-payer rate control systems. By 1980, 27 states had
some form of hospital rate setting. Of these, four required all payers
to participate.[21] Among the all-payer rate control states, New York

Table 1.3   Average Annual Changes in Per Capita Spending
for Health Care, 1980–1991

	Total	*Hospital*	*Physician*
U.S. Average	9.3%	8.7%	10.4%
California	7.6	6.7	8.8
Michigan	8.4	8.0	8.5
Oregon	8.6	8.5	9.0
Florida	9.2	8.7	10.0
Minnesota	9.6	8.4	11.7
New York	9.7	8.9	11.6
Massachusetts	9.8	8.2	13.8

Note: Includes hospitals, physician services, and prescription drugs.
Source: ProPAC, June 1994.

and Maryland stand out as having the most successful programs and ones that have been in place for the longest period of time.

Studies conducted in the 1980s suggested that these all-payer programs did have a positive effect on controlling total hospital spending. A study by Carl Schramm and colleagues concluded that, for the six states with a rate control program between 1976 and 1984, the rates of growth in spending for a hospital stay were 3–4 percent less annually than for those states without such a program. The cumulative effect of this consistently lower spending increase in the rate-setting states between 1976 and 1984 totaled 87 percent.[22] But containing hospital spending is not the same as controlling total health care expenditures. More recent information cast doubt on the long-term positive effects of these programs. As shown in Table 1.3, New York and Massachusetts, two rate control states, had the largest increases in total *per capita* health care spending of the ten largest states between 1980 and 1991. In contrast, California, which is generally considered to have the greatest competition among managed care plans, had the lowest per capita rate increase. The evidence, therefore, questions the long-term effectiveness of these regulatory systems, or at least suggests that if they are to be truly effective, they must go beyond controlling only the prices of inpatient care.

Fragmented and vacillating policy efforts

Although various cost control efforts have been tried over the past several decades, the United States has never successfully attempted a nationwide and systemwide initiative. No cost-containment program has ever covered all of the major health care payers and all sectors of the delivery system. Various partial-payer programs did achieve some cost reductions for the services controlled or the payers covered, but often at the expense of shifting costs to noncovered services and payers.

In short, fragmented cost-containment efforts have had limited success in controlling total expenditures or in changing the fundamental factors that have shaped the U.S. health care system. In addition, U.S. health care policy has been characterized by vacillation between government regulation and market competition. Trusting neither approach and knowing there would be "losses" under each, government policymakers have been unwilling to implement either a full system of market competition or a comprehensive regulatory approach. The net result has been an uncontrolled system leading to steadily rising U.S. health care spending.[23] Other countries have not been so timid, at least on the regulatory side.

How Foreign Countries Control Their Health Care Expenditures

Health care expenditures in the United States, whether measured on a per capita basis or as a percentage of GDP, far exceeds that found in other industrialized nations. Interestingly, even though U.S. expenditures are higher, the U.S. norm is for far fewer hospital days—about one-half that of OECD countries—and fewer visits to physicians.[24] On the other hand, the price of a hospital stay or a physician visit far exceeds that charged in other industrialized countries. These higher prices result from more services being provided per day and per hospital admission as well as higher wages and profits earned by health care workers and health care institutions. In addition, more expensive technologies are available in the United States, and they are used less effectively. This results in lower use rates and higher costs per unit of service. For example, whereas the average occupancy rate of acute care hospitals in OECD countries in 1990 was 78.5 percent, in the United States it was 69.5 percent.[25] Also, as shown in Figure 1.5, the United States operates far more of the most expensive medical technology facilities, such as open heart surgery units and organ transplant centers.

Why have other countries been successful in controlling such

Figure 1.5 Comparative Availability of Selected Medical
Technologies, 1992–1993

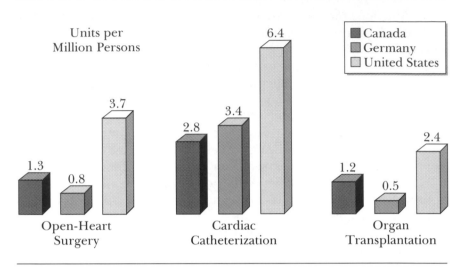

Source: Dale A. Rublee, *Medical Technology in Canada, Germany, and the United States.* © Stuart Altman, 1994.

factors? Can such techniques be as successful in the United States? Also, will the "side effects" of employing such techniques in the U.S. market be so negative that they should not be transplanted even if they could be? Since, in the long run, demand factors, including the willingness to pay higher and higher rates, determine the supply of services and, therefore, the level of expenditures, how have the payers for health care in these other countries been able to arrest these demand factors?

Top-down expenditure control

The German and Dutch health care systems have experienced similar trends in health care spending. Both systems underwent large rates of increase in the early 1970s and then through government intervention imposed a series of tight sector-specific expenditure controls. For the most part, these expenditure controls have been effective in keeping health care spending in line with the growth in each country's national income. By establishing total sector budgets and distributing funds to private payer groups in accordance with these budgets, the central authority is assured that total spending will remain within the budgets established. These "top down" total expenditure control approaches are in sharp contrast to the U.S. market approach (a bottom-up system), in which each supplier and managed care organization establishes its own fees or premiums; through competition among these groups total spending is kept in line.

Health expenditure levels in these two European countries are determined in the context of other social programs and the inevitable trade-offs among them. In Germany, reunification costs have led to the need for more stringent health care cost controls. In the Netherlands, the trade-off appears to be between acute care and chronic care. Of course, the performance of the overall economy is an additional constraint in both countries, since premiums are directly linked to wages.

A top-down regulatory approach, while successful at keeping total costs under control, seems to generate significant inefficiencies in the provision of services. With fixed budgets, providers do not have to be as responsive to patient needs. Further, the system provides little incentive to be efficient in the delivery of services. Once budgets are expended, providers are forced to cut back services, particularly for those illnesses that are not life-threatening or an emergency.

Perhaps even more important in terms of efficiency, sectoral budgets prevent substitutions among sectors. What makes the sectoral approach especially unresponsive to change is a separate physician budget. Physicians significantly affect all services, but there is no incentive for them in such a system to use less expensive settings or to constrain service use in other sectors. In the United States, the fee-for-service or capitation systems permit facilities and providers to benefit from reorganization. The growth in outpatient care, ambulatory and surgical centers, and subacute care are examples of delivery system changes in the United States that have not developed as readily under the European sector-specific budgets. These new delivery system additions, if used correctly and as substitutes for more expensive and less desirable services, can provide a net benefit to a system. But if not used correctly, they can easily become add-ons that make the system even more inefficient and expensive (this occurred in the United States in the 1970s and 1980s). Either by regulation or through self-interest, the appropriate trade-offs must be made between the old and the new services. One of the strongest attributes of a competitive capitated system is that it does more in terms of providing the appropriate incentives for selecting the right mix of new and old services.

As foreign governments have taken over the responsibility for setting expenditure levels, they have in effect established income policies for health care workers. Both the wage levels paid and the number of health care professionals employed are directly or indirectly determined by national policy. The opponents of regulation have often referred to the "tar baby" attribute of regulation. This has become evident in Germany and the Netherlands: as controls in one sector become effective, other sectors fall out of line. This forces regulatory activities to expand to other sectors. The result has been expansion in both the scope and breadth of the cost-containment regulations throughout the economy. Further, in some ways government actions are constrained because of potential negative effects on politically powerful segments of the health care system.

Lessons for the United States

The actions of foreign countries in containing health care expenditures provide an insight into the natural consequences of implementing cost controls in a largely fee-for-service system. In a fee-for-service system with no effective budget constraint, prices cannot be controlled without regulation. As a result, price controls are likely to be established first using small units of services. Eventually, this leads to controlling more aggregate units of services, which incorporate the volume of services as well as price. The unit basis for which payments are set can vary from individual physicians and hospitals to regional budgets, or even national budgets for certain services.

Since the public sector controls the levels of investment in most countries, the rates of growth of capital formation and its diffusion are limited. This is a major factor in explaining differences in expenditure levels between the United States and other countries. New procedures and expensive treatments are developed at a much faster rate in the United States. Furthermore, the ready availability of private financing in the United States accelerates the diffusion of these new procedures.

In looking at the options for controlling expenditures in the United States in light of foreign experiences, the key issue is whether expenditure regulations will be needed and, if so, what type. Such regulations appear to be less relevant for the United States today and surely less politically acceptable as the health care system becomes predominant based on market competition and capitated managed care. The issue could, however, loom large in the future if the competitive system fails to bring total health care expenditures more in line with national income. Even if some regulation is necessary, it should be designed to be compatible with the most positive forces of a competitive system, namely, incentives to produce services more efficiently. To do this, the United States could develop all-payer rates for small units of payment (e.g., a hospital per diem). By setting rates for small units, the incentive for managed care organizations to control the number of admissions and the length of a hospital stay would be maintained. At the other extreme, the United States could return to the concept of an overall budget for a geographic area. Within these limits, organizations could compete on the basis of premiums. Those qualified plans with the lowest premiums would be assured a greater market share.

The Competitive Approach

In recent years, the growth of health care expenditures has slowed considerably. Is this slowing permanent or is it only a temporary pause in the long-term upward trend? What caused this slowdown and to what extent is it related to the widespread adoption of managed care by the under-65 population?

After 1987, the rate of increase in health care spending relative to the growth in the nation's income accelerated, reaching a peak in 1992. The relative rate of growth fell sharply in 1993 and was close to zero in 1994. Important as this reverse trend is, it is not the first time such a sharp reduction has occurred. As shown in Figure 1.6, the relative growth in health care spending has fallen to zero or become negative three other times since 1970. In each of these first three cases, a positive growth rate resumed after a brief period because the underlying dynamics of the industry had not changed. There are high hopes that this pattern will not repeat itself in the middle 1990s. Even if expenditures continue to grow, they are expected to do so at more moderate rates. For the first time, a broad-based competitive insurance market has emerged that is dominated by capitated managed care plans. This market appears to be exerting substantial pressure on health care providers to become more efficient and to cut costs on a permanent basis. One indication of the strength of this new

Figure 1.6   Rates of Change of Percentage of Gross Domestic
Product Spent on Health Care, 1970–1994

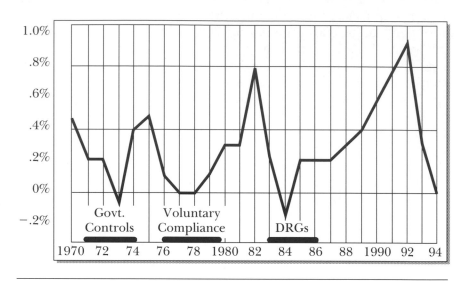

Source: Health Care Financing Administration. © Stuart Altman, 1995.

price competition on provider costs is the dramatic reductions in the cost of treating an average hospital admission. Whereas the cost of a hospital admission was growing in real terms at between 4 and 5 percent between 1986 and 1992, it grew at only 1.8 percent in 1993 and actually declined by 0.7 percent in 1994 (Figure 1.7).

There is little doubt that the growth in managed care enrollments contributed to this decline. But while managed care plans have for some time been reducing the volume of services, particularly hospital days, only a small portion of these savings have been translated into lower premiums. In an analysis of the medical payout rate of several large for-profit managed care plans, it was shown that most of these plans retained 30 to 40 percent of the premium dollar in the early 1990s. These for-profit managed care organizations used retained premium dollars for advertising, administrative costs, expansion, and profits. This retention rate seems in excess of what would be expected if this industry were in long-term competitive equilibrium. Clearly, monopoly profits are being made. Whereas such higher sums previously went to the providers of care, they now go to the managed care organizations. These plans have been able to force providers to

Figure 1.7   Annual Change in Hospital Costs per Case, Inpatient
and Outpatient Services, 1987–1994

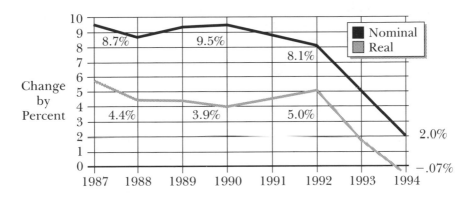

Source: AHA National Hospital Panel Survey, CPI-U. © Stuart Altman,
1995.

lower prices to them because of the availability of an excess supply of
health care services, particular hospital capacity, and the ready availability of specialists. As often happens in fast-changing markets, not
enough managed care plans have been taking advantage of this situation and therefore only limited price competition exists at the consumer level. It takes significant competition among managed care
plans to translate lower provider service costs into premium reductions and ultimate reductions in health care expenditures.

This situation, however, may be changing. Some recent evidence
suggests that such competition is now taking place. The Group Health
Association of America in December 1994 announced that "for the
first time, premiums for people getting health care from HMOs will
decline."[26] They report that "the typical HMO member can expect a
1.2 percent reduction in 1995 compared with a 5.6 percent premium
increase in 1994." In California, a large purchasing organization for
state and county employees (CalPERS) has negotiated sizable discounts in premiums from these managed care plans for 1995.

Premium competition is what competition among managed care
plans should be all about. If it continues to exist, then one of the three
underlying inflation factors, monopoly profits, will be controlled. To
achieve continued price reductions, however, individuals, firms, and
the government will have to pay more attention to price and become

aggressive buyers of health insurance plans. They must be conscious of premium differences in otherwise similar plans and be prepared to switch among plans based, in part, on relative prices. To ensure this, consumers will have to bear more of the cost burden for choosing a health plan with higher premiums. This cost consciousness can be accelerated if employer premium contributions are set at a fixed rate regardless of the cost of the plan chosen by the employee, with the premium amounts that exceed the employer contribution having to be paid entirely by the employee. A more controversial component of increasing cost conciousness would be to do away with the income tax subsidy for health insurance either entirely or at least for that portion that exceeds the lowest or average cost plan in the region. In addition, all plans should be required to offer a set of standardized benefits so that consumers can select intelligently among plans. Finally, better mechanisms to create accurate risk-adjusted premiums are sorely needed to limit the ability of plans to benefit by selecting better health risks.

The need to require consumers to bear the costs of selecting a more expensive plan is not a problem for those who have the financial ability to supplement employer or government payments. But the issues are more complicated for those individuals covered by Medicaid and Medicare. For the Medicaid program, states can set budgets and force recipients into managed care plans. But these recipients cannot supplement the budget constraint or switch plans at will. Therefore, states must be cautious about setting these budgets too tight and they should monitor the quality and accessibility of the care provided. Medicare must also be cautious as it moves away from its open-ended choice policy. But it must move. Currently, Medicare has been able to control the price it pays for inpatient hospital care and the total amount it pays for physician services. It has not, however, been able to control the number of hospital admissions or the growth in outpatient care, home health services, or post-acute care. This is why Medicare spending is rising faster than private health care spending. It may be that Medicare will have to separate the various population groups it covers and allow those who have the capacity to pay more and to choose different options to enter the competitive system. For those too frail, too sick, or too poor for such options, an alternative strategy must be developed. For these individuals, emphasis should be focused on personalized care management, rather than managed care. The difference is that the former tries to tailor the care used more to the personal needs of the patient, while the latter uses organizational controls to constrain service use. Individuals should be able to move between categories, depending on their changing economic circumstances and health status, and the funding for both categories should come from the same pool of funds, so that two separate systems are not created—one for those who are healthy or wealthy and another for those who are poor or sick. Clearly, if a competitive managed care system truly becomes the nation's cost control mechanism, then Medicare must be included, at least partially. Medicare must also restructure itself not as a third-party payer of services, but as an organization offering multiple managed care options.

Significant competition among managed care plans should generate continued pressure to constrain the amounts paid to providers and also to return most of these savings to the ultimate consumers. Thus, in terms of total health care expenditures, both price and volume increases will be constrained. But questions remain about whether the rate of technological change will be slowed by such a competitive system. If it is not slowed, the ultimate effect of such competition on total expenditures will be limited.

Managed care is built on the continued existence of third-party insurance coverage and the commitment of each plan to provide a comprehensive range of services. Since insurance facilitates the demand for more services, managed care plans in order to be responsive to consumer demand will still wish to provide what is perceived as relatively easy access to high-quality care and to include the most advanced treatment methods where appropriate. While managed care plans will likely become more thorough in evaluating the cost-effectiveness of treatments and will likely introduce cost-saving technologies where possible, these plans will probably not withhold many new treatments. As a result, the impact of new technologies on rising expenditures are not likely to be significantly altered. Thus, the United States may have to consider nonmarket or regulatory approaches at some point for rationalizing the introduction and utilization of new technologies. Such regulations—if they are to do more good than harm—should be consistent with the positive aspects of a market-oriented system. But, for now, such a regulatory apparatus should be kept in the closet.

Conclusion

A great deal is known today about the factors driving health care expenditures and about feasible approaches for addressing the varying causes of rising costs. The experiences of foreign countries have shown how to control total health care expenditures using a top-down regulatory system (if that is the only goal). But inefficiencies and a lack of responsiveness to some patients result from regulating prices and quantities of services. Further, it is evident that piecemeal solutions will not work. Most important, if the United States is truly interested in slowing the rate of growth in health spending, it must commit to developing a budget constraint for health care through either a top-down regulatory approach or an approach based on market forces. The nation must also commit to staying the course once the approach is chosen. Given the national preference for private initiatives and limited government, competition among managed care plans seems at present to be the only viable option.

Competition among managed care plans has the potential to be both comprehensive and responsive to the rapid changes in the health care delivery system. But it also has the potential to retain much of the savings from a more efficient system rather than translating them into lower premiums, and there are questions about its effectiveness with regard to limiting the long-run growth in total health expenditures. Finally, concern persists that capitation could change the incentives so much that providers deny needed services to some patients. Therefore, it would be wise public policy to create a national monitoring entity to observe and assess the progress of the U.S. health care system in achieving the twin goals of providing needed coverage to all, or most, Americans, and of doing so in a cost-effective manner.

Data should be gathered on what happens to provider prices, to service utilization patterns of various population groups, to premiums, and to the introduction and utilization of new technologies under a health care system dominated by managed care. Also, the impact of a competitive system on medical education and on long-term investments in biomedical research must be assessed. This information will allow an assessment of whether a competitive managed care system is working and of whether improvements in the delivery system are adequately translated into lower premiums. This quasi-public monitoring entity would be charged with observing the changing structure of the health care system and the efficiency that such changes generate, and with evaluating the trade-offs made by the health care system between controlling health care expenditures and possibly reducing quality or access to health care services. This national body would have neither the authority to determine health care expenditures nor any mechanisms for steering the health care system.

However, by monitoring the trends and describing the trade-offs to the public and to the relevant policy units at the private and public levels, it might help the United States to achieve a more balanced growth rate of national health care expenditures.

Acknowledgments

The authors give special thanks to Lori Cavanaugh and John Cai for their help with this manuscript.

Notes

1. U.S. Department of Health and Human Services, *HHS News Release* (Washington, DC: U.S. Department of Health and Human Services, 22 November 1994).
2. H. Aaron, *Serious and Unstable Condition: Financing America's Health Care* (Washington DC: The Brookings Institution, 1991).
3. J. Newhouse, "An Iconoclastic View of Health Care Cost Containment," *Health Affairs* 12 (1993, Supplement): 152–71.
4. W. Schwartz, "In the Pipeline: A Wave of Valuable Medical Technology," *Health Affairs* 13, no. 3 (1994): 70–79.
5. Congressional Budget Office, *Rising Health Care Costs: Causes, Implications, and Strategies* (Washington, DC: Congressional Budget Office, April 1991).
6. Personal health care expenditures exclude government public health care spending, which is included in total national health care spending.
7. G. Schieber, J. Poullier, and L. Greenwald, "Health System Performance in OECD Countries," *Health Affairs* 13, no. 4 (1994): 100–12.
8. G. Schieber, J. Poullier, and L. Greenwald, "Health Spending, Delivery and Outcomes in OECD Countries," in J. Iglehart, ed. *Debating Health Care Reform: A Primer from Health Affairs* (Bethesda, MD: Health Affairs, Project HOPE, 1993), 162–71.
9. Prospective Payment Assessment Commission (ProPAC), *Medicare and the American Health Care System: Report to Congress* (June 1995).
10. K. Levit, A. Sensnig, C. Cowan, H. Lazenby, P. McDonnell, D. Won, L. Sivarajan, J. Stiller, C. Donham, and M. Stewart, "National Health Expenditures, 1993," *Health Care Financing Review* 16, no. 1 (1994): 247–94.
11. Levit et al. 1994.
12. ProPAC 1995.
13. B. Weisbrod, "The Health Care Quadrilemma: An Essay on Technological Change, Insurance, Quality of Care, and Cost Containment," *Journal of Economic Literature* 29 (June 1991): 523–52.
14. S. Altman and J. Eichenholz, "Inflation in the Health Industry: Causes

and Cures," in *Health: A Victim or Cause of Inflation?* edited by M. Zubkoff (New York: Milbank Memorial Fund, 1976), 7–30.

15. Thomas, 1993 to come from author.
16. Yondorf et al. 1985 to come from author.
17. D. Salkever and T. Bice, "The Impact of Certificate-of-Need Controls on Hospital Investment," *Milbank Memorial Fund Quarterly* (Spring 1976): 185–214.
18. ProPAC 1995.
19. ProPAC 1995.
20. ProPAC 1995.
21. K. Davis, G. Anderson, D. Rowland, and E. Steinberg, *Health Care Cost Containment* (Baltimore, MD: Johns Hopkins University Press, 1990), 95.
22. C. Schramm, S. Renn, and B. Biles, "Controlling Hospital Cost Inflation: New Perspectives on State Rate Setting," *Health Affairs* 5, no. 3 (1986): 22–33.
23. S. Altman and M. Rodwin, "Halfway Competitive Markets and Ineffective Regulation: The American Health Care System," *Journal of Health Politics, Policy and Law* (Summer 1988): 323–39.
24. Schieber et al. 1993.
25. Schieber et al. 1993.
26. Group Health Association of America, *HMO Performance Report* (December 1994).

2

Redefining Private Insurance in a Changing Market Structure

Deborah J. Chollet

Abstract. This discussion on likely changes and challenges for the health insurance industry over the coming decade assumes that significant national reform of health care financing for the privately insured population will not occur—or, if it does, that it will mirror the insurance market reforms that many states already have undertaken.

First, the changes in private insurance coverage during the past several years are considered, with particular attention to the erosion of employer-based coverage and to the rising influence of public insurance programs—especially Medicaid—on the private insurance market. Next is a description of the changing web of state laws and regulations governing private health insurance. At this writing, virtually every state has enacted or is considering reforms of the small group market to limit what many perceive as unfair or destructive insurer practices and to set new ground rules for competition among insurance arrangements. The changing nature of private insurance contracts in the United States is considered next. Evolving from conventional fee-for-service contracts, private insurance is increasingly a complex mixture of capitation, partial capitation, and reinsurance of capitated arrangements. Finally, this chapter discusses three issues of increasing importance in shaping the marketplace for private insurers: (1) the federal preemption of states' regulatory authority over self-insured employer plans; (2) emerging state regulation to restructure competition in the health insurance and health care markets; and (3) the growing interest of both federal and state governments in medical savings accounts to finance health insurance and health care spending.

Owing both to its great success and its considerable failures, the private insurance industry is at an important crossroads.

The industry's success is demonstrated by the fact that a majority of Americans participate in private insurance plans. Private insurance plans cover nearly 70 percent of all Americans under age 65.[1] Among Americans aged 65 or older, two-thirds report coverage by a private insurance plan, typically in the form of a Medicare supplement plan.

Private insurance pays for about one-third of all health care delivered in the United States, and for about one-half of all health care that is financed by third-party payers (including Medicare and Medicaid). In 1993, private insurance financed 49 percent of all physician services and 36 percent of all hospital care.[2]

Further, most Americans who have private insurance are reasonably satisfied with it in the context of their overall health care arrangements. In fact, the general satisfaction of insured Americans with their own health care arrangements has been a major factor in the failure of reform proposals that would significantly change the choices and financing available to people who are insured together with those who are not.[3,4]

Despite these achievements of private insurance, the industry's failures are compelling. Conventional insurance shelters consumers—as would any financial intermediary—from the financial consequences of their decisions. As a result, consumers are inclined to use more health care and more amenities bundled into health care than they would were they not insured. And because they reward health care providers for delivering more care regardless of provider efficiency or the effectiveness of care, insurers that pay on a fee-for-service basis have long been regarded as a leading culprit behind the nation's extraordinary, spiraling health care costs. In this regard, private insurance may also play an important role in the quality of care problems posed by the delivery of unnecessary health care services.

The rising cost of health care and, consequently, health insurance has created problems of affordability for the insurance industry. Insurers have responded to employers' demands for lower-cost coverage by taking a number of actions, including underwriting medical risk more stringently and redesigning contracts to reduce coverage and plan liability. Insurers also have begun to alter their traditional relationships with health care providers to encourage more efficiency in health care delivery.

These measures notwithstanding, every year a smaller proportion of Americans report having any private insurance coverage at all. Between 1989 and 1993, the proportion of people under age 65 with private insurance coverage declined by more than 5 percentage points. Most of this coverage loss was associated with a decline in the number of dependents covered by employer-sponsored plans. Despite recent growth in employer coverage of workers, the purchase of individual private coverage, and continued substantial growth in Medicaid coverage, the number of Americans without coverage from any source—private insurance or public programs—increased by 6.5 million between 1989 and 1993. In 1993, 41 million Americans (18.1 percent of the population under age 65) were uninsured.

The Changing Structure of Health Care Financing in the United States

Most Americans under age 65 are covered by private health insurance and, most often, by a plan offered by their employer or a family member's employer. While this has not changed during the past several decades, in recent years ongoing erosion of the coverage offered through employer plans has become a matter of substantial concern. The estimated number of people under age 65 covered by employer plans has declined in every year for which data are available: in 1993, these plans covered about 4 million fewer Americans under age 65 than in 1989 (Table 2.1).

While this erosion of coverage has continued at very nearly the same annual rate since 1989, most recently the *distribution* of coverage loss has changed dramatically. In 1993, the number of people reporting coverage as dependents dropped sharply while the number of people reporting coverage as employees rose for the first time in this decade. These changes in employer-based coverage are consistent with a long-term decline in the willingness of employers to subsidize dependents' coverage and with increasingly competitive labor markets. They also are important indicators of rapid changes in the way workers are compensated and in the management of employer-based plans.

At least some of the loss of dependents' coverage in employer plans between 1992 and 1993 was offset by growth in the number of people under age 65 covered by some other private insurance arrangement—presumably individual coverage. The growth of individual coverage—in the aggregate, fully offsetting the loss of employer coverage—suggests that the individual market may be more hospitable for large segments of the population than many had presumed, especially in the wake of reforms in some states that prohibit medical

Table 2.1 Number and Percent of Population under Age 65 with Health Insurance Coverage from Selected Sources: 1989, 1992, 1993

	1989		1992*		1993		Percentage Change†	
	Number (millions)	Percent	Number (millions)	Percent	Number (millions)	Percent	1989– 1992	1992– 1993
Total population under age 65	213.7	100.0%	223.8	100.0%	226.2	100.0%	3.3%	1.1%
Private insurance, total	160.3	75.0%	157.4	70.4%	157.6	69.7%	–2.4%	0.1%
Employer plan	141.8	66.4%	138.6	61.9%	137.6	60.8%	–2.8%	–0.7%
Covered as employee	71.2	33.3%	68.9	30.8%	72.0	31.8%	–3.3%	4.5%
Covered as dependent	70.6	33.1%	69.7	31.1%	65.6	29.0%	–2.3%	–5.9%
Individual policy	18.6	8.7%	19.0	8.5%	20.8	9.2%	1.3%	9.5%
Public program	26.2	12.2%	34.3	15.3%	36.4	16.1%	27.6%	6.1%
Medicaid	18.5	8.7%	26.5	11.8%	28.9	12.8%	38.2%	9.2%
Any insurance, total	179.3	83.9%	184.0	82.2%	185.3	81.9%	1.7%	0.7%
Uninsured, any source	34.4	16.1%	39.8	17.8%	40.9	18.1%	12.0%	2.8%

Source: The Alpha Center. Tabulations of the March 1990, 1993, and 1994 Current Population Surveys (U.S. Bureau of the Census). *Note:* Population includes noninstitutionalized persons only, and excludes members of the military and their families.

*Survey responses have been reweighted to the 1990 Census and may differ from earlier, unreweighted estimates published elsewhere.

†Percentage changes between 1989 and 1992 are calculated using the original (1980-based) CPS population weights for 1992; percentage changes between 1992 and 1993 are calculated using the new (1990-based) CPS population weights.

underwriting and discourage wide variations in insurance rates. Also, many have argued[5] that a system of individual coverage, were it sufficiently encouraged by tax policy, would create an intrinsically fairer and more flexible system than the current system of employer-based coverage. For adherents of this philosophy—including advocates of medical savings accounts—the unusual growth of individual coverage reported since 1992 may support a cautious optimism. The trend certainly merits further and careful consideration.

These changes in private coverage notwithstanding, the growth in public sector coverage and the continued growth of the uninsured population are the most compelling features of the structure of health care financing in the United States. Between 1989 and 1992, the number of people under age 65 who qualified for Medicaid coverage increased 38 percent, and then by another 9 percent between 1992 and 1993. In 1993, an estimated 13 percent of the nonelderly population either received or were eligible for Medicaid coverage, including nearly one-quarter of children under age 18. Among children under age 7, 32 percent were covered by Medicaid (see Table 2.2). This expansion of Medicaid to cover significantly larger numbers of low-income working-age Americans and, especially, larger numbers of children has been the single greatest change in the structure of health care financing during the past decade.

Despite the rapid expansion of Medicaid coverage, the number of uninsured has also continued to grow. Between 1990 and 1993, the nonelderly population without insurance coverage from any source—neither coverage from a private insurance plan nor eligibility for a public program—increased by 12 percent. This population grew another 3 percent between 1992 and 1993.

From a policymaker's perspective, the high cost of health care and, concomitantly, the rising number of uninsured, ebbing coverage from employer-based plans, and rapidly growing eligibility for Medicaid have become the defining features of health care financing in this country. From the perspective of the private sector, the defining features of health care financing in the United States are the speed and pervasiveness of ongoing fundamental change, fusing the financing and delivery of care in ways that are unprecedented in other developed nations. Paradoxically, these two perspectives on the U.S. systems of health care financing are consistent.

State Medicaid programs historically have paid providers "at the margin," in some states paying rates that are only a fraction of the payment normally made by a private insurance plan for the same service.[6] And while the uninsured probably consume much less health

Table 2.2 Number and Percent of Children and Adults Eligible for Medicaid, 1993

	Age 0–6	Age 7–17	All Children	Age 18–64	All Nonelderly
Number of persons (millions)	8.8	7.8	16.6	12.3	28.9
Percent within age group	31.5%	19.1%	24.1%	7.8%	12.8%

Source: The Alpha Center. Tabulations of the March 1994 Current Population Survey (U.S. Bureau of the Census).

care than they might were they insured, the care that they do receive is characteristically more expensive and more likely to be partly or entirely uncompensated. In real terms, growth of Medicaid coverage and the uninsured population each induce providers to shift significant costs to private insurance plans, further raising the cost of private plans and inciting ever more stringent cost management of these plans. More stringent cost management may take any number of forms: increased reliance on capitation, placing providers at risk both for management of the cost of enrollee care and for the uncompensated care that they may provide to other patients; more stringent negotiation of rates and terms with preferred providers; reduced payments as a percent of charges in fee-for-service plans; or simple savings at the bottom line, such as reducing or eliminating employer contributions to coverage.

However, growth of Medicaid coverage may also have some positive implications for private insurance plans. Recognizing the general opposition of employers to mandates that would expand private group coverage as well as the strictures imposed on the states by the federal Employee Retirement Income Security Act (ERISA), which broadly protects employer health and welfare plans from state regulation, some states have begun to view expanded Medicaid coverage as a way to address the problem of growing noncoverage.[7] Expanding Medicaid to resolve the significant social and economic problems posed by rising numbers of uninsured people affords employers some political respite, even while potentially exacerbating the cost problems of employers that sponsor health insurance plans. Ironically, efforts under way in the 105th Congress to institute block grants for federal Medicaid funding could remove the states' only practical option for resolving the problem of large uninsured populations without mandating employer-based coverage.

State Reform of Private Health Insurance Markets

Large firms in the United States are significantly more likely to sponsor health insurance plans for their workers than are small firms. In 1993, only 24 percent of workers in firms with fewer than ten workers reported being covered through an employer-sponsored plan, compared with 69 percent of workers in firms of 1,000 or more. However, workers without coverage from their own employer plan are only moderately more likely to work for a very small firm than for a very large firm (see Table 2.3).

Table 2.3   Number and Percent of Private Sector Workers Covered by their Own Employer-Sponsored Health Insurance Plan, by Size of Firm, 1992 and 1993

Number of Workers in Firm	1992			1993		
	Number of Workers Covered (Millions)	Workers Covered as a Percent of all Workers	Workers Not Covered as a Percent of All Workers Not Covered	Number of Workers Covered (Millions)	Workers Covered as a Percent of all Workers	Workers Not Covered as a Percent of All Workers Not Covered
All Workers	66.6	52.9%	100.0%	68.8	54.3%	100.0%
1–10	5.1	20.5	33.5	7.0	25.8	34.5
11–24	4.2	37.2	12.0	5.2	41.2	12.8
25–99	8.9	51.4	14.2	9.1	53.7	13.6
100–499	11.5	62.5	11.6	11.7	63.8	11.4
500–999	4.7	66.1	4.1	5.3	66.6	4.5
1000+	32.1	68.8	24.6	30.5	69.6	23.0

Source: The Alpha Center: Tabulations of the March 1993 and 1994 Current Population Surveys (U.S. Bureau of the Census).

The lower likelihood that a small firm will offer a health insurance plan has been attributed to the characteristics of small-firm employment, as well as to various features of the small-group insurance market. Small firms employ, on average, both younger and older workers than large firms. Younger employees, by virtue of their lower earnings and lower health risk, are believed to have less demand for health insurance in lieu of cash wages. Older employees represent substantially higher health risk than the average and, therefore, higher insurance cost.

Competition for workers in small firms apparently also affects the willingness of employers to offer a health insurance plan. Surveys of small firms that do not sponsor a health insurance plan typically find that affordability is the most important reason for not offering a health plan to their workers. However, many small-firm employees are insured elsewhere and employers often can successfully compete for labor without offering a health plan. In one recent survey of small firms that did not sponsor health benefits, coverage of workers from another source and the ability to hire workers anyway were cited as the second and third most important reasons for not offering health insurance to workers (see Table 2.4).[8]

The importance of plan cost as a deterrent to employers that might otherwise sponsor health insurance benefits has led many states to consider opportunities for subsidizing employer spending for health insurance. To date, such subsidies have typically taken the form of experimental private programs.[9] Relatively few states have sought

Table 2.4   Reasons Small Employers Give for Not Offering Health Insurance, by Order of Importance

1. Too expensive
2. Many employees insured elsewhere
3. Employees can be hired without providing insurance
4. Firm not sufficiently profitable
5. Employees do not want insurance
6. Cannot find an acceptable plan
7. Company turned down for coverage because of company size
8. High employee turnover
9. Lack of information or difficulty judging plans
10. Employees cannot qualify because of preexisting conditions
11. Company turned down because of type of business

Source: The Alpha Center. Reprinted from W. David Helms et al. "Mending the Flaws in the Small Group Market," Health Affairs 11, no. 2 (Summer 1992): 8–27.

to subsidize the cost of health insurance plans for small groups either directly or in the form of employer tax credits against the cost of a health insurance plan.[10] However, neither direct subsidies in the form of reduced premiums nor state tax credits for small employers that initiate a health insurance plan for their workers have achieved significant market penetration among small groups that were not already insured.[11,12,13]

Rather than subsidizing the price of insurance to small groups, most states have attempted only to stabilize the small-group market by restricting insurers' pricing behavior and underwriting practices. These strategies presume that medical underwriting and wide price variations constitute deterrents at least to small groups' maintaining coverage, if not to the decision to initiate coverage. By the end of the 1994 legislative session, all but five states (Alabama, Hawaii, Michigan, Nevada, and Pennsylvania) had enacted some type of small-group insurance reform.

The most common type of reform enacted by the states is the establishment of allowable "rate bands," that is, intervals within which insurers can vary their premiums around the average rate calculated across their own full book of business. In states with rate bands, each insurer is required to set insurance rates for the products that it offers as if the demographics of the buyers of each product were distributed in the same way as the demographics of all buyers collectively across all of its products. Thus, insurers can vary rates to reflect differences in benefits, but are limited in the extent to which premiums may reflect the demographics of enrollment in particular plans. The most common restriction on rate variation enacted by the states has been that proposed by the National Association of Insurance Commissioners (NAIC) in model legislation; in effect, the current NAIC rate bands allow insurers to offer premiums that vary by as much as 2:1.

While 45 states have enacted rate bands of some type, at this writing only 17 have enacted rate bands that are narrower than those proposed by the NAIC. Of these, seven have enacted legislation requiring insurers to use "modified" or "pure" community rates to price their products, although in most of these states the community rating law has not yet become effective.[14] Typically, modified community rating statutes allow insurers to vary premiums for each product to reflect the age structure of the insured group, as well as family size and geography. Some allow insurers also to use additional factors such as gender, industry, group size, and (in Florida) tobacco use to price insurance products. Only one state—New York—has required small-group insurance products to be priced at the "pure" community rate since 1994, allowing insurers to vary their small-group rates only for family size and geography. However, both New Jersey and Maine have enacted comparable statutes, both to become effective in 1997.[15]

Typically in conjunction with restrictions on how widely insurance prices may vary, many states have enacted legislation limiting insurer underwriting practices. At this writing, 38 states require insurers to offer small-group coverage on a guaranteed-issue basis. In these states, insurers cannot deny coverage to any group on the basis of health status or prior claims experience. Forty-three states require insurers to renew coverage to all groups that they currently insure, sometimes in addition to guaranteed issue of first coverage. And 41 states have legislated portability statutes, limiting the ability of insurers to deny, limit, or exclude coverage for preexisting conditions when the group (or individual within the group) has been continuously insured for some period of time.

These laws—those that limit premium variation as well as those that limit or prohibit medical underwriting—are intended to stabilize the small-group market by forcing insurers to accept and aggregate risk into larger pools. Laws that limit premium variation discourage insurers from splintering their business into small risk pools and prohibit insurers from pricing products to reflect extraordinarily high actual or anticipated claims experience within those small pools. In states that have enacted portability laws, insurers are prohibited from issuing contracts that limit the plan's risk exposure related to new participants. Instead, they are required to offer coverage to the entire group for the full scope of benefits covered by the plan.

These types of laws may have some predictable effects. First, and perhaps most perversely, they make coverage more costly for insured groups that represent relatively low risk. With insurance priced at the average in a diverse risk pool, predictably low-risk groups will subsidize predictably high-risk groups within the pool. Thus, estimates of the effects of pure community rating on the price of insurance coverage to insured groups uniformly project substantially higher insurance premiums for approximately 20 percent of insured lives, but commensurately lower insurance premiums for only about 10 percent of insured lives for the same type of coverage.[16] While early evidence about the effect of community rating in New York suggests that in fact some good risks might have left the insurance market in response to higher insurance prices (or, alternatively, might have abandoned some conventional insurance plans for self-insured or managed care plans), this effect apparently has been very small.[17]

Second, the inability of insurers to limit the risk associated with individual participants (by denying coverage or restarting preexisting condition exclusions) or to price in a manner that reflects known risk may cause insurers to reconsider the risk exposure inherent in their plan designs. At present, the most common internal limits on liability in private insurance plans relate to coverage for mental health and substance abuse, home health, and hospice care. A substantial minority of fee-for-service plans also place internal limits on coverage for inpatient hospital care (32 to 39 percent, weighted by number of enrolled workers) and inpatient physician care (21 to 25 percent).[18]

If fee-for-service indemnity plans, in particular, respond by more aggressively redesigning benefits, they may generate still wider differences in the design of fee-for-service plans compared with tightly managed HMOs. To the degree that HMOs are able to manage high-use participants to control plan cost and offer attractive prices in the market, these changes may encourage still greater HMO enrollment among consumers seeking fuller insurance coverage in lieu of unrestricted choice of providers.[19] Indeed, early experience in Vermont suggests that accelerated enrollment in managed care plans may be one result of enacting narrow rate bands together with a guaranteed issue.[20]

Finally, these kinds of insurance laws may be expected to drive from the market very small insurers—those with aggregate business that is too small to ensure a normal distribution and average level of risk. These laws may also be expected to encourage small employers whose plan size puts them within the scope of the statute to convert to a self-insured plan, to the extent that these plans enjoyed favorable insurance prices that are no longer available to them.

However, New York's early experience with pure community rating, as well as Vermont's experience with very tight rate bands, indicates that very few insurers flee the market following the substantial restriction of insurance pricing and underwriting. The persistence of even very small insurers in the market may be an artifact of the very large market share that historically has been held by open-season, community-rated Blue Cross and Blue Shield plans (which claim to have already absorbed a disproportionate share of bad risk), as well as the flexibility to modify plan design that commercial insurers still enjoy. Similarly, New York has no evidence that employers responded to pure community rating by converting to self-insurance. However, a general softening of the health insurance market in 1994—with falling prices and rising insurer profit margins—probably contributed to market stability in states that had implemented major insurance reforms.

The Changing Nature of Insurance Contracts

✓Possibly the most dramatic change in health insurance during the past decade has been the rapid and ongoing growth of capitated insurance arrangements. ⌐Enrollment in conventional HMO plans that place physicians on staff or hold them in more or less tightly bound networks with full or partial capitation has soared. As of 1994, HMO membership was growing by more than 11 percent per year and was expected to exceed 50 million by year-end, accounting for approximately one-third of the nonelderly population enrolled in private insurance plans (see Figure 2.1). Investigations of whether managed care plans reduce health care costs have provided no conclusive

Figure 2.1   Enrollment in HMOs, 1985 to 1995 (Projected)

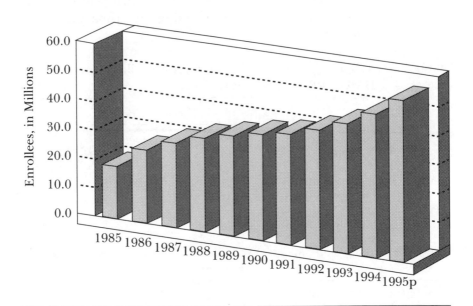

Source: Group Health Association of America 1995.

evidence. However, a significant body of research indicates that the potential for lower cost rests with HMOs, since enrollees in these plans are less likely to use certain types of expensive care.[21]

As various forms of managed care have grown, and as traditional indemnity plans have sought to compete by instituting closer prospective utilization review, physicians and hospitals have begun to respond by developing and marketing capitated contracts directly. These entities—generically called physician-hospital organizations, or PHOs—are roughly patterned after the famed Mayo Clinic and are explicitly intended to compete with more conventional, insurer-initiated HMOs and PPOs.

Nevertheless, emerging PHOs have formed intricate financial relationships with conventional insurers. In one survey of PHOs,[22] only 3 percent of surveyed PHOs were owned by insurers, but a significant number (39 percent) had exclusive contracts with an insurer, and nearly half (47 percent) used an insurer as a third-party administrator.[23]

At least some PHOs are indistinguishable from HMOs in the way that they contract risk (see Table 2.5). For example, in the above survey, the primary hospital accepted at least some risk in 42 percent of the PHOs (and in 73 percent of PHOs with annual budgets of $1 million or more), but typically shared risk with the PHO entity.[24] However, in fewer than one-half of PHOs did either the primary care phy-

Table 2.5   Relationship to Insurers and Typical Allocation of Risk in HMOs, PPOs, and PHOs

	Usual Relationship to Insurers	Provider Bears Risk		
		Primary Care Services	Specialty Services	Hospitalizations
HMO	Owned by insurer or competes with insurers	●	—	—
PPO	Owned by insurer or contracts with one or more insurers	—	—	—
PHO	Contracts with one or more insurers	—	—	●

● Typically fully capitated.
—May be fully capitated, partially capitated, or paid by the contracting entity on a fee-for-service basis.

sicians or the specialty physicians bear risk on contracts, although physicians were substantially more likely to bear risk in large PHOs than in small ones. In fact, the low probability that physicians in PHOs bear risk may be the feature that most distinguishes the structure—and ultimately the performance—of emerging PHOs from more conventional HMO networks.

While PHOs may represent a new wrinkle in the now familiar concept of managed health care delivery, they portend some important changes in the market for health insurance, as well as in the market for health care services. In markets where they are emerging quickly, PHOs may represent a "white flag" raised by physicians who historically have opposed managed care contracting out of concern over possible loss of economic and professional control. The apparent popularity of exclusive contracts with insurers suggests that, at least in some cases, physician opposition to managed care may have been more a matter of financial interest and reluctance to change than of concern over economic and professional autonomy.

Furthermore, the PHOs that ultimately compete most successfully with more conventional HMOs may do so by emulating some of their salient features—in particular, by developing staff model or strong group practices in which primary care physicians bear risk collectively or individually. In turn, heightened competition for enrollees among increasingly similar capitated arrangements may begin to drive down the price of managed care plans even in markets in which individual insurance buyers—employers and individuals—have not organized to exert market power. The extraordinary profits reported by HMOs (particularly in markets where HMO penetration is high) suggest a failure of active competition among managed care plans. If this failure is resolved in a maturing system with more players, the already rapid growth of enrollment in managed care plans will accelerate.

Despite the potential benefits of emerging competition, the rapid growth of unconventional forms of insurance poses some significant regulatory challenges. The federal government historically has had no role in regulating insurance arrangements to ensure solvency or consumer protection, having recognized these responsibilities to be the purview of the states in 1945.[25] While states have developed some expertise in regulating and monitoring conventional insurance plans to protect consumers, very few states have assembled the staff or experience to regulate integrated managed care enterprises as insurance arrangements.

Similarly, only a few states have begun to grapple with the consumer protection issues raised by limited provider networks, developing and distributing standardized quality information to consumers. Instead, most states have hoped that growing competition among managed care plans would force the development and distribution of information on quality so that consumers can make informed choices. However, managed care plans that are seeking to distinguish themselves from one another in the market are likely instead to develop products that are increasingly complex and information that discourages direct comparison—strategies similar to those undertaken by conventional insurance plans. The few states that have taken the lead in developing comparable information on quality (comparing either the whole state or a particular market segment) have done so anticipating that competition will fail to produce the necessary information for consumers.

In many states, regulation of HMOs and other managed care plans falls to the Department of Health as a provider licensing function, not to the Department of Insurance. Solvency standards for HMOs vary from state to state, and in states where the Department of Insurance exercises little or no oversight over managed care plans, these plans might not participate in the state guaranty fund. In such cases, consumers are unprotected in the event of the insolvency of the managed care plan, although the contracts that link providers in the plan may protect them (unlike indemnity plan participants) from liability for charges incurred but not paid.

However, even in states with Department of Insurance oversight of managed care plans, these departments are characteristically unprepared to oversee provider-related issues, such as quality monitoring and reporting. Thus, conventional state regulation of insurance, as well as conventional state and federal antitrust standards, are likely to require broad reevaluation and change as various forms of managed care systems predominate in the health insurance market.[26] Some states have chosen to address the cross-cutting issues that managed care plans raise by moving all oversight of health care financing and delivery into a single "superagency."[27]

Issues at a Crossroads

Much of the discussion of health care reform as it would affect private insurance has crystallized around three issues: ERISA's preemption of the state's authority to regulate employer plans, the formation of insurance purchasing cooperatives, and the potential for national legislation that would allow tax-qualified medical savings accounts. Each of these issues is discussed below.

ERISA preemption

ERISA preempts all state regulation of employer-sponsored health and welfare plans. Consequently, while the states have the authority to regulate insurance products marketed to employee groups, they are not authorized to regulate employer plans directly. With respect to self-insured employer plans, the states have no regulatory authority at all. Both the federal courts and the U.S. Supreme Court have construed ERISA broadly to protect employer plans from state laws that require coverage of particular medical services or coverage of workers or qualified dependents in particular circumstances.[28] Since its enactment in 1974, ERISA's preemption clause has become the basis for major controversy between those who would "level the playing field" to resolve problems of the uninsured and the cost of health care, and those who believe that self-insured plans have been important innovators, especially with respect to managing health care costs.

As the states have begun to address the problems of uninsured populations and uncompensated care, they increasingly have been challenged by self-insured employer plans that claim federal protection under ERISA. For example, in 1994, a U.S. District court struck down Connecticut's newly created uncompensated care financing scheme on the grounds that the state's tax on gross hospital earnings and patient services is preempted by ERISA, although the court clarified that the state does have authority to impose such a tax on charges paid by insured plans.[29] However, in a similar case (*Travelers et al.* v. *Pataki*) brought before the U.S. Supreme Court in 1995, New York's authority to tax and redistribute hospital revenues to offset differences in hospitals' uncompensated care burdens was upheld, narrowing the interpretation of ERISA's preemption provision.[30] Still, employer mandates legislated in three states (Massachusetts, Oregon, and Washington) may not be implemented without relief from ERISA's preemption.[31,32]

Aside from issues related to state initiatives for broader financing of health care, the ERISA preemption also raises important issues related to the states' conventional responsibilities to ensure consumer protection. While relatively large self-insured plans are generally

Table 2.6   Percentage of Workers in Insured versus Self-Insured
Employer-Sponsored Health Plans, by Establishment
Size, 1992–1993

	Establishments with Fewer than 100 Employees, 1992	Establishments with 100 Employees or More, 1993
Insured Plans	68	53
Fee-for-service	41	20
PPO	13	10
Prepaid HMO	14	23
Self-insured plans	32	46
Fee-for-service	27	30
PPO	5	16
Prepaid HMO	—	—

Source: U.S. Department of Labor, Bureau of Labor Statistics, *Employee Benefits in Small Private Establishments,* Bulletin 2441 (May 1994); and, *Employee Benefits in Medium and Large Private Establishments,* Bulletin 2456 (November 1994).

more vocal in opposing any state infringement on their ERISA protections, in fact a large proportion of self-insured firms are quite small. Available data from the U.S. Department of Labor indicate that nearly one-third of insured workers in firms with fewer than 100 employees are covered by a self-insured plan (see Table 2.6). Moreover, unpublished data from a Robert Wood Johnson Foundation survey of employer plans indicate that, in some states, self-insured plans are surprisingly common even in firms that employ fewer than ten workers.[33]

Self-insured plans are particularly likely to be fee-for-service indemnity plans and may or may not include a PPO arrangement. ERISA does not require self-insured plans to hold reserves or to meet solvency standards to protect workers and their dependents in the event of the insolvency of the employer and, therefore, of the self-insured plan. Moreover, ERISA does not make available to insured workers any means of redressing complaints about the administration of the plan, short of pursuing legal action in a federal court. For patients and families who are contending with a serious illness, this form of redress is likely to be deeply inadequate.

The ongoing conflict between the states' interest in resolving critical problems of financing care and ERISA's broad protection of self-insured employer plans does not appear to be headed toward simple resolution. For example, legislation introduced in the 104th

Congress by Senators Graham (FL) and Hatfield (OR) would have provided "shotgun" waivers of the ERISA preemption to particular states where ERISA impedes implementation of the states' broad health care reforms. But a bill introduced in the 105th Congress only months later by Congressman Fawell (IL) would expand ERISA's protections to all multiple-employer welfare arrangements (called MEWAs). (Under current law, the states may prohibit MEWAs from self-insuring.) If enacted, such legislation could move most private health insurance activity out of the sphere of the states' regulatory authority and consumer protections in favor of ERISA's loose federal oversight.

Reshaping the market: health insurance purchasing cooperatives

In their most generic form, health insurance purchasing cooperatives are organizations that combine employer groups or individuals for the purpose of buying insurance. They are intended to help small buyers bargain for lower health insurance premiums both by consolidating their purchasing power and by achieving greater administrative efficiencies in enrollment and premium collection. The idea of health insurance purchasing cooperatives was central to the 1994 national reform debate and, as a voluntary measure, remains popular among state legislators. Since 1992, at least 20 state governments across the country have enacted laws authorizing the establishment of health insurance purchasing cooperatives.[34]

Purchasing cooperatives have developed in both the private and public sectors. In May 1992, private purchasing cooperatives (that is, voluntary associations of private employers to purchase health insurance locally or regionally) were operating in at least 45 states and included both large and small employers.[35] While state-sponsored cooperatives were originally established to purchase health insurance for state employees, some also allow voluntary participation by county and municipal workers or other public entities such as school districts. However, voluntary participants and others included in a purchasing cooperative may be bargained separately if they represent substantially different risk than mandated participants.[36]

Existing purchasing cooperatives commonly exercise significant policymaking authority in a number of areas in order to improve competition among products, maximize the cooperatives' market power, and maximize the value of health care purchasing in the cooperative. To improve competition among health insurance plans (and also to discourage biased selection among plans), purchasing cooperatives typically standardize the design of benefits offered through the cooperative. In addition, cooperatives may exclude insurers and/or negotiate premiums (actions that are universal among private cooperatives but not universal among public cooperatives)[37] and may initiate self-insured plans. Increasingly, both private and public cooperatives are also concerned about the quality of health care purchased through the cooperative, and are adopting systems of quality monitoring and feedback to enrollees, health plans, and participating health care providers.[38]

As purchasing cooperatives develop and mature, they are emerging as a key influence in the market for health insurance. In markets in which managed care penetration is low, purchasing cooperatives have been instrumental in encouraging the development of managed care plans.[39] In markets such as Minneapolis, where managed care penetration is very high and the consolidation of the market into relatively few very large HMOs has begun to impede competition, the area's large private purchasing cooperative is attempting to restore competition by initiating *intraplan* bidding and negotiation with particular provider groups and hospitals affiliated with participating plans.[40] The ability of successful purchasing cooperatives to craft the health insurance market in which they wish to participate is a signal accomplishment and, as a model of competitive market management, a distinguishing feature of the evolving system of health insurance in the United States.

Medical savings accounts

Patterned on the idea of tax-qualified individual retirement accounts, the concept of individual medical savings accounts has become familiar to most students of health policy.[41] In general, medical savings accounts would offer a tax-exempt savings option for individuals, from which individuals could purchase health insurance, health care services, or both. Under current law, a similar type of account may be offered within a tax-qualified employer-sponsored cafeteria plan.[42]

Advocates of medical savings accounts commonly stress the several advantages that they might offer relative to the current system of tax-exempt employer-sponsored health insurance. If use of medical savings accounts displaced conventional employer-based coverage, workers could decouple their health insurance plans from their place of employment. Workers and nonworkers alike would be free to purchase any plan available in the market and would not risk having to change plans because they change jobs. Thus, a system of medical savings accounts would achieve full and automatic portability. This advantage is increasingly important in an environment of managed care plans where changing health insurance plans may mean also changing one's personal health care providers.

Medical savings accounts may also ease the problems experienced by part-time, seasonal, or self-employed workers in financing health insurance coverage. In two-worker families or among workers with multiple jobs, medical savings accounts may facilitate the merging of contributions from several employers. The same tax advantages enjoyed by employed workers also could be made available to self-employed workers and parents engaged in family care.

Finally, advocates of medical savings accounts emphasize the inequity of the current distribution of tax preferences for employer-based coverage. This inequity arises from two sources: first, the graduated structure of the federal income tax (and sometimes also state and local income taxes) raises the value of a tax-exempt dollar to high-income taxpayers above the value of that same dollar to taxpayers with lower income and, therefore, a lower marginal tax rate. This inevitable consequence of a graduated income tax is the basis for the argument by many economists that refundable tax credits would be a fairer means of encouraging health insurance coverage through the tax code. Individual medical savings accounts would greatly facilitate the administration of a system of refundable tax credits in lieu of the current exemption of employer contributions to health insurance benefits.

While these advantages of medical savings accounts are attractive to many constituencies, they also pose some very difficult problems. First, by decoupling employer sponsorship of a health insurance plan from employer contributions to the plan, medical savings accounts would facilitate employers' freezing or reducing their contributions to health insurance for some or all workers and their dependents. Even if workers' wages were increased by the amount that employers now contribute to health insurance, it is unlikely that all workers now covered by an employer plan would elect to place the full wage differential in a medical savings account for the purpose of buying health insurance. Furthermore, many workers who would buy coverage might seek to buy less insurance than they have now—either by purchasing "catastrophic" coverage (that is, coverage with a very high deductible), narrow coverage (such as a cancer policy), or coverage with low limits. Absent a requirement that everyone purchase at least some coverage, some workers who are now covered would choose to buy no coverage at all.

Critics of medical savings accounts argue that these choices would result in an increase in the number of low-income consumers—who are financially the most vulnerable and may also have the greatest health care needs—being underinsured or uninsured entirely. While the questions of no insurance or underinsurance (as well as other related issues, such as the likelihood of reduced financing for preventive services) might be addressed by defining in law the minimum design of a qualified health insurance plan, this type of regulation would in general be seen as antithetical to the free market principles of medical savings accounts.

By decoupling employers from the financing of health care, a system of medical savings accounts also would reduce employers' interest in managing the cost of health insurance plans. While this might be attractive to many employers, it poses a problem for health care costs in general. Where employers have asserted their purchasing power, either individually or collectively, they believe that they have been successful in moderating their own costs and, in some areas of the nation, health care costs marketwide. Critics of medical savings accounts do not foresee that a comparable vehicle for cost management would necessarily emerge as employers disengage. Instead, they are concerned that underinsured consumer decisions would guide the health care services market and that information about value in the health care market would be less accessible to individual consumers than it is even to large employers.

Critics of medical savings accounts have also expressed concern about the greater administrative cost that might characterize an individualized system of insurance coverage. The validity of this issue is difficult to appraise, however, since a system of medical savings accounts would probably redistribute administrative costs from employers into the price of the plan that workers are buying.[43] If consumers changed insurance plans less often as a result of improved portability, and as electronic information systems become more widespread, administrative costs in the aggregate might even decline. Nevertheless, it is difficult to believe that a system that might rely ever more heavily on individual purchasing agents and individualized marketing could achieve the efficiency of large-group purchasing.[44]

Finally, critics of medical savings accounts are concerned that, to achieve the same level of health insurance coverage, a system of refundable tax credits would be more costly to the federal government than the present system of tax-exempt employer contributions. Unwilling to support greater tax expenditures, they reason, the Congress would attempt to legislate a low-cost version of refundable tax credits. Critics fear that such a system might inadequately fund low-income consumers and would segment the health care system if low-risk or higher-income consumers chose to use medical savings accounts to finance catastrophic coverage rather than invest in plans that offered more complete coverage for health care services.[45] Either result would place low-income consumers at risk because greater risk segmentation could make conventional, full-coverage health insurance plans (including managed care plans) prohibitively expensive, and because political momentum for developing a more adequate system of financing might be lost.

Conclusion

While still the principal source of private health insurance in the United States, employer-based health insurance has eroded significantly as health care costs have continued to rise. Most recently, this pattern of erosion has taken a particular turn: employer coverage of workers rose in 1993, but a decline in employer coverage of dependents more than offset the improvement in coverage among workers. Individually purchased coverage is rising, but not so rapidly as to offset the historic decline in employer coverage among the population under age 65. Medicaid coverage has soared to include growing numbers of the low-income working population without access to employer plans.

To public policymakers and analysts, the growing numbers of the uninsured and the fact that an increasing number of low-income workers and their families without employer coverage rely on expanded eligibility for Medicaid have become a litmus test for the performance of the private insurance system. To date, these indicators reflect important failures of the private insurance system to control costs effectively and to offer reliable health care financing to the broad spectrum of workers and their families.

In the absence of national reform of health care financing, many states have undertaken to reform the private insurance market within their borders. Small-group and individual insurance reforms are intended to address some insurer practices that have been considered the most egregious, especially denial of coverage and prohibitive pricing to individuals and groups with health problems. Whether these reforms stabilize insurance markets, reorganize competition, and broaden voluntary insurance coverage remains to be seen. Early evidence suggests that the states' small-group reforms have probably resolved some consumer problems and have not produced flight from the market by either insurers or purchasers. Nevertheless, these reforms are unlikely to offset the ongoing erosion of employer coverage where it exists.

While more aggressive state reforms to redistribute the burden of uncompensated health care or to reverse the erosion of employer coverage have been impeded by ERISA, the private insurance market is nonetheless undergoing revolutionary change. Some argue that this change offers the best hope for developing an efficient, flexible, and workable system of health care financing, improving the quality of care, stabilizing costs, and broadening access to financing. Some point to the growth and maturation of managed care systems and the growing experience of voluntary purchasing cooperatives as hallmarks of this changing market. And some advocate medical savings accounts as a means of accelerating and perhaps redirecting private market change toward more individualism in the purchase of insurance.

While private employers and public policymakers alike are guardedly optimistic that ongoing changes will force better value in the health care market, it seems unlikely that they will broaden voluntary insurance coverage enough to resolve the driving issue of the 1994 national health care reform debate—the persistently large proportion of the population that is uninsured. Nevertheless, the fast-changing private insurance market may offer a new platform for crafting solutions to this problem, as both private and public purchasers learn how to induce better performance in the financing and delivery of health care.

Acknowledgments

The author wishes to express appreciation to Stacy Halbert of Alpha Center for his assistance in tabulating the Current Population Survey, and to Stan Jones and Uwe Reinhardt for thoughtful review and comments. The opinions expressed in this chapter are those of the author and should not be attributed to Alpha Center.

Notes

1. All information about sources of private insurance coverage are supported by Alpha Center tabulations of the March Current Population Survey for the referenced years and reflect counts of the civilian noninstitutionalized population under age 65.
2. K. R. Levit, A. L. Sensenig, C. A. Cowan, H. C. Lazenby, P. A. McDonnell, A. K. Won, L. Sivarajan, J. M. Stiller, C. S. Donham, and M. S. Stewart, "National Health Expenditures, 1993," *Health Care Financing Review* 16, no. 1 (Fall 1994): 247–94.
3. R. J. Blendon, T. S. Hyams, and J. M. Benson, "Bridging the Gap Between Expert and Public Views on Health Care Reform," *Journal of the American Medical Association* 269, no. 19 (19 May 1993): 2573–78.
4. D. Yankelovich, "The Debate That Wasn't: The Public and the Clinton Plan," *Health Affairs* 14, no. 1 (Spring 1995): 7–23.
5. See, for example, M. V. Pauly, P. Danzon, P. Feldstein, and J. Hoff, "A Plan for 'Responsible National Health Insurance,'" *Health Affairs* 10, no. 1 (Spring 1991): 5–25.
6. Physician Payment Review Commission, *Annual Report to Congress* (Washington, DC: PPRC, 1991), chapter 15.
7. See, for example, J. Holahan, T. Coghlin, L. Ku, D. J. Lipson, and S. Rajan, "Insuring the Poor through Medicaid 1115 Waivers," *Health Affairs* 14, no. 1 (Spring 1995): 200–17.
8. Typically, industry groups and firms that are characterized by low rates of own-employer coverage also "import" significant amounts of employer-based dependents' coverage. This importing behavior represents a significant real subsidy to small firms, especially to firms with 10–24 workers, and a significant self-imposed real tax on large firms. See D. Chollet, "Employer-Based Health Insurance in a Changing Work Force," *Health Affairs* 13, no. 1 (Spring 1994): 315–26.
9. For example, supported by the Robert Wood Johnson Foundation's Health Care for the Uninsured Program (HCUP), a number of states and nonprofit groups have tested different methods to make health insurance both more affordable and available to uninsured small businesses and individuals. Eleven demonstration projects became operational under the program between 1986 and 1992: ten developed new insurance products or subsidized existing products, and one developed a health insurance information and referral service. See W. D. Helms, A. K. Gauthier, and D. J. Campion, "Mending the Flaws in the Small Group Market," *Health Affairs* 11, no. 2 (Summer 1992): 8–27.
10. Oregon, Massachusetts, and Florida have each attempted to use employer subsidies and tax incentives during the past six years to raise rates of employer coverage in small firms. In Oregon, which offered small business tax credits from 1989 to 1993, only about 26,000 persons ever enrolled in tax-credited plans. See D. J. Lipson, "Keeping the Promise?

Achieving Universal Health Coverage in Six States." Report to the Henry J. Kaiser Foundation (Washington, DC: Alpha Center, September 1994). However, some studies have suggested that the time-limited nature of these tax credits discouraged employers from taking advantage of them. See U.S. General Accounting Office (GAO), *Access to Health Insurance: State Efforts to Assist Small Businesses,* GAO/HRD-92-90 (May 1992).

11. W. D. Helms, "Lessons from Voluntary Efforts to Expand Health Insurance Coverage and Implications for Health Care Reform." Testimony presented to the United States Senate Committee on Finance (1 February 1994).

12. Lipson 1994.

13. C. G. McLaughlin and W. Zeller, "The Shortcomings of Voluntarism in the Small-Group Insurance Market," *Health Affairs* 11, no. 2 (Summer 1992): 28–40.

14. New York's law became effective in 1994; Connecticut's, Florida's, and Washington's laws became effective in 1995; Maine's and New Jersey's laws will become effective in 1997; and Colorado's law will become effective in 1998.

15. Selected provisions of the states' small-group community rating laws are summarized in D. Chollet and R. Paul, "Community Rating: Issues and Experience." (Washington, DC: Alpha Center, December 1994), monograph.

16. This result directly follows from the skewed distribution of risk in any large risk pool: relatively few participants incur the vast majority of plan cost. Therefore, averaging risk within the pool (rather than discriminating by known risk) will raise premiums for the majority of participants— directly in proportion to the amount the overall risk distribution is skewed. If applied to the small-group market, these results rest on the following logic: relatively few individuals in the population of workers and their dependents represent extraordinary risk. However, the participation of one or several of these individuals in a small group significantly raises the group's average claims experience relative to that of small groups in which such individuals do not participate. If the number of small groups exceeds the number of high-risk individuals in the population (or if high-risk individuals are not randomly distributed among small groups), then the average claims experience among small groups is distributed in roughly the same way as individual claims experience is distributed among the population. Thus, application of community rates by competing insurers creates "winners" and "losers" among small groups, which would not be the case if the groups were experience-rated.

17. Chollet and Paul 1994.

18. D. Chollet, "Major Provisions of Employer Group Plans." Report to the Health Care Financing Administration (Washington, DC: Alpha Center, November 1993).

19. An empirical literature evaluating the cost-effectiveness of HMO management of chronic care patients is only just emerging. This literature

suggests that HMOs have had only limited experience with chronic care management for older patients, but may be developing more extensive experience in chronic care management within their pediatric practices. See, for example, T. Fama, P. D. Fox, and L. A. White, "Do HMOs Care for the Chronically Ill?" *Health Affairs* 14, no. 1 (Spring 1995): 234–43.

20. Chollet and Paul 1994.
21. R. H. Miller and H. S. Luft, "Managed Care: Past Evidence and Potential Trends," *Frontiers of Health Services Management* 9, no. 3 (1993): 3–37.
22. Hamilton/KSA, H&HN, AAPHO/IHDS Survey of 109 PHOs in 1994, cited in: Terese Hudson, "Growing Pains," *Hospitals and Health Networks* 69, no. 1 (5 January 1995): 42–45.
23. The representativeness of the Hamilton/KSA survey is unknown.
24. The PHOs questioned in this survey also were heavily capitalized by hospitals. Hospitals controlled 63 percent of capital; physicians controlled 26 percent. Outside investors controlled less than 1 percent of capital among all PHOs surveyed.
25. The McCarran-Ferguson Act (Public Law 15) exempts insurance from certain federal insurance regulation to the extent that the individual states actually regulate insurance. It also provides that most other federal laws are not applicable to insurance, unless they are specifically directed at the business of insurance. See B. T. Beam, Jr., and J. J. McFadden, *Employee Benefits*, 3rd ed. (Dearborn, MI: Financial Publishing, Inc., 1992).
26. See, for example, J. Johnsson, "Feds Take Aim at PHOs," *American Medical News* (23/30 January 1995): 1.
27. R. Paul and D. Chollet, "Administrative Structures for Health Care Reform: The Allocation of States' Responsibilities under Health Care Reform" (Washington, DC: Alpha Center, March 1995), monograph.
28. For example, in 1985, the Supreme Court ruled that state law mandating coverage of mental health benefits was inapplicable to ERISA plans in *Metropolitan Life Insurance Co. and Travelers Insurance Co. v. Massachusetts*. In a more recent case, a federal court ruling interpreted ERISA as protecting an employer that altered the plan design explicitly to limit AIDS-related benefits (*McGann v. H&R Music Company*).
29. *Connecticut Hospital Association v. Pogue*, DC Conn, No. 3:94 CV01224 AVC (17 November 1994).
30. At this writing, litigation brought respectively by an HMO and by the Health Insurance Association of America on behalf of its members in New York challenges New York's risk-adjustment regulation related to community-rated health insurance plans. The plaintiffs have charged that this regulation is a violation of ERISA's preemption, to the extent that it affects the minimum-premium policies available to self-insured plans.
31. While it is clear that Washington's mandate would require exemption from ERISA, it is uncertain whether implementation of the employer mandate statutes in Massachusetts and Oregon would violate ERISA. See P. Butler, *Roadblock to Reform: ERISA Implications for State Health Care Initia-*

tives (Washington, DC: National Governors' Association, 1994). ERISA also blocks full implementation of Florida's health care reforms. While Florida did not require employers to provide coverage, it required the legislature to revisit this question. Florida's 1992 law provided that "employers shall be mandated to provide such coverage" if coverage among employees and their dependents was not at a level acceptable to the legislature by 31 December 1994.

32. ERISA grandfathered Hawaii's employer mandate, which was enacted prior to 1974. Under ERISA, Hawaii is the only state that is able to mandate that employers offer or contribute to health insurance for workers or their dependents.

33. Supported by the Robert Wood Johnson Foundation's *State Initiatives in Health Care Reform* program, this survey was conducted by RAND in eight states in 1993 and 1994.

34. Intergovernmental Health Policy Project, George Washington University, "Purchasing Alliances: Strengthening Small Group Clout," *State Health Notes* 15, no. 191 (31 October 1994): 4–5.

35. GAO 1992.

36. In their examination of one private purchasing cooperative, the GAO concluded that voluntary participation did result in higher-risk groups enrolling in at least one private cooperative. Both Minnesota and Washington also have found that the diverse membership in their state purchasing cooperatives (including Medicaid beneficiaries) necessitates that the states negotiate separately for some groups in the cooperative. U.S. General Accounting Office (GAO), Access to Health Insurance: Public and Private Employers' Experience with Purchasing Cooperatives (GAO/HEHS-94-142), 1994.

37. Even in states in which public purchasing cooperatives enjoy wide discretionary authority to determine the number and type of carriers offered, most still contract with a large number of carriers. For example, as of May 1994, the California Public Employee Retirement System (CalPERS) included 22 carriers, but limited new contracts to plans that introduced HMO coverage to unserved areas of the state. For 1994, the Health Insurance Plan of California (HIPC) received bids from 25 carriers and contracted with 18 (see GAO 1994). However, Florida's Community Health Insurance Plans (CHPAs)—available to firms with 50 or fewer employees, state employees, and Medicaid beneficiaries—may not negotiate premiums, nor may the CHPAs exclude any state-certified health plan.

38. For example, Minnesota's private Business Health Care Action Group (BHCAG) fostered establishment of the $2 million Institute for Clinical Systems Integration to facilitate continuous quality improvement and better integration of the health care delivery system. As of 1994, CalPERS requires plans to submit during the rate renewal process data on a list of preventive service delivery indicators as well as some indicators of the quality of health status management in the plan. Florida's CHPAs

will issue "report cards" on the quality of care offered through CHPA plans. The CHPA report cards will reflect incidence rates for selected services or outcomes, patient satisfaction, costs, and accreditation.

39. In 1984, the Wisconsin state employee cooperative restricted plans offered through the cooperative to two self-funded fee-for-service plans and to HMOs, tripling enrollment in HMOs that year. See GAO 1994.

40. R. Cunningham, "MN Business Group Fosters New Wave of Competition," *Medicine and Health Perspectives* 49, no. 14 (3 April 1995).

41. Pauly and Goodman describe one version of medical savings accounts and review many of the arguments that have been raised against earlier versions of the concept. M. V. Pauly and J. C. Goodman, "Tax Credits for Health Insurance and Medical Savings Accounts," *Health Affairs* 14, no. 1 (Spring 1995): 125–39.

42. Commonly, these accounts are established as companion plans to a menu of health insurance plan options, and are not part of a broader cafeteria plan. In such cases, they typically are called "Section 125 plans," after the section of the Internal Revenue Code that recognizes qualified cafeteria plans. Organized in this way, employers usually make no contribution to the account. Employee contributions are "use or lose"; that is, any unused balances must be forfeited to the plan at the end of the tax year.

43. In a system of group coverage, large employers, especially, bear significant administrative costs directly that do not appear in the price of their insurance plans. In a more individualized system of coverage, the administrative costs no longer supported by employers would appear in the plan premium, raising administrative costs as they are now measured. However, if workers captured the value of employers' direct administrative costs in the form of higher wages, in principle they could also make higher contributions to their medical savings accounts.

44. To a great degree, the health insurance purchasing alliances proposed in 1994 by the Clinton administration were constructed in response to these cost concerns. Available to employer groups and individuals alike, these alliances would have emulated the prudent purchasing behavior that characterizes the large firms that have invested in aggressive cost management. In addition, by standardizing and consolidating information, alliances potentially would have held marketing costs in check and simplified the market to an extent that would have allowed consumers to sidestep the services of insurance agents.

45. Research evidence related to individual retirement accounts (IRAs) suggests that higher-income families are more likely to contribute to these accounts than lower-income families. See S. F. Venti and D. A. Wise, "The Determinants of IRA Contributions and the Effects of Limit Changes," in Zvi Bodie, J. B. Shoven, and D. A. Wise, eds. *Pensions in the U.S. Economy* (Chicago: University of Chicago Press, 1988): 9–52. Moreover, contributions to IRAs appear to represent no net saving among households that contribute, but instead are a transfer of savings from taxable to nontaxable forms. See W. G. Gale and J. K. Scholz, "IRAs and

Household Saving," *The American Economic Review* 84, no. 5 (December 1994): 1233–60. Whether similar results would occur with medical savings accounts would depend on whether contributions to medical savings accounts are voluntary and on the level and distribution of refundable tax credits that would support them.

3

Rationing Health Care: What It Is, What It Is Not, and Why We Cannot Avoid It

Uwe E. Reinhardt

> Your phrase "price rationing" makes applesauce of the word "rationing," which is becoming yet another classification that does not classify.
> —Columnist George F. Will, in a letter to the author

Abstract. The word "rationing" has come to play a central role in the national health policy debate. Alas, it is also one of the most misunderstood of words. Its injection into the debate has generated far more heat than light.

This chapter reviews the definition of "rationing" preferred by the profession that takes as its task the study of how individuals and society respond to and deal with scarcity, namely, the economics profession. It will be shown that economists usually consider all limits on the distribution of a scarce good or services to be "rationing," whether that limit takes the form of a price barrier or some method of non-price allocation—for example, queues or allocation by lottery. To make a distinction between allocation through freely competitive markets and other forms of resource allocation, economists distinguish between "price rationing" and "non-price rationing." This is a meaningful distinction. Adoption of the economist's definition of "rationing" would greatly clarify the national health policy debate.

Next, the discussion turns to the controversial proposition, commonly made by most economists and a handful of their allies in the medical profession, that an *economically efficient* health care system will inevitably engage in the pervasive withholding of services that may be sought by patients and their physicians, and that it will do so to enhance the quality and efficiency of the health care system overall. If managed competition lives up to its current billing, it will entail rationing of precisely that sort. Unfortunately, the individualist tradition of the United States, as it expresses itself in the tort system, may seriously hinder managed competition from achieving its stated goal.

Finally, this chapter offers some conjectures on the approach to rationing likely to be taken by the United States health care system in the twenty-first century. It is argued that, far from having been inconclusive, the most recent congressional debate on health care reform actually gave official sanction to a three-tiered health system, with fairly severe rationing in the bottom tier and virtually none in the top tier. While such tiering has always been present in the U.S. health care system, the phenomenon has hitherto been treated as a blemish to be removed by government—now it will probably remain a permanent fixture.

If there is one word that is more frequently used than any other in health care policy debates, and one that is more often than not misused, it probably is the word "rationing."

During the three decades following World War II, Americans had gradually persuaded themselves that rationing health care was unethical and that it could be avoided permanently. For a while it appeared that, uniquely in the industrialized world, the United States actually had succeeded in implementing that idea at the level of practice. The vast majority of Americans were very well insured for the cost of health care, either at their place of work or through government programs. Through open-ended reimbursement systems—either passively paid "charges" or "retrospective full-cost reimbursement"—both public and private insurance carriers effectively opened their treasuries to the providers of health care, and these providers could tap these treasuries almost at will. Not surprisingly, the health care system established more physical capacity, and more technically sophisticated apparatus, than doctors and hospitals could sensibly use. As a consequence of this abundance, neither money nor bricks and mortar nor human resources were ever spared in responding to the illnesses that well-insured Americans presented to their health care system.

Although the 10 to 15 percent of the population without health insurance often did encounter financial barriers to this abundant capacity, it is not surprising that the great majority of well-insured Americans came to believe quite sincerely that the denial of medically beneficial services for economic reasons was not only immoral, but also unnecessary. Thus, the very idea of rationing health care became anathema in the debate on health policy, which was conducted mainly by very well-insured and well-to-do Americans.

The financial burden of this abundance, however, soon came to vex even the staunchest defenders of the American health care system. By the early 1980s, the United States had spent about 30 percent more per capita on health care than had the next most expensive health system in the world, neighboring Canada.[1] After about 1960 and until the early 1990s, the health care component of the U.S. gross domestic product (GDP) tended to outpace the rest of the GDP by an average of close to 3 percentage points,[2] a trend not matched by any other country. By 1993, close to 14 percent of the GDP was being consumed by health care. By that time, no other country had exceeded even 10 percent.[3] In 1993, the Congressional Budget Office (CBO) forecast that U.S. health care spending would reach 18.9 percent by the year 2000.[4] Further extrapolation of this trend to the mid-twenty-first century implied that close to 50 percent of the GDP would go to health care alone by the year 2050.[5]

 It has become evident to all thoughtful observers of the health care system that the nation will soon break off the health care spending trend followed in the past three decades. It will also be evident to any thoughtful observer that such a break will entail the rationing of health care in one way or another, even if that very thought today remains anathema among the general public. In this respect, the United States will simply return to the fold of the rest of the industrialized world, albeit with a uniquely American approach to the task.

Because the topic of rationing cannot be avoided much longer in the national debate on health care policy, it may be useful to explore in a detached manner what that term actually means, and also to speculate on the manner in which the United States will ration health care in the coming decades.

"Rationing" in the Vernacular

According to *Webster's Collegiate Dictionary*, "to ration" means "to distribute equitably."[6] That definition conjures up an image of benign intent. One thinks of calamities—a famine or a war—in which a civilized community decides to allocate the available, limited supply of basic necessities on the basis not of the individual's ability to pay, but on some other criterion of need or merit. The precise algorithm of rationing chosen in particular contexts is based on some widely shared social ethic—for example, that all members of the community should share equally in the limited supplies, or that women and children be given preference, or that the weak and the sick be favored. Rationing in that context is deemed good.

In the recent debate on national health care reform, however, the word "rationing" took on a more sinister meaning. Commentators who attributed rationing to this or that health care reform proposal typically did not imply thereby that the plan proposed to "distribute health care equitably." On the contrary, they aimed that word as a lethal blow.

One of the arguments most frequently hurled against President Clinton's ill-fated Health Securities Act, for example, was that this plan would *lead* to rationing of care. This argument suggests by implication that the United States does not now ration health care, and that it need not do so in the future. As noted in the introduction, for the vast majority of well-insured Americans rationing health care will, indeed, be a novel idea and a threat. But millions of low-income American families without comprehensive health insurance must have found themselves perplexed by the assertion that health reform might "lead" to rationing. It is well known that these Americans have for decades gone without the proper health care at the proper time, either because they lacked the money to purchase the needed care, or because they lived in areas that had been bypassed by an otherwise abundantly endowed health care system.

In a recently completed study, research assistants approached private medical practices pretending to be Medicaid patients in need of care; 63 percent of them were denied care because of their Medicaid coverage.[7] It is known that, other socioeconomic factors (income, family status, location, and so on) being equal, uninsured Americans receive, on average, only about 60 percent of the health care services received by equally situated insured Americans.[8] This appears to be true even for the subgroup of adults whose health status is poor or only fair.[9] Studies have shown that uninsured Americans relying on the emergency rooms of heavily crowded public hospitals experience very long waits before being seen by a doctor, sometimes so long that they simply leave because they are literally too sick to wait any longer.[10] After controlling statistically for the effects of diagnosis, race, hospital type, and other relevant variables, a study of a large cohort of about 30,000 newborns in California found that uninsured infants received substantially fewer health care services than did otherwise similar, insured newborns, and that babies covered by Medicaid received fewer services than privately insured babies.[11] Studies have found that, after careful statistical control for a host of socioeconomic and medical factors, uninsured Americans tend to die in hospitals from the same illness at up to triple the rate that is observed for equally situated insured Americans[12] and that, over the long run, uninsured Americans tend to die at an earlier age than do similarly situated insured Americans.[13]

Evidently, commentators who warned darkly that this or that proposed health care reform plan would "lead" to the rationing of health care in America did not regard as "rationing" the withholding of health care from uninsured Americans unable to pay for their own care. These commentators apply the term "rationing" only to the act of withholding of goods or services from someone for reasons other than ability to pay, for example, the withholding of a diagnostic procedure from someone who would be willing and able to pay the going free-market rate for the service but who is forced to stand in a queue for that care, or is simply denied it by administrative fiat. This form of rationing is common in countries with socialized health insurance systems (e.g., Canada and the United Kingdom), where health care may be free at point of service and where fees paid the providers of care are low, but where patients often have to queue up for elective surgery and for diagnostic tests that are not critically needed immediately.

Other students of American health care, however, evidently would apply the term "rationing" to the withholding of health care over price as well. In an op-ed piece harshly critical of the Clinton plan, Bernadine Healy, M. D., formerly director of the National Institutes of Health, argued that the exclusion of screening mammography for women in their 40s from the President's standard benefit package constitutes "rationing" of that procedure.

> When combined with global budgeting, the new health plan becomes a methodology of health care rationing. Under this plan, a woman is being forced to buy services she might not want, and is being deprived of services she does want—such as mammography—*unless she is able to come up with the extra after-tax dollars on top of the already expensive mandatory Clinton health "premium."*[14] (Italics added)

If one applies Healy's interpretation of the term "rationing" consistently, then one would have to describe as "rationing" the exclusion of any medical procedure, supply, or device from a *collectively* financed health benefit package—whether it be under collectively financed public or private health insurance—even if patients are free to purchase the excluded items with their own after-tax funds, as they would have been under the Clinton plan.[15] In other words, in Healy's view the current health care system surely already does ration screening mammography pervasively,[16] even for women in their 50s and early

60s, because millions of American women who are not covered by Medicare lack insurance coverage for screening mammography, and many of them are too poor to afford regular screening with their own meager after-tax budgets. Indeed, consistent application of Healy's expansive interpretation points to wholesale rationing of many types of health care in our current health system, for many private insurance policies exclude this or that procedure from coverage and, as noted, millions of Americans do not have any health insurance coverage in the first place.

Other authors have made similar arguments. In response to Henry J. Aaron's and William B. Schwartz's by now classic *The Painful Prescription: Rationing of Hospital Care,* Merrill and Cohen[17] wondered when, if ever, Americans might be prepared to contemplate a more systematic, ethically defensible form of rationing health care in place of the haphazard rationing already in practice. Aaron and Schwartz, incidentally, wrote their classic book about rationing without ever explicitly defining that term. Apparently they meant by it the comparison of the benefits and costs of particular medical procedures in decisions on their use,[18] and they thought that everyone clearly understood that letting costs enter into clinical decisions by way of benefit-cost analysis obviously implied rationing.

Given the varying interpretations imposed on the term "rationing," it may be useful to explain how economists define that term in their discussions of resource allocation in general. In a nutshell, economists make a distinction between "price rationing" and "non-price rationing" and consider both types of rationing proper.

"Rationing" in Economics

Economists define their intellectual terrain as "the study of how individuals and societies respond to and deal with limited resources."[19] Central to this definition are the notions of *scarcity* and *choice.* By *scarcity* economists mean that the available supply of most desirable things will typically be insufficient to satisfy the demand for them that would obtain if they were distributed freely without exacting any sacrifice whatsoever from the recipient. By *choice* economists mean that individuals and societies have or should have some flexibility in deciding how scarce resources ought to be allocated to competing ends. As one popular adage among economists puts it: "For economists there is no

Heaven or Hell, because in Heaven there is no *scarcity*, and in Hell there is no *choice*."

Price rationing versus non-price rationing

There are only a few ways for society to allocate scarce resources among its members; among them:

- Allocation to the highest bidder, through the free market;
- Allocation on a first-come, first-served basis;
- Allocation by lottery; and
- Allocation on the basis of administrative discretion.

In economics, all four methods of allocation (not only the nonmarket algorithms) are considered "rationing." Economists call the free-market allocation "price rationing." All other allocations are called "non-price rationing."

In their leading textbook on microeconomic theory at the intermediate level, for example, Michael L. Katz and Harvey S. Rosen instruct students that

> if bread were free, a huge quantity of it would be demanded. Because the resources used to produce bread are scarce, the actual amount of bread has to be *rationed* among its potential users. Not everyone can have all the bread they could possibly want. The bread must be *rationed* somehow; the [money] price system accomplishes this in the following simple way: Everyone who is willing to pay the equilibrium [market-clearing] price gets the good, and everyone who is not, does not.[20] (Italics added)

To quote from another recent textbook in first-year economics:

> Scarcity implies that commodities must be rationed. *Prices ration commodities on the basis of willingness to pay.* Those who are willing to pay more get the commodity; those who are only willing to pay less do not. When a price ceiling is imposed, [money] prices no longer serve this socially useful function. The market no longer rations the amount provided to the market among the competing consumers. Therefore, an alternative rationing device that does not depend upon price must be devised. . . . There is simply no way around the rationing problem.[21] (Italics added)

Most other textbooks in freshman economics contain similar passages. To be sure, after making the very useful distinction between *price rationing* (really, money-price rationing) and *non-price rationing* (i.e., rationing by methods other than money-prices), economists usually go on to argue that non-price rationing typically triggers unintended side effects that make non-price rationing inherently less economically *efficient* than rationing by money-prices and that, therefore, make rationing by money-price the inherently superior allocation method.

The inefficiency attributed to non-price rationing is thought to flow from two distinct sources. First, if non-price rationing of a scarce commodity is coupled with a strict prohibition of a secondary market in which people can trade their allocation for money or for other things, then such rationing may bestow that commodity on some persons who do not crave it much, if at all, leaving other persons who truly do crave it with less. It is self-evident that overall social welfare could be enhanced by allowing such parties to exchange the thing for money in mutually beneficial exchanges.

But, second, even if such mutually beneficial trades in a secondary market were tacitly or explicitly allowed under non-price rationing, the need to organize that secondary market would require more *real* resources (mainly time, but possibly other resources too) than would be used up by a simple free-market allocation from the outset.

In making this argument, however, economists are not unaware that their prescription may meet objections on ethical grounds. They counter these objections with the proposition that, if society really wished to help low-income individuals gain access to a particular, scarce commodity—such as health care or education—then the most economically efficient method of reaching that goal would be simply to redistribute appropriate amounts of money from the rich to the poor, and then to let the poor bid for that commodity in the free market with money-prices, alongside the rich, letting the chips fall where they may.

That proposition, in turn, is based on either one of two important, tacit assumptions. First, one could assume that the free-market allocation of scarce commodities actually will be preceded by a redistribution of money in sufficient amounts to make possible an ethically acceptable distribution of scarce commodities among members of society. Alternatively, one simply could assume that the distribution of income and wealth that prevails in a democracy at any point in time (after taxes and subsidies) must be ethically acceptable to society at large, because otherwise that distribution would not prevail.[22] On either assumption, the distribution of commodities begotten by price rationing in a freely competitive market ought to be judged ethically acceptable as well. If neither assumption is valid, then normative prescriptions based on the criterion of economic efficiency rest on very shaky ground.

In any event, whatever economists wish to assume about the prevailing income distribution, professional standards oblige them to say something quite *explicitly* about the ethical acceptability of that distribution when they recommend price rationing in free markets as the inherently more *efficient* and hence *superior* allocation method, particularly when that prescription is applied to the context of health care.

The concept of "efficiency" in economics

Along with the term "rationing," the term "efficiency" probably is one of the most widely used and most widely misunderstood terms in discussions on public policy. In the vernacular, use of the term "efficiency" is almost always fuzzy. In their professional writings and in the classroom, economists use a very precise definition of the term. Unfortunately, that definition is so technical and complex that it spans entire textbook chapters that bedevil even doctoral students in economics.[23]

The most compact definition of the term used by economists, and found in every textbook on economics, is the following:

> A particular allocation of resources among members of society is said to be efficient when no person can be made better off through a reallocation of these resources without making someone else worse off.[24]

Economists call this situation *Pareto efficient,* after the nineteenth century Italian economist Vilfredo Pareto who first defined efficiency that way. This celebrated definition does have its uses at the abstract level of theory. But rarely is it helpful in applied policy analysis, because there are so few situations in the real world in which public policymakers can reallocate resources without making at least someone worse off and, thus, sorely upset. Politicians know this only too well, as do practicing economists outside the confines of their classrooms.

A more intuitively appealing interpretation of efficiency, sometimes used by practicing economists, is that among several alternative policies—*with all of them designed to achieve exactly the same goal*—the most efficient policy is the one that reaches that same specified goal with the least expenditure of real resources (human labor, energy, materials, land, and so on). That definition is easily grasped by the layperson, and it does find uses in applied policy analysis.

Now it is immediately apparent from this more pragmatic defi-

Figure 3.1   Efficiency versus Social Desirability: Is More Efficient Necessarily Better?

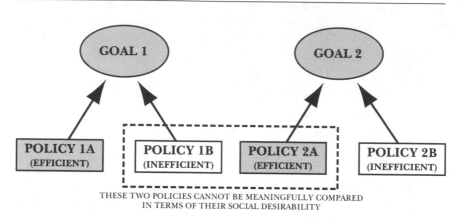

THESE TWO POLICIES CANNOT BE MEANINGFULLY COMPARED
IN TERMS OF THEIR SOCIAL DESIRABILITY

nition of efficiency that one cannot use that definition to rank alternative policies in terms of their social desirability, *unless all of them lead to precisely the same ultimate outcome,* a point illustrated visually in Figure 3.1. To illustrate this point concretely, an inefficient policy under which all children receive appropriate immunizations is not *ipso facto* less desirable than a superbly efficient policy that succeeds in immunizing only half of the nation's children, and no properly trained economist would ever argue otherwise. Instead, he or she would search for more efficient approaches that succeed in immunizing all children, if that were the goal society sought to attain. Stated in plain English, that proposition seems obvious.

It follows from the preceding discussion that it is just not meaningful to rank alternative methods of rationing health care solely in terms of their relative economic efficiency, unless one *explicitly* declares the prevailing distribution of income as optimal in the sense that this distribution would make possible an ethically acceptable allocation of the available health care resources, if these resources simply were allocated to people bidding the highest money-prices for them. It is surprising and distressing how many otherwise well-educated commentators on health policy fail to grasp this simple point when they distinguish between the "market approach" (i.e., money-price rationing), on the one hand, and "rationing" (i.e., non-price rationing), on the other.

A proposed nomenclature

The gist of the preceding discussion is that the conventional use of the term "rationing" in the national health policy debate is not helpful. That usage sometimes implies that rationing occurs only if people are denied access to something for which they would have been willing and able to pay money. It has led to the strange notion that "rationing" of health care is never acceptable, unless the access to care is denied because of the sick person's inability to pay for the needed care. There is no evidence that this notion has broad support among the American people, and there is much evidence that it has not.[25]

Indeed, in their research on the behavior of firms and their customers, Kahneman, Knetsch, and Thaler[26] report that Americans often prefer waiting in a queue to the use of higher prices in the face of shortages, even in the context of commodities other than health care. In responses to one survey on the optimal allocation of tickets to football games, for example, 75 percent of the respondents considered auctioning of tickets to the highest bidders as "least fair" and 68 percent considered allocation by queue "most fair." In terms of a preferred allocation method, rationing by queue outranked rationing by lottery, and by a huge margin both outranked rationing by auction. One may safely assume that, if the public holds these sentiments on football games, it is likely to hold them with even greater force in the context of health care.

Suppose, for example, one asked any random sample of Americans the following concrete question:

> Assume that a scarce health care resource (a transplantable organ, a highly skilled surgeon, or a dialysis machine) could be allocated to only one of two patients: one the child of a low-income gas station attendant and the other the child of a wealthy executive. Should that scarce resource be allocated to the child whose family is able to bid the highest money-price for it?

It is doubtful that a majority of Americans would respond in the affirmative. It is doubtful even that a majority of professional American economists would respond in the affirmative. Yet this question goes to the heart of the question of how scarce health care resources in general ought to be allocated to members of society. If rationing by price and ability to pay is not to be used in this particular instance, then when does it become legitimate, even in health care?

A preferable usage of the term "rationing" would be to apply it to *all* methods of allocating scarce resources to competing ends—as most textbooks in economics do—and then to make the meaningful distinction between price rationing and non-price rationing. That distinction automatically invites further thought on both the economic and the ethical implication of either form of rationing. Specifically, it might force policymakers to categorize the broad set of goods and services now lumped together under the generic label "health care" into those they might allow to be rationed by price and ability to pay and those for which that allocation mechanism would trigger strong objections on ethical grounds, given the prevailing distribution of income. A useful first exercise in a workshop on health economics and policy might be to construct such a list.

Furthermore, when economists do advocate price rationing as an inherently superior method of allocating scarce resources—even for health care—it behooves them to precede their normative prescriptions with an *explicit* statement on their assumptions about the underlying distribution of income, like a highly visible warning label.

One such statement might be that the analyst considers the prevailing (after-tax and after-subsidy) distribution of income ethically acceptable and, therefore, regards any distribution of health care that the prevailing distribution of income might beget as ethically acceptable as well. Alternatively, if economists do not regard the prevailing distribution of income as ethically acceptable, then their normative propositions ought to be *explicitly* conditioned on the assumption that a proper redistribution of income will precede the application of these normative propositions. Either way, an *explicit* statement on this point would alert the user of normative economic analysis to its ethical dimensions. Simply to sweep the issue of the underlying income distribution under the rug, by assuming that this issue is well understood, strikes at least this author as dubious professional practice. It is like prescribing a drug without warning the patient of possible side effects.

The more precise usage of the term "rationing" advocated here would do much to enhance the clarity of the national health care policy debate. It would also serve as a reminder that the rationing of health care cannot simply be wished away from the American health care system. As already noted, the United States has always rationed health care for at least some segment of its population, and always will. In fact, economists would argue that any health care system that does not somehow ration health care is *ipso facto* inefficient, a point constantly made not only by economists,[27] but by some physicians as well.[28,29]

Why Efficient Health Systems Ration Health Care

When economists are asked what percentage of its gross national product a nation should spend on health care, they usually equivocate that there is no concrete answer to that question. At the level of theory, however, economists can always offer a crisp and clear answer, one that emerges from the following fundamental principle drummed into the head of every first-year economics student:

> An individual, an organization, or an entire nation should continue to devote real resources (human labor, raw materials, energy, land, and equipment) to one particular activity only up to the point at which the extra benefits yielded by adding extra resources to that activity just cover the benefits that are foregone by not producing the most valued good or service that is not being produced in an alternative activity because the real resources have been diverted to the first activity.

Economists call these foregone benefits the "opportunity costs" of the particular activity that is being endowed with the extra resources, or simply the "incremental" or "marginal" costs of expanding that activity.

The application of this fundamental economic principle to health care is as straightforward as it is shocking to physicians, politicians, and patients:

> Added real resources should be devoted to health care only if the incremental benefits they yield there cover the opportunity cost of the resources diverted from other fields. For example, at the most applied, micro-economic level, the principle means that an additional diagnostic test should not be undertaken if the added cost of that test cannot be justified by the added benefits it yields, even if the test reliably yields demonstrable added medical benefits.

For as long as health economists have plied their trade, they have propagated this principle with the diagram reproduced in Figure 3.2.[30] The horizontal axis of that diagram represents a nation's (or a health plan's) utilization of health care in a given year. The vertical axis represents a monetary measure of the costs and benefits associated with additional utilization of health care.

For the purposes of the highly abstract level at which economists develop this diagrammatic illustration, it is acceptable to assume that

Figure 3.2   A Hypothetical Benefit-Cost Curve for Health Care

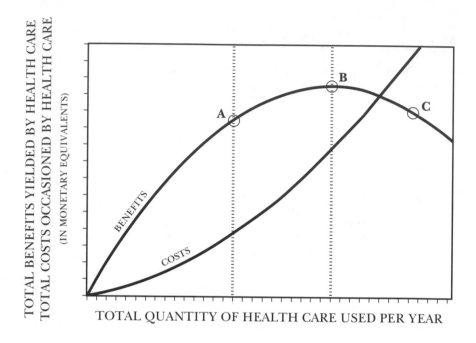

the use of "health care" can be measured by some imaginary, quantitative, standard unit of care whose opportunity cost in terms of real resources can be expressed in monetary units. Because additional real resources for health care must be bid away from displaced alternative uses at ever higher opportunity costs (in terms of foregone alternative benefits), it is reasonable to suppose that the health care cost curve bends upward, as it does in Figure 3.2.

The second curve in Figure 3.2 measures the benefits from diverting additional resources to health care. At this level of abstraction, it is simply assumed that it is possible somehow to measure the incremental enhancements of a nation's quality of life obtained with additional expenditure of resources on health care, and that these added benefits can be meaningfully measured in terms of monetary units. In fact, of course, measuring the clinical outcomes from health care is difficult enough. Assigning them a monetary value is even more problematic.[31]

Now it is reasonable to assume that, in any given period, the *incremental* benefits yielded by additional use of health care are positive, but only up to a point. In Figure 3.2, that point is identified by the letter B. Beyond that point (that is, in the range from point B to C and beyond), further use of health care actually harms patients. There is mounting scientific evidence that at least some U.S. health care—some experts would argue a substantial quantity of it[32]—lies on this downward-sloping segment of the cost-quality curve where health care actually harms patients. Citing a large study recently conducted by researchers at Harvard University[33] and similar studies, *Business Week* recently reported that as much as 40 percent of invasive heart procedures currently being administered to American patients are of doubtful value.[34] Some experts have argued that the elimination of that waste could spare this nation a decision to ration health care for years to come.[35] Although the precise magnitude of this waste can surely be debated, few students of the U.S. health care system doubt that there is a great deal of it.

It would, of course, be nonsense to regard the withholding of health care on the downward sloping segment of the benefit-cost curve as "rationing," even if a particular physician and his or her patients erroneously believe that the curve still slopes up at that point (i.e., that added medical benefits could be had by this or that procedure widely judged ineffective among clinical experts). The more appropriate term for such withholding is "rationalizing." It is not doing the patently wrong thing.

While no one can argue with rationalizing health care in this sense, the question is whether a case can be made for retreating even to the left of point B, down toward point A on this health care benefit-cost curve. Many practicing physicians might object to such a strategy for they have been conditioned by years of training to fight for their patients' health to the utmost, which means point B on the curve. When consumers are ill and they are therefore "patients," they probably share the physician's view, even though they may deplore our "wasteful health care system" when they are healthy. As the fundamental principle articulated earlier suggests, however, economists would judge the *optimal* point on the benefit-cost curve to be something like point A, at which point the *incremental* benefit from additional health care (actually the slope of the benefit line) just covers the *incremental* cost of that additional health care (the slope of the cost curve).

√In other words, and in plain English, economists openly advocate that an efficient health care system is one that withholds from patients health care services (those on segment A-B of the benefit-cost curve) that would have yielded patients positive medical benefits. Because this straightforward proposition remains politically incorrect in public forums, many economists may be reluctant to offer it quite that bluntly in testimony before the Congress or on television. They may even be reluctant to remind their own attending physician of it when they or their loved ones are sick. But that is the proposition they offer when they are well,[36] and that is what they teach.

To just about every noneconomist, however, the economist's prescription never makes sense and is seen as blasphemous. The problem is not only that economists never have been able actually to put monetary values on the hypothetical benefit curve. The problem is a general revulsion at letting considerations of cost enter clinical decisions at all. At this time, for example, few politicians would have the courage openly to advocate that Medicare should weigh benefits against costs when it makes decisions on whether or not a particular procedure should be covered by Medicare. Similarly, few politicians would have the courage to propose that the Food and Drug Administration should explicitly weigh costs versus benefits in its approval of new drugs or medical devices. Even hints at such a sensible strategy are still being met with howls of "rationing!"

And there this important issue rests. Throughout the most recent debate on health policy, Americans have steadfastly refused to confront it. Until that debate is properly joined, however, a stiff price will be paid for this ostrich-like posture. Included in that price will be capricious barriers to the development of managed competition, apparently this nation's preferred strategy for cost and quality control. If managed competition does its job properly, the U.S. health care system will ration pervasively and judiciously.

Rationing under Managed Competition

Consider again the illustrative drawing in Figure 3.2. The retreat from the downward sloping segment of the health benefit-cost curve (B-C and beyond) is one of the major openly stated objectives pursued by the advocates of managed competition, who seek to displace the traditional fee-for-service method of compensating the provider of health care with a system under which the providers of care are strictly budgeted in advance, by means of prepaid capitation payments.

Under the traditional fee-for-service system, every medical practice and hospital, and every department within those facilities, functions as a so-called *profit center* whose revenues and profits increase in direct proportion with their levels of activity. Naturally, these profit centers have strong financial incentives to maximize the use of resources in the treatment of illness. They are forever subject to the suspicion that, wittingly or unwittingly, the resource intensity of their medical treatments will be pushed well beyond the economically most efficient level (point A on the benefit-cost curve) at least as far as point B and, quite often, even onto the patently wasteful segment B-C. If this method of compensating the providers of health care is coupled with virtually first-dollar health insurance coverage, then there is relatively little that third-party payers can do from a distance to prohibit these forays into inefficiency. It is this open-ended system that had persuaded the majority of Americans to view rationing health care as somehow un-American.

The only hope to endow a fee-for-service system with some measure of countervailing power is the imposition of high deductibles and coinsurance on patients, in the manner now being proposed for the Medical Savings Account (MSA) model. Under this model, insurance coverage in any given year would set in only after the insured individual has spent a "deductible" of, say, $1,500 on health care out of pocket without the benefit of insurance. (For a family, this deductible might be $3,000.) The individual could finance this out-of-pocket deductible out of a tax-sheltered medical savings account into which he or she would be able to deposit up to $1,500 per year out of pre-tax income. (For a family, the tax-sheltered deposit might be up to $3,000.) If the individual had traditionally received comprehensive coverage from an employer, that employer would henceforth provide insurance coverage only for expenditures in excess of the $1,500 deductible and deposit the savings in premium costs achieved by replacing the comprehensive policy with the high-deductible policy into the employee's medical savings account. In a recent study of MSAs, the American Academy of Actuaries has estimated that these premium savings might be on the order of $500 to $550 for an individual.[37]

Such an approach does offer patients the advantage of free choice of doctor and hospital *at the time of illness.* It also offers physicians a high degree of professional independence—certainly the freedom to practice as a self-employed professional. Perhaps that is why organized medicine is now favorably disposed to MSAs. But this approach to cost control does have two shortcomings.

First, deductibles and coinsurance would make individual patients active cost control agents only up to the maximum risk exposure written into their MSA contract. For example, if catastrophic, first-dollar coverage sets in after a family has absorbed, say, $3,000 in out-of-pocket expenses per year, then neither patients nor those who treat them have any economic incentive to observe economy in that treatment. On the contrary, under fee-for-service compensation, the incentive will be to leave no stone unturned in diagnosing and treating the patient. Here one should be mindful that, in any given year, the bulk of national health care spending is concentrated on a relatively small number of patients. About 1 percent of the American population tends to account for about 30 percent of all health care spending in any given year, about 5 percent of the population tends to account for close to 60 percent of all spending, and about 10 percent of the population tends to account for close to 75 percent of all annual health spending.[38] These data suggest that, in the absence of managed care for insured expenditures above the out-of-pocket deductible, the MSA approach would leave a large portion of national health care spending unprotected by cost controls from the patient's side.

Critics of the MSA see a second potential drawback of that approach—its lack of clinical accountability. Precisely because of the freedom of choice the MSA approach offers patients and the professional independence it accords physicians, the fragmented medical treatments made possible by the MSA approach make it difficult to hold any particular physician or institution clinically and economically accountable for the resources they use in the treatment of particular illnesses, other than in the eyes of sick patients who may not be able to make that complex assessment properly.

The dream among many health policy analysts and politicians always has been an arrangement under which the providers of health care can be held measurably accountable for the impact that their resource use has on the quality of life of an *entire, well-defined population* under these providers' care. The ability to render that kind of accounting is one of the major advantages claimed for the alternative to MSAs, namely, comprehensive, virtually first-dollar insurance coverage, but coupled with *capitated managed care*.

The MSA approach to cost control relies exclusively on rationing decisions originating on the demand side, that is, from the patient. Patients are made to feel the financial consequences of their choices at two points: first, when they purchase insurance coverage and, second, when they are ill and still within the limits of the maximum annual out-of-pocket payment to which their insurance contract exposes them. Because the providers of health care are paid on a fee-for-service basis, they have no financial incentive to withhold services a patient may want and is willing and able to pay for. Capitated managed care, on the other hand, employs a quite different two-tiered system of rationing: it relies on price rationing that originates on the demand side when patients purchase comprehensive, virtually first-dollar insurance coverage; but it is coupled with rationing that originates on the supply side when patients are ill and need treatment. Supply-side rationing is driven by the fact that, under capitation, every provider of health care is effectively a *cost center* whose profits fall with increases in their level of activity. Capitation therefore is the economic engine that drives managed care.

Under capitated managed care, supply-side rationing is implemented on the basis of practice guidelines. Ideally these guidelines are to be based on what is known as "clinical outcomes research," that is, systematic research on what works and what does not work in clinical medicine. Both the federal government and the private sector are now heavily engaged in promulgating such guidelines. At the federal level, they emerge from research funded by the Agency of Health Care Policy Research (AHCPR), which is part of the Department of Health and Human Services (DHHS). In the private sector, they are being developed by the various medical specialty societies and also by employee benefit consulting firms. As *The New York Times* recently reported,[39] one of the most influential among these consulting firms is Milliman & Robertson (M&R), whose guidelines are now widely used by private insurance companies, especially by the capitated health plans. These private sector guidelines appear to be quite rigorous. As *The New York Times* reports, for example, the M&R guidelines call for a stay of not more than one day for a normal delivery and of not more than two days for a delivery with cesarean section, and outpatient treatment only for a mastectomy. Insurers who apply the M&R rules probably do not like to see that practice described as "rationing." As will be argued further on, however, it certainly is a form of supply-side rationing. There is merit in acknowledging it openly, because that type of rationing does have its defenders in the scientific community.

Capitated managed care has gained wide support among politicians in recent years, across a broad range of the political spectrum. It is now being advanced in the Congress as the ideal cost control mechanism for both the Medicaid and the Medicare programs, possibly along with MSAs. A central idea proposed by the advocates of capitated managed care is that the integrated health plans competing for enrollees under that arrangement should be held formally *accountable* for their economic and clinical performance: hence, the commonly used name "Accountable Health Plans" or AHPs for these networks. The standards for accountability will necessarily be *averages* over the entire enrollee population. These population averages may be satisfaction scores elicited from patients, population-based immunization rates, rates of screening for sundry medical conditions, morbidity rates (such as disability days), and mortality rates, all properly adjusted for the socioeconomic composition of an AHP's enrolled population.

Confronted with the task of owning up to these population-based standards, an AHP's first step in enhancing its average scores will be to eliminate any service thought to be inappropriate. Earlier, we have called this "rationalizing." Given a fixed, prepaid annual budget, however, an AHP can enhance its overall *average* performance standards by rationing health care outright. In terms of Figure 3.2, this means retreating beyond the top of the benefit-cost curve (point B), down to point A, at which point added spending indeed yields added medical benefits, albeit small ones. It involves the withholding from some patients of potentially beneficial health care, purely for economic reasons. To cite from a paper delivered by Dallas Salisbury, president of the Employee Benefit Research Institute, to a conference entitled *Making Choices: Rationing in the U.S. Health System:*

> Because medicine is as much an art as a science, rationing medical care by guidelines and gatekeepers may be the most direct route to quality. It may be time to worship rationing as both the route to quality and as an economic necessity.[40]

Strict application of the M&R guidelines probably is intended to be precisely this type of rationing.

William B. Schwartz, M. D., coauthor with Henry Aaron of the previously cited *The Painful Prescription,* and always a thoughtful and candid observer of U.S. health care, recently put it similarly in an interview with *The Internist:*

> I do think HMOs will have an important role in cost-containment *because they have a wonderful mechanism for rationing care.* Managed care has a system that makes it possible to control how much and what kind of expensive care is delivered. But in the absence of rationing, I don't think managed care can do much to help us.[41] (Italics added)

Evidently, Schwartz' comment was meant to be neither facetious nor cynical. On the contrary, he meant to commend the future role of HMOs (and other forms of Accountable Health Plans) in our health system. By "a wonderful mechanism for rationing care," Schwartz apparently had in mind the ability an HMO has to allocate a fixed resource budget among classes of patients in a way that will maximize the overall, average health status of the entire population enrolled in the HMO, even if some patients may be forced to make do with less than they would have had under the open-ended fee-for-service system. Such a reallocation of resources is far more difficult under the uncoordinated, traditional fee-for-service system. Indeed, further on in the interview, Schwartz criticizes the explicit rationing system adopted for its fee-for-service Medicaid program by the state of Oregon. Under the Oregon program, the medical interventions are ranked by estimated benefit-cost ratios and then funded, in descending order of benefit-cost ratio, as far down as the appropriated budget for Medicaid permits. As Schwartz observes:

> Oregon ranks interventions and then pays for all care down to the point that funds run out. In other words, low benefit uses of interventions lying above the cut-off point are fully funded, while high benefit uses of technologies that fall below the cut-off point are excluded from support.[42]

Although Schwartz' criticism is on the mark, one nevertheless must admire the citizens of Oregon for admitting openly that any appropriation implies rationing and that, under a fee-for-service system, rationing must be made explicit, Schwartz' criticism notwithstanding.

In an article entitled "Rationing Resources While Improving Quality," David M. Eddy[43] presents illuminating illustrations of the reallocation Schwartz and others would prescribe for HMOs. In short, Eddy shows with concrete examples ways to enhance the quality of care through what he openly admits is *rationing*, and how HMOs are ideally suited to implement such a policy. Similar material was more recently presented by Grumbach and Bodenheimer in an article entitled "Painful vs. Painless Cost Control."[44]

Fundamental to Eddy's analysis is the premise that, in its current *modus operandi*, the U.S. health care system underuses many high-value medical interventions (for example, diagnostic tests with a very low yield of detected illness) and overuses many low-value interventions. In terms of Figure 3.2, Eddy argues that the U.S. health care system currently leaves patients distributed all along this curve, both to the left and to the right of the economically efficient point A. He then proceeds to present concrete examples—among them, breast cancer screening, cholesterol treatment, and ionic versus nonionic contrast agents—to illustrate numerically how a reallocation of resources among patients in various risk classes could reduce both overall costs and the overall death rate for an HMO's population at risk. By implication, he argues that this type of reallocation could and should be made for the entire U.S. population.

In connection with breast cancer screening, for example, Eddy proposes a reallocation of screening mammography away from women younger than 50 or older than 75 and toward women between ages 50 and 75. In his illustration, this reallocation of resources would "simultaneously decrease the number of breast cancer deaths [in the hypothetical health plan] by about 33 percent and reduce overall cost of breast cancer screening by about 30 percent."[45] But there is a major catch in his prescription, which he is quick to acknowledge honestly and explicitly. To quote him at length on this important point:

> The catch is that the strategy, depending on how strictly it is applied, will either discourage the use of or deny coverage for interventions that for some particular individuals might have benefit. That is where the rationing comes in. Whether it is "soft" rationing by discouraging use, or "hard rationing" through denial of coverage, from the point of view of patients and their physicians who cannot get covered something they want, the quality of care went down, not up. The fact that patients can always receive an uncovered service if they are willing to pay for it will not mollify their displeasure very much.[46]

Just how displeased some people will be by that prospect can be gauged by the previously cited commentary by Bernadine Healy, who used Eddy's example as the basis for her assertion that President Clinton proposed to ration health care.[47]

The reallocation proposed by Eddy also is apt to bring the wrath of the media onto the managers of capitated health plans, because the media thrive on individual tragedies and not on changes in population averages. In fact, the very idea of judging capitated Accountable Health Plans by performance standards that are *averaged* over their entire population of enrollees clashes with this nation's fiercely individualist tradition, a tradition that raises anecdotes in the media and in the courtroom to such importance. That tradition also looks askance at depriving one individual of something he or she desires purely for the sake of enhancing the *average* health status or quality of life of some collectivity. Clinician David Eddy, economists, and the advocates of managed competition may well be able to demonstrate to a sophisticated readership that an Accountable Health Plan had best concentràte its capacity to perform screening mammography on women aged 50 to 75. That same demonstration is unlikely to assuage a 45-year-old woman who was refused coverage for a screening mammography that she had desired and who subsequently developed breast cancer. That woman is likely to sue the AHP instead, especially if she can cite experts such as Bernadine Healy[48] in support of her claim.

In a private communication with this author, Mark Pauly has taken issue with Eddy's approach: "It docs not matter whether reallocating screening mammography away from 45-year-old women toward 55-year-old women will simultaneously decrease the number of breast cancer deaths and reduce overall screening costs,'" argues Pauly. "What matters is whether screening [45-year-olds] is worth what it costs 45-year-olds. There is no budget constraint (yet) imposed on HMOs, so why does Eddy keep developing models that assume that there is a fixed budget?"

According to Pauly, in "a proper (non-tax-subsidized[49]) competitive market, HMOs would compete [for enrollees] by offering [them] attractive rationing/premium combinations." Consumers would have to know or guess what degree of rationing they would be likely to experience in various HMOs and select the point on the rationing-premium trade-off curve that they like best, given their budgets. Figure 3.3 illustrates this idea at the conceptual level, here with only three competing HMOs. The scheme envisaged by Pauly is analogous to choosing from a menu of prepaid vacation packages, some with luxury accommodations and some with more constrained accommodations. "You pay your money up front," writes Pauly; "they ration you when you get to Greece."

Pauly raises an important point. In principle, unless the competing HMOs really are confronted by an externally fixed budget and then are evaluated on population-based, average performance measures, it is not clear why they would deny 45-year-old women screening mammographies *if these women were willing to pay the extra premium that might be necessitated.* Indeed, there is no reason why an HMO would not offer a 45-year-old woman screening on a fee-for-service basis, even if that service is not in the benefit package covered by its capitation premium.

In practice, of course, the market might not work quite as

Figure 3.3   The Economist's Conception of Health Plan
Competition

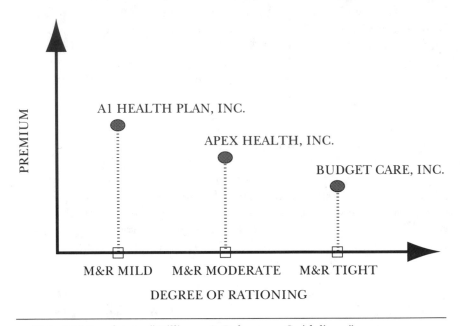

Note: M&R refers to "Milliman & Robertson Guidelines."

smoothly as Pauly envisages. For one, it would be extremely difficult for prospective patients to visualize the premium-rationing trade-off frontier Pauly has in mind, if for no other reason than that the competing HMOs will do everything in their power to camouflage the rationing they actually will do. The slogan "We at Apex Health Care Inc. ration harshly. But we're cheap!" is not likely to grace billboards soon. Information on rationing would at best be second-hand, informal, and crude.

If the honest marketing envisaged by Pauly cannot be achieved—and it most probably will not even be attempted—then the HMOs and other AHPs that *are* held accountable for population-based performance averages probably will engage in the rationing advocated by Eddy. Once consumers have chosen an HMO and paid their premium, that premium effectively constitutes a fixed budget for the duration of the contract. In the HMOs' eyes, and in the eyes of those who judge them, they will profit by "rationing resources to raise the overall quality of their care," to use Eddy's phrase.

Rationing in Twenty-First Century U.S. Health Care

Eddy's elegant analysis leaves us where the rubber hits the rough road of politics. Fundamental to his idea of rationing toward greater efficiency is a redistribution of resources among people. That redistribution makes the matter *ipso facto* political.

Eddy's vision is idealistic. It is based on the notion that there is such a thing as a "community," and that the members of that "community" would be content to see health care resources flow to those members with the most pressing medical need for them, rather than to those who are willing to bid the highest money prices for them. In this country, at this time, that is not a politically marketable proposition. There is no sign that it will ever be a marketable proposition.

Whatever one may think about Congress' tortuous recent debate on health care reform, it did serve to flush out more clearly than ever before the politically dominant social ethic that has driven U.S. health care policy so far and that is likely to drive it deep into the twenty-first century. That ethic is decidedly not egalitarian. It is simply inconceivable, for example, that America's well-to-do would ever countenance an arrangement under which they might be denied marginally beneficial health services (e.g., diagnostic screening tests for low-risk groups) so that other Americans can receive added health care with substantially higher medical benefits (e.g., screening tests for high-risk groups, prenatal care, and so on). Nor is there any evidence that America's well-to-do are in a mood, at this time, to finance with more tax money additional health care that might yield quite substantial medical benefits for low-income families, even if that policy would not deprive the well-to-do of the merely marginal medical benefits they desire. The operative political slogan at this time is "no added taxes, no added entitlements." Eddy's rational prescription for rationing toward greater efficiency can be applied in the United States at most within layers of economic classes, and even then only with great difficulty.

If one deciphers the code words used in the most recent congressional debate on health care reform, one concludes that a working majority of the U.S. Congress (and possibly of the U.S. population at large) views health care as essentially a *private consumption* good of which low-income families might be accorded a basic ration, but whose quality and availability should be allowed to vary systematically with family income. As Congressman Dick Armey (R-Texas) has put it in his unique and refreshingly candid style:

> Universal coverage is just a euphemism for the welfarization of health care. Obviously we would hope everybody would enjoy health care, but . . . health care is just a commodity, just like bread, and just like housing and everything else.[50]

The sentiment expressed by Congressman Armey seems to be fairly widespread in the Congress, although it is not usually expressed this bluntly. Instead, it is encoded in words such as "empowerment," "free choice," "personal responsibility," the "freedom to choose whether or not to be insured and what coverage to purchase," and so on. Practically, however, all of these code words add up to the notion that well-to-do Americans should be empowered to allocate their ample budgets between health care and other things as they choose, and that low-income Americans be empowered to do likewise with their low income, plus whatever subsidies Congress may or may not bestow on them. The popular battle cries of "no added taxes" and "no added entitlements" suggest that any such subsidies will be small.

This now politically dominant view officially sanctions a three-tiered American health system. In terms of the imagery developed in Figure 3.2, Americans will continue to be distributed all along the benefit-cost curve in health care. Many will receive too little health care (relative to clinically determined need) and others too much.

Rationing in the bottom tier

For uninsured Americans who are poor or near poor, the current patchwork of public hospitals and clinics will be reserved and perhaps expanded. That arrangement will confront these Americans with two forms of rationing: *price rationing* at the nexus of the decision whether or not to contact the health care system at times of illness, and *non-price rationing* by health care providers, once contact with the health care system has been made.

Non-price rationing will be forced on public hospitals and clinics through the fixed budgets they will be allocated, chiefly by local governments that are under perennial fiscal siege. These public health care facilities can be expected to find themselves permanently underfunded, as they usually have been in the past, thus forcing on them severe limits to their physical capacity. Such limits on physical capacity, in turn, will beget the long queues that have always been the classic instrument of rationing.[51] Lack of adequate funding will also limit the medical technology available to the health care professionals working in these public institutions. Objective commentators would call this budget-driven withholding of technology rationing as well.

The uninsured will increasingly be herded into these beleaguered public institutions, because the ever steeper price discounts extracted from private hospitals by Medicare, Medicaid, and private health plans will rob private hospitals of the financial cushion they have hitherto used to finance the considerable charity care they have been able to offer the uninsured. It is doubtful that private institutions will be inclined to remain society's health insurer of last resort as they find themselves under severe fiscal siege. In fact, there is something contradictory in the popular notion that satisfactory cost control must come first before added millions can be brought under insurance coverage, when the very act of successful cost control would destroy the fiscal basis of the implicit catastrophic health insurance that has traditionally been provided by the nation's private hospital system.

If one adopts the comprehensive definition of rationing employed by economists and advocated in this chapter, then surely one can agree that patients in the bottom tier of the U.S. health care system will likely be rationed out of needed health care for years to come, as they already have been in the past. Perhaps the time is at hand to acknowledge frankly the permanence of this bottom tier in the U.S. health care system, and to concentrate the main thrust of future public health policy on the quality of that bottom tier. Practically, this will mean strengthening the Public Health Service at the federal, state, and local levels. In effect, the Assistant Secretary for Health of the U.S. Department of Health and Human Services will become the Secretary in charge of the bottom tier.

Rationing in the middle tier

The employed, broad middle class will be enrolled in the newly emerging health plans, such as HMOs. As noted, these plans will be budgeted prospectively, on a per capita basis, through competitively bid premiums. To control their outlays, they necessarily must limit the patient's choice of doctor and hospital at time of illness.

Americans in this middle tier will experience both *price rationing* and *non-price rationing.* While at this early time in the development of managed competition there probably is no correlation between the premiums charged by a capitated health plan and the quality of the health care it provides, it is reasonable to suppose that eventually there will emerge a positive correlation between these two dimensions, once the market has squeezed the current waste out of the system. The higher premiums of some Accountable Health Plans (AHPs) are then likely to reflect better benefits—whether they be more luxurious facilities, more high-tech facilities, shorter wait times for appointments with physicians or with specialized equipment, more medical specialists, and so on, as well as point-of-service riders that offer patients some ability to receive care outside of their own health plan, or riders that finance high-cost experimental procedures. It would be naive to assume that the relatively unregulated price competition among AHPs expected in the decade ahead can proceed without at least some *price rationing* of care among members of the competing AHPs.

Aside from the *price rationing* that will occur at the stage when consumers select among health plans, there also will be the *non-price rationing* toward greater efficiency within AHPs described in the previous section. Ideally, the physicians within an AHP will apply that form of non-price rationing tacitly and implicitly, in a manner similar to the gentle dissuasion reportedly used by British physicians under the British National Health System.[52] In the American context, however, rationing through gentle dissuasion might nevertheless trigger rancor and lawsuits at the fringes, if a patient's health thereafter turns for the worse. Thus, the bite of this form of rationing ultimately will be determined by the courts.

The top tier

Finally, well-to-do Americans will continue to enjoy an open-ended, free-choice, fee-for-service health care system without rationing of any form, even in instances where additional care is of dubious clinical or economic merit. Well-to-do Americans will demand no less, and they will always have it, because they are willing and able to pay for it. As the *Wall Street Journal* recently reported,[53] one already discerns a trend in business to bestow on top management more generous health insurance plans than are made available to the rank and file. In the article, a spokesperson for the Walt Disney Company is reported to have explained that the company's deluxe executive health plan "frees people [executives] from the administrative duties of selecting from a menu of insurance choices. That's time they don't have to be distracted from the job."[54] Reportedly, the Guarantee Mutual Life Company of Omaha promotes its deluxe *Exec-U-Care* plan with the slogan: "For you and your executives who deserve more."[55] This development is not surprising. It is a reasonable forecast that the distinction between executive and rank-and-file plans will grow sharper with time.

One can readily understand the strong preference among high-income Americans for the traditional free-choice, fee-for-service medicine to which they have long been accustomed. One can equally understand the politician's respect for that preference. It would be very difficult to argue that Americans should not be allowed to spend their own money as they see fit.

A question for Congress to ponder, however, is whether that upper tier merits continued public support through the tax preference now accorded employer-provided health insurance. Although such contributions clearly are part of total compensation, they are now excluded from taxable income. As the Progressive Policy Institute,[56] the conservative Heritage Foundation,[57] and many economists have long pointed out, it is a highly regressive tax preference, because its benefits accrue primarily to the upper-income classes. Remarkably, at the urging of the small-business lobby this regressive tax preference may be extended even further in the years ahead to self-employed persons of all income groups.

The same question arises in connection with health care reform proposals that build on the idea of the so-called tax-exempt Medical Savings Account.[58] Under these proposals, individuals would purchase super-catastrophic health insurance policies with very high deductibles and cover those deductibles out of an MSA into which they could make annual, tax-deductible deposits up to a certain amount. Individuals covered by employers would have the catastrophic policy provided by the employer who would also make deposits to the MSA. Although the premium and the deposit paid by the employers would be treated as a normal, tax-deductible payroll expense, neither that deposit nor the premium would count as the employee's taxable income. Evidently, such an arrangement would extend the tax preferences even to health spending that is not now tax sheltered, namely, the deductibles and coinsurance now paid by patients. That circumstance has two important consequences.

First, the plan necessarily would force Congress to stipulate in minute detail what types of personal health care could and could not be financed with the tax-sheltered MSA. That task would certainly not be any easier than the definition would be of any congressionally stipulated benefit package under any other health care reform plan—including the President's—and it would trigger lobbying by providers seeking to have their services included in the tax-preferred package. Over time the official benefit package would surely grow to include ever more marginal services.

That development would heighten the inherent regressivity of the MSA. There is every reason to believe, for example, that the MSA mechanism would eventually allow high-income Americans facing a marginal income tax rate of 50 percent to have their teeth cleaned regularly at half price (that is, at a cost in terms of *after-tax* dollars equal to 50 cents per dollar billed by the dentist). By contrast, families facing a marginal income tax rate of 15 percent would purchase that same procedure at a cost of 85 cents of *after-tax* income per dollar billed by the dentist.

The widespread political support for this tax shelter, and for tax-sheltered MSAs, reflects a distinct social ethic. That conclusion only reinforces the central theme of this section, namely, that a working majority of Congress now favors a health care system tiered by income class, with relatively severe rationing of health care at the bottom and relatively little at the top.[59] To what extent this politically dominant vision for U.S. health care faithfully reflects the independent preferences of the so-called "grass roots" is a subject best explored by political scientists. Whatever the case may be, however, it is difficult to imagine that the Congress of the United States will soon contemplate moving the health care system toward the one-tiered structure that is still being endorsed, officially, by most politicians.

Finally, there is the question of where the nation's elderly fit into this three-tiered health care system. Because they are so politically powerful, the elderly have traditionally been able to fend off any attempt to limit their freedom of choice among doctors or the benefits covered by Medicare. At the time of this writing, however, Congress is actively exploring a major restructuring of the program. For the elderly, that restructuring might turn out to be a mixed blessing.

On the one hand, Congress would like to offer the elderly a choice among alternative private insurance products, in addition to the traditional Medicare program. The private options might include comprehensive coverage under capitated managed care (e.g., HMO coverage), and a high-deductible, fee-for-service insurance product, coupled with a medical savings account to cover the high deductible. To make this wider choice among private insurance products possible, Medicare would issue the elderly an annual voucher whose value would be adjusted for the individual's age and gender and for other risk factors identified with the individual's geographic location.

While the elderly ought to welcome this wider choice of insurance products, they might be asked to pay for it by assuming more or all of the risk of health care cost inflation. To date, Medicare has been effectively a *defined-benefit* program, that is, it has promised to bestow on the elderly a defined package of benefits, whatever these benefits might cost the Medicare program (i.e., the taxpayer). Under that approach the taxpayer has to assume the risk of inflation in the cost of these promised benefits. Under a voucher approach, that risk might be shifted entirely to the elderly if Congress decided arbitrarily to limit annual increases in the value of the vouchers, totally abstracting from inflation in the cost of health care. In that case, the Medicare program would become a *defined contribution* program. If the defined contribution were tightly constrained, the Medicare program would eventually evolve toward a multitiered insurance program for the elderly.

It is, of course, possible to combine the benefit of wider choice among insurance programs with the *defined benefit* feature of Medicare. This could be achieved simply by tying increases in the value of the annual voucher to some price index for health care in general. Alternatively, it could be achieved by offering the elderly for their annual voucher the traditional Medicare coverage, without any diminution in its benefits. That approach would leave the risk of health care cost inflation on the shoulders of the taxpayer, and it would place there the added burden that adverse-risk selection on the part of the elderly could drive up the overall cost of the Medicare program. This might occur if relatively healthier elderly persons chose private insurance products with added benefits, leaving a relatively sicker pool for the traditional Medicare program. Unless the size of the annual vouchers could be adjusted for such adverse-risk selection, it could easily drive up the cost of the entire program.

Conclusion

The objective of this chapter has been to review alternative definitions of the term "rationing," to propose a preferred definition of the term and, finally, to explore in what manner the United States and other industrialized nations are likely to ration health care in the twenty-first century. Three distinct definitions of rationing have been identified:

1. To ration is to distribute equitably.

2. Rationing occurs only when someone willing and able to pay money for something is somehow denied access to it.

3. Rationing is *any* allocation of a scarce supply of a good or service to users who would otherwise want more of it, including charging a money price sufficient to limit demand to the available supply.

The first definition, found in *Webster's Collegiate Dictionary,* describes the ostensible motive of nations, such as Canada and the European nations, who admittedly do implicitly ration certain of their health services for everyone through government-imposed limits on physical capacity. Such rationing is widely decried in the United States, although it is tacitly practiced here as well in public hospitals and clinics. Whatever one may think of this approach to allocating health care, if one wishes to be fair to Canada and the European nations, one should acknowledge at least the egalitarian precept upon which that approach to rationing is based.[60]

The second definition of rationing tends to be preferred by those who would like to make a distinction between allocating health care through the free play of market forces and various alternative allocative algorithms, including the implicit rationing practiced by other nations. Unfortunately, as that second definition of rationing is applied in practice, it tends to suggest that free-market allocations of health care through money prices are inherently superior to alternative allocations, regardless of the actual distribution of health care among members of society. In the end, it tacitly endorses the notion that health care should be allocated to individuals chiefly according to their ability to pay for it. Such an algorithm could be defended on certain theories of distributive justice—for example, the strictly libertarian theory. But that theory of justice should be openly endorsed by the adherents to this definition of rationing, so that the merits of the underlying ethic can be debated forthrightly. That is rarely, if ever, done in this country.

Finally, the third definition of rationing embraces all forms of resource allocation. It is therefore inherently value-neutral. It seems to be the definition preferred by many economists, if perhaps not all. Adherents to this definition distinguish between price rationing (i.e., rationing through money prices) and non-price rationing (i.e., all other forms of rationing). In the author's view, much clarity could be gained in the national health care policy debate if this, the economist's usage, became the standard definition of rationing.

In a treatise that gained wide currency on Capitol Hill during the recent health reform debate, economist William J. Baumol[61] argues that it appears very difficult to achieve significant productivity gains in the production of health care (and education as well), a phenomenon now known in the literature as "Baumol's Disease." Baumol's proposition remains controversial among economists, primarily because it is so difficult to define "productivity" in this context. Even so, to the extent that Baumol's thesis is even near the mark, it implies that we cannot expect much long-run relief from sustained health care cost pressures through price deflation that is driven by productivity gains. (Such productivity gains, for example, have vastly reduced the prices of consumer electronics and of information processing.) If one couples Baumol's thesis with the assumption that health care and general education will continue to be viewed as basic necessities that ought to be made available to all citizens, regardless of their income, then one is led to the conclusion that these two basic human services are likely to absorb an ever growing share of the gross domestic product. That prospect, of course, makes it all the more compelling to be utterly forthright on the issue of rationing, for that will become a chief mechanism for constraining at least somewhat the growth in spending on these two commodities. It is not helpful simply to define that problem away through judicious code words, pretending thereafter that the rationing of health care can be avoided forever in the United States. The nation has not been able to avoid rationing in the past, and will not be able to avoid it in the future. The nation has merely lacked the courage to admit to rationing forthrightly and to debate the merits of alternative forms of rationing in good faith.

Acknowledgments

The author would like to thank Janet Kline, Congressional Research Service, Library of Congress, and Mark V. Pauly, University of Pennsylvania, for their many helpful comments on the first draft of this chapter. Any remaining shortcomings are, of course, entirely the author's.

Notes

1. G. J. Schieber, J.-P. Poullier, and L. Greenwald, "Health System Performance in the OECD Countries, 1980–1992," *Health Affairs* 13, no. 4 (Fall 1994): 100–12.
2. V. R. Fuchs, "The Health Sector's Share of the Gross National Product," *Science* 247(2 February 1990): 534–38.
3. G. J. Schieber et al. 1994, 101, Exhibit 1.
4. Congressional Budget Office (CBO), *Trends in Health Spending: An Update.* (Washington, DC: U.S. Government Printing Office, June 1993), 2.
5. If X_o denotes the percentage of the GDP spent on health care in a base year (e.g., 1990) and d denotes the percentage points by which the annual growth spending on health care exceeds that of the rest of the GDP, then the percentage of the GDP spent on health care in some future year t can be calculated with the simple equation

$$X_t = \frac{e^{dt}}{e^{dt} - 1 + (1/X_o)}$$

where e is the natural constant 2.71828, found on most hand-held calculators. For example, if the base year 0 is 1990 and the future target year is the year 2050, then t would be 60. If d were 3 percentage points (.03), then dt would be equal to (.03)60 = 1.8. To obtain $e^{1.8}$ one enters 1.8 into the calculator and then hits the button marked e^x, to obtain 6.0496475. Health care spending in 1990 had been about X_o = .125 or 12.5% of the GDP. It follows that X_{60} (health care spending as a percentage of the GDP forecast for the year 2050) would then be 6.0496475/[6.0496475 − 1 + (1/.125)] = .4635 or 46.4%. If one had chosen the year 2000 as the base year (so that t would be 50) and taken the CBO forecast that health care spending then would be 18.9% of the GDP (X_o = .189), then one would predict health care spending as a percentage of GDP in the year 2050 as 51.1%.
6. *Webster's Ninth New Collegiate Dictionary* (Springfield, MA: Merriam-Webster Inc., 1989), 977.
7. Cited in "The Ultimate Denial: Rationing is a Reality," *Issue Scan: Quarterly Report on Health Care Issues and Trends from Searle* 4, no. 2 (Summer 1994): 5.
8. Congressional Budget Office (CBO), *Behavioral Assumptions for Estimating the Effects of Health Care Proposals* (Washington, DC: Congressional Budget Office, November 1993): viii, Table 3.
9. S. H. Long and M. S. Marquis, *Universal Health Insurance and Uninsured People: Effects on Use and Costs: Report to Congress* (Washington, DC: Office

of Technology Assessment and Congressional Research Service, Library of Congress, 5 August 1994): Figures 1, 4.

10. A. L. Kellerman, "Too Sick to Wait," *Journal of the American Medical Association* 266, no. 8, (28 August 1991): 1123; D. W. Baker and C. D. Stevens, "Patients Who Leave a Public Hospital Emergency Department without Being Seen by a Physician," *Journal of the American Medical Association* 266, no. 8 (28 August 1991): 1085; A. B. Bindman, K. Grumbauch, D. Keane, L. Rauch, and J. M. Luce, "Consequences of Queuing for Care at a Public Hospital Emergency Department," *Journal of the American Medical Association* 266, no. 8 (28 August 1991): 1091.

11. Study published in *Journal of the American Medical Association* (18 December 1991) and cited in *The New York Times* (18 December 1991): A26.

12. J. Hadley, E. P. Steinberg, and J. Feder, "Comparison of Uninsured and Privately Insured Hospital Patients," *Journal of the American Medical Association* 265, no. 3 (16 January 1991): 374–79.

13. P. Franks, C. Clancy, and M. Gold, "Health Insurance and Mortality," *Journal of the American Medical Association* 270, no. 6 (1995): 737–41.

14. B. Healy, "Mammograms—Your Breast, Your Choice," *The Wall Street Journal* (28 December 1993): A10.

15. In this connection, see *President Clinton's Health Care Reform Proposal and Health Security Act as presented to Congress on October 27, 1993* (Chicago, IL: Commerce Clearing House, Inc., 1993): Section 1003, 15.

16. M. I. Brown, I. G. Kessler, and F. G. Rueter, "Is the Supply of Mammography Machines Outstripping Need and Demand? *Annals of Internal Medicine* 113 (1990): 547–52.

17. See, for example, J. C. Merrill and A. B. Cohen, "The Emperor's New Clothes: Unraveling the Myths about Rationing," *Inquiry* 24 (Summer 1987): 105–109.

18. H. A. Aaron and W. B. Schwartz, *The Painful Prescription: Rationing of Hospital Care* (Washington, DC: The Brookings Institution, 1984).

19. See, for example, J. K. Kearl, *Principles of Microeconomics* (Lexington, MA: D. C. Heath & Co., 1993), 2. Close variants of this definition are offered in every introductory textbook on economics.

20. M. L. Katz and H. S. Rosen, *Microeconomics* (Homewood, IL: Richard D. Irwin, Inc., 1991), 15–16.

21. J. R. Kearl 1993, 288.

22. The author would like to thank Mark V. Pauly for reminding him of the possible legitimacy of that assumption.

23. For a general explanation of efficiency at the intermediate level, see Katz and Rosen, 1991, Chapter 11, pp. 403–44. For an extensive discussion of the philosophical underpinning of the word "efficiency" in the context of health care policy, see U. E. Reinhardt, "Reflections on the Meaning of *Efficiency:* Can Efficiency be Separated from Equity?" *Yale Law & Policy Review* 10, no. 2 (1992): 302–15. See also U. E. Reinhardt, "On the Economics and Ethics of 'Rationing' Health Care," in *Who Lives, Who Dies, Who Decides: The Ethics of Health Care Rationing,* Hearing before the Special Committee on Aging, United States Senate, 102nd Congress, 1st Session,

June 19, 1994, Serial no. 102–4. (Washington, DC: U.S. Government Printing Office, 1992): 17–35.

24. See, for example, J. E. Stiglitz, *Economics* (New York: W. W. Norton & Company, 1993), p. 380.

25. R. J. Blendon and K. Donelan, "The Public and the Emerging Debate over National Health Insurance," *The New England Journal of Medicine* 273, no. 3 (19 July 1990): 208–12. See also U. E. Reinhardt and H. Taylor, "Does the System Fit?" *Health Management Quarterly* (Third Quarter, 1991): 2–10.

26. D. Kahneman, J. L. Knetsch, and R. H. Thaler, "Fairness and the Assumptions of Economics," *Journal of Business* 59, no. 4, pt. 2 (1986): S285–99; and D. Kahneman, J. L. Knetsch, and R. H. Thaler, "Fairness as a Constraint on Profit Seeking: Entitlements in the Market," *The American Economic Review* 76, no. 4 (September 1986): 728–41.

27. T. A. Sheldon and A. K. Maynard, "Is Rationing Inevitable?" In *Rationing in Action,* edited by R. Smith (BMA Publications, 1993), Ch. 1, pp. 3–14.

28. D. M. Eddy, "Health System Reform: Will Controlling Costs Require Rationing Services?" *Journal of the American Medical Association* 272, no. 4 (27 July 1994): 324–28; and D. M. Eddy, "Rationing Resources While Improving Quality," *Journal of the American Medical Association* 272, no. 10 (14 September 1994): 817–24.

29. J. M. Eisenberg, "A Guide to the Economic Analysis of Clinical Practices," *Journal of the American Medical Association* 262, no. 20 (1989): 2879–86.

30. V. R. Fuchs, "Health Care and the U.S. Economy: An Essay in Abnormal Physiology," *Milbank Memorial Fund Quarterly* 50, no. 2, pt. 1 (April 1972): 211–37. Figure 1 on page 214 is one of the first published renditions of the famous diagram in the health economics literature.

31. See U. E. Reinhardt, "Global Budgeting in German Health Care: Insights for Americans," *Domestic Affairs* (Winter 1993-1994): 159–94, especially the section entitled, "Some Philosophical Perspectives on Global Budgeting," 185–94.

32. R. H. Brook and M. E. Vaiana, *Appropriateness of Care* (Washington, DC: The National Health Policy Forum, George Washington University, June 1989).

33. M. McLellan, B. J. McNeil, and J. P. Newhouse, "Does More Intensive Treatment of Acute Myocardial Infarction in the Elderly Reduce Mortality?" *Journal of the American Medical Association* 272, no. 11 (1994): 859–66.

34. M. McNamee, "When Less Is More in Coronary Care," *Business Week* (3 October 1994): 60.

35. R. H. Brook and K. N. Lohr, "Will We Need To Ration Effective Health Care?" *Issues in Science and Technology* 3, no. 1 (Fall 1986): 68–77.

36. V. R. Fuchs 1972.

37. American Academy of Actuaries, *Medical Savings Accounts: Cost Implications and Design Issues* (May 1995), ii.

38. M. L. Berk and A. C. Monheit, "The Concentration of Health Expenditures: An Update," *Health Affairs* 11, no. 4 (Winter 1992): 145–49.

39. A. Myerson, "Helping Insurers Say No," *The New York Times* (20 March 1995).
40. Employee Benefit Research Institute, *Making Choices: Rationing in the U.S. Health System* (Washington, DC: Employee Benefit Research Institute, April 1993), 1.
41. W. B. Schwartz, M. D., in an interview with *The Internist,* September 1994: 17.
42. Schwartz 1994, 18.
43. D. M. Eddy, "Rationing Resources While Improving Quality," *Journal of the American Medical Association* 272, no. 10 (1994): 817–824.
44. K. Grumbach and T. Bodenheimer, "Painful vs. Painless Cost Control," *Journal of the American Medical Association* 272, no. 18 (9 November 1994): 1458–64.
45. Grumbach and Bodenheimer 1994, 818.
46. Grumbach and Bodenheimer 1994, 820.
47. See B. Healy 1993.
48. Healy 1993.
49. Pauly refers here to the exclusion of employer-financed health insurance from taxable income and the tax-deductibility of at least part of health insurance premiums for the self-employed.
50. Quoted in *The Wall Street Journal* (23 November 1993): A4.
51. See A. L. Kellerman 1991.
52. See H. J. Aaron and W. B. Schwartz 1984.
53. G. Anders, "Employee Health Benefits May Be Fine, But Look at What Some Executives Get," *The Wall Street Journal* (25 October 1994): B1, B5.
54. Anders 1994, B5.
55. Anders 1994, B1.
56. J. D. Rosner, "A Progressive Plan for Affordable, Universal Health Care," in W. Marshall and M. Schram, *Mandate for Change* (New York: Berkley Books, 1992), 107–28.
57. S. M. Butler, "A Policymaker's Guide to the Health Care Crisis. Part I: The Debate over Reform," *Heritage Talking Points* (Washington, DC: The Heritage Foundation, 12 February 1992).
58. J. C. Goodman and G. Musgrave, *Patient Power: The Free Enterprise Alternative to Clinton's Health Plan* (Washington, DC: Cato Institute, 1994).
59. For a penetrating critique of Medical Savings Accounts, see M. V. Pauly, *An Analysis of Medical Savings Accounts: Do Two Wrongs Make a Right?* (Washington, DC: American Enterprise Institute Press, 1994).
60. See, for example, Sheldon and Maynard 1993, 12.
61. W. J. Baumol, "Social Wants and the Dismal Science: The Curious Case of the Climbing Costs of Health and Teaching," *Proceedings of the American Philosophical Society* 137, no.4 (1993): 612–37.

4

The New Organization of the Health Care Delivery System

Stephen M. Shortell and Kathleen E. Hull

Abstract. The U.S. health care system is restructuring at a dizzying pace. In many parts of the country, managed care has moved into third-generation models emphasizing capitated payment for enrolled lives and, in the process, turning most providers and institutions into cost centers to be managed rather than generators of revenue. While the full impact of the new managed care models remains to be seen, most evidence to date suggests that it tends to reduce inpatient use, may be associated with greater use of physician services and preventive care, and appears to result in no net differences either positive or negative with regard to quality or outcomes of care in comparison with fee-for-service plans. Some patients, however, tend to be somewhat less satisfied with scheduling of appointments and the amount of time spent with providers. There is no persuasive evidence that managed care lowers the *rate* of growth in overall health care costs within a given market. Further, managed care performance varies considerably across the country, and the factors influencing managed care performance are not well understood.

Organized delivery systems are a somewhat more recent phenomenon representing various forms of ownership and strategic alliances among hospitals, physicians, and insurers designed to provide more cost-effective care to defined populations by achieving desired levels of functional, physician-system, and clinical integration. Early evidence suggests that organized delivery systems that are more integrated have the potential to provide more accessible coordinated care across the continuum, and appear to be associated with higher levels of inpatient productivity, greater total system revenue, greater total system cash flow, and greater total system operating margin than less integrated delivery forms. Some key success factors for developing organized delivery systems have been identified. Important roles are played by organizational culture, information systems, internal incentives, total quality management, physician leadership, and the growth of group practices.

This chapter describes the growth and evolution of managed care and organized delivery systems, the research evidence regarding managed care and organized delivery systems, and the likely future organization of the health system in light of recent trends and evidence. It also highlights some of the more important public policy implications of the new health care infrastructure.

The U.S. health care system is in the midst of transformation. Even in the absence of national reform legislation, major changes in the organization of the health care system have been occurring at a rapid pace since the early 1980s. Health practitioners and administrators are by now well acquainted with the broad outlines of these changes as reflected in the growth and evolution of managed care and, more recently, in the movement toward organized delivery systems striving to achieve greater integration of health care services along a continuum of care. These two forces—managed care and organized delivery systems—are separate but closely linked developments that have emerged in response to several conditions in the health care environment, including pressures to contain costs, increasing demands for value and accountability, growing recognition of the importance of primary and preventive care, and the prospect of meaningful state- and national-level health care reform initiatives evolving over the coming years.

Pressures to contain costs mounted in the 1980s as health care spending spiraled upward at a dizzying pace. Years of health care spending growth rates well above overall economic growth rates meant that health spending was consuming an ever larger share of total economic output over time. Under current conditions, health expenditures are projected to top $1.7 trillion, or 18.1 percent of the gross domestic product (GDP), by the year 2000.[1] This cost escalation has commanded the attention of both private and public purchasers of health care. Private business has seen its health care spending rise as a share of after-tax corporate profits, and employees have seen a larger proportion of their compensation taken up by health benefits.[2] Government purchasers of health care have also faced the consequences of rapidly rising costs, and in this era of constrained revenue growth and massive budget deficits, these increases have provoked serious concern.[3] Higher health care costs have contributed to budget difficulties at all levels and may be squeezing out spending on other needed programs.

While the quest for effective cost control has been the dominant force behind the growth of managed care and organized delivery systems, other pressures also have had a significant impact. Demands for value and accountability have grown louder as purchasers of health care, particularly employers, have sought more hard evidence on the quality, effectiveness, and appropriateness of the care they are buying. This demand for value has highlighted the need for better measurement of quality and outcomes; ways to continuously improve the care being delivered; and higher levels of continuity, coordination, and comprehensiveness of care. Preventive and primary care, too, have gained greater recognition, and the focus has increasingly been placed on health maintenance and wellness in addition to diagnosis and treatment of disease. The prevailing acute care paradigm (medical attention only after a patient has become ill) is eroding and may eventually be replaced by a more holistic approach to health. Under the new paradigm, health care providers may be encouraged and provided incentives to regard improved community health status as their overarching goal.

Cost control and other pressures have been at work for more than a decade, but more recent political developments making national health care reform a prominent issue have also stimulated changes in the health care system. Candidate Bill Clinton made the promise of health care reform central to his 1992 presidential campaign, and President Clinton made development of a health care reform proposal a top priority early in his administration. Although the Clinton proposal spawned competing initiatives and no legislation emerged in 1994, the Clinton plan did help to define the parameters of the health care debate. If managed competition was to play a central role, insurers and providers who organized themselves to provide comprehensive care in an environment of increasingly capitated payment would clearly have a stronger position in the post-reform era. As a result, the anticipation of significant national reform caused existing trends toward managed care and organized systems of care to accelerate.

Broadly defined, *managed care* includes not only HMOs and preferred provider organizations (PPOs), but also "managed fee-for-service" plans in which a traditional indemnity plan is complemented by some utilization management features. The core concept unifying all forms of managed care is the attempt to control costs by reducing unnecessary use of health care services. An *organized delivery system* is a network of organizations that provides or arranges to provide a coordinated continuum of services to a defined population and is willing to be held clinically and fiscally accountable for the outcomes and health status of the population(s) served.[4] Many systems will own or be closely aligned with an insurance product. While many unanswered questions still remain about both the effects of managed care and the performance of organized delivery systems, we know more about the former than the latter. For quick review, we highlight some of the major findings.

Summary of Major Research Findings on Managed Care

- Most forms of managed care are effective in reducing health care utilization, especially inpatient care.

- Health maintenance organizations (HMOs) also appear to reduce utilization of tests, procedures, or treatments that are expensive or that have lower-cost alternatives.

- Some forms of managed care may lead to higher utilization of certain types of services, including physician visits and preventive care.

- Some direct evidence suggests that managed care plans—particularly HMOs and managed fee-for-service plans—are able to reduce health costs of enrollees. The evidence of lower utilization of inpatient care provides additional indirect support for the cost-saving potential of managed care.

- Only very limited evidence exists to show that lower managed care costs lead to lower systemwide health costs.

- There is emerging evidence that greater HMO penetration is associated with lower growth in costs as reflected in lower FFS and HMO premiums.

- There is no evidence of lower quality of care under managed care, but there is some evidence of lower patient satisfaction compared with fee-for-service plans. However, most HMO patients rate their care highly.

- Evaluations of Medicare and Medicaid managed care programs suggest that publicly insured individuals in managed care enjoy access to care that is comparable to or better than access under traditional Medicare and Medicaid arrangements.

- There is preliminary evidence of cost savings in Medicaid managed care programs in the range of 5 to 15 percent.

These findings suggest that policies and decisions that encourage greater enrollment of Americans in managed care plans may hold some promise as a cost-effective way of delivering services. The degree to which such benefit is achieved, however, will vary greatly across the country as a function of the type of managed care plan involved, local market forces, socioeconomic and demographic characteristics of populations, historical practice patterns, the political economy of local employers and providers, and related factors. In the process, increased attention is likely to be paid to such issues as provider choice, access to specialist care, outcomes of care, patient satisfaction, and the ability of managed care plans to care for disadvantaged and vulnerable populations over time. The challenge is to strike a balance between protecting the interests of providers and patients and the need to give managed care plans sufficient freedom to develop innovative cost-effective approaches to providing services.

Summary of Major Research Findings on Organized Delivery Systems

- There is some evidence that organized delivery systems that are more integrated have the potential to provide more accessible care across multiple delivery points, for example, from primary care to hospital care to home care.

- Evidence is emerging that organized delivery systems experience greater inpatient productivity and have greater total revenue, cash flow, and operating margins than other systems.

- There is some evidence that delivery systems that are more integrated can demonstrate marked reductions in length of hospital stay, and that under capitation they have the potential to reduce per member per month payments by 26 to 35 percent.

- Almost no work has been done evaluating the quality of outcomes of care in organized delivery systems, but emerging data from Kaiser Permanente of Northern California suggest outcomes as good as or better than those of other providers in California.

- While there is a paucity of research on the performance of organized delivery systems, ongoing work has identified some of the key ingredients that such systems will need in order to meet their objectives. These include (1) the ability to do population-based health planning and needs assessment; (2) the ability to determine system size based on the results of population-based planning; (3) the ability to assume the financial risk of caring for defined populations based on achieving appropriate levels of physician and clinical integration of services; (4) the development of information systems that can track patients and providers across the continuum of care and provide data on cost, quality, and outcomes of care; and (5) the need for new management and governance structures that support the new models of health care delivery.

The Growth of Managed Care

Most forms of managed care combine at least some of the following elements:

- Attempts to influence or "manage" providers' decisions about patient care by various mechanisms;
- Prepayment for care, whereby purchasers make capitated payments to managed care firms and enrollees face very limited out-of-pocket costs;
- Networks of preferred or required providers, which impose some limitation on freedom of choice for the enrollee;
- Payment terms with providers other than traditional fee-for-service payment, such as discounted fees, capitation, salary, bonuses and withholds, and other payment terms; and
- Primary care "gatekeepers" who coordinate care and control referrals to specialty care.

Managed care is perhaps best understood as a spectrum of service or product types, ranging from plans that incorporate only one or two of the defining elements just described, to plans that include all of the defining elements (see Table 4.1). Managed care in its various forms has grown rapidly since the early 1980s (see Figures 4.1 and 4.2). An additional 2.6 million people are enrolled in other HMO products such as open-ended plans.[5] HMO enrollment growth has been greatest in urban areas, with market penetration in several metropolitan

Table 4.1   Defining Elements of Managed Care Plan Types

Defining Elements	*Plan Types*				
	"Managed" FFS	*PPO*	*Point-of-Service*	*HMO*	
Attempt to influence or "manage" patient care decisions of providers	Yes	Sometimes	Yes	Yes	
Prepayment for care	No	No	Sometimes	Yes	
Use of networks of preferred or required providers	No	Yes	Yes	Yes	
Payment terms with providers other than traditional fee-for-service	Sometimes	Yes	Yes	Yes	
Use of primary care "gatekeepers"	No	Sometimes	Sometimes	Yes	

Figure 4.1   Growth of Managed Care Enrollment by Plan Type

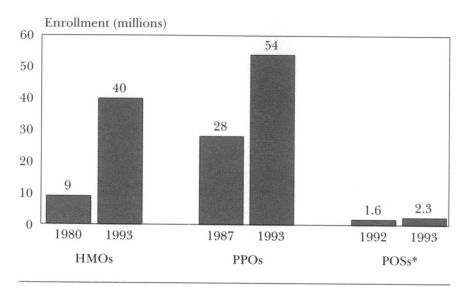

* Point-of-service plans (open-ended HMO products only).
Sources: InterStudy (HMO & POS data); American Managed Care & Review Association (PPO data).

areas now exceeding 40 percent. High levels of urban HMO penetration have not been confined to one or two geographic regions: in April 1994, areas with the highest penetration included metropolitan areas in the East, the West, the Midwest, and the Southwest.[6]

While the growth of HMOs has attracted much attention, partly because their use of capitated payment and closed panels of providers makes HMOs so distinct from the traditional indemnity model, the growth of PPOs has also been significant (see Figures 4.1 and 4.2). The rapid growth of PPOs may result from their combination of managed care cost control features (attractive to payers) and their greater freedom of provider choice relative to HMOs (attractive to consumers).

Point-of-service plans represent a new high-growth area within managed care (see Figures 4.1 and 4.2). Under point-of-service plans, enrollees have the option of using the plan's closed panel of providers at little or no out-of-pocket cost or using outside providers and paying a significant copayment. These plans differ from PPOs in several ways: the copayment rate for using nonpanel providers is generally

Figure 4.2   Growth of Managed Care Plan by Plan Type

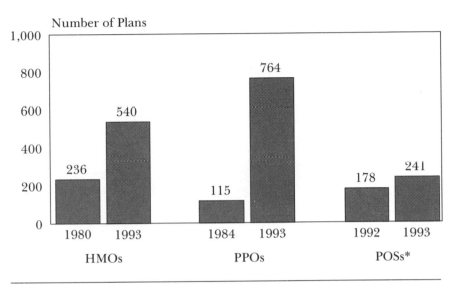

* Point-of-service plans (open-ended HMO products only).
Sources: InterStudy (HMO and POS data); SMG Marketing Group (Figure 1.2 is McPlans in H.G.3).

higher than in PPOs, and the in-plan care arrangements tend to more closely resemble HMOs (greater use of primary care gatekeepers, more active management of provider decision making, and so forth). Point-of-service plans can be offered as an option within an HMO plan (also known as an open-ended HMO product) or can be offered as a stand-alone plan. In 1990, overall point-of-service enrollment accounted for 5 percent of employees with health insurance.[7] By 1993, this proportion had risen to 9 percent.[8] Like PPOs, point-of-service plans offer the attractive combination of potential cost savings without rigid restriction of choice of provider.

The combined enrollment growth of HMOs, PPOs, and point-of-service plans has radically reshaped the private insurance market within a relatively short period of time. A recent survey of nearly 2,000 public and private employers found that 51 percent of employees were enrolled in either an HMO, a PPO, or a point-of-service plan in 1993 (see Figure 4.3), compared with 29 percent just five years earlier. The survey also found that fewer employees were given the option to choose a fee-for-service plan: 90 percent of employees re-

Figure 4.3   Employer-Sponsored Group Health Insurance
Enrollment, by Plan Type, 1993

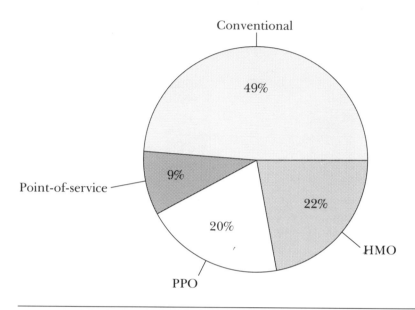

Source: J. Gabel, D. Liston, G. Jensen, and J. Marsteller, "The Health Insurance Picture in 1993: Some Rare Good News," *Health Affairs* 13, no. 1 (1994): 327–36.

ceiving health insurance could choose a conventional plan in 1988, but only 65 percent had that option in 1993.[9]

A final growth area in the private insurance market has been the use of utilization management practices within conventional indemnity plans, or "managed fee-for-service." By 1992, enrollees in conventional plans could expect to face a wide range of utilization management practices, including preadmission certification for inpatient care (78 percent of employees), utilization review (72 percent), mandatory second opinion for surgery (40 percent), large claims management (73 percent), incentives for ambulatory surgery (31 percent), and penalties for non-urgent emergency care use (35 percent).[10] A recent survey shows that 83 percent of managed care plans and HMOs regularly conduct clinical studies of quality of care and 74 percent of plans profile practice patterns.[11]

While managed care has grown to dominate the private insurance market, the picture is somewhat different in the major publicly sponsored insurance programs, Medicare and Medicaid. Enrollment of Medicare and Medicaid beneficiaries in managed care programs has increased over time, and the ability of Medicare beneficiaries to choose participating HMOs and Medicaid managed care programs varies by state. However, managed care enrollment in the public programs is still much lower in proportional terms than in the private insurance market. Publicly insured individuals have limited incentive to enroll in managed care programs when enrollment is voluntary, since they will sacrifice some freedom to choose their own providers (except under certain types of Medicare HMO contracts). To date, all Medicare HMO enrollment and most Medicaid managed care enrollment has been voluntary, although there is current interest in expanding HMO opportunities for Medicare beneficiaries and state interest in mandatory managed care programs for Medicaid recipients has been growing rapidly.

In Medicare, the push for HMO enrollment gained momentum with the passage of the Tax Equity and Fiscal Responsibility Act (TEFRA) of 1982, which enhanced the incentives for HMOs to enroll Medicare beneficiaries in risk contracts. As of July 1993, nearly 2.2 million people were enrolled in Medicare HMOs and approximately 1.7 million of these enrollees (78 percent of the total) were covered under TEFRA risk contracts.[12] These TEFRA risk enrollees represented roughly 5 percent of all Medicare beneficiaries.

Use of managed care within the Medicaid program has also grown in recent years. Increasingly, states have turned to managed care as a potential solution for rapidly rising program costs, an inadequate supply of primary care providers willing to participate in traditional Medicaid arrangements, and the uneven quality of care. Managed care in Medicaid is a "continuum of models" ranging from comprehensive prepaid models (in which plans receive capitated payment to provide all covered services) to fee-for-service gatekeeper models (in which traditional fee-for-service payment arrangements are maintained, and a per capita case management fee is paid to providers for coordinating the patient's care).[13] States wishing to use managed care in their Medicaid programs have two options. First, the Omnibus Budget and Reconciliation Act (OBRA) of 1981 gave states the opportunity to apply for program waivers to gain exclusions from program requirements in the areas of statewide implementation of the program, comparability of services, and beneficiary freedom of choice in selecting providers. These are called Section 1915(b) waivers, in reference to the relevant portion of the Social Security Act. In addition, states can experiment with managed care through research and demonstration waivers—called Section 1115 waivers—granted under a separate waiver process. While these options have been available to states for many years, recent explosive growth in Medicaid program costs and enrollment have severely strained state budgets, giving added impetus to experimentation with Medicaid managed care.

Enrollment in Medicaid managed care programs more than doubled between 1987 and 1992, to 3.6 million enrollees (or 12 percent of the overall Medicaid population). As of early 1993, 36 states had at least one Medicaid managed care program in operation, and an additional 13 states were planning to implement programs. All of the existing programs target the AFDC population within Medicaid, and some target other groups within Medicaid as well.[14,15] Fee-for-service gatekeeper programs have been the fastest growing type of managed care within Medicaid, mainly because states have had difficulty attracting providers to capitated models because of inadequate payment rates, higher financial risk, and greater administrative burden.[16]

As managed care has grown in terms of total enrollment and market share, in both the private insurance market and in public programs, it has also grown in diversity of product offerings and organizational forms. There has also been a blurring of distinctions among plan types. HMO plan categories such as "staff model," "group model," "IPA," "network model," and "mixed model" continue to be used, despite the fact that they do not usefully delineate differences among plans. These differences include methods of reimbursement to primary care and other providers (salary, capitation, or fee-for-service), use of financial incentives to control provider behavior (such as risk pools for inpatient and specialty care), utilization management practices, the practice settings of the primary care providers (solo or small group practice versus large group practice), whether participating providers also see non-HMO patients in their practice, and the presence or absence of a middle tier between the HMO and the primary care providers (i.e., whether the HMO contracts directly with the physician or contracts with an organization that in turn reimburses the physicians).

These kinds of variables may affect plan performance by shaping the financial and nonfinancial incentives facing primary care physicians, the key decision makers in HMOs.[17] The inability to distinguish among plans along these critical dimensions makes it difficult for researchers and policy analysts to compare the impacts of such factors on plan performance and, ultimately, to determine which plan arrangements are most successful in controlling costs while maintaining access, quality, and patient satisfaction.

From Managed Care to Organized Delivery Systems

The trend toward greater integration of services and providers into coordinated systems of care is due in part to the growth of managed care. In fact, the most advanced organized delivery systems[18] are found in those markets with the greatest degree of managed care penetration. Incentives for providers to join such systems include possible cost advantages, access to capital for expansion and development, and access to management support services and systems.[19] Integration has occurred in two ways: *horizontally,* when similar providers join together to form larger groups and systems, and *vertically,* when providers at different stages in the continuum of care join together to form more comprehensive delivery systems.[20]

Horizontal integration has been most noteworthy among two provider types: hospitals and physicians. Among hospitals, horizontal integration has occurred with the formation of multihospital systems. Multihospital systems are defined as two or more hospitals owned, leased, sponsored, or contract managed by a central organization.[21] The greatest activity in the formation of hospital systems was seen between 1984 and 1990, when the number of multihospital systems rose from 250 to a peak of 311. Since 1990, the number of multihospital systems has declined somewhat, to 283 systems in 1993, but most of this decline is probably the result of merger and consolidation activities among systems.[22] Such consolidation is having a marked effect on hospital capacity and use. For example, in some markets such as Minneapolis-St. Paul, hospital consolidation between 1981 and 1992 resulted in a reduction of 3,840 beds (42 percent decline), and a 1.0 million decline in inpatient days (42 percent decline) with 21 percent fewer admissions and a 24 percent decline in average length of stay.[23]

Among physicians, horizontal integration has occurred as the number of medical group practices has risen and the proportion of patient care physicians practicing in groups has increased. A medical group practice consists of three or more physicians practicing together. The early 1980s were a particularly active period, with the number of medical group practices increasing from 10,762 in 1980 to 15,485 in 1984, more than a 40 percent increase within the span of just four years.[24] Growth continued through the remainder of the 1980s and into the 1990s, but at a somewhat slower rate. In 1979, just over one in four nonfederal physicians (26.2 percent) practiced in a group setting; by 1991, nearly one in three physicians (32.6 percent) were in groups.[25] In more advanced managed care markets (such as Minneapolis), the percentage of physicians practicing in groups increased from an already high 58.4 percent in 1979 to 95 percent in 1993. The percentage of multispecialty groups grew from 21.1 percent in 1979 to 36.0 percent in 1993, and the percentage of group practices with over 25 full-time equivalent (FTE) physicians grew from 4.7 percent to 19.9 percent.[26] In the future, the number of group practices may stabilize or even decline, as existing groups expand and consolidate, while the proportion of physicians practicing in groups is likely to continue to increase.[27,28]

More recently, traditional hospital-based systems have begun to link vertically with physician groups and other entities to form systems of care embracing a broad continuum of services that have been previously defined as organized delivery systems. The definition does not require that all entities have a common ownership.[29] Rather, it allows for a variety of contractual arrangements and strategic alliances.[30,31] What ties the system or network together, however, is its clinical and fiscal accountability for a defined population(s).

It is not known how many systems or networks in the United States meet the definition of an organized delivery system, but over 40 percent of U.S. hospitals ($n = 2,842$) belong to the nearly 300 hospital systems currently in existence.[32] Recent surveys, however, suggest that a smaller percentage of these hospitals belong to organized delivery systems; estimates range from 12.6 percent[33] to 24 percent.[34] An additional 47 percent of hospitals, however, report that they plan to develop or will be part of an organized delivery system in the near future.[35] Most of the integration activities, however, are confined to hospitals and physician group practices, with less attention given to other components of the continuum of care such as ambulatory surgery, home health care, skilled nursing care, hospice care, and related activities. There are also geographical limitations to the ability to provide coordinated care across the continuum to defined populations. For example, only 20 percent of all community general hospitals (representing 402 urban-based local systems) are located within 60 miles of the largest urban parent hospital.[36] Further, only about 14 percent ($n = 56$) of these local hospital systems have sufficient nucleus or presence in a given market (e.g., four or more hospitals and at least one hospital with greater that 285 beds) to form the basis for a regional delivery system.

Large multispecialty group practices such as the Mayo Clinic, the Cleveland Clinic, and the Ochsner Clinic, as well as selected staff and group model HMOs such as Kaiser Permanente and Group Health Cooperative of Puget Sound, operate in addition to hospital-based systems and in many cases have preceded them. Some of the newer systems and networks are organized around physician groups such as the Mullikin Medical Group and the Friendly Hills Medical Group in Southern California. In addition, insurance companies such as Aetna, Prudential, Cigna, and Blue–Cross Blue Shield are organizing provider networks in selected markets across the country.

Core Characteristics of Organized Delivery Systems

While models of organized delivery systems are many and various, they share common core characteristics and imperatives. These include the need to

- Provide a continuum of care embracing primary care, acute care, and chronic care management to defined populations;
- Assume financial risk;
- Produce and use clinical and financial outcome data;
- Achieve requisite levels of horizontal and vertical integration;
- Achieve higher levels of physician integration; and
- Achieve needed levels of clinical integration of services in local markets.

Continuum of care and population-based care

Systems must provide or arrange to provide a comprehensive array of services that includes prevention, wellness, and health promotion as well as acute care and rehabilitative, restorative, and maintenance care to defined populations. These populations may include enrollees in managed care plans of one form or another, people living within a defined geographic area, people in need of special services, or some combination of the three. Purchasers are interested in reducing the transaction costs of monitoring dozens of different contracts while recognizing that some carve-out contracts (e.g., substance abuse and psychiatric services) may still be needed. Also, consumers are interested in being part of a delivery system that reduces the cost of searching for providers and services themselves and that can provide them with more coordinated care as they require different types of care at various points in time. Pressures to reduce the costs of hospital care are also driving efforts to develop more efficient and coordinated post-hospital services, including subacute units, home health agencies, and hospice care. Finally, organized delivery systems must locate the various elements of the continuum sufficiently close to the desired populations to be served. Thus, not only must the full continuum of care be offered, but it must also be offered in geographically accessible locations.

Financial risk

New forms of payment are increasing the pressure on providers to assume financial risk. Capitation pays a set rate per member per month to manage the care of enrollees for a fixed period of time and to provide a defined set of benefits. Such payment creates incentives to keep enrollees as healthy as possible and, when illness strikes, to restore the patient's health as cost-effectively as possible. This means that delivery systems must actively manage clinical care in new ways. Some emerging evidence suggests that interdisciplinary teams using protocols and pathways, continuous quality improvement/total quality management (CQI/TQM) approaches, care management systems, and outcome reporting systems will be required in order to manage such risk effectively.[37]

Clinical and financial outcomes data

As biomedical, clinical, and health services research expands knowledge regarding the efficiency and effectiveness of various medical treatments and interventions, health care delivery organizations must systematically study and record the results of their efforts. Information systems must be able to integrate clinical and financial data and link patients and providers across the continuum of care. The resulting data must be used for both internal continuous improvement of quality of care and for external accountability purposes.

Horizontal and vertical integration

Horizontal integration allows the coordination of care at the same stage of patient treatment—for example, coordination among radiology, lab, and intensive care units within a given hospital or coordination of such services across hospitals. Vertical integration allows the coordination of care across different levels of patient treatment; for example, between the hospital and the physician's office or between the hospital and the home health care agency. Given the increased emphasis on outpatient, ambulatory, and primary care, vertical integration has emerged as an increasingly important determinant of an organized delivery system's ability to offer coordinated care.

Physician integration

The growth of managed care and capitated payment has meant that hospitals and physicians must work more closely together in order to manage risk. Also, greater emphasis on outcomes reporting requires closer linkages among the different components of the delivery system. In response, a number of new models of hospital-physician linkages have emerged, including independent practice associations or group practices without walls (GPWWs), management service organizations, physician-hospital organizations, foundations, salaried staff models, and equity models. An *independent practice association* (IPA) involves an organization of independent physicians who come together for purposes of negotiating managed care contracts. The physicians typically practice in solo or small partnership settings throughout the community and are primarily linked together through various mechanisms to review and manage patient utilization. A *management services organization* (MSO) is an entity whereby a hospital or health system offers a variety of practice management support services to physicians.[38] The MSO may also own the physical assets of physician practices. A *physician-hospital organization* (PHO) is typically a jointly owned 50/50 arrangement between physicians and hospitals that jointly assumes risk in providing care to enrollees associated with managed care contracts.[39] The PHO may be open to all physicians affiliated with the hospital or system (i.e., open model) or more selective, based on those physicians who practice cost-effective care and who share the system's vision (i.e., closed model). A *foundation model* involves the purchase of the nonphysical assets of physician practices or medical groups and the provision of all marketing and management services to support the practices and groups.[40] Physicians usually form a professional services corporation, which contracts exclusively with the foundation to provide services. The foundation, in turn, negotiates and manages contracts with purchasers. *Salaried models,* of course, involve employment of physicians by a hospital or system. Finally, *equity models* involve financial arrangements whereby participating physicians can share in the increased market value of a practice arrangement that has been built through their efforts.

Clinical integration

Clinical integration is defined as the extent to which patient care services are coordinated across the activities, functions, personnel, and units of the delivery system in order to maximize the value of care delivered to patients. The ultimate test of the newly emerging organized delivery systems will be whether or not they offer increased value to patients and to the communities served. Everything else is subordinate to this end. Existing research suggests that this considerable challenge will require pervasive organizational change on multiple fronts.[41]

Organized delivery systems face the twin challenges of *differentiation* and *integration*.[42] The challenge of differentiation means that sufficient services must be offered in terms of both *breadth* and *depth*. A sufficient breadth of services will cover the desired geographic marketplace. Such services include primary care centers, clinics, home health, hospices, acute care, and nursing homes. A sufficient depth of services will provide multiple facilities and units of the same type in order to meet demand. The challenge of integration lies in coordinating the broad continuum of care across the geographic market of interest. Here the depth required for adequate geographic coverage may pose an integration challenge in terms of duplicative facilities and units; for example, multiple home health agencies, hospices, hospitals, and the like. Appropriate integrative mechanisms must be established to assure that cost-effective care is provided across the geographic market of interest. The need to simultaneously differentiate and integrate represents the internal logic of organized delivery systems[43] and is critically dependent on "right sizing" the system.

Alternative Models

Figure 4.4 depicts four alternative models or approaches to organizing the delivery system.[44] The figure assumes a defined population that has insurance coverage for a predetermined set of benefits. The hospital/health system–led model may currently be the most prevalent form, owing primarily to the financial, organizational, and leadership resources and expertise of these systems. A major potential disadvantage, however, is the overemphasis on acute care, which focuses

Figure 4.4   Four Alternatives to Organizing Integrated Delivery Systems

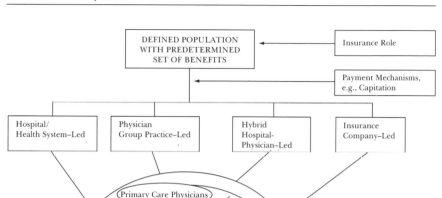

Source: Adapted from S. M. Shortell, R. R. Gillies, and D. A. Anderson, "The New World of Managed Care: Creating Organized Delivery Systems," *Health Affairs* 13, no. 4 (Winter 1994): 46–64.

on filling hospital beds, as opposed to population-based delivery models such as those based on capitated payment.[45,46]

The system or network can also be organized around physician group practices. These groups own or lease hospital beds as needed, as well as developing linkages with other components of the system. An advantage of the physician-led approach is its closeness to patients and the alignment of economic incentives with the primary provider of care, the physician. Under capitation, physicians have every incentive to use all resources prudently in meeting patient needs. However, many physician groups do not have the necessary size, capital reserves, or organizational and managerial expertise to run an integrated delivery system.

A third approach is to combine the hospital/health system– and physician group–led models into a hybrid health system–physician-led organized delivery system. Many hospital-led systems, in fact, have created "subsidiary" hospital-physician organizations for the purposes of aligning economic interests and pursuing managed care contracts. However, the hospital-physician-led integrated delivery system goes beyond the mere pursuit of contracts to form integrated management and governance structures that oversee the entire continuum of care for defined populations. This model has many potential advantages in that it combines the financial and organizational resources and expertise of hybrid health systems with the clinical focus of physicians and their closeness to the patient. Its success, however, demands a great deal of trust between hospitals and physicians, strong leadership on both sides, and a commitment to working through problems. It also requires sufficient balance between primary care physicians and specialists.

Finally, the integrated delivery system may be organized around insurance companies. Insurance companies bring the advantages of expertise in administration of actuarial claims, and in marketing to the network. A major disadvantage is that they typically do not understand the delivery of patient care and the complex professional and institutional relationships that must be maintained across the continuum of care.

While there is no evidence to date on the comparative performance of these different models, it may be that the hybrid health system–physician-led model has the greatest potential to meet most of the criteria for delivering cost-effective care to populations. For example, by linking the capital resources and managerial expertise of hospital/health systems with physician delivery capabilities, the hybrid models can potentially provide a more comprehensive continuum of care than hospital-led or physician-led models alone. This, however, depends on the extent to which primary care capacity is expanded and on primary care providers playing a greater leadership role in system development. The ability of the hybrid model to assume risk depends greatly on the extent to which the physicians are organized into groups supported by relevant clinical and financial information systems. Again, this is most likely to occur where the resources of both the hospital and the physician are brought together. Certainly, the hybrid model has great opportunities to achieve both horizontal and vertical integration as well as physician integration. As subsequently described, existing research indicates that physician integration is strongly related to clinical integration.[47] With regard to the ability to differentiate and integrate simultaneously, many hospitals have the capital resources to add components of the system but need physician input in order to appropriately integrate these into a cohesive network of services. Insurance-led models will probably be least likely to meet the core characteristics of an effective system, but insurers may well be critical partners in many of the evolving systems and networks. This is particularly true where insurers can link with strong hospital/ health system and physician leadership. Longstanding examples of such hospital-physician-insurer models include Kaiser Permanente and Group Health Cooperative of Puget Sound and, more recently, the Cigna-Lovelace Medical Group arrangement in Albuquerque, New Mexico.

Past Performance of Managed Care

Can managed care deliver the desired cost control while maintaining or improving outcomes, access, and satisfaction? The answer depends on the type of managed care examined and the definition of acceptable results along various dimensions of performance. Most research on the performance of managed care has focused on comparisons with fee-for-service performance, particularly in the areas of costs and utilization of services. These findings are limited due to the problems of selection bias and wide variations in the characteristics of individual plans. Selection bias occurs when individuals with certain characteristics tend to select enrollment in a certain plan type more frequently than others. For example, younger and healthier people may be more likely to join HMOs, creating what is termed "favorable selection" for HMOs. In fact, there is some evidence that people who use health services less frequently are more likely to join HMOs[48] and PPOs.[49,50] Selection bias makes it difficult to determine whether performance differences among plans are the result of actual differences in the plans or merely a reflection of differences in their enrollees. Direct comparisons among plans are difficult, because plans may differ along many important dimensions, such as benefits package, cost-sharing provisions, and methods for reimbursing providers. Despite these issues, the body of research on managed care is now sufficiently mature to permit making some definitive statements, particularly regarding the performance of HMOs.

Utilization

The goal of managed care is to control costs by reducing unnecessary care. A good deal of convincing evidence reports that some types of managed care reduce inpatient utilization compared with fee-for-service plans. A comprehensive review of 54 studies of network-based managed care programs found that, controlling for selection bias, HMOs generally had lower hospital admission rates, fewer hospital days per enrollee, and shorter lengths of stay than FFS plans.[51] In some cases, admission rates were 26–37 percent lower in HMOs than with FFS.

Despite the fact that PPOs have been in existence for over a decade, no rigorous research findings exist on inpatient use in PPOs compared with FFS or other forms of managed care. For "managed FFS" plans, however, some significant findings suggest that utilization management practices within the FFS setting can reduce inpatient use on the order of 5–13 percent for inpatient admissions and 5–12 percent for inpatient days.[52–55]

Reductions in inpatient utilization have also been observed among publicly insured managed care enrollees. Results from a study comparing Medicare HMO enrollees with Medicare FFS enrollees found no differences in admission rates between the two groups, but both length of stay and inpatient days per 1,000 beneficiaries were almost 17 percent lower for the HMO enrollees.[56] Medicare HMO enrollees were more likely than FFS enrollees to receive care in a skilled nursing facility, suggesting that some of the reductions in inpatient care for HMO enrollees may have been achieved by substituting skilled nursing care for hospital inpatient care when possible. Medicaid managed care programs implemented by states since the early 1980s have varied greatly in their program designs, making it difficult to generalize about the effects of managed care in Medicaid. Most of the more methodologically rigorous studies of Medicaid managed care have found no differences in levels of inpatient use in these programs compared to traditional Medicaid.[57,58]

While managed care has produced some clear reductions in inpatient use in the private sector, and to a lesser extent in the public sector, research findings on the impact on outpatient care are more mixed. Studies comparing physician visits in HMOs and FFS plans are divided, with half suggesting higher physician visit rates in HMOs and half suggesting lower rates.[59] But the research clearly indicates that HMO enrollees consistently receive more preventive services and health promotion activities than their counterparts in FFS. Studies also suggest that the use of tests, procedures, and treatments that are expensive or that have a lower-cost alternative is more than 20 percent lower in HMOs than in FFS plans.[60] These findings suggest that, even though HMOs may not reduce outpatient use as measured by physician services, they deliver a different mix of care, placing greater emphasis on preventive care and less reliance on expensive interventions.

Evidence on outpatient use in PPOs is scant and inconsistent. One of the stronger studies found that PPO enrollees used more physician services per episode of care than FFS enrollees.[61] To the extent that PPOs do not apply tough utilization review procedures to their outpatient services, higher outpatient use is not entirely unexpected, since participating providers have an incentive to make up the income they lose on discounted fees by increasing the volume of services provided.

In the public programs, some types of outpatient care have been reduced while others may have increased under managed care.[62,63] However, a review of Medicaid managed care programs found that programs using FFS payment to the primary care provider were more likely to see an increase in physician visits. Almost all of the Medicaid managed care programs with separate data on emergency department use reported lower utilization of this type of care, and most reductions exceeded 20 percent. In addition, a large proportion of the programs reported decreases in the use of ancillary services and prescription drug use.[64]

Costs

Limited recent evidence comparing costs in HMOs with FFS plans shows inconclusive or conflicting results.[65] In the RAND Health Insurance Experiment (HIE), using data from the late 1970s, researchers estimated that expenditures for patients who were randomly assigned to a staff-model HMO were 28 percent lower than for patients assigned to a FFS plan with no cost sharing. Most of the difference resulted from lower hospital admission rates for the HMO enrollees.[66]

For PPOs, no convincing evidence is available to indicate their ability to reduce the health costs of their enrollees. While some studies have shown that PPOs can reduce costs for outpatient mental health services[67,68] and for inpatient care, research findings also suggest that PPOs may actually increase outpatient or physician care costs.[69,70] Studies have produced conflicting findings on whether PPOs reduce total costs per enrollee.[71,72] These findings suggest the potential importance of applying utilization management practices to outpatient as well as inpatient care in PPO settings, in order to counteract the incentive for physicians to increase their volume of services under discounted fee arrangements. Some evidence shows that managed FFS plans are able to reduce enrollees' total health costs, primarily by achieving reductions in inpatient costs. Recent well-designed studies of managed FFS plans have reported inpatient spending reductions of 6–8 percent, leading to overall expenditure reductions of 4–6 percent per enrollee.[73,74]

Evidence for cost savings in public managed care programs is mixed, partly because of the ways in which cost savings are defined for these programs. Evaluations of Medicare and Medicaid managed care tend to focus on cost savings to Medicare or Medicaid (as the purchaser of care), rather than on overall cost savings. Managed care enrollees in public programs may consume fewer health care resources than their FFS counterparts, but if the Medicare or Medicaid program is paying the managed care provider a rate higher than the cost of the care in the FFS setting, the program does not see any cost savings. For example, an evaluation of Medicare HMO enrollment in risk contracts found that the use of HMOs did not produce savings for the Medicare program, despite lower utilization among HMO enrollees, because the formula for setting Medicare capitation rates does not adequately adjust for selection bias. The Medicare beneficiaries who chose to enroll in HMOs turned out to be healthier on average than the Medicare population as a whole. Because of this selection bias, the Medicare program spent 5.7 percent more for enrollees' care than it would have paid under the usual FFS arrangements.[75] The Medicare program's experience with risk contracting suggests that public programs seeking program savings through the use of capitated contracts must refine the approach for setting capitation rates to better account for selection bias.

The picture is somewhat brighter for cost savings produced by managed care in Medicaid. Some of the most convincing evidence comes from the Arizona Health Care Cost Containment System (AHCCCS), a statewide alternative Medicaid program featuring mandatory enrollment in capitated health plans. During its first nine years of operation (fiscal years 1983–1991), AHCCCS achieved significant cost savings over the estimated cost of a traditional Medicaid program, despite higher administrative costs. Cumulative cost savings for acute care beneficiaries for the nine-year period exceeded $100 million, and costs per enrollee in 1991 were estimated to be 19 percent lower than in a traditional Medicaid program.[76,77] Some evidence also suggests savings in the range of 5 to 15 percent in other Medicaid managed care programs.[78]

Only very limited evidence suggests that managed care results in lower systemwide costs. No persuasive evidence has been produced yet on the actual impact of managed care on overall health spending at the national or regional level. Early studies also failed to show that HMO market share had a significant impact on overall hospital expenditures in local areas. However, more recent studies have linked both HMO market share and PPO plan growth to lower hospital expenditures in the state of California.[79]

Evidence regarding the rate of growth of managed care costs is mixed. Two studies, one using data from 1976 to 1981 and the other from 1984 to 1986, found no evidence of lower growth in HMO costs (as measured by HMO premiums) compared with FFS costs.[80,81] But studies using more recent data, one covering the period 1985–1992 and the other 1988–1991, found HMO penetration to have a negative effect on the rate of growth of indemnity insurance premiums in the one case and on HMO premiums in the other case.[82,83] On the public side, Arizona's alternative Medicaid program (AHCCCS) also provides evidence of lower cost growth in addition to lower cost levels. AHCCCS acute care spending increased at an average annual rate of 6.8 percent between 1983 and 1991, compared with an estimated annual growth of 9.9 percent in a traditional Medicaid program.[84]

Quality, access, and patient satisfaction

Skeptics have questioned whether managed care plans achieve their cost savings at the expense of quality of care, adequate access to care, and patient satisfaction. Research findings can be broadly summarized as showing that quality of care is equivalent and sometimes better than under FFS plans, while access to care and patient satisfaction are generally acceptable but possibly lower than under FFS plans. The majority of research evidence on these dimensions comes from the HMO setting, and these findings cannot always be generalized to other managed care arrangements.[85] A review of studies with data from 1980 and later found that almost all studies determined that the quality of care in HMOs was better than or equivalent to quality in FFS plans; the only inferior-quality findings for HMOs came from observations of enrollees with mental health problems.[86]

Evaluations of the quality of care received by managed care enrollees in public programs indicate that the quality is comparable to the care received by traditional Medicare and Medicaid enrollees, although some studies have identified concerns that less than adequate care is being provided in some situations.[87,88] For Medicaid managed care, most studies of quality of care have focused on a small number of common treatments or services and have concluded that the quality of care in managed care programs is at least as good as, if not better than, quality in the traditional Medicaid programs. However, the quality of care received by both managed care and traditional Medicaid enrollees is often substantially lower than quality of care in non-Medicaid settings and often falls short of generally accepted medical standards for the treatment of specific conditions.[89,90]

Most results from recent and early HMO studies using patient ratings indicate somewhat lower patient satisfaction in HMOs compared with FFS plans, although most studies also found that HMO enrollees rate their plans highly.[91–93] HMO enrollees also rate the financial aspects of their plans more highly than do FFS enrollees.[94] There is a lack of evidence on patient satisfaction and access to care in PPOs and managed fee-for-service plans. In the public programs, patient satisfaction appears to be somewhat lower in managed care, but access appears to be at least equal to, if not better than, access in FFS Medicare and Medicaid.[95–97] An evaluation of Medicare HMOs determined that HMO and FFS enrollees enjoyed equal access to ambulatory care for several common chronic medical problems.[98] A review of studies of Medicaid managed care programs in several different states concluded that access is generally equal to, or better than, access in traditional Medicaid.[99]

The Future of Managed Care

Research to date provides some insight into where managed care has been, but it can only hint at where managed care is headed.[100] Recent trends reflect rapid growth of the managed care market, and continuing enrollment gains seem likely. Enrollment patterns of the past several years suggest that purchaser and consumer preferences are shifting toward those forms of managed care that offer a relatively high level of provider choice, either through providing a broad network of providers (as in IPA-model HMOs) or by allowing enrollees to receive out-of-network services with at least partial coverage from the plan (as in PPOs, and more recently in point-of-service plans). And, as vertical integration of providers advances, it seems clear that more and more managed care enrollees will receive their care from larger, organized delivery systems.

Some analysts have predicted that three interrelated developments will occur as managed care continues to evolve: (1) concentration of purchasing power will increase as employers steer more business to lower-cost plans and to a limited number of managed care firms to gain greater economic leverage with plans; (2) market share will be concentrated among a few leading firms in most local markets, and less successful firms will merge, fail, or be acquired; and (3) managed care firms will size their provider networks to achieve increased enrollee volume per provider, giving managed care organizations greater economic leverage over providers and leading to increased attention to the provider selection process.[101]

In the regulatory and legislative arena, managed care plans are likely to face increasing efforts by government to control their operations in order to protect consumers and providers. Two types of legislation designed to place limits on the selective contracting practices of managed care firms are "any willing provider" and "essential community provider" provisions. Any willing provider laws require health plans to contract with any providers willing to meet the plan's terms and conditions, while essential community provider proposals require plans to contract with any interested providers in their service area who are deemed "essential" to the community. Any willing provider laws existed in 21 states as of June 1994, and an additional 19 states are considering any willing provider proposals.[102] Most of the early any willing provider laws focused on pharmacy services, but the scope of providers covered has broadened considerably among many of the newly proposed and enacted laws. Some provider groups assert that such laws are necessary to protect providers from being unfairly excluded from managed care networks and to preserve an adequate range of provider choice for consumers. The managed care industry, however, argues that any willing provider laws are cost-increasing measures that limit the ability of managed care plans to develop networks of appropriate size and provider mix. A study commissioned by the Group Health Association of America (GHAA) concluded that any willing provider laws lead to both higher administrative costs and higher health care costs in managed care networks, estimating that such laws could increase administrative costs by as much as 127 percent and health care costs by as much as 18 percent for a "typical" HMO.[103]

Essential community provider protections represent a narrower variation on the same theme of controlling the terms of provider participation in managed care. These proposals are designed to protect certain classes of providers thought to be at a particular disadvantage in competitive markets dominated by managed care plans, by assuring that these providers will be allowed to participate in managed care networks in order to survive. Providers deemed "essential" under different versions of various proposals included community health clinics, maternal and child health clinics, substance abuse treatment providers, children's hospitals, small rural hospitals, rural health clinics, and family planning clinics, among others.

From the perspective of these vulnerable providers, the growth of managed care poses serious dilemmas. These providers often see a higher proportion of patients with costly and difficult health problems, and they serve many patients with inadequate or no insurance coverage. If expanding managed care networks take away their insured patients (probably mostly Medicaid recipients), these providers may be left with a large uncompensated care burden. In addition, many former patients now covered by managed care plans may still come back to these providers for further care, especially if they have established relationships with individual caregivers or if these community providers seem better attuned to patients' needs. At the same time, these providers often lack the capital and management expertise to develop viable competing care networks. Managed care groups, however, have opposed essential community provider proposals on the grounds that they would unduly constrain their ability to develop networks with true cost-saving potential.

Other legislative initiatives targeting managed care plans have also cropped up around the country. A recent review of this legislation identified three broad categories: networking legislation, utilization review regulation, and benefit mandates.[104] Networking legislation influences the design of managed care networks, usually by restricting the ability of managed care plans to offer incentives for enrollees to use networks, limit subscribers' choice of provider, contract with a limited set of providers (e.g., any willing provider laws), or offer financial incentives to providers. Many aspects of managed care plan design could be affected under these laws. Utilization review regulation runs the gamut from simple registration requirements to more strict controls on the review practices employed by managed care plans. Benefit mandates require plans to cover specified services, and a more expansive set of mandates is sometimes applied to managed care plans than to indemnity plans. The review of existing legislation identified 31 states with networking legislation, 30 states with comprehensive utilization review laws, 10 states with more limited utilization review laws, and a variety of mandated benefits, ranging from a low of 9 in Alabama to a high of 37 in Connecticut.[105]

The proliferation of legislative and regulatory controls targeting managed care plans does raise concerns about the possible impact on plans' cost performance. In addition, some of the regulatory effects are uneven in that regulations cover certain types of providers but not others. For example, providers covered by provisions of the federal HMO Act of 1973 face requirements not imposed on many newer managed care entities. There is a growing realization at the state level that laws may have to be changed or expanded to respond to developments in the market. In general, the challenge in the future will be finding an appropriate balance between the desire to protect the interests of providers and patients and the need to give managed care plans enough freedom to develop innovative cost-saving approaches.

Success Factors in Managed Care

Given the research evidence on managed care performance and likely future trends, what will be the critical success factors for managed care plans? At the level of plan characteristics, the following factors will prove increasingly important over time:

- *Physician relationships.* Successful plans will encourage physicians to make the mental shift from viewing their role as practicing a no-holds-barred, "heroic" style of medicine to that of making the best clinical choices for a population of patients under given resource constraints. Some factors that may facilitate this shift include reimbursement arrangements that remove incentives to provide too much care,[106] greater involvement of physicians in the management and/or governance of the plan, and contracting with physicians who see most or all of their patients under managed care arrangements.[107]

- *Information systems.* Successful plans will use sophisticated information systems to better coordinate care, adjust risk, monitor outcomes, and improve quality.

- *Flexibility.* Successful managed care firms will offer a sufficient variety of plan types (or options within plans), giving them the ability to tailor their products to the needs of a wide range of purchasers and consumers. All other things being equal, firms that can offer this kind of "one-stop shopping" should enjoy a competitive advantage.

- *Size and ownership.* Successful plans will more likely be relatively large and more likely will be part of a regional or national firm with adequate capital to finance growth.

In addition, several characteristics of local markets may influence performance of plans:

- *Regulatory climate.* Plans may do better in markets where regulatory burdens (capital and reserve requirements, required benefits, etc.) are less stringent.[108]

- *Involvement of corporate purchasers.* Plans may fare better in markets with active corporate interest in restraining health costs. There is evidence that organized corporate action, such as formation of health care coalitions, encourages the growth of managed care plans.[109]

- *Physician attitudes.* Markets with a higher proportion of younger physicians and a higher proportion of physicians in group practice may be more hospitable to managed care plans. Research also suggests that higher physician-population ratios are associated with larger HMO market share.[110]

- *Community profile.* Managed care plans may also have an edge in markets with higher income and higher rates of in-migration, since people are less likely to have firm preferences for certain providers. However, the evidence on this point is shaky.[111]

Performance of Organized Delivery Systems

Unlike the work on managed care, little systematic research has examined the comparative performance of organized delivery systems with regard to access, cost, quality, or outcomes of care. This is due both to the relatively recent emergence of such systems and to problems of collecting reliable, comparable performance data at the level of an overall system or network, as opposed, for example, to collecting data on individual hospital performance. As a result, this section must largely frame the issues involving the performance of such systems and suggest the kinds of research and measures that will be useful to policymakers, payers, managers, and providers alike. Something is known, however, regarding one of the precursors of organized delivery systems, namely, the multihospital systems that largely emerged in the 1970s and 1980s. In addition, scattered information describes the performance of such organized delivery systems as Kaiser Permanente and some of the newly emerging organized delivery systems being examined in the Health Systems Integration Study.[112]

Access

While, theoretically, organized delivery systems can improve access to care by offering more of the continuum of care through a wider distribution network, there is little evidence to indicate the extent to which this actually occurs. Previous research, for example, found that hospitals belonging to a system provided no greater number of services to their communities than freestanding hospitals, nor did system hospitals provide any greater amount of charity care than freestanding hospitals.[113] Not-for-profit systems, however, did provide more out-of-hospital services (i.e., outpatient, home health, and the like) than did for-profit systems.[114,115] Recent case studies also suggest that organized delivery systems that are more integrated can improve access by offering more convenient care through primary care satellite offices, smoother transitions among caregivers and facilities, longer office hours, and greater use of minor emergency centers.[116]

Costs

No consistent evidence shows that hospitals belonging to systems operate more efficiently (e.g., lower cost per adjusted admission) than non-system hospitals,[117] nor that system hospitals are any more profitable than non-system hospitals.[118,119] Recent evidence, however, does suggest that hospitals belonging to more *integrated* health care delivery systems with closer coordination among all of the component parts of the system have higher inpatient productivity (measured by number of FTEs per adjusted admission), and that these systems overall experience greater total revenue, cash flow, and total operating margin than less integrated systems.[120] Further, there is some evidence that hospitals belonging to more integrated systems do better financially than their market area competitors on a composite index involving market share, cash flow, operating margin, capital expense load, and related measures.[121] Also, a recent study of California hospitals suggests that hospitals belonging to systems have higher price-cost margins and profitability than random collections of independent hospitals.[122] Recent evidence also suggests that some integrated systems can achieve rapid reductions in length of stay in response to capitated payment pressures, for example, reducing Medicare length of stay within one month from 6.6 to 5.1 days and reducing the average length of stay for coronary artery bypass graft surgery patients after one year from 10 days to 6.5 days.[123] These reductions may be due to the ability of such systems to structure a continuum of care from preadmission to postdischarge using less resource-intensive treatment modalities, resulting in lower cost per hospital episode of illness.[124] It is also estimated that integrated systems that are capitated can reduce per member per month cost of hospital care.

Quality and outcomes of care

Whether or not more integrated systems offer higher quality of care or achieve outcomes superior to those of less integrated systems is largely unknown. Most recently, a concerted effort has been made to develop quality report cards[125] and related outcome measures.[126,127] Kaiser Permanente of Northern California has recently used such measures to benchmark its performance on cardiovascular care against statewide data.[128] Kaiser Permanente appears to be performing as well or better than the statewide data. Kaiser has improved cardiovascular outcomes by such measures as home care for heart attack and bypass patients, walk-in cholesterol screening programs, automated tracking systems for people with high lipid levels, and home blood pressure monitoring education. Finally, some evidence suggests that nursing homes that are part of systems that provide a broad continuum of care services experience better patient outcomes.[129]

Success Factors in Organized Delivery Systems

While there is a dearth of evidence regarding the comparative performance of organized delivery systems, existing research has identified some key factors that appear to be associated with organizing such systems and networks.[130–132] These include the imperatives to

- Conduct population-based community health status needs assessment;

- Use population-based data to calculate appropriate system and network size in terms of primary care providers, specialty providers, acute care beds, nursing homes, home health, hospice, and related components of the continuum of care;

- Assume financial risk for the provision of care to established populations; and

- Produce relevant, accurate, and timely data on cost, clinical, and functional health status outcomes of care for patients as well as health status indicators for the population at large.

These are challenging tasks requiring considerable clinical and managerial leadership, new ways of delivering patient care, innovative management and governance models, and new relationships between physicians and systems of care.

Reflecting many of the above challenges, system CEOs have indicated that their greatest concerns are to

- Improve measures of cost, quality, and outcomes of care;

- Improve risk management;

- Speed up the pace of downsizing acute inpatient bed capacity;

- Accelerate the formation of physician group practices;

- Increase the number of primary care physicians and related primary care providers;

- Determine how to best structure medical education and residency programs; and

- More effectively meet the health needs of the poor and those with inadequate financial coverage for care.[133]

While the preceding challenges are daunting, they are mostly under the control of system clinicians, leaders, and managers. Other factors, however, such as mixed financial incentives, patients without adequate insurance coverage, and various regulatory policies are not directly under system control. These represent areas for public policy intervention; interventions that could shape the continued evolution of managed care and encourage or discourage the growth of organized delivery systems.

Public Policy and Strategic Choices

The rapid growth and spread of both managed care and organized delivery systems suggest a number of important strategic choices facing policymakers and practitioners right now. In the area of managed care, key considerations include:

Protecting against undertreatment in managed care plans. Undertreatment includes inadequate or inappropriate care or insufficient access to needed care. Within a relatively short period of time, the dominant financing mode in the U.S. health care system has shifted from fee-for-service arrangements, with strong incentives for overtreatment, to managed care, in which plans may have strong incentives to encourage undertreatment of patients. The difficult challenge for both policymakers and managed care practitioners will be to develop methods for managing and paying providers that strike the optimal balance between reducing unnecessary care and protecting patients from undertreatment. The issue of potential undertreatment is particularly important for special populations—such as the elderly, the chronically ill, and children with special needs—who often have greater health care needs and costs.

Reducing the rate of cost growth for managed care plans. No convincing evidence suggests that managed care costs grow more slowly than FFS costs. While national health care spending growth appeared to slow in the early 1990s,[134] it is too early to tell whether this was a temporary reaction to the possibility of health care reform or the beginning of an important trend. Policymakers should revisit some of the options proposed by managed competition advocates for making health consumers more price-sensitive (changes in the tax treatment of health benefits, more cost sharing, better comparative data on plans, and so forth). Such changes would increase the incentive of managed care plans to keep annual cost increases low. Plan managers will have to devise fair but effective methods to control the use and diffusion of expensive technologies, given the growing consensus that advances in medical technology are a major cause of the high growth rate of health care costs.[135]

Maintaining competition among managed care plans over time. Some observers predict increasing concentration of managed care market share over time, and a few large plans control most of the business in some markets. If this scenario emerges, policymakers will have to consider whether consumer choice of health plans is being reduced beyond an acceptable point. In addition, monopoly conditions at the local level could adversely affect the cost and quality of care. The growing involvement of for-profit firms in managed care may heighten the need for safeguards. Policymakers should already be considering public policy responses to ensure consumer choice, competitive pricing, and high quality of care. These responses could include development of standardized performance measures and requirements that plans collect and publish data on these measures.

Protecting the clinical autonomy of caregivers in the face of extensive review of individual clinical decisions and strong financial pressures to reduce the amount of care provided. Under various "economic credentialing" practices, for example, physicians face financial penalties and even expulsion from managed care networks for providing too many high-cost services. The essence of managed care is eliminating costly, unnecessary services. But physicians must retain enough freedom to continue to make their patients' well-being their top priority. The issue takes on added importance with the growing dominance of for-profit managed care plans.

Ensuring the survival of important but vulnerable institutional providers that serve training and safety net functions, such as academic medical centers, public hospitals, and community health centers. By their very nature, these institutions tend to serve patients with above average risks and conditions. In the absence of universal insurance coverage, the growth of managed care threatens to leave these providers with a patient population made up solely of those who have the greatest need and the least ability to pay—a situation that cannot be sustained indefinitely. Protective legislation, such as essential community provider laws, may represent one solution.

The growth of organized delivery systems also poses policy and management challenges distinct from managed care. These can be organized around two key questions: *First, to what extent (if any) should public policy encourage the formation of such systems? Second, to what extent and in what ways should public policy hold such systems accountable?*[136]
Regarding the first question, should any incentives be established to encourage organized delivery systems in the absence of more definitive evidence concerning their performance? (It must be recog-

nized that the current delivery system is enormously fragmented and has acknowledged deficiencies.) Intuitively, the concept of organized delivery systems has great appeal, and the existing evidence, however embryonic, suggests the possibility of positive benefits. Whether or not legislation can be developed that specifically encourages the formation of organized delivery systems, the need to create incentives that would encourage more coordinated and cost-effective health care delivery of whatever specific organizational form is evident. Among the tasks that national and state policymakers could take on in this regard are the following:

Promote the development of payment systems that encourage common financial incentives for providers. Perhaps the most important task of all, this will ensure compatible motivations for hospitals, physicians, and others to provide more integrated care. The current mixture of fee-for-service, discounted prices, DRG-based payment, partial capitation payment, and full capitation payment (and various combinations) creates directly contradictory financial incentives and intensifies conflicts among hospitals, physicians, and other providers. Little progress will be made in achieving clinical integration of care at the local community level until common financial incentives are created for hospitals, physicians, and others to work together.[137] The greatest potential for promoting integrated care lies with capitated payment that aligns the economic incentives of all providers. The Health Systems Integration Study demonstrated a tendency for those systems involved with a greater degree of capitated payment to be further along in their clinical integration efforts.[138]

Develop a reasonably comprehensive common benefit package. This will also facilitate the provision of more coordinated, cost-effective care. A benefit package that is too narrow will simply perpetuate divisions among acute inpatient care, primary care, home health care, and long-term care. A splintered or incomplete benefit package, such as carve-outs for mental health, substance abuse, and long-term care, can only result in a fragmented delivery system. There are, of course, trade-offs between the comprehensiveness of a benefit package and the ability to pay for it, on the one hand, and the ability of providers to deliver more coordinated care, on the other. Benefit design as well as payment incentives are the twin pillars on which public policy must be built in regard to alignment with delivery system incentives. Establishing a defined benefits package also assists purchasers in evaluating price, utilization, and outcome differences in plans and providers.

Change existing licensure and certification laws to permit more flexible use of health professionals. Providing more coordinated care across the continuum requires a different type of health professional. Physicians, nurses, therapists, and other caregivers must have multiple skills, an ability to work in teams, and a willingness to take responsibility for managing the entire process of care associated with an episode of illness. This will require professionals trained in multiple areas who can work across traditional boundaries and tasks. This, in turn, will require more flexible certification and licensure laws at state and federal levels, particularly with regard to scope of practice and nonphysician providers. Increasing reliance should be placed on institutional and system licensure for personnel using performance and outcome standards rather than an overreliance on formal educational requirements.

Change existing accreditation standards. Accrediting bodies should refocus their task from accrediting individual institutions to accrediting systems, networks, and core processes of care that cut across the continuum of care. Accrediting individual institutions simply reinforces the fragmentation in the delivery system. The Joint Commission on Accreditation of Healthcare Organizations (JCAHO) is taking the lead in this area by developing processes for accrediting systems and networks and by revising their standards to focus on core organizational, managerial, and clinical processes associated with delivery of care.

Rethink the application of antitrust laws. Antitrust policy requires prudent application. Decisions ought to be based on the ability of merging or consolidating providers to provide evidence of improvements in community health status and cost-effective care. The dangers of creating potential monopolies must be weighed against the dangers of wasteful competition based on narrow-minded pursuit of institutional survival at any cost. Issues involving "any willing provider" laws and "essential community providers" must be closely scrutinized and physician self-referral laws that may mitigate against creating more coordinated patient care delivery must be examined. A distinction should be made between preserving patient freedom and promoting competition with regard to selecting a delivery system for care versus structures and decisions made by providers designed to provide more continuous, cost-effective care to patients within a given system.

Set aside funds for the development of clinical and health status information systems. The lack of information systems that could link patients and providers across the continuum of care is a major barrier to the integration of health care delivery. Such information is needed both for external accountability and for internal continuous improvement. External funding for the development of clinical and health information systems will help build an infrastructure that "raises all boats in the harbor."[139]

Policymakers should also consider provisions to encourage specifically the formation of organized delivery systems. For example, provisions for reinsurance could be made to delivery systems to locate in low-income inner-city and low-income rural areas where health care needs are greatest. An alternative would be to provide risk-adjusted capitated payments to such delivery systems, but reinsurance may still be needed given the challenges of equitably risk-adjusting payments at this point in time. Consideration should also be given to developing amendments to existing state insurance laws that would allow regionally organized delivery systems to subcapitate to other hospitals or physician groups. In addition to making provisions for reinsurance, allowing subcapitation and risk-adjusting payments, consideration should be given to providing loan guarantees for capital formation to encourage the development of organized delivery systems in targeted markets across the country. These loan guarantees could be made on a time-limited temporary basis, perhaps for a period of four to five years. Similarly, subsidies or loan guarantees could be provided to organized delivery systems for the formation of physician group practices. Existing research suggests that the formation of group practices is a key element in integrating physicians into systems of care and, more important, achieving needed levels of clinical integration.[140] Again, this would be needed only for a limited period of time, perhaps for four to five years, after which the majority of physicians would be organized into groups of one form or another. Consideration should also be given to developing matching funds to provide information system development grants or loans specifically to organized delivery systems. Such systems are most likely to have additional resources to leverage outside investments that could result in information systems that link patients and providers across the continuum of care. Finally, state health policy could include incentives for organized delivery systems to work with the public health system, the social services system, and related community groups to encourage needed integration for population-based delivery.[141] Examples could include government-assisted reinsurance; lowering the requirements for financial reserves,[142] reduced regulatory requirements, access to low-cost loans for new program development, and relief from certain antitrust provisions.

With regard to the second question asked earlier, what can be done to hold organized delivery systems accountable? For example, should certification standards be established? If so, what should be included? What criteria of access, cost, quality, and outcomes should be expected from such systems? One approach would be to link some of the incentives outlined in the preceding pages to achievement of certain accountability objectives. For example, organized delivery systems could be required to publish annual "balanced scorecards" of system performance that would include access, cost, quality, and outcome criteria. These scorecards would resemble scorecards used by some leading companies in the business sector.[143,144] *Access* criteria could include the percentage of Medicaid at and below and near poverty line for which the system provides care along with information on waiting time for appointments and waiting times in offices; *financial* criteria could include cost of services provided per enrolled member adjusted for health status and cost per person for selected high-volume conditions and procedures; *quality* criteria could rely on the provision of appropriate care consistent with established guidelines and protocols for selected conditions such as congestive heart failure, asthma, and diabetes; and *outcome* criteria could include risk-adjusted mortality and morbidity data for such procedures as coronary artery bypass graft surgery and total hip replacement, in addition to use of functional health status measures such as the Short Form 36 and related patient satisfaction data. Some states are already developing such criteria; for example, Minnesota plans to use a 30-minute, 30-mile rule regarding location of facilities.[145] States should also consider requiring organized delivery systems to specify the type and range of services they can deliver as well as the geographic distribution of their providers. Over time, measures based on communitywide health status and benefits could be developed (e.g., incidence of infant mortality, preventable mortality and morbidity, immunization rates, and low birthweight).[146,147] The extent to which organized delivery systems influence these indicators in meaningful ways, particularly in forming partnerships with other community agencies that share responsibility for community health and well-being, can be determined.

Conclusion

Imagine a situation in which community leaders, clinical caregivers, health care executives, policymakers, and purchasers worked together as an interdisciplinary team to design a delivery system for their community. What would they create? It would likely be something other than the piecemeal, fragmented, gerrymandered delivery systems that currently exist in most communities throughout the United States. The delivery system currently specializes in suboptimization at the same time that there appears to be a growing outcry for more integration.[146] Both third-generation managed care models and the provision of such care within the context of more organized delivery systems appear to hold potential for meeting changing consumer, purchaser, and policymaker expectations. At present, the evidence supporting various models of managed care is greater than that supporting the various approaches to organized delivery systems. More research is needed to address such questions as: Do organized delivery systems provide more cost-effective care per capita? Which models demonstrate superior performance? Do organized delivery systems sustain such performance over time? How do the different types of organized delivery systems and their performance vary by urban versus rural location[147–150] and across different market characteristics?

While greater evidence is needed on all of these questions, the U.S. health care system is rapidly restructuring and reorganizing itself with or without the evidence. What is particularly needed is an accurate description of these fast-moving changes and "evaluation on the fly" of these changes as they emerge. Clearly, U.S. hospitals and U.S. physicians are no longer a cottage industry. A new infrastructure has emerged, and any attempts to reform the U.S. health care system, whether market-based or legislation-based, at either the state or federal level, must take these changes into account.

Acknowledgments

The authors are grateful to Lauren LeRoy and Gail Warden for their comments on an earlier draft of this chapter. Appreciation is also expressed to Alice Schaller for her assistance in the preparation of the chapter.

Notes

1. S. T. Burner, D. R. Waldo, and D. R. McKusick, "National Health Expenditures Projections Through 2030," *Health Care Financing Review* 14, no. 1 (Fall 1992): 1–29.
2. C. A. Cowan and P. A. McDonnell, "Businesses, Households, and Governments: Health Spending, 1991," *Health Care Financing Review* 14, no. 3 (Spring 1993): 227–48.
3. Cowan and McDonnell 1993.
4. S. M. Shortell, R. R. Gillies, D. A. Anderson, J. B. Mitchell, and K. L. Morgan, "Creating Organized Delivery Systems: The Barriers and Facilitators," *Hospital and Health Services Administration* 38, no. 4 (Winter 1993): 447–66.
5. InterStudy, *The InterStudy Competitive Edge* 3, 2 (Minneapolis, MN: InterStudy, 1994).
6. InterStudy, *Metropolitan Market Update to The InterStudy Competitive Edge* 3, 2 (Minneapolis, MN: Decision Resources, Inc., 25 April 1994).
7. E. W. Hoy, R. E. Curtis, and T. Rice, "Change and Growth in Managed Care," *Health Affairs* 10, no. 4 (Winter 1991): 18–36.
8. J. Gabel, D. Liston, G. Jensen, and J. Marsteller, "The Health Insurance Picture in 1993: Some Rare Good News," *Health Affairs* 13, no. 1 (Spring 1994 [I]): 327–36.
9. Gable et al. 1994.
10. Health Insurance Association of America, *Source Book of Health Insurance Data, 1993* (Washington, DC: HIAA, 1993).
11. M. Gold, R. Hurley, T. Lake, T. Ensor, and R. Berenson, *Arrangements between Managed Care Plans and Physicians: Results from a 1994 Survey of Managed Care Plans* (Washington, DC: Physician Payment Review Commission, 1995).
12. InterStudy 1994, *The Interstudy Competitive Edge.*
13. U.S. General Accounting Office (GAO), *Medicaid: States Turn to Managed Care to Improve Access and Control Costs* (Washington, DC: GAO, 1993).
14. GAO 1993.
15. AFDC recipients are those families that also receive cash assistance through the federal/state entitlement program, Aid to Families with Dependent Children. AFDC and AFDC-related recipients, who are mostly poor women and their children, represent 70 percent of the Medicaid-eligible population but account for less than 30 percent of total program costs.
16. GAO 1993.
17. W. P. Welch, A. L. Hillman, and M. V. Pauly, "Toward New Typologies for HMOs," *Milbank Quarterly* 68, no. 2 (1990): 221–43.

18. These systems have also been referred to as integrated delivery systems (IDS), integrated service networks (ISNs), and integrated delivery networks (IDNs). We use the term *organized delivery system* rather than *integrated* because the latter is a value-laden term that involves an evaluation of the extent to which a given system or network is, in fact, integrated.

19. Witt/Kiefer, Ford, Hadelman & Lloyd, "Integrated Delivery Systems and Networks: Surveys of Medical Group Practices, Healthcare Systems and Hospitals," In *The 1994–1995 Healthcare Alliance and Network Sourcebook.* (New York: Faulkner & Gray, Inc., 1994).

20. D. A. Conrad and W. L. Dowling, "Vertical Integration in Health Services: Theory and Managerial Implications," *Health Care Management Review* 15 (1990): 9–22.

21. American Hospital Association, *Guide to the Health Care Field, 1994 Edition* (Chicago: AHA, 1994).

22. American Hospital Association. 1994. Unpublished table.

23. J. E. Kralewski, "Consolidation of the Health Care Marketplace and Anti-Trust Policy: The Minnesota Experience," Working Paper (Minneapolis, MN: Institute for Health Services and Policy Research, University of Minnesota, 1995).

24. P. L. Havlicek, *Medical Groups in the U.S.: A Survey of Practice Characteristics, 1993 Edition* (Chicago: American Medical Association, 1993).

25. Havlicek 1993.

26. Kralewski 1995.

27. P. L. Havlicek, Telephone correspondence on 14 September 1994.

28. The American Medical Association does not make official projections regarding the number of group practices or the number of physicians practicing in groups.

29. J. Goldsmith, "The Illusive Logic of Integration," *Healthcare Forum Journal* 37 (1994): 26–31.

30. H. S. Zuckerman and A. D. Kaluzny, "Strategic Alliances in Health Care: The Challenges of Cooperation," *Frontiers of Health Services Management* 7, no. 3 (Spring 1991): 3–23.

31. W. L. Dowling, "Alliances as a Structure for Integrated Delivery Systems," in *Partners for the Dance: Forming Strategic Alliances in Health Care,* edited by A. D. Kaluzny, H. S. Zuckerman, and T. C. Ricketts III (Ann Arbor: Health Administration Press, 1995).

32. American Hospital Association 1994.

33. American Hospital Association, *Guide to the Health Care Field, 1993 Edition* (Chicago: AHA, 1993).

34. F. Cerne, "The Fading Stand Alone Hospital," *Hospital and Health Networks* 68, no. 12 (20 June 1994): 28–29.

35. Cerne 1994.

36. R. D. Luke, "Local Hospital Systems: Forerunners of Regional Systems?" *Frontiers of Health Services Management* 9, no. 2 (Winter 1992): 3–51.

37. S. M. Shortell, J. L. O'Brien, J. M. Carman, R. W. Foster, E. F. X.

Hughes, H. Boerstler, and E. J. O'Connor, "Assessing the Impact of Continuous Quality Improvement/Total Quality Management," *Health Services Research* 30, no. 2 (June 1995): 377–401.

38. Dowling 1995.
39. Dowling 1995.
40. Dowling 1995.
41. S. M. Shortell, R. R. Gillies, and D. A. Anderson, "The New World of Managed Care: Creating Organized Delivery Systems," *Health Affairs* 13, no. 5 (Winter 1994): 46–64.
42. Shortell, Gillies, and Anderson 1994.
43. Shortell, Gillies, and Anderson 1994.
44. Shortell, Gillies, and Anderson 1994.
45. Shortell et al. 1993.
46. R. E. Hurley, "The Purchaser-Driven Reformation in Health Care: Alternative Approaches to Leveling Our Cathedrals," *Frontiers of Health Services Management* 9, no. 4 (Summer 1993): 5–35.
47. R. R. Gillies, S. M. Shortell, D. A. Anderson, J. B. Mitchell, and K. L. Morgan, "Conceptualizing and Measuring Integration: Findings from the Health Systems Integration Study," *Hospital and Health Services Administration* 38, no. 4 (Winter 1993): 467–89.
48. F. J. Hellinger, "Selection Bias in Health Maintenance Organizations: Analysis of Recent Evidence," *Health Care Financing Review* 9, no. 2 (Winter 1987): 55–63.
49. J. E. Billi, C. G. Wise, S. I. Sher, L. Duran-Arenas, and L. Shapiro, "Selection in a Preferred Provider Organization Enrollment," *Health Services Research* 28, no. 5 (December 1993): 563–75.
50. J. Zwanziger and R. R. Auerbach, "Evaluating PPO Performance Using Prior Expenditure Data," *Medical Care* 29, no. 2 (February 1991): 142–51.
51. R. H. Miller and H. S. Luft, "Managed Care Plan Performance Since 1980: A Literature Analysis," *Journal of the American Medical Association* 271, no. 19 (18 May 1994): 1512–19.
52. P. J. Feldstein, T. M. Wickizer, and J. R. C. Wheeler, "Private Cost Containment: The Effects of Utilization Review Programs on Health Care Use and Expenditures," *The New England Journal of Medicine* 318, no. 20 (19 May 1988): 1310–14.
53. T. M. Wickizer, J. R. C. Wheeler, and P. J. Feldstein, "Does Utilization Review Reduce Unnecessary Hospital Care and Contain Costs?" *Medical Care* 27, no. 6 (June 1989): 632–47.
54. R. M. Scheffler, S. D. Sullivan, and T. H. Ko, "The Impact of Blue Cross and Blue Shield Plan Utilization Management Programs, 1980–1988," *Inquiry* 28 (Fall 1991): 263–75.
55. R. K. Khandker and W. G. Manning, "The Impact of Utilization Review on Costs and Utilization," in *Health Economics Worldwide,* edited by P. Zweifel and H. E. Frech III (The Netherlands: Kluwer Academic Publishers, 1992).
56. R. S. Brown, D. G. Clement, J. W. Hill, S. M. Retchin, and J. W.

Bergeron, "Do Health Maintenance Organizations Work for Medicare?" *Health Care Financing Review* 15, no. 1 (Fall 1993): 7–23.

57. R. E. Hurley, D. A. Freund, and J. E. Paul, *Managed Care in Medicaid: Lessons for Policy and Program Design* (Ann Arbor, MI: Health Administration Press, 1993).

58. J. L. Buchanan, A. Leibowitz, J. Keesey, J. Mann, and C. Damberg. *Cost and Use of Capitated Medical Services: Evaluation of the Program for Prepaid Managed Health Care.* (Santa Monica, CA: RAND Corporation, 1992).

59. Miller and Luft 1994.

60. Miller and Luft 1994.

61. D. W. Garnick, H. S. Luft, L. B. Gardner, E. M. Morrison, M. Barrett, A. O'Neil, and B. Harvey, "Services and Charges by PPO Physicians for PPO and Indemnity Patients: An Episode of Care Comparison," *Medical Care* 28, no. 10 (October 1990): 894–906.

62. Brown et al. 1993.

63. Hurley, Freund, and Paul 1993.

64. Hurley, Freund, and Paul 1993.

65. Miller and Luft 1994.

66. W. G. Manning, A. Leibowitz, G. A. Goldberg, W. H. Rogers, and J. P. Newhouse, "A Controlled Trial of the Effect of a Prepaid Group Practice on Use of Services," *The New England Journal of Medicine* 310, no. 23 (7 June 1984): 1505–10.

67. K. B. Wells, S. D. Hosek, and S. M. Marquis, "The Effects of Preferred Provider Options in Fee-for-Service Plans on Use of Outpatient Mental Health Services by Three Employee Groups," *Medical Care* 30, no. 5 (1992): 412–27.

68. Zwanziger and Auerbach 1991.

69. Garnick et al. 1990.

70. Zwanziger and Auerbach 1991.

71. S. D. Hosek, S. M. Marquis, and K. B. Wells, *Health Care Utilization in Employer Plans with Preferred Provider Organization Options* (Santa Monica, CA: The RAND Corporation, 1989).

72. Zwanziger and Auerbach 1991.

73. Wickizer, Wheeler, and Feldstein 1989.

74. Khandker and Manning 1992.

75. Brown et al. 1993.

76. N. McCall, C. W. Wrightson, L. Paringer, and G. Trapnell, "Managed Medicaid Cost Savings: The Arizona Experience," *Health Affairs* 13, no. 2 (Spring 1994, Part II): 234–45.

77. The cost savings achieved by AHCCCS are impressive, but must be interpreted with caution, because the study had to compare the Arizona program's costs to costs in traditional Medicaid programs in other states, since Arizona never had its own traditional Medicaid program.

78. Hurley, Freund, and Paul 1993.

79. Miller and Luft 1994.

80. J. P. Newhouse, W. B. Schwarz, A. P. Williams, and C. Witsberger, "Are

Fee-for-Service Costs Increasing Faster than HMOs' Costs?" *Medical Care* 23, no. 8 (August 1985): 960–66.

81. Wickizer, Wheeler, and Feldstein 1989.
82. T. M. Wickizer and P. J. Feldstein, "The Impact of HMO Competition in Private Health Insurance Premiums, 1985–1992." *Inquiry* 32 (Fall 1995): 241–51.
83. D. Wholey, R. Feldman, and J. B. Christianson, "The Effect of Market Structure in HMO Premiums." *Journal of Health Economics* 14 (1995): 81–105.
84. McCall ct al. 1994.
85. D. Freeborn and C. H. Pope, *Promise and Performance in Managed Care: The Prepaid Group Practice Models* (Baltimore, MD: Johns Hopkins University Press, 1995).
86. Miller and Luft 1994.
87. Brown et al. 1993.
88. D. G. Clement, S. M. Retchin, R. S. Brown, and M. H. Stegall, "Access and Outcomes of Elderly Patients Enrolled in Managed Care," *Journal of the American Medical Association* 271, no. 19 (18 May 1994): 1487–92.
89. GAO 1993.
90. D. Balaban, N. McCall, and E. J. Bauer, *Quality of Medicaid Managed Care: An Evaluation of the Arizona Health Care Cost Containment System (AHCCCS)* (San Francisco: Laguna Research Associates, 1994).
91. Miller and Luft 1994.
92. A. Davies, J. E. Ware, R. H. Brook, J. R. Peterson, and J. P. Newhouse, "Consumer Acceptance of Prepaid and Fee-for-Service Medical Care: Results from a Randomized Controlled Trial," *Health Services Research* 21, no. 3 (August 1986): 429–56.
93. H. S. Luft, *Health Maintenance Organizations: Dimensions of Performance* (New York: John Wiley & Sons, 1981).
94. Miller and Luft 1994.
95. Brown et al. 1993.
96. GAO 1993.
97. N. McCall, E. D. Jay, and R. West, "Access and Satisfaction in the Arizona Health Care Cost Containment System," *Health Care Financing Review* 11, no. 1 (Fall 1989): 63–77.
98. Brown et al. 1993.
99. GAO 1993.
100. K. Davis, S. Collins, and S. Morris, "Managed Care: Promise and Concerns," *Health Affairs* 13, no. 4 (Fall 1994): 178–85.
101. R. H. Miller and H. S. Luft, "Managed Care: Past Evidence and Potential Trends," *Frontiers of Health Services Management* 9, no. 3 (1993): 3–37.
102. Atkinson & Company, *The Cost of "Any Willing Provider" Legislation* (Washington, DC: Group Health Association of America, 1994).
103. Atkinson & Company 1994.
104. D. Ermann and J. Richmond, "Managed Care Arrangements: Barriers

to Cost Savings Potential," *Medical Care Review* 51, no. 2 (Summer 1994): 125–48.

105. Ermann and Richmond 1994.
106. A. L. Hillman, M. V. Pauly, and J. J. Kerstein, "How Do Financial Incentives Affect Physicians' Clinical Decisions and the Financial Performance of Health Maintenance Organizations?" *The New England Journal of Medicine* 321, no. 2 (13 July 1989): 86–92.
107. L. R. Burns, J. A. Chilingerian, and D. R. Wholey, "The Effect of Physician Practice Organization on Efficient Utilization of Hospital Resources," *Health Services Research* 29, no. 5 (December 1994): 583–603.
108. D. R. Wholey, J. B. Christianson, and S. M. Sanchez, "The Effect of Physician and Corporate Interests on the Formation of Health Maintenance Organizations," *American Journal of Sociology* 99, no. 1 (July 1993): 164–200.
109. Wholey, Christianson, and Sanchez 1993.
110. J. B. Christianson, S. M. Sanchez, D. R. Wholey, and M. Shadle, "The HMO Industry: Evolution in Population Demographics and Market Structures," *Medical Care Review* 48, no. 1 (Spring 1991): 3–46.
111. Christianson et al. 1991.
112. Shortell et al. 1993.
113. D. Ermann and J. Gabel, "Multi-Hospital Systems: Issues and Empirical Findings," *Health Affairs* 3, no. 1 (Spring 1984): 51–64.
114. Ermann and Gabel 1984.
115. H. S. Zuckerman, "Multi-Institutional Systems: Their Promise and Performance," in *Multi-Institutional Systems,* edited by L. E. Weeks (Chicago: Hospital Research and Educational Trust, 1979).
116. D. C. Coddington, K. D. Moore, and E. A. Fischer, *Integrated Health Care: Reorganizing the Physician, Hospital, and Health Plan Relationship* (Englewood, CO: Center for Research in Ambulatory Health Care Administration, 1994).
117. S. M. Shortell, "The Evolution of Hospital Systems: Unfulfilled Promises and Self-Fulfilling Prophecies," *Medical Care Review* 45, no. 2 (Fall 1988): 177–214.
118. G. S. Levitz and P. P. Brooke, Jr., "Independent vs. System-Affiliated Hospitals: A Comparative Analysis of Financial Performance, Cost, and Productivity," *Health Services Research* 20, no. 3 (August 1985): 315–39.
119. M. J. McCue and J. R. Lynch, "Financial Assessment of Small Multi-Hospital Systems," *Hospital and Health Services Administration* 32 (May 1987): 171–89.
120. Shortell, Gillies, and Anderson 1994.
121. Shortell, Gillies, and Anderson 1994.
122. D. Dranove and M. Shanley, "Cost Reductions or Reputation Enhancement as Motives for Mergers: The Logic of Multihospital Systems," *Strategic Management Journal* 16, no. 1 (January 1995): 55–74.
123. The Advisory Board Company, *Capitation Strategy* (Washington, DC: The Advisory Board Company, 1994).
124. D. A. Conrad, T. Wickizer, C. Maynard, T. Klastorin, D. Lessler, A. Ross,

N. Soderstrom, S. Sullivan, J. Alexander, and K. Travis, "The Impact of Managed Health Care on Hospital Efficiency: A Look Inside the 'Black Box,'" unpublished paper, 1994.

125. P. J. Kenkel, "Health Plans Face Pressure to Find 'Report Card' Criteria That Will Make the Grade," *Modern Healthcare* 24, no. 2 (10 January 1994): 41–42.

126. National Committee on Quality Assurance, *Healthplan Employee Data Information Set (HEDIS)*, Version 2.0. (Washington, DC: NCQA, 1993).

127. D. R. Nerenz, B. Zajac, and H. S. Rosman, "Consortium Research on Indicators of System Performance," *Joint Commission Journal on Quality Improvement* 19, no. 12 (1993): 577–85.

128. J. Mangano, "Evidence on Health Care Report Cards," *Quality Management Update* (Oakland, CA: Kaiser Permanente of Northern California, October, 1994).

129. J. S. Zen, W. E. Aaronson, and N. D. Rosko, "Strategic Groups, Performance, and Strategic Response in the Nursing Home Industry," *Health Services Research* 29, no. 2 (June 1994): 188–205.

130. Shortell et al. 1993.

131. Shortell, Gillies, and Anderson 1994.

132. J. E. Kralewski, A. deVries, B. Dowd, and S. Potthoff, "The Development of Integrated Service Networks (ISN's) in Minnesota," Report prepared for the Minnesota Legislative Oversight Committee (Minneapolis, MN: Institute for Health Services and Policy Research, University of Minnesota, 1994).

133. *Health Systems Integration Study CEO Roundtable* (Napa, CA, 1993).

134. K. R. Levit, C. A. Cowan, H. C. Lazenby, P. A. McDonnell, A. L. Sensenig, J. M. Stiller, and D. K. Won, "National Health Spending Trends, 1960–1993," *Health Affairs* 13, no. 5 (1994): 14–31.

135. R. A. Rettig, "Medical Innovation Duels Cost Containment," *Health Affairs* 13, no. 3 (Summer 1994): 7–27.

136. Shortell, Gillies, and Anderson 1994.

137. Shortell, Gillies, and Anderson 1994.

138. Shortell, Gillies, and Anderson 1994.

139. M. J. Field, K. M. Lohr, and K. D. Yordy, eds., *Assessing Health Care Reform* (Washington, DC: National Academy Press, 1993).

140. Shortell et al. 1993.

141. Field, Lohr, and Yordy 1993.

142. Alpha Center, "Integrated Service Networks: New Rules to Play By," *State Initiatives* (September-October 1994): 5.

143. R. S. Kaplan and D. P. Norton, "The Balanced Scorecard—Measures That Drive Performance," *Harvard Business Review* (January-February 1992): 71–79.

144. R. S. Kaplan and D. P. Norton, "Putting the Balanced Scorecard to Work," *Harvard Business Review* (September-October 1993): 134–47.

145. Alpha Center 1994.

146. J. Christianson and I. Moscovice, "Health Care Reform and. Rural Health Networks," *Health Affairs* (Fall 1993): 58–75.

147. Nerenz, Zajac, and Rosman 1993.
148. S. M. Shortell, R. R. Gillies, D. A. Anderson, K. L. Morgan-Erickson, and J. B. Mitchell, *Re-making Health Care in America: Building Organized Delivery Systems* (San Francisco: Jossey Bass, 196).
149. National Committee on Quality Assurance 1993.
150. Christianson and Moscovice 1993.

5

Strategic Issues for Managing the Future Physician Workforce

David A. Kindig

Abstract. Physician workforce issues were among the most hotly debated components of the recent national health care reform effort. What are the United States' goals for its physician workforce? Will market forces be adequate to achieve these goals, or will regulatory intervention be needed? This chapter provides public and private policymakers with a framework for arriving at reasonable conclusions about this important subcomponent of national health policy.

Physician supply and requirements are discussed first. A picture of the current U.S. physician workforce is presented, together with details of its size and the physician-to-population ratio. Future growth of the physician workforce is projected, and future requirements are discussed along with the potential for both surpluses and shortages in some areas. Graduate medical education, a crucial topic in this discussion, is covered. The issue of substitution of nonphysician providers for physicians is considered next, with special attention paid to the capabilities of nonphysician providers in performing certain tasks, as well as the productivity and cost-effectiveness questions involved.

While the physician supply in the United States may be adequate overall, gaps in service and problems with access to services persist in many rural and inner-city areas. The geographic distribution of the physician workforce and the balance of subspecialists and generalists are addressed. Other topics of discussion include the need for greater minority representation in the physician workforce and the evolving role of the physician executive.

Finally, this chapter ends with a wrap-up of policy considerations and themes central to the new delivery system of the twenty-first century. These themes include market forces versus regulation, cost containment and workforce cost-effectiveness, the global role of the United States, and nonfinancial barriers to access to care, as well as the impact of technology and the role of physician scientists.

While the fundamental issues facing a reformed health care delivery system are adequacy of coverage, cost-effectiveness, and improved population health status, the issues of the supply, distribution, and competency of the physician workforce to support these goals will continue to have major importance. Significant bipartisan support for some policy changes in the physician workforce composition was evident in the 1994 debate over the Clinton administration's Health Security Act and other congressional proposals. The failure of the national health care reform effort has left us with two questions: What are the goals for the physician workforce? And will market forces be adequate to achieve them, or is some regulatory intervention still needed?

The period of the late 1960s was characterized by concerns that the physician supply would be inadequate to meet the demands of the newly enacted Medicare and Medicaid programs. A variety of federal and state incentives resulted in a doubling of medical school graduates at that time. The peak of the increased number of physicians produced by that change will not be realized until about 2015. In addition, the late 1960s saw great concern over the issue of physician geographic distribution, particularly of generalists. The policy response was to create a large variety of service and educational programs, such as community health centers, the National Health Service Corps, the expansion of Family Medicine, the development of the collaborative professions of nurse practitioners and physician assistants, and many curriculum experiments and innovations.

A second period began in 1980 with the publication of the report of the Graduate Medical Education National Advisory Committee (GMENAC), which noted the rapid rise in the number of physicians and warned of an impending surplus of subspecialists.[1] Despite growing concerns about rising medical care costs, the laissez-faire environment of the 1980s did not provide an opportunity for significant discussion or policy intervention in this area. The geographic distribution issue was reopened in the light of rural hospital closures and the AIDS epidemic, and the growth of managed care systems reemphasized the issues of future supply of physicians and subspecialists, and the requirements they must meet.

The Council on Graduate Medical Education (COGME) is an

independent policy body that reports to Congress and to the secretary of the Department of Health and Human Services (DHHS) on physician workforce issues. COGME has identified several key findings regarding the physician workforce:[2,3]

- The United States has too few generalists and too many sub-specialists.

- The current physician-to-population ratio is adequate; further increases will do little to enhance the health of the public or to address the problem of access to care, and will hinder efforts to contain costs.

- Problems of access to medical care persist in rural and inner-city areas.

- The racial and ethnic composition of the nation's physicians does not reflect the general population and contributes to access problems for underrepresented minorities.

COGME has also concluded that failures in this market as well as inappropriate current regulatory incentives require national policy intervention, although of a decentralized and flexible nature. Other analysts and groups favor more centralized microregulatory approaches.

In contrast, the growth of capitated managed care has led some to question whether governmental regulation is necessary or appropriate, since such market forces might produce self-correcting workforce production discipline not possible in the open-ended fee-for-service system.

In addition to ongoing physician workforce issues such as overall size, geographic distribution, and specialty composition, new challenges will face integrated delivery systems and workforce planners. Such challenges include the workforce implications of managed care, population-based workforce requirements, the demographic imperative for more minority physicians, the need for physicians to substitute for residents if total supply is reduced, the implications of reduced domestic production of physicians and the entry of international medical graduates (IMGs), the appropriate balance of physician and midlevel providers, the need for physician scientists, and the determination of the physician executive role in integrated delivery systems.

A number of strategic choices about workforce policy will have to be made in the next few years, and by a number of groups. Delivery systems and purchasers will have to decide on the mix of generalists, subspecialists, and other providers that will meet their needs for cost-effective and high-quality care. Many local "experiments" in alternative mixes will be undertaken, and results will be disseminated through provider networks long before researchers identify or assess their validity or generalizability. Particularly difficult choices will face providers remaining in fee-for-service practice.

Private sector organizations will have to decide on what their public policy strategy on workforce issues will be. State legislatures especially will be faced with decisions regarding medical school support, Medicaid graduate medical education funding, and legislation about "any willing provider" as well as professional practice acts. As physician compensation is affected, the medical profession may attempt to limit overall physician supply, as can now be seen in Canada. Antitrust considerations will affect such private sector and professional organization activities as raising the standards of educational quality. Public-private "medical education academic endowments" may be created at state or metropolitan levels as preservation of academic centers in alignment with their social responsibility is considered.

Federal public sector policy choices will take place primarily in the realm of funding policy for graduate medical education through Medicare and Medicaid, and decisions will have to be made about identifying and describing the nation's goals for the physician workforce and delineating ways to align funding policy with those goals. The issue of immigration is a federal policy choice, to be applied either indirectly through funding policy or directly through immigration policy. If reduction in the numbers of residents trained is attempted, then the federal government will have to decide if it will become partners with states and the private sector in setting up transition programs for those states and metropolitan areas that are currently dependent on IMG residents for service in underserved areas. In the absence of universal coverage, the federal government and state governments will have to decide on how much safety net access they will continue to provide in rural and inner-city areas with chronic shortages of generalist providers, as well as for core educational support for generalist physicians and nonphysician providers (NPPs). The level of domestic production of physicians, such as recently suggested by the Pew Commission, will be focused at the state level, since the federal government plays almost no role in undergraduate medical education. The ability of government to affect private schools of medicine, including osteopathy, and of nursing is minimal.

Physician Supply and Requirements

The balance between expected future physician supply and future requirements is as much an issue today as it was during the 1970s, when initial concerns about a possible shortage of physicians turned to projections of a potential surplus. In a major study in 1980, GMENAC used an epidemiologically driven, specialty-specific, "adjusted need–based" methodology to predict a near balance of generalists and a significant excess of subspecialists by 1990 and 2000.[4] Despite methodologic criticism,[5] the GMENAC study remains the most thorough physician workforce research ever conducted. It is of some interest, therefore, that Jonathan Weiner's major physician workforce effort of 1994,[6] using a totally different methodologic approach (studying managed care demand for physicians' services) produced a similar result. What is the evidence that the United States may be overproducing physicians, particularly subspecialists, and what would the implications of this be for public and private policy choices?

Supply

Projections of too few or too many physicians point to an imbalance in supply and requirements. The federal Bureau of Health Professions Supply Model, widely used by researchers and policymakers for this component of workforce dynamics, ages the existing supply with death and retirement estimates and then adds new entrants from either domestic or international sources. New entrants from both sources have resulted in a 59 percent increase in patient care physicians per 100,000 population, from 111.5 in 1950 to 181.7 in 1990, as displayed in Figure 5.1.[7] For purposes of this discussion, patient care physicians include allopaths and osteopaths whose primary professional activity is in patient care, but excludes residents and fellows and those not involved in patient care, such as teachers, researchers, and administrators.[8] The U.S. physician supply for 1992, separated by category, is presented in Table 5.1. Figure 5.1 also shows that physician supply is projected to increase to 218.9 per 100,000 population by 2010. This assumes the following: that the annual output of allo-

Figure 5.1   Patient Care Physician Supply and Ratios per 100,000
Population under Current PGY1 Scenario and Specialty
Output, Actual (1950–1990) and Projected (2000–2020)

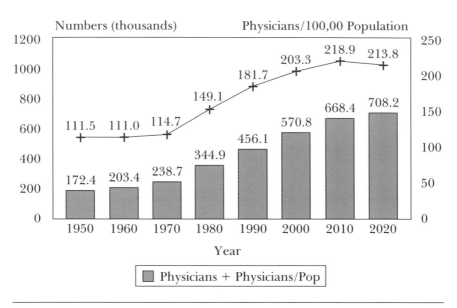

Year

Physicians + Physicians/Pop

Note: PGY1 at 140% USMGs, resident output at 30% generalists/70% specialists.

Source: 1950–1990 data adjusted by BHPr from AMA Physician Masterfile and unpublished AOA data. Projections from BHPr physician supply model.

pathic and osteopathic schools stays constant from 1997 until 2020 at 15,900 and 1,900 graduates, respectively; that the United States continues to train 140 percent of U.S. graduates in graduate medical education; and that 80 percent of IMGs are projected to remain in the United States at the completion of their residency training.

This overall growth has been characterized by slight increases in the number of generalist physicians and much larger increases in the number of subspecialists, as illustrated in Figure 5.2. Given current levels of resident specialty choice, the 2020 level is anticipated to reach approximately 66 patient care generalists and 148 patient care subspecialists per 100,000 population.

Whereas projections of supply are much more reliable than projections of requirements, they are nevertheless quite sensitive to

Table 5.1   U.S. Physician Supply, by Category, 1992

	MD	DO	Total	Per 100,000 Population
Total	653,062	32,229	685,291	267.5
Total active	597,406	30,317	627,723	245.0
Teaching	7,983	310	8,293	3.2
Research	16,367	31	16,398	6.4
Administration	14,923	202	15,125	5.9
Not classified	22,913	4,451	27,364	10.7
Patient care residents and fellows*	93,596	5,542	99,138	38.7
Patient care†				
General/family practitioner‡	63,209	10,636	73,845	28.8
General medicine‡	73,757	1,054	74,811	29.2
General pediatrics‡	32,961	391	33,352	13.0
Obstetrics and gynecology§	29,062	611	29,673	11.6
Emergency medical services	13,169	1,165	14,334	5.6
General surgery	27,875	488	28,363	11.1
Medical specialties¶	41,164	1,346	42,510	16.6
Surgical specialties**	57,498	1,191	58,689	22.9
Psychiatry	27,773	467	28,240	11.0
Hospital based++	47,219	1,434	48,653	19.0
Other	27,937	998	28,935	11.3

Note: Data derived from American Medical Association and American Osteopathic Association (1993) masterfiles.

*This equals 15.8 percent of total active physicians.

†Patient care physicians minus residents and fellows total 461,405 or 180.1 per 100,000 population. This is 73.5 percent of total active physicians.

‡These three specialties together equal 71 per 100,000 population or 39.4 percent of patient care physicians minus residents and fellows.

§This equals 6.4 percent of patient care physicians minus residents and fellows.

¶Includes medical subspecialties, pediatric subspecialties, dermatology, and neurology.

**Includes orthopedics, ophthalmology, urology, and all others.

++Includes radiology, anesthesiology, and pathology.

Source: D. Kindig, "Counting Generalist Physicians." *Journal of the American Medical Association* 271, no. 19 (1994): 1505–07.

changing domestic output of physicians, IMG entry and retention, and retirement rates. In addition, population projections must be kept in mind when projecting supply; increased population projections from the 1990 census resulted in lowered estimates of active physician supply for the year 2020.

Figure 5.2   Generalist and Specialist Patient Care Physician Supply
Ratios per 100,000 Population under Current PGY1
Scenario and Specialty Output, Actual (1965–1992) and
Projected (2000–2020)

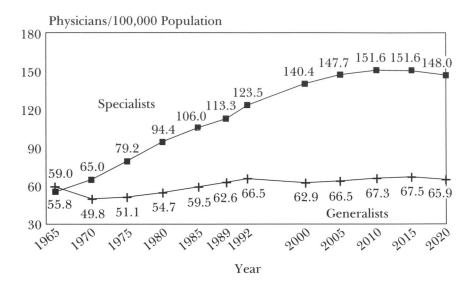

Note: PGY1 at 140% USMGs, resident output at 30% generalists/70%
specialists.

Source: 1965–1992 data adjusted by BHPr from AMA Physician Masterfile
and unpublished AOA data. Projections from BHPr physician supply model.

Requirements, shortages, and surpluses

Estimating future requirements is difficult, and it is essential to state
the assumptions underpinning the forecasts. The GMENAC report
cited earlier used specialty-specific panels to review the expected epi-
demiology of disease in future populations, to estimate the number of
physician equivalents "needed" for each specialty, to assess physician
productivity and substitution of midlevel personnel, and to calculate
requirements by specialty for the years 1990 and 2000. The result was
a generalist requirement of 72 per 100,000 population and a subspecialist requirement of 106 per 100,000 population in 2000. Comparing
these figures with a midpoint of supply projections at that time,

GMENAC estimated a near balance of generalists and a significant surplus of subspecialists for 1990 and 2000.

More recently, utilization of physicians by managed care organizations has been used to project the "demand" for physicians in a new delivery system. Unfortunately, these estimates have to rely almost exclusively on data from group-staff HMOs, since this type of organization has such data readily available. Such HMOs are not the predominant form of managed care, however, and their patient population is not identical to that of the United States as a whole. Weiner has recently provided estimates that correct for these factors as completely as possible.[9] His projections are still based on data from group-staff HMOs, but he adjusts for age, for out-of-plan use, for the uninsured, and for physician productivity in different types of plans; he also makes estimates of the degree of managed care penetration. He arrives at patient care (minus residents) generalist requirements of 59 per 100,000 population and subspecialist requirements of 82 per 100,000 population for 2000. Based on his supply projections, these translate into a surplus of 140,000 subspecialists and a potential surplus of 12,000 to 29,000 generalists.

The Bureau of Health Professions has made similar managed care physician requirements projections, using somewhat different estimates of HMO utilization and productivity.[10] Their requirements figures come to 77 generalists and 96 subspecialists per 100,000 population, and therefore they project correspondingly greater shortages of generalists and a lower surplus of specialists.

The figures just cited have been those accepted in the main by such policy bodies as COGME and the Physician Payment Review Commission (PPRC) in rendering policy advice about graduate medical education reform, and were reflected in the Clinton Health Security Act workforce provisions as well as the Mitchell and Gephardt reform proposals in Congress. Two authors, however, disagree with the assessment of a surplus of total physicians and specialists. Schwartz and colleagues made projections for internal medicine based on the assumption that every city of population greater than 50,000 (and possibly, every city of greater than 30,000) needs a subspecialist in every field.[11] Based on this, they predicted a shortage of 7,000 medical subspecialists in cities of this size by 2000. Also, as Schwartz and colleagues argue, after making adjustments for projected declines in resident and female physician productivity, that demand for physician services will increase 1.3 percent per capita per year, based largely on the needs of new technology and increased coverage; their assumptions and projections result in a balance of supply and requirements by 2000.[12] They indicate that "widespread rationing" as the result of cost containment could constrain demand and lead to an imbalance in supply and requirements.

Recently, Cooper summarized the evidence for achieving a "balanced" physician workforce.[13] He agrees with the studies just cited that a level of 70 to 80 generalist physicians may be appropriate; but, based on adjustments to the current managed care experience, he asserts that about 120 subspecialists per 100,000 population will be needed. He reports that the number of subspecialists per 100,000 population has grown at about three per year over the past 25 years and comments that two per year would have produced the level of 120 subspecialists that he recommends. This assessment of need is the difference between his estimates and those based primarily on the managed care experience, which have built in flat or negative growth rates for subspecialists.

Comparing supply with requirements allows consideration of whether the workforce will be in balance. Figures 5.3 and 5.4 compare the requirements estimates with potential supply over the next several decades. They assume a continuation of the current pattern of 140 percent total residents to U.S. medical graduates at three different specialty mixes of the output. A 40 percent generalist component puts supply in the middle of the requirements range, while ratios of 30:70 and 50:50 lie just under and over the range, respectively. For specialists, all three supply ratios lie considerably over the managed care requirements range; only the 50:50 scenario approaches the 120 subspecialists per 100,000 level recommended by Cooper.

Graduate Medical Education Reform

Physician supply in the United States comes from two sources: domestic production and international migration. In domestic medical education, prospective physicians spend four years in medical school after college (undergraduate medical education) and then spend three to eight years of residency training in a given specialty (graduate medical education). International migration usually occurs in residency training, but can funnel directly into licensure and practice.[14] International medical graduates (IMG) can either be noncitizens or U.S. citizens (USIMG).

Figure 5.3   Generalist Patient Care Physician Supply and
                 Requirements under Alternative Specialty Production
                 (or Output) Scenarios and Current PGY1 at 140
                 Percent of U.S. Medical Graduates

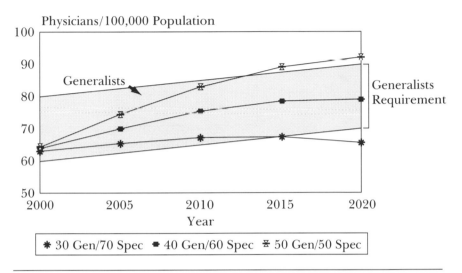

Source: Bureau of Health Professions and Council on Graduate Medical
Education, 1995.

Direct federal support of undergraduate medical education is
quite limited at the current time; undergraduate medical education
is largely supported from tuition, research grants, practice income,
and state support in the case of public schools. Medicare and, to a
lesser extent, Medicaid, however, provides major direct support for
graduate medical education through its direct and indirect formula
contributions to teaching hospitals.

Because of this federal financial support, reform of graduate
medical education was the most hotly debated workforce policy issue
under discussion in the 1994 national health care reform debate.
Many policy bodies and politicians expressed concern that future imbalance in supply and requirements would tend only to exacerbate
lack of access to generalists and to continue fueling the escalation of
medical expenditures partially attributable to increasing numbers of
subspecialists.

A growing literature argues that generalists can provide certain

Figure 5.4   Specialist Patient Care Physician Supply and
Requirements under Alternative Specialty Mix
Scenarios and Current PGY1 at 140 Percent of U.S.
Medical Graduates

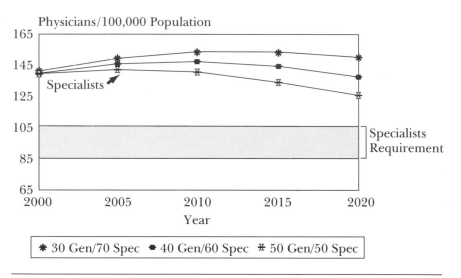

Source: Bureau of Health Professions and Council on Graduate Medical
Education, 1995.

services in a more cost-effective manner than subspecialists,[15] and estimates of the cost savings that would result from changing the mix of
specialists have been made.[16] In examining variations in total health
expenditures across states, the total number of physicians per 100,000
population was a significant predictor of higher expenditures, while
the number or percentage of generalists was not significant, supporting the argument that the ratio of specialists to population is the important factor in increasing costs.[17]

　　Figures 5.3 and 5.4 illustrate the imbalance in future supply and
requirements; these were the basis for COGME's goal to reduce the
number of residency positions to 110 percent of domestic medical
graduates. This was derived from examining the requirements data
presented previously and the resulting professional judgment that the
problem of excess physicians was serious and that decreased output
was necessary. It was not seen at that time to be politically feasible to
reduce domestic output of medical schools, so the reductions would

Figure 5.5 Total Residents and U.S. Medical Graduate Residents; International Medical Graduates as a Percentage of All Residents

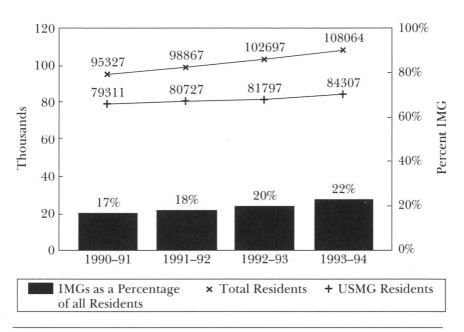

Source: AAMC, SAIMS Database 1994, plus unpublished updated material, AOA, Biographical Records (unpublished data).

have to come from the IMGs who make up 29 percent of residents in addition to the domestic output (Figure 5.5). The 110 percent figure was chosen to allow all domestic graduates a residency training spot and a 10 percent increase for IMGs.

In addition to recommending reductions in total resident positions, COGME also recommended that the reduced output be balanced equally between generalists and subspecialists; this came to be known as the "110/50:50" policy.[18] This would have been achieved by creating an all-payer pool of Medicare graduate medical education dollars and dollars derived from a surcharge on private insurance premiums; these funds would have been administered by a national body that would distribute workforce dollars to training institutions in accord with a 110/50:50 allocation. COGME developed the idea of graduate medical education consortia of local medical schools and

Figure 5.6   Generalist Patient Care Physician Supply and
Requirements under Alternative Specialty Output
Scenarios and PGY1 at 110% of U.S. Medical Graduates

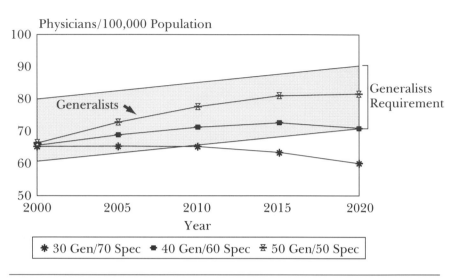

Source: Bureau of Health Professions and Council on Graduate Medical
Education, 1995.

teaching hospitals that would distribute positions among institutions based on federally determined generalist and subspecialist targets. Figures 5.6 and 5.7 are companions to Figures 5.3 and 5.4 and indicate the impact of a 110 percent policy at various generalist-to-subspecialist ratios; it is clear that subspecialist supply begins to approach requirements of a managed care scenario only under such conditions.

Other groups such as the PPRC and the Association of American Medical Colleges adopted similar positions, but with less specificity. PPRC recommended a centralized allocation mechanism, with program level specialty-specific review based on program quality. This approach was embraced in the Health Security Act and in several congressional reform proposals.

Opponents of any regulatory intervention argued that market forces would produce needed reforms, and that teaching hospitals would be damaged in their patient care and academic functions; this was most strongly argued by eastern U.S. teaching hospitals, which

Figure 5.7   Specialist Patient Care Physician Supply and
                 Requirements under Alternative Specialty Output
                 Scenarios and PGY1 at 110% of U.S. Medical Graduates

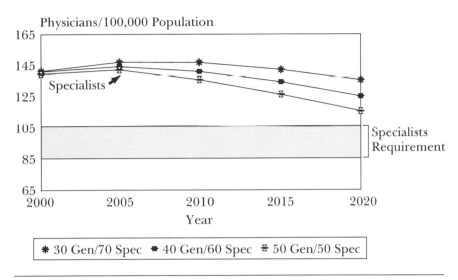

Source: Bureau of Health Professions and Council on Graduate Medical
Education, 1995.

are very dependent on residents for service needs and on Medicare
medical education dollars for financial stability. An academic perspective on a market approach was published by Dranove and White[19] in
which they present arguments against market failure in the areas of
demand inducement, imperfect information, and moral hazard. They
do not address the issue of the training market being separate from
the market of practice. They call for changes in federal funding for
residencies, physician payment reform, relaxation of licensing regulation for nonphysician providers, and a focusing of NIH research
grants on cost-reducing technology.

A thoughtful market-sensitive argument was put forward by
Reinhardt in an article entitled "Planning the Nation's Health Workforce: Let The Market In."[20] Reinhardt suggests that academic leaders
should do a much better job of informing potential residents about
the market for various specialties, so that they can make better-
informed choices about their future careers. He also calls for restruc-

turing financing incentives so that "teaching hospitals and ambulatory care facilities serving this function lack powerful economic incentives to impose their own narrow economic imperatives upon the student's or society's interests." Reinhardt also warns of the likely political fallout from any failed governmental action in these cynical times, and warns that "it is a politically charged . . . game at which the government just cannot win any glory."

Supporters of intervention have argued that the teaching hospital market is not connected to the market of population need; that Medicare payment policies have been responsible in large part for the increasing number of residents (20 percent from 1988 to 1993); that teaching hospital service needs should not drive national physician production policy; that resident substitution by nurse practitioners and physician assistants is possible;[21] that the shortage of generalists is causing problems for managed care plans as well as for geographic subareas; and that public funding requires public accountability.[22]

The failure of federal health care reform efforts did not allow for national political resolution of this issue. It is unlikely that any significant policy changes will emerge in the current Congress. Some observers contend that market pressures have been underestimated, and that these pressures will result in a significant lowering of subspecialist incomes, which in turn will influence medical student choice of specialty. It is critical that local anecdotal data be gathered in as systematic a way as possible, since it takes several years for trends to be reflected in traditional databases and published research. State efforts must be monitored carefully as well. It is possible that market forces and state efforts may be able to enhance and stabilize generalist production, although finding resources to replace the federal dollars underpinning generalist residencies will be critical if significant cuts are made for federal deficit reduction.

It is less clear how markets or states would be able to reduce the total output of residents, although there has been speculation about domestic medical school closures; however, as many as seven new schools of osteopathy are opening or are planned. Reductions in the number of IMG residents or the proportion of subspecialists is less likely through state or market forces, since neither mechanism has much leverage over teaching hospital resident numbers. Current COGME efforts, in focusing on potential changes in Medicare GME policy, are recommending that support for IMG residents be gradually reduced to 25 percent of the current baseline, upweighting for nonhospital educational experiences (particularly those in public health centers), and rationalizing the payment formulas under Medicare managed care contracts.[23] While Medicare is only a single payer, it is large enough and has paid for GME so well in the past that such policy changes could be effective, although total financial support to teaching hospitals would determine the impact of this proposal. Finally, private and public support should be identified for demonstration and transition efforts in states, such as New York, that train and retain large numbers of IMGs, but have become dependent on them for service delivery in needy areas. Transition funds to allow the replacement of these residents with nonphysician providers or a targeted National Health Service Corps Resident Replacement Force are ideas worth serious consideration.

A final consideration is that of domestic medical school output. Because the system is being strongly influenced by organizational and economic practices that minimize physician utilization, the United States may see excesses of both generalists and subspecialists in the future. This will not only require reductions in the IMG component, but will call into question domestic production as well, such as the recent report of the Pew Health Professions Commission calling for 20 percent reductions in domestic physician production. Population-based future requirements backcast into alternative combinations of domestic production and IMG entry would help to elucidate the public policy choices of the next decade.

Nonphysician Providers

A policy review on the physician workforce cannot avoid considerations of advanced practice nurses and physician assistants, sometimes referred to as midlevel providers or nonphysician providers. In addition to substituting for some physician work, NPPs provide care-enhancing services that go beyond what physicians provide.

The growth and development of the NPP role in the United States and Canada occurred in the late 1960s and early 1970s. The role of NPPs was initially conceived of as complementing physician general and subspecialty practice; however, the need for inner-city and rural providers in underserved areas encouraged the development of the fields. An excellent recent review of the NPP field has been produced by the Association of Academic Health Centers.[24] The number of active physician assistants grew to about 23,000 and active nurse practitioners to about 24,000 by 1993.

The issue of NPP substitution for physicians is of renewed current interest for two reasons: because their use has increased in many managed care systems for reasons of cost control and because the Clinton Health Security Act proposed to increase their training and utilization significantly to cover newly enfranchised populations. Even with the failure of national health care reform, this issue has increased the tension between organized medicine and nurses regarding the boundaries between the professions.[25,26]

The question of NPP substitution centers on two issues: capability and cost-effectiveness. Most studies support the claim that NPPs can provide safe and effective care that is consistent with training and supervision. The debate focuses on what tasks in which specialties lie outside of that boundary. Political advocates of nursing have claimed that nurses can do the majority of what primary care physicians do, and this naturally engenders a counterreaction of equal political passion. Most studies of effective practice and cost-effectiveness date to the mid 1970s. An excellent review is that of Record.[27] She makes the following observations: that the range of delegation is very broad (from 2 percent to 90 percent), that some of the delegation studies are actual and some are potential, that delegation increases with practice size, and that delegation may be related to the consultation rate. Record cites and seems to endorse the findings that at least 90 percent of office visits for children are functionally delegable as well as 80 percent of adult office visits.

GMENAC included a factor for NPP delegation in determining its physician requirements. They estimated that 12 percent of adult ambulatory care, 15 percent of ambulatory pediatrics, and 20 percent of ambulatory obstetrics/gynecology could be provided by NPPs; these actual rates were reduced from the ideal in large part because of expectations of an increasing physician supply.

A major study on NPPs was produced by the Office of Technology Assessment in 1986.[28] OTA makes the claim that "NPPs working under physician supervision can increase total practice output by 20–50% . . . depending on practice setting, responsibilities delegated, severity and stability of patient illness, and how physicians choose to use the free time that results from delegating tasks." The main study that they cite to back up these conclusions (which currently are widely circulating in the policy community) is an unpublished working paper by Hauser that claims that 60–80 percent of primary care can be provided without physician consultation; this paper cannot be located either by the OTA staff or the consulting firm that did the work.

Nonetheless, the shift from potential task delegation to increase in practice output is conceptually important in thinking about the substitution-productivity equation.

A widely cited 1993 meta analysis done by the American Nurses Association[29] indicated that the number of studies adequately controlling for differences in patient intensity and risk was not sufficient to draw conclusions on regarding comparative physician and NPP cost-effectiveness. The analysis concludes that "NPs [nonphysician providers] and CNMs [certified nurse midwives] had patient outcome equivalent or slightly better when compared to physicians. Given these outcomes and the lower costs associated with education and employment, these nurses practicing in advanced practice roles are cost effective providers of primary care services."

Lomas and colleagues made projections on the overall impact of NPP substitution on physician requirements in Ontario,[30] making adjustments for many of the variables cited previously and introducing the important concept that, as the number of delegated services increases, the services increase in complexity and cost-effectiveness falls. They conclude that 20–32 percent of Ontario's general practitioners could be replaced by NPPs and recommended policies phasing this in over 20 years.

NPP utilization practices in managed care organizations were reported by Weiner in 1986.[31] He reported an average of 27 NPPs per 100,000 enrollees but noticed marked variability across HMOs: delegation ranged from 6 to 47 percent of adult visits and ranged from 0 to 26 percent of pediatric visits. Rentmeester[32] found that several group–staff model HMOs increased a physician's panel size by 30–50 percent when one NPP was added into the practice. A more current description of NPP use in one Kaiser plan is described by Hooker, whose study also includes specialty use.[33] Hooker indicates that NPPs are viewed as equally productive as physicians, and that they prescribe similarly to physicians, are as satisfactory to members, and are economically viable alternatives at current salary and training costs.

Market force economics and consumer attitudes will require delivery organizations to grapple with the issue of nonphysician providers in the early twenty-first century. The following summary considerations will be important in identifying both public and private sector organizational directions on this issue.

1. There is a difference between potential and actual substitution. Many of the studies reporting the highest potential range of substitution are based on what "can" be done safely and while retaining good quality, but these levels are rarely achieved in practice. In addition, actual substitution depends on the willingness of physicians to delegate, training of physicians in appropriate NPP utilization, organizational setting (larger practices and managed care organizations being more favorable), cost-effectiveness, legal and financial barriers, and competition between physicians and NPPs. Supervision must increase as the percentage of tasks delegated increases, and as the complexity of tasks delegated increases. Some critics of delegation claim that comparisons are not being made on severity-adjusted panels or tasks.

2. In some areas, NPPs may be pricing themselves out of the market. In general, the issues of productivity and cost-effectiveness seem to support the NPP role. In managed care organizations making extensive use of NPPs, a physician's panel size is commonly increased by 50 percent with an NPP addition. Based on such managed care productivity, a model for estimating the impact of NPPs on physician supply was produced.[34] One of many possible combinations indicated that if the addition of one NPP to a physician generalist practice increased the panel size by 40 percent, a doubling of the number of generalist NPPs would have allowed a reduction in 1990 of generalist physicians from 182,000 to 164,000. Estimates of costs must include relative estimates of salary, benefits, supervision, and training costs, as well as any other costs to the organization and practice. However, as NPP salaries rise in relation to physician salaries, NPP cost-effectiveness diminishes.

3. NPP substitution may not be equally achievable in all settings. The higher incidence of NPP substitution in managed care organizations and large groups has implications for utilization increases in the future as these forms of practice increase. Whether the experience in staff model HMOs will be replicated in the larger and faster-growing IPA models is doubtful, however, since they lack the organizational structure and practice environments that have produced increased NPP utilization in other models.

4. Most research on NPP utilization has been done in the area of primary care. There is anecdotal experience in the subspecialties, but almost nothing on productivity and cost-effectiveness. It may be that greater opportunities exist in subspecialty substitution in the future, due to the relatively higher salary levels and the possibility that too many subspecialists may be a greater problem than not enough generalists, although the competition from "too many" subspecialists may limit this in the fee-for-service sector.

5. The use of NPPs as substitutes for residents shows great promise. Such substitution in effect would both shorten resident's work weeks and respond to reductions in specialty residencies if they are mandated. In this case, cost-effectiveness is less important since the price of getting the work done will be compared with staff physician substitutes[35]; cost-effectiveness in this context relates to overall health expenditures, which should be less, with fewer subspecialists produced for the practice pool.

6. The issue of physician competition is a very serious one, at least in the short run. Even as the cost-effectiveness of NPPs is demonstrated, the fact remains that the United States has a large and rapidly expanding pool of physicians. Unless this growth can be truncated, adding NPPs could add to overall expenditures instead of contributing to reductions. This point of view was presented in a 1984 editorial by Spitzer,[36] in which he says, "The most important factor in economic viability of NPs will be their level of remuneration. Their push for economic parity with primary care MDs will vitiate earlier studies on their cost effectiveness, and will result in lessened support from government. In Canada, the surplus of primary care MDs has all but precluded a legitimate role for NPs in the health system of any province." In fact, this is precisely what has occurred in the United States over the past 15 years. There is a "zero-sum" aspect to this workforce dynamic; the generalist-enhancing reform discussion provided a bully pulpit stimulus for potential increases in the output of generalists of all types. Current efforts, such as those currently underway by a joint workgroup of COGME and the Nursing Advisory Committee on Nursing Education and Practice to quantify the joint requirements for physicians and NPPs, are critically important.[37]

Geographic Distribution and Underservice

Concerns about adequate physician supply in some urban and rural areas has dominated the approach of many legislators to physician workforce reform. Policy concern about geographic distribution dates in the modern era to the late 1960s and early 1970s, when a number of national and state initiatives, such as the development of family medicine, the National Health Service Corps, Community and Migrant Health Centers, Area Health Education Centers, loan repayment programs, and medical school admission and curriculum reform, were developed to ensure an adequate or appropriate number and type of physicians across geographic areas. How has adequacy been conceptualized, and what progress has been made?

Generalist distribution

A recent review of the concepts of adequacy and underservice was compiled in a 1991 supplemental issue of the *Journal of Rural Health*.[38] Attention has centered on the federal criteria for designating Health Professions Shortages Areas (HPSAs) and Medically Underserved Areas (MUAs).[39] Almost all efforts have focused on shortages of primary care providers, and little attention has been paid to subspecialists or to the possibility of "overservice."

Determination of shortages or surplus within a geographic area requires definition of the area as well as development of criteria for adequacy for the type of resource being considered. Most initial HPSAs were county based, but later requirements for "rational service areas" provided for groups of adjacent counties, that is, portions of metropolitan and nonmetropolitan counties that are distant from the county's resources or "socioeconomically distinct," or that encounter access barriers to resources. In addition, state officials were given prerogatives in the late 1980s for their own designation criteria. The importance of the choice of area can be illustrated with respect to geographic variation in the supply of generalist physicians; the percentage of generalists in the United States at the county level is 63 percent while at the state level it is 37 percent.

Once the geographic area has been defined, what criteria are used to determine if adequacy, shortage, or surplus obtains? For the federal HPSAs, which are primarily used to allocate National Health Service Corps personnel, the ratio of primary care physicians to population has been the predominant criterion. Initially conceptualized as any area that has less of a physician-to-population ratio than 1:4,000 (25 per 100,000), it is currently set at 1:3,500 (29 per 100,000). A higher "level 2" criterion of 1:3,000 (33 per 100,000) is set for areas with unusually high need or insufficient capacity. A "level 3" ratio of 1:2,000 (50 per 100,000) was identified to approximate a "target ratio" of adequacy.

Table 5.2 indicates the current number of HPSAs designated and

Table 5.2 Health Professional Shortage Areas, by Metropolitan/Nonmetropolitan Classification, 1994

	Number of Designations	Percentage of All Designations	Population of Designated HPSAs	Percentage of HPSA Population
Primary Medical				
HPSA Totals	2,577	100%	45,188,521	100%
Metropolitan	796	30	23,075,806	51
Nonmetropolitan	1,781	70	22,112,715	49

	Practitioners Needed to Remove Designations	Percentage of Practitioners Needed to Remove Designations	Practitioners Needed to Achieve Target Ratios	Percentage of Practitioners Needed to Achieve Target Ratios
Primary Medical				
HPSA Totals	5,085	100%	11,708	100%
Metropolitan	2,902	57	6,322	54
Nonmetropolitan	2,183	43	5,386	46

Source: Department of Health and Human Services, Health Resources and Services Administration, 1994 on HPSA.

Table 5.3   Generalist Physicians in Nonmetropolitan Counties,
Supply and Number Needed to Reach 50 per 100,000
Population, by Region, 1975 and 1990

	Supply 1975	Needed 1975	Supply 1990	Needed 1990
New England	29.7	260	72.5	4
Mid-Atlantic	21.5	949	50.9	181
South Atlantic	11.0	3,677	47.8	1,069
East South Central	7.0	2,674	46.0	725
East North Central	18.1	2,975	47.8	675
West North Central	20.7	2,439	53.1	489
West South Central	11.8	2,518	44.9	651
Mountain	13.6	1,323	53.9	267
Pacific	10.9	990	60.2	124
Total		17,805		4,185

Source: Unpublished data, Wisconsin Network for Health Policy Research, 1994.

the number of physicians needed to meet shortage and adequacy standards. It can be seen that 5,085 practitioners would be required to "remove" the HPSA designation, and that 11,708 would be required to achieve a "target ratio" of 50:100,000. These requirements are approximately divided between metropolitan and nonmetropolitan areas and have remained at approximately the same level over the past 15 years. Table 5.3 displays the change from 1975 to 1990 in nonmetropolitan counties; despite significant increases in all regions, the number of generalists still needed is 4,185. Significant numbers of NPPs practice in underserved areas and practitioner shortage strategies should take into account the maximum effective participation of NPPs along with generalist physicians.

It is possible to dismiss such numbers as a very small percentage of all practicing physicians, or to presume that continuing increased supply will trickle down into the remaining underserved areas. However, rural and inner-city areas experiencing persistent underservice are characterized by high levels of poverty. Many individuals are without insurance and therefore lack the market power to attract physicians; it is only federal and state public programs such as Community Health Centers and the National Health Service Corps that have kept the ratio of generalists to population as favorable as they are. Under universal coverage, the delivery systems would have expanded capacity to reduce these needs significantly, perhaps leaving only the most severely depressed and isolated areas in need of a public infrastructure. In the absence of universal coverage, federal and state government bear the responsibility to continue existing efforts and to expand them to meet the remaining need. Given the output of medical schools and residencies, and market forces that favor generalism, new resources should be concentrated on adequate practice support in the remaining underserved areas; this should be thought of in a highly targeted way. An evaluation should be made regarding the relative effectiveness of Medicare Part B bonus payments[40] with direct support such as Community Health Centers and National Health Service Corps in the remaining areas of underservice. Finally, in a period of federal and state budget constraints, it should be remembered that without current educational and delivery safety net efforts current indicators would be much worse.

Subspecialist distribution

Almost all attention has been turned toward areas with shortages of generalists. How should adequacy of physician supply of subspecialists be considered? Should the concept of overservice be further developed? Currently subspecialist representation varies considerably across geographic areas. The editors of the supplemental volume previously cited made the following observation:

> There is a general understanding that larger nonmetro counties or urban areas will have higher per capita levels of certain services, reflecting the cost and quality rationale for centralizing some specialized services. On the other hand, there is an expectation that more common and routine services including primary care and emergency care, be available in all geographic areas within a certain distance or travel time. Unfortunately, moving beyond these generalizations is quite difficult because of limitations in our understanding of need and demand characteristics of different areas, and the relationship between health services and health.[41]

Figure 5.8 displays the bivariate relationships between physicians per 100,000 population by specialty and size of health service area. It can be seen that the number of physicians, already expressed in per capita terms, varies substantially across health service areas (HSAs) of different population sizes. Only family medicine has lower levels of physicians as population size increases. This is offset by an increase in general internal medicine and pediatrics, although the total number of generalists is higher in the HSAs with larger populations. Most sub-

Figure 5.8   Physician Specialty Distribution by Health Service Area
Size, 1990

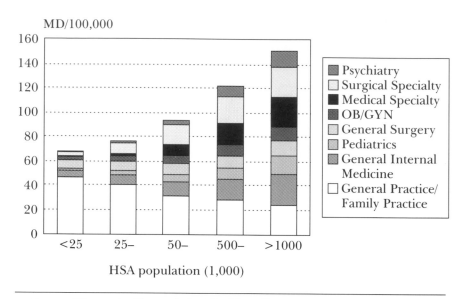

Source: Wisconsin Network for Health Policy Research, 1994.

specialties increase with population (general surgery is an interesting
exception). Increases in the medical and surgical subspecialties are
not unexpected; the significant increase in psychiatry deserves further attention and explanation.

Other bivariate relationships have also been described, such as
those for race and commuting patterns.[42,43] Multivariate analysis of
supply is different for each specialty. For all physicians, about 50 percent of the variance can be explained. Positive relationships are seen
for population, for hospital beds per capita, for per capita income, for
the number of medical school graduates, and for lower percentages
of outbound commuters. When regional dummy variables are included, the North Central, South, and Western regions of the country,
in that order, are associated with substantially lower levels than the
Eastern United States.

Market forces in areas with high managed care penetration will
reduce subspecialist levels in these plans, but the fate of the remainder
in the fee-for-service "compartment"[44] is unclear. Early retirement,
retraining as generalists and outcome analysts, continued physician-

induced demand, and lowered incomes have all been discussed. The uncertain impact of new biomedical and information technology will undoubtedly affect all geographic areas. Perhaps the major unanswered policy question is whether or not an oversupply of subspecialists will result in public policy that reduces overall output of physicians through either domestic production or immigration or both.

Diversity in the Physician Workforce

There is a great imbalance between the minority population in the United States and minority representation in the physician workforce. COGME indicated that, whereas African Americans, Hispanics, and Native Americans will constitute about 25 percent of the U.S. population by 2000, they represent only 10 percent of entering medical students, 7 percent of practicing physicians, and 3 percent of medical faculty. The period from 1975 to 1990 saw an 18.5 percent increase in minority population and only 7 percent in minority medical student enrollment. If population parity between the number of minority physicians and the minority population is a goal, much remains to be done; 1990 census data show a white physician:white population ratio of 251 per 100,000 population, while comparable figures for African Americans, Hispanics, and Native Americans are 71, 129, and 48, respectively.[45] Significant increases in minority population are expected in the coming decades. In addition to longstanding deficits in the number of African American and Native American physicians, the situation for Hispanics may be the most critical in the future, given demographic projections for that group and the fact that historically most Hispanic physicians have been IMGs.

Nickens and coauthors[46] have recently reported on the status of the American Association of Medical Colleges "Project 3000 by 2000," a program designed to increase minority enrollment before the end of the century. The authors report some progress toward this goal; number of matriculants has increased from 1,470 in 1990 to 1,863 in 1993. Three approaches are considered important and effective: magnet health science high schools; articulation agreements among high schools, colleges, and medical schools; and science education partnerships. A recent report by the Institute of Medicine entitled "Balancing the Scales of Opportunity" has an even broader agenda, one linked to future national productivity.[47]

Achieving a closer balance is important for two reasons: (1) minorities tend to practice in minority populations and underserved areas, and (2) minority physicians reduce cultural and linguistic barriers to care. As health status improvement becomes the goal of the system and particularly if universal coverage is achieved at some future date, an increase in minority physicians will be critical for health plans in culturally diverse populations. This difficult issue has resisted the best efforts to date of academia and government and the private sector. It must reemerge as a critical policy and research priority. Fruitful avenues for exploration include regional medical education consortium strategies and entry level strategies through allied health and midlevel providers. As one major health plan executive recently stated, "This is no longer only a social imperative, it is a business imperative."

The Role of the Physician Executive

Physician executives, or medical managers, are defined as those physicians who spend the majority of their time in management. Historically, they have made up between 3 and 4 percent of the physician supply. In the past they have primarily limited their activities to medical education and medical staff activities,[48] but recently a new role has emerged for physician executives as major players on the corporate team. As integrated delivery systems emerge, and the physician-organization relationship becomes more important, the physician executive will play a boundary-spanning role. Physician executives will mediate between clinical practice and business fundamentals, in such areas as clinical cost-effectiveness, physician performance improvement, medical ethics, and managed care-group practice relationships. A recent survey of CEOs of a variety of health organizations indicated that physician executives will play an important role in organizational performance in the next five years; the most important functions were judged to be evaluation of practice patterns for efficiency, improved quality improvement activities, effective relations with medical staff, and participation in establishing the strategic directions of the organization.[49]

Many current and aspiring physician executives are increasing their skills and knowledge through continuing education programs in the American College of Physician Executives and in graduate education such as that offered at the University of Wisconsin, Madison.[50] Whereas dramatic increases in the numbers in these roles are not expected, the importance of the role in managing the system will continue to increase and be critical in the emerging new delivery system.

Policy Considerations

A number of generic themes emerge from this discussion of workforce issues. These themes will be central to a consideration of workforce issues for the new delivery system of the twenty-first century.

1. Market forces versus regulation. Whereas this consideration applies most fully to the central health care reform issues of universal coverage and cost containment, it is critical to workforce issues as well. Existing incentives may produce market distortions, and market failure is not unknown in the health care field. The most prominent current example relates to GME reform, where market force advocates oppose regulatory allocation schemes, believing that the cost-containment pressures will result in any changes in workforce composition that are warranted. Others argue that the production markets of teaching hospitals are not connected to the market needs of the world of practice, and that current Medicare residency training financing creates incentives for specialist production. With regard to geographic distribution, it was argued in the early 1980s that an overall increasing supply of physicians would improve geographic distribution; while this has happened to some extent, not much change has taken place in urban and rural shortage areas. Whether universal coverage would create enough financial incentive to attract generalists into these areas is unknown; neither is the relative future income expectations that would alter current specialty choice. Careful tracking of changes in local markets must be carried out to determine if the markets of the teaching hospital and the world of managed care–dominated practice are developing connections. If not, some regulatory intervention may be required to reduce both domestic production and immigration in order to reduce aggregate supply.

2. Cost containment and workforce cost-effectiveness. Those who are convinced that growth in the number of physicians and specialists is not a problem are implicitly assuming that the growth in health expenditures that has been responsible for past trends will continue as well. The Congressional Budget Office (CBO) currently indicates that, without reform, expenditures will approach 20 percent of GDP by

2002. With this kind of growth, increased utilization of all resources will continue, including physician generalists and specialists, whether they are contributing to health status improvement or not. Only in a framework in which the product of the health care system is defined as units of health status per dollar expended will alternative workforce composition be realized. It must be noted that CBO projections have included very conservative assumptions about the impact of managed care and managed competition on national health care expenditures. Miller and Luft[51] recently pointed out that alternative assumptions are plausible and should be built into sensitivity analysis.

Even in this context, greatly increased knowledge about the cost-effectiveness of alternative workforce arrangements is needed. The growing bodies of evidence about the cost-effectiveness of generalist physicians, and the most cost-effective mix of generalists and specialists for given conditions, must be greatly expanded on and validated. The beginnings of cost-effectiveness analysis of midlevel practitioners from the 1980s must be seriously revisited in the light of today's salary structure and practice arrangements. Population-based workforce models are needed; this will allow local areas to determine the most cost-effective and appropriate mix of professionals and paraprofessionals for their needs. Emphasis may begin to be placed as much on the issue of overservice as it has been on underservice in the past.

3. The global role of the United States. Current thinking about overall U.S. workforce policy highlights the important role the United States plays in supporting emerging systems in other parts of the world. While health is fundamentally a local product, the global economy affects it as well. What roles will U.S. health professionals play globally, both in terms of technology development and systems development? The GME debate may be seen as xenophobic by some, to the degree that it has recently concentrated on reducing the number of foreign residents training in U.S. teaching hospitals in an era of potential domestic excess. But this consideration should not decrease the transfer of skills to the developing world. It should be possible to develop policy that accommodates both purposes. The United States has much to learn from other countries and systems, particularly in the area of public health and nonmedical inputs as a cost-effective way to improve population health status.

4. The impact of technology and the role of physician scientists. Serious attention must be paid to the impact of new technology on workforce composition and distribution. Obviously, this relates to the issue of cost-effectiveness, but it stands alone as well. It is widely assumed that advances in biomedical science such as genetic engineering will continue to require more specialized resources than in the past, but it is conceivable that the net impact might be the reverse as chronic disease and degeneration is reversed. Kirschner and coauthors[52] have made convincing arguments for continuing investment in biomedical research and for not reducing innovation prior to the stage of development when cost-effectiveness is feasible. Maintaining an adequate supply of physicians is important for achieving this goal, but it accounts for a very small number of physicians and must be dealt with in a very targeted way aligned with biomedical research support. Reducing the overall number of physicians or residents will have minimal if any independent impact on the supply of such scientists.

Also, developments in information systems may decrease the geographic population gradient previously assumed for specialized services. Kassirer has suggested that the rapid growth of computer-based electronic communication, the fact that a new generation is increasingly comfortable with electronic transfer of information, and the shift toward giving patients more responsibility for health care decisions may mean that such technology "will replace a substantial amount of care now delivered in person." Kassirer speculates that the United States may need "fewer primary care physicians, nurse practitioners, and even specialists than is being predicted today."[53]

5. Nonfinancial barriers to access and health status. National health care reform was leading to universal coverage for basic health care services in the short term. Whenever this happens, attention will shift to workforce issues associated with nonfinancial barriers such as culture, language, social support, and individual behavior, and interfaces with other sectors such as education, environment, and welfare. The roles that education, income disparity, and social hierarchy play in producing the socioeconomic status gradient in morbidity and mortality will have profound impact on workforce size and balance of essential competencies.[53]

Notes

1. Department of Health and Human Services (DHHS), *Report of the Graduate Medical Education National Advisory Committee*, Vols. 1–7, Pub. no. (HRA) 81, (Hyattsville, MD, 1980), pp. 651–57.
2. M. Rivo and D. Satcher, "Improving Access to Health Care Through

Physician Workforce Reform," *Journal of the American Medical Association* 270 (1993): 1074–78.

3. Council on Graduate Medical Education (COGME), Fourth Report to Congress and DHHS (Rockville, MD: U.S. Department of Health and Human Services, 1994).

4. DHHS 1980.

5. U. Reinhardt, "The GMENAC Forecast: An Alternative View," *American Journal of Public Health* 71, no. 10 (1981): 1149.

6. J. Weiner, "Forecasting the Effects of Health Reform on U.S. Physician Workforce Requirement," *Journal of the American Medical Association,* 272 (1994): 222–30.

7. Council on Graduate Medical Education (COGME), Seventh Report to Congress and DHHS (Rockville, MD: U.S. Department of Health and Human Services, 1995).

8. D. Kindig, "Counting Generalist Physicians," *Journal of the American Medical Association* 271 (1994): 1505–07.

9. Weiner 1994.

10. COGME 1995.

11. W. B. Schwartz, et al., "Are We Training Too Many Subspecialists?" *Journal of the American Medical Association* 259, no. 2 (1988): 233–39.

12. W. B. Schwartz, et al., "Why There Will Be Little or No Physician Surplus Between Now and the Year 2000," *The New England Journal of Medicine* 318, no. 14 (1988): 892.

13. R. A. Cooper, "Seeking a Balanced Physician Workforce for the 21st Century," *Journal of the American Medical Association* 272, no. 9 (1994): 680–87.

14. F. Mullan, et al., "Medical Migration and the Physician Workforce: International Medical Graduates and American Medicine," *Journal of the American Medical Association* 273, no. 11 (1995): 1521–27.

15. S. Greenfield, et al., "Variations in Resource Utilization among Medical Specialties and Systems of Care," *Journal of the American Medical Association* 267 (1992): 1624–30.

16. K. Grumbach and P. Lee, "How Many Physicians Can We Afford?" *Journal of the American Medical Association* 265, no. 18 (1991): 2369–72.

17. D. Kindig and D. L. Libby, "Setting State Health Spending Limits," *Health Affairs* 13, no. 2 (Spring 1994): 288–89.

18. D. Kindig and D. L. Libby, "How Will Graduate Medical Education Reform Impact on Specialties and Geographic Areas?" *Journal of the American Medical Association* 272, no. 1 (1994): 37–42.

19. D. Dranove and W. White, *Clinton's Specialist Quota: Shaky Premises, Questionable Consequences* (Washington, DC: AEI Press, 1994).

20. U. Reinhardt, "Planning the Nation's Health Workforce: Let the Market In," *Inquiry* 31 (Fall 1994): 250–63.

21. J. Stoddard, D. Kindig, and D. Libby, "Graduate Medical Education Reform: Service Provision Transition Costs," *Journal of the American Medical Association* 272, no. 1 (1994): 53–58.

22. D. Kindig, "Specialist Glut, Generalist Shortage," OpEd, *Washington Post* (7 September 1994).
23. COGME 1995.
24. Association of Academic Health Centers, *The Roles of Physicians' Assistants and Nurse Practitioners in Primary Care* (Washington, DC: AAHC, 1993).
25. J. P. Kassirer, "What Role for Nurse Practitioners in Primary Care?" *The New England Journal of Medicine* 330, no. 3 (1994): 204–205.
26. M. O. Mundinger, "Advanced Practice Nursing: Good Medicine for Physicians?" *The New England Journal of Medicine* 330, no. 3 (1994): 211–13.
27. J. C. Record, M. McCally, and S. O. Schweitzer, "New Health Professions after a Decade and a Half: Delegation, Productivity, and Costs in Primary Care," *Journal of Health Politics, Policy, and Law* 5, no. 4 (1980): 470–97.
28. Office of Technology Assessment, "Nurse Practitioners, Physicians' Assistants, and Certified Nurse Midwives: A Policy Analysis," *Case Study 37* (U.S. Congress, 1986).
29. S. A. Brown and D. E. Grimes, "A Meta-Analysis of Process of Care, Clinical Outcomes, and Cost Effectiveness of Nurses in Primary Care Roles" (Washington, DC: American Nurses Association, 1993).
30. J. Lomas and G. Stoddart, "Estimates of Potential Impact of Nurse Practitioners on Future Requirements for Physicians," *Canadian Journal of Public Health* 76 (1985):119–23.
31. J. Weiner, D. M. Steinwachs, and J. W. Williamson, "Nurse Practitioner and Physician Assistant Practices in Three HMOs," *American Journal of Public Health* 76, no. 5 (1986): 507–11.
32. K. Rentmeester and D. Kindig, Report to the Robert Wood Johnson Foundation, 1995.
33. R. S. Hooker, "The Roles of Physicians' Assistants and Nurse Practitioners in a Managed Care Organization," in *The Roles of Physician Assistants and Nurse Practitioners in Primary Care* (Washington, DC: AAHC, 1993).
34. D. Kindig and N. Kaufman, "How Much Physician Work Can Nurse Practitioners and Physician Assistants Do?" Submitted for publication, 1995.
35. Stoddard, Kindig, and Libby 1994.
36. Bureau of Health Professions, Integrated Primary Care Workforce Requirements, 1995.
37. See also W. D. Spitzer, "The NP Revisited—Slow Death of a Good Idea," *The New England Journal of Medicine* 310, no. 16 (1984): 1049–51.
38. D. Kindig and T. Ricketts, "Issues and Trends in Availability of Health Care in Rural America," *Journal of Rural Health, Supplemental Issue* 7, no. 4 (1991).
39. R. Lee, "Current Approaches to Shortage Area Designation," *Journal of Rural Health* 7 (1991): 437–50.
40. Physician Payment Review Commission, *Annual Report to Congress* (Washington, DC:PPRC).
41. Kindig and Ricketts 1991.

42. D. Kindig and W. Hong, "The Relationship Between Nonmetropolitan Commuting Patterns and Utilization of Health Resources in Nonmetropolitan Counties of the U.S.," *Medical Care* 30 (1992): 1154–58.

43. D. Kindig and Y. Guo, "Physician Supply in Rural Areas with Large Minority Populations," *Health Affairs* 12 (Summer 1993): 177–83.

44. A. R. Tarlov, "HMO Enrollment Growth and Physicians: The Third Compartment," *Health Affairs* 5 (Spring 1986): 23–35.

45. Association of American Medical Colleges, *Minority Students in Medical Education, Facts and Figures VII* (Washington, DC: AAMC 1993).

46. H. W. Nickens, T. P. Ready, and R. G. Petersdorf, "Project 3000 by 2000: Racial and Ethnic Diversity in U.S. Medical Schools," *The New England Journal of Medicine* 331, no. 7 (1994): 472–76.

47. Institute of Medicine, *Balancing the Scales of Opportunity: Ensuring Racial and Ethnic Diversity in the Health Professions.* (Washington, DC: National Academy Press, 1994).

48. D. Kindig and S. Lastiri, "Administrative Medicine: A New Medical Specialty?" *Health Affairs* 5 (Winter 1986): 146–156.

49. N. C. Dunham, D. A. Kindig, and R. Schulz, "The Value of the Physician Executive Role in Organizational Effectiveness and Performance Health Care Management Review," *Health Care Management Review* 19, no. 4 (1994): 56–63.

50. D. Kindig, "Administrative Medicine at the University of Wisconsin/Madison," *Journal of Health Administration Education* 7 (1989): 734–737.

51. R. H. Miller and H. S. Luft, "Estimating Health Expenditure Growth under Managed Competition," *Journal of the American Medical Association* 273, no. 8 (1995): 656–62.

52. M. W. Kirschner, E. Marincola, and E. O. Teisberg, "The Role of Biomedical Research in Health Care Reform," *Science* 266 (7 October 1994): 49–51.

53. J. P. Kassirer, "The Next Transformation in the Delivery of Health Care," *The New England Journal of Medicine* 332, no. 1 (1994): 52–53.

54. N. E. Adler, T. Boyce, M. A. Chesney, S. Cohen, S. Folkman, R. L. Kahn, and S. L. Syme, "Socioeconomic Status and Health: The Challenge of the Gradient," *American Psychologist* (January 1994): 15–24.

6

States and Health Care Reform: The Importance of Program Implementation

Dennis F. Beatrice

> It must be remembered that there is nothing more difficult to plan, more doubtful of success, nor more dangerous to manage than the creation of a new system. For the initiator has the enmity of all who would profit by the preservation of the old institutions and merely lukewarm defenders in those who would gain by the new ones.
>
> —Machiavelli, *The Prince*

Abstract. The recent debate on national health care reform marked another case of policy being considered without reference to how—or even if—it could be implemented. The debate revolved around broad issues, such as universal versus partial coverage, mandatory versus voluntary alliances, and the respective roles of government and the market in health care. The ease or even the possibility of successful implementation was not an ingredient in evaluating proposals.

The burden of making health care reform work falls to the states. Whether in response to national reform or in implementing their own programs, they must move from a general reform blueprint to an actual program that delivers services. The hands-on role of the states in designing and operating programs makes their implementation duties both unavoidable and critical.

This chapter explores implementation issues that should be considered an integral part of planning for health care reform, at both the federal and the state level. The chapter has two goals. First, it makes a case for altering the usual approach to designing reform and recommends paying attention to implementation early in the policy process, rather than treating it as an afterthought. Second, it is intended to help policymakers design implementable programs and anticipate pitfalls. To achieve these goals, it examines the state role in health care reform; state capacity to carry out this role; examples of state health care reform initiatives and lessons for implementation drawn from these efforts; and barriers to successful implementation. The chapter concludes with recommendations for policymakers.

Machiavelli's words, written over 400 years ago, continue to resonate today, and the debate on national health care reform reminded us just how hard it is to create a "new system."

The difficulty of accomplishing change is compounded by the fact that the policy process focuses on *what* to do about a problem, but not *how* to do it. Neglect of workable ways to turn a broad policy vision into a program that works is endemic to the policy process. As Richard Nathan noted: "Implementation is the short suit of American Government. We promise the moon and plan as if we were installing a light bulb."[1] Our failure to plan for implementation contributes to the public belief that government does not work, that it is unresponsive and incompetent, and that it lurches from crisis to crisis.

The late, lamented debate on national health care reform marked another case of policy being considered without reference to how—or even if—it could be implemented. The debate revolved around broad issues, such as universal versus partial coverage, mandatory versus voluntary alliances, and the respective roles of government and the market in health care. Eventually, attention turned to outlining a proposal for a program that could be cobbled together and enacted by Congress. The ease or even the possibility of successful implementation was not an ingredient in evaluating proposals.

The burden of filling this gap, of paying attention to the hard realities of making health care reform work, would have fallen to the states. The states cannot escape this role; whether in response to national reform or in implementing their own programs, they must move from a general reform blueprint to an actual program that delivers services. The hands-on role of the states in designing and operating programs makes their implementation duties both unavoidable and critical.

A Tough Job

States face a difficult task in implementing health care reform, whether under their own initiatives or as part of a future national reform plan. In a little-noticed warning accompanying its "scoring" of the 1994 crop of reform proposals, the Congressional Budget Office (CBO) noted that government simply might not have been able to carry out the responsibilities imposed by most of the leading reform bills that were before Congress. The CBO concluded that no matter which of the leading plans Congress had chosen, potential administrative problems made them all equally problematic, and there was a "significant chance" that the changes envisioned could not be implemented.[2]

The CBO noted several components of the leading plans that would have placed heavy burdens on states. Building and operating a program of subsidies to low-income persons was cited as a particular challenge. Difficulties included determining eligibility for subsidies, reconciling overlapping subsidies for low-income families and low-income children and pregnant women, and performing year-end income checks to ensure that subsidized families received the appropriate level of help.[3] The General Accounting Office (GAO) concluded at about the same time that, based on experience with Medicaid eligibility, the task of documenting eligibility for and setting levels of subsidies under health care reform would be extremely difficult.[4]

Implementing state reform programs is no less daunting a task. The Washington State Health Care Reform Act of 1993, for example, mandated dozens of studies and analyses to address issues raised by the reform program, and literally hundreds of items appeared in a workplan prepared by the state agencies charged with converting the legislation into a working program.[5] The experience of other states that have taken the lead in health care reform is similar.

The bottom line is that, under the best of circumstances, it is a tough job to implement health care reform. This difficulty makes it even more essential that implementation receive early and serious attention in the reform process and that all relevant intelligence be gathered sufficiently in advance of the implementation effort.

The State Role in Health Care Reform

The state role in health care has always been substantial.[6] It has included protecting the public health and safety, providing health care services directly through state agencies and institutions, paying for health care services, licensing and training health care providers, and regulating providers and their activities in the health care marketplace. Health care reform may change the content of these roles and add new functions, but state responsibility will remain. Required state roles in implementation are thus fundamental, but they have not been given their due, front and center, in the health care reform debate.

It is impossible to capture the full range of activities required in the states to implement either federal or state health care reform. Tasks vary by type of reform chosen, individual state circumstances, and how much will be new to the state—the size of the learning curve—in implementing reform. Some activities will be extensions of existing responsibilities, like insurance regulation, while others will be new, such as establishing purchasing groups.

Framework

Larry Brown has suggested five tasks that are especially important to workable state implementation of health reform: (1) regulation, perhaps to oversee the behavior of providers and patients, and certainly to monitor budgets; (2) information, to guide management of the system, inform consumers, and assure quality; (3) planning, to organize the state role, even in a market-driven environment; (4) negotiation, to reach and maintain equitable arrangements with providers, consumers, and among government agencies; and (5) reorganization, to provide for effective governance of the reform effort.[7] States also must assure that service delivery systems, which might change substantially under reform, are adequate to the task, that public health functions are performed, that cost control is implemented and policed, that legal challenges to reform are met, that subsidies are delivered to low-income individuals and perhaps small businesses, that rules for participation by health plans are defined and monitored, and that an adequate corps of health care professionals is maintained and deployed where needed.

Careful consideration of the actual performance of a reform plan along these implementation dimensions could help policymakers choose models for reform. Amidst uncertainty and the varieties of political pressure, it is only sensible to make the ability to implement the reform plan an important criterion for choosing an approach to reform.

Complexity and importance

Even apparently straightforward implementation tasks are complex. To set up a purchasing alliance, for example, requires that states set geographical boundaries; certify participating health plans; oversee governance of the alliance; assure financial solvency; monitor plan marketing practices and quality of care; set enrollment, disenrollment, and grievance procedures; monitor the collection and distribution of premiums; provide for outreach to enroll eligible clients; define data collection and reporting requirements; determine whether and how public employees fit within the alliances; "risk-adjust" payments, to minimize the incentive for plans to enroll healthy, low-cost persons; make services equitably available to underserved and low-income areas; assure access for needed specialty services; and determine whether and how essential community providers are to be made part of the alliances.

Each element of reform spawns a similarly enormous set of state implementation responsibilities. And these state actions are far-reaching. State implementation decisions have an obvious impact on poor and uninsured individuals brought into the system under reform. The future of public hospitals and clinics that have historically served these populations will also have their future shaped by state decisions: will they receive extra reimbursement to offset the costs of providing care to persons with greater needs? Will their participation in managed care plans or provider networks be mandated, or will they have to compete in the marketplace with all other providers?

The public sector is such a large purchaser of services that state implementation decisions will affect the entire health care marketplace. How well implementation is handled will in large part determine whether the goals of reform, whatever they may be—universal coverage, cost control, or insurance market reform—are achieved. The shape of the reformed system, and whether reform will mean chaos, will depend on the effectiveness of the states in performing their roles and on the hundreds of decisions they will make while implementing reform.

State Capacity to Implement Reform

So much depends on the implementation efforts of states. If states lack the capacity to implement health care reform, an operational meltdown may result. The Congressional Budget Office questioned the ability of states to implement reform, and former CBO director Robert Reischauer observed that "the financial and economic problems associated with systemic health reform are minor considerations when compared to the administrative and implementation challenges that would be posed by any of these plans."[8] A discussion of some of the factors that affect state capacity to implement health care reform follows.

Capacity varies

Capacity among the states is uneven. While some states have the administrative resources to mount a credible implementation effort, and a history of innovation that would spur them to try, many states do not start with these advantages. For example, the General Accounting Office reviewed the health insurance regulation efforts of states and found wide variation in their authority, their oversight role, and the resources they have committed to the job.[9] Even the best prepared and most experienced states will find it difficult to implement reform; the rest face a nearly impossible task, since they will have to build basic capacity while undertaking the complex new functions of health care reform.

Political chaos has great political costs in the short run. But not all states will make the up-front investment to reduce these risks. Richard Nathan has espoused a strategy of "help the best and push the rest"[10] in the context of encouraging state flexibility in health care reform. This approach may turn out to be even more critical on the implementation front, but the push given to those least able to implement reform will have to include substantial doses of financial and technical assistance.

Paying for implementation

Health care is expensive: subsidizing the health care coverage of low-income persons is a financial burden for states. Paying for the implementation of health care reform will be a tremendous additional burden as well. Management information systems must be established or upgraded and administrative capacity must be increased. States that took the lead in health care reform incurred millions of dollars in new costs for initial information system upgrades and to make nominal staff additions before reform would even have begun. A national reform program could have included funds to help states implement reform, but such help was never certain. Its absence would have constituted the greatest unfunded mandate ever. Without national reform, states will have to fund their own implementation efforts, and

the extremely low rates of administrative spending devoted to Medicaid are not sustainable under health care reform—the tasks are
simply too numerous and complex.

Many hard-pressed states are not in a position to incur these
costs. The result is likely to be insufficient attention to implementation
tasks, as states try to make do with personnel and other resources
borrowed from existing programs. Implementation is never easy, and
implementation "on the cheap" is a recipe for failure. A broad-based
use of purchasing alliances could offer relief from this financing prob
lem, as a portion of premiums could be used to defray state administrative expenses. But without alliances or federal help, states must
commit their own funds to implement reform. The danger is that they
will not make this commitment (or will not be able to make it—after
all, states must balance their budgets), and the already shaky prospects for successful implementation will become shakier.

The intrusion of politics

States face the same political obstacles and interest group politics that
marked the national health care reform debate. The fact that a number of states have overcome these obstacles and passed significant reform initiatives on their own is a tribute to state leadership and a
reflection of the fact that states have less opportunity to discuss problems than to address them. But politics still impinges on the implementation of state reform.

Continuity is a particular challenge in the fast-moving world of
state government. Commitment over time is needed to complete reform in stages—the usual state approach—and to address the inevitable problems that arise. A Florida state legislator instrumental in his
state's reform effort noted: "The legislative mentality is to deal with
an issue and move on. The most difficult thing for legislators to do is
return (in the next session) and do the same issue again, and that's
what health care reform requires."[11] If the political will to act is lost—
for instance, because of a change in the governorshp—reform is at
risk. The delay experienced by Massachusetts in implementing its
universal coverage system was largely attributable to the departure of
its principal advocate, Governor Michael Dukakis, and the failure to
build bipartisan support for reform. In short, staying the course is a
key ingredient in successful state implementation of reform, but pa-
tience, time, and commitment are finite resources.

The importance of organizations

Elected officials propose and enact reform plans, but organizations and the people that staff them implement these initiatives. As a result, organizational structure and capacity will affect the ability of states to implement reform. The structure to put in place for planning and managing reform is an important early state decision, and one that will have implications for all subsequent elements of reform.

Many organizational arrangements are possible, including splitting implementation tasks among existing agencies; putting one agency in charge; using a newly established commission; or taking a "Governor's Cabinet" approach, where gubernatorial staff run the effort, drawing in agency staff as needed. States have made various decisions about the organization of reform. For example, Washington's reform law has established a new entity to take the lead on implementation, while Tennessee's ambitious plan to enroll Medicaid and low-income people in managed care is run by existing staff. It is too soon, and research is needed, to determine whether one organizational approach or another results in more successful implementation. For now, all that can be said is that new administrative structures will be needed to perform new tasks and to assume expanded responsibilities.

Organizational capacity is another key issue—the amount of implementation that state agencies can accomplish with the resources they have, and the degree and kind of flexibility they have to obtain more. Owing to the nature of civil service and to arcane procurement rules, state agencies often have trouble recruiting staff with the skills needed to function in the new world of health care reform. Pay scales often fall behind those in the private sector, executive recruitment is rarely used to find the best people, and simply obtaining permission to hire enough (or any) new staff can be a challenge.

Much of what must be done to implement reform is new: organizations cannot rely on their standard operating procedures. Too often, organizations are geared up to regulate the health care system of the 1980s, and implementing health care reform requires that they cope with the more integrated, market-driven, managed care–reliant system of the 1990s. The inability to recruit enough staff with the right skills puts state implementers at a disadvantage, especially compared with the sophisticated provider and insurance organizations they are called upon to negotiate with and monitor.

Moreover, implementing reform means that state administrators simply have more to do. For example, setting eligibility policy for Medicaid is challenging enough; establishing eligibility for all uninsured persons in a state magnifies the task. Demands on staff time and agency resources increase faster than their capacity to respond in terms of staff, information systems support, and expert help. As a result, performance of the new functions required to implement reform is likely to lag. This problem is compounded by the fact that it is difficult to build capacity in the public sector. There is widespread distaste for increasing the size of government—current public attitudes toward government do not bode well for gathering support to build capacity to implement health care reform. The prognosis also may not be good for building and sustaining public support for reform. These factors make it likely that a mismatch will exist between what states are called upon to do under health care reform and their capacity to perform the required tasks.

Residual state health programs

Although reform efforts receive most of the attention, even comprehensive health care reform leaves the majority of state health activities untouched. For example, almost half of every state Medicaid budget is devoted to institutional care for the elderly and disabled, and most health care reform proposals have not addressed long-term care. A catch-22 situation is created in the states: if resources are diverted to implement reform, existing programs costing hundreds of millions of dollars and serving tens of thousands of vulnerable people may suffer; if resources remain with established programs, implementation of reform may fail. The need to balance old and new programs creates another source of tension in state implementation of reform; the need to address that balance further strains already limited capacity.

Lessons for Implementation from State Health Care Reform Efforts

Despite their constraints, states have acted aggressively to enact and implement reform. Six states (Florida, Hawaii, Massachusetts, Minnesota, Oregon, and Washington) have committed to providing coverage for all of their citizens and have enacted specific approaches and financing mechanisms, such as subsidy programs and employer mandates, to achieve the goal.[12,13]

Comprehensive state programs

Florida has focused its efforts on creating 11 purchasing alliances (called Community Health Purchasing Alliances or CHPAs) that can be used by businesses to obtain more affordable coverage for their employees. CHPAs are designed to facilitate comparison and selection of health plans by consumers and to handle administrative functions, such as contracting with health plans that meet established criteria. In addition, all small-market insurance carriers must offer basic and standard benefit plans set by the insurance department.

Hawaii acted first on health care reform, and in 1974 required that employers provide health insurance for all employees working more than 20 hours per week and that the employer pay at least 50 percent of the cost. Hawaii also limits the employee's share of the premium as a percentage of income. The program offers low-cost insurance to persons with incomes below 300 percent of poverty and subsidizes the cost of premiums on a sliding scale.

Massachusetts passed legislation in 1988 imposing an employer mandate, but its implementation has been delayed and its eventual fate is in doubt, as the governor and legislature debate the future shape of reform. Massachusetts has also enacted a variety of insurance reform measures for businesses with fewer than 25 employees, a health insurance plan for children under the age of six, with subsidies for children in families with income under 400 percent of poverty, and a subsidy program for unemployed workers and their families.

Minnesota has combined subsidized health insurance to low-income uninsured families and individuals, reform of the private health insurance market, and cost containment. Health insurance coverage is not mandated, but is available on a subsidized basis. An individual mandate is slated to go into effect in 1997. The program makes subsidies available to persons with incomes below 275 percent of poverty, and enrollees pay premiums based on their ability to pay. Insurance reform has been an important part of Minnesota's program, as has cost containment built around expenditure targets that seek to control growth in health care expenditures and insurance premiums.

Oregon has implemented the most widely discussed state health care reform plan. It expands Medicaid coverage to all residents with incomes up to 100 percent of the poverty level and pays for the expansion by replacing a defined set of benefits in Medicaid with coverage based on prioritized diagnoses and treatments—the so-called rationing element of the plan. A "pay or play" system is also created: employers are required to offer health insurance to their employees or pay into a state fund that will be used to pay for employee coverage.

Washington has enacted perhaps the most comprehensive state health care reform initiative. It mandates that a uniform benefit package be made available to all residents of the state. The law creates voluntary health insurance purchasing cooperatives, available to any individual or business, to make insurance more affordable to small employers and the self-employed. A phased-in 50 percent employer contribution is required, with subsidies available to low-wage businesses. Subsidies are offered to individuals below 200 percent of poverty, and will be financed through taxes on alcohol and cigarettes, insurance premiums, and hospitals' gross incomes. The state will set maximum rates that certified health plans may charge for the uniform benefit package, and will establish a maximum health care inflation rate that will be lowered over time until it matches the growth in personal income.

Incremental reform

While only a handful of states have enacted comprehensive reform, practically every state has made important changes in parts of their health care systems. Eleven states have adopted the purchase of cooperative initiatives, like Florida, to make care available and affordable to small businesses and uninsured individuals. Medicaid expansions to cover pregnant women and children have been widely pursued, and a number of states have chosen to subsidize coverage for children in families with incomes above the Medicaid limits. Many states are seeking cost containment by promoting managed care and managed competition, as well as through more regulatory mechanisms such as limiting allowable insurance premium rate increases, setting rates for providers, and renewing interest in health planning.

Insurance market reforms have been implemented in dozens of states. These reforms seek to guarantee issuance and renewal of insurance coverage, and to make coverage portable, limit preexisting condition limitations, and apply community rating. Two dozen states operate medical high-risk pools that offer coverage to individuals who cannot obtain it through the regular insurance market. A number of states have sought to change the buying habits of consumers through tax incentives and Medical Savings Accounts. Some states have provided a state tax break for unincorporated small businesses, the self-employed, and individuals purchasing coverage for themselves—groups that do not benefit from the same federal tax subsidy as individuals who receive coverage through larger businesses. Six states have adopted Medical Savings Account legislation that permits these accounts to be established on behalf of individuals, employees, or families. Designed to be used in conjunction with high-deductible "catastrophic" health plans, nonmedical withdrawals are penalized and deposits may be rolled over to accumulate from year to year. The intent of these plans is to make consumers as cost-conscious about their health care purchases as they are about everything else they buy.

Managed care

Another group of states, including, notably, Tennessee and Rhode Island, have made dramatically increased use of managed care for Medicaid recipients—and many uninsured individuals—the centerpiece of reform. Sixteen percent of Medicaid enrollees are now in some form of managed care, up from 10 percent in 1990 and 1 percent in 1983. States are following the trend of growth in HMO enrollment among the general population; states are not "leading with the poor" on managed care.

Several factors contribute to the momentum for managed care. States are desperate to control their health care spending, and many believe that managed care will have that controlling effect. State policymakers also believe that managed care means better care for low-income people, with improved coordination of services and increased use of primary care physicians in place of clinics and emergency rooms. Finally, the menu of other cost-saving techniques is not attractive—to save money, a state can cover fewer people, provide fewer services, reduce payment to providers, or employ a range of usually limited utilization review devices. None of these options is very appealing, and managed care looks good by comparison. A number of waiver requests that will allow additional states to enroll large segments of their Medicaid and uninsured populations in managed care are pending with the federal government.

The reach and the grasp

States have made tremendous progress in implementing reform, and the public by a wide margin now prefers state-based rather than national solutions to reform.[14] But despite their best efforts, the first lesson of state health care reform is that states cannot do the job alone.

States lack the financial resources, organizational capacity, control over the health care system, and flexibility (primarily on federal law and regulation) to implement comprehensive reform on their own. A recent study showed that even the states with the best track record on reform (Hawaii, Minnesota, and Oregon) were only able to cover between one-fifth and one-third of the uninsured population through their reform efforts.[15] This indicates that even the most ambitious and well-implemented reform program cannot assure universal coverage or provide for comprehensive cost control.

Perhaps most importantly, state health reform efforts may be bogging down. The failure of national health care reform reduced the momentum for change. Changes in governorships and party control of state legislatures has endangered some state efforts. Possible Medicaid caps and other cuts in federal funding would reduce the already limited resources available to states to finance reform, and would shift state attention from reform to retrenchment. While greater use of block grants might increase states' flexibility to act, it is likely that less federal money will flow to the states, further straining their financial capacity to implement reform. Some states may not have the staying power to implement reform: Washington is scaling back its reform plan, Florida is moving more slowly than planned, and Minnesota has shifted to a less ambitious timetable for full implementation.

States can do (and have done) a great deal—making a substantial dent in the number of uninsured in a state is a major accomplishment. Incremental reforms have addressed some of the most egregious problems in the health care system, and the use of managed care continues to grow in the states. But *federal* participation and help is necessary if reform is to deal fully with the core issues of cost and access, and this federal participation will have to take a more tangible form— such as funds to subsidize coverage for low-income persons—than simply increasing state flexibility.

The trade-off between speed and effectiveness of reform

"Do you want it right or do you want it fast?" This admonition also applies to implementing state health care reform. States have learned that there is a trade-off between implementing reform quickly and having implementation proceed more deliberately. Many states, such as Washington and Minnesota, have adopted a sequential model, where components are added to reform as the system (and its administrators) are prepared to absorb them. The risk of this strategy is that events will intervene to delay or block reform—a key manager may leave state service, a governor may lose an election, or opponents of reform may take the opportunity provided by sequential reform to organize in an effort to block continued progress.

On the other hand, by implementing reform quickly, a state can avoid these problems. Political will does not dissipate and opposition does not have time to coalesce. But these benefits come at a price. Consider the case of Tennessee's implementation of TennCare, its program to move the Medicaid population into managed care. The state attempted to implement the program in record time. In just a few months, all 750,000 Medicaid recipients were enrolled in two statewide and ten regional managed care organizations. Seven of these were newly established. In addition, over 300,000 previously uninsured people were also enrolled. The speed of implementation was made even more striking by the fact that Tennessee had limited previous experience with managed care—only 30,000 Medicaid beneficiaries had been enrolled in managed care prior to TennCare.

As might have been expected, implementation did not proceed smoothly. Many plans were not ready to receive the volume of patients assigned. Physician opposition to the plan caused many of them to sign up with plans late or not at all, leaving many individuals to choose a plan without knowing whether or not their doctor participated. Many individuals did not know where to go for care, and confusion was widespread—at the peak of implementation overload, 7,000 calls per hour were coming into 250 toll-free lines the state had hastily established. The situation appears to have improved, although physician opposition remains strong and some confusion persists about where patients are to go for care.

But the plan *was* implemented, opponents did not derail it, and problems are being addressed. There is a clear choice to be made: implement reform slowly and risk being stopped short of full implementation, or implement quickly, face some level of chaos, and troubleshoot problems over time. There is no one right choice. The lesson is to be strategically knowledgeable in considering the pros and cons of rapid versus sequential implementation, and not to stumble into an implementation strategy unaware of the trade-offs.

Mixed approaches: the market and the public sector

It is common to rely on a mix of public and private sector organizations to implement policy. For example, Medicare uses private intermediaries to run the program and process claims. The Job Training

Partnership Act (JTPA), which serves as the principal job training resource for welfare recipients and other low-income individuals, operates as a joint public/private enterprise. Moreover, developments in the health care marketplace are outpacing changes in public policy, and these leading private sector efforts can help guide and support state health care reform.

There is no reason to believe that states should adopt other than a mixed public/private model of reform. States have limited capacity to carry out the major functions needed to implement reform, and they must enlist help. At the same time, the public sector spends huge sums of money on health care and is responsible for large populations of vulnerable people, and these responsibilities cannot be ceded entirely to the private sector. The likely result, therefore, is a mixed system, with state government and private organizations, such as insurance companies, health care plans, physician group practices, and hospitals, sharing implementation tasks.

Purchasing alliances illustrate the likely emergence of mixed public/private administrative structures. Although the mega-alliances proposed in the Clinton plan and several congressional alternatives died with national health care reform, a number of states are using alliances to help provide coverage to those who cannot obtain it or afford it on their own, such as small businesses and uninsured individuals. California, Florida, and Texas have enrolled thousands of people in these alliances, and nearly half of the businesses that join alliances in Florida are providing insurance to their workers for the first time.[16] The Health Insurance Plan of California (HIPC) has brought thousands of small firms together into a purchasing pool and has reduced premiums by 15 percent.[17]

While these alliances use private insurance and negotiated arrangements with health plans, states finance a substantial portion of the care provided through alliances, set standards for alliance operations, and monitor alliance and health plan performance. Combined public standard-setting and financing, coupled with private sector operational responsibility, can support a winning strategy for implementing reform. State officials should seek out and actively help to build these public/private arrangements; the private sector as well as the federal government should be courted as a partner.

Integrating public programs into reform

Many health care reform proposals combine acute care services under Medicaid with other groups in the private insurance market. By this change, policymakers aim to eliminate categorical distinctions among low-income people and to create common criteria for insuring these groups. Washington, for example, is integrating its Medicaid population with other publicly financed populations, such as state employees. Others, notably Tennessee, are bringing the uninsured into managed care plans with Medicaid beneficiaries.[18]

State reform proposals are moving more slowly toward integration of Medicaid with other population groups than did 1994's crop of federal proposals, perhaps reflecting states' clearer sense of the dangers and difficulties of integrating Medicaid into the private insurance system. Proposals to "cap" Medicaid spending would make integration even more difficult; as Medicaid funds are squeezed by a cap, the difference between what Medicaid and private insurance would pay for services will increase, making providers less willing to give both groups equal access.

This is an important issue for state health care reform. Vulnerable low-income people, especially Medicaid recipients, could be put at risk if the transition to a unified system is handled badly. State health care reformers must tread carefully in this area.

Providers serving the poor, such as public hospitals and community health centers, are also at risk under reform. A recent report states: "Health care reform may threaten the viability of public hospitals and clinics that may not be able to compete in a new environment, marked by managed care, stiffer price competition, and less opportunity for cost shifting. To the extent that these providers are considered essential, states may financially assist these institutions in making the transition to a more competitive environment."[19] States may wish to make special provisions to protect these institutions, such as requiring health plans to contract with providers who have long-standing links to low-income people. States must decide what, if any, premium they are willing to pay to keep safety net providers viable as the health care system changes. As with integrating Medicaid, caution is needed: safety net providers are the only resource available for vulnerable people if new health care systems fail them.

Barriers to Successful Implementation of Health Care Reform

It is critical to identify barriers to the implementation of health care reform. As one observer noted: "Anticipating difficulties may permit them to be alleviated; being warned about roadblocks can lead to an altered route, not abandonment of the trip."[20] There will be no shortage of barriers for states to overcome. This chapter has already suggested several of them, including a complex and confusing array of functions to be sorted through and organized; many complex and new functions to be carried out; limited organizational capacity to do the job; the high cost of implementation, and the difficulty of maintaining commitment to reform over time. The following areas must be addressed if barriers are to be overcome and if health care reform is to be implemented.

Federal-state relations: flexibility, accountability, and the art of the deal

The year of grand reform plans was 1994; 1995 was the year of intergovernmental relations in health care reform, with a focus on identifying deals that can be struck between the federal and state governments. The astute policymaker will not ask what each level of government can do alone, but what they can do together, and how responsibilities will be divided among levels of government.

If national reform had been enacted, the issue would be how to draw the lines of authority between the federal and state governments. In general, the federal government would have set broad guidelines for reform, such as global budgets or caps on spending, basic benefit plans, a framework for financing reform, and a package of health insurance market reforms. It would also have adjusted this framework over time as lessons were learned during implementation.

Within this framework, states would have performed the broad set of tasks suggested in this chapter, including policing alliances and health insurers, promoting access and creative arrangements for delivering care, and monitoring quality.

The failure of national reform has changed the nature of the federal-state relationship in reform, but not its importance or its contentiousness. One veteran observer of federalism concluded that "states feel victimized by the federal government . . . state administrators—particularly good state administrators and good governors and people who want to do things well—feel that they are on the receiving end of a very, very long pipeline that has no feedback loops whatever; that there is no way in which Washington understands what they need; and there is no way in which Washington is systematically learning from them."[21] On the other hand, many in the federal government resist granting broad discretion to the states, fearing that they will stress cost control to the point of putting at risk persons dependent on government services.

The difference in perspective will be played out on two major issues: the Employee Retirement and Income Security Act (ERISA) and federal waivers to permit states to continue to experiment with health care reform.

ERISA

Enacted in 1974 in response to concerns about the management of pension plans, ERISA applies to all employee benefit plans, including health plans. Businesses that leave the regulated insurance market and opt to self-insure receive protection under ERISA, which in turn exempts them from state insurance regulations and, through court interpretations, from many other state mechanisms necessary to control health care costs and expand access. Nationwide, nearly two-thirds of the insured working population are in firms that self-insure.[22]

ERISA is a critical barrier to comprehensive state health reform. Its greatest impact results not from its requirements, but rather from what it prevents the states from doing. ERISA precludes states from requiring all employers to offer health insurance, from regulating or taxing self-insured plans, from taxing or assessing surcharges on employer welfare benefit plans, and from mandating that specific benefits be covered by employer health plans. Without exemptions from the provisions of ERISA, states cannot implement employer-based tax-financed plans, "pay or play" employer mandates, provider taxes earmarked for coverage of the uninsured, or uncompensated care pools that use a surcharge on rates to expand coverage. Even the effectiveness of insurance market reform is reduced by ERISA, since self-insured plans are exempted from their provisions. Broad court interpretations of ERISA could also stop states from enacting individual mandates or publicly funded plans that supplant employer-based coverage.[23]

States are hamstrung by these restrictions and maintain that the provisions preclude even modest efforts to cover the uninsured, let alone comprehensive reform. Several leading reform states, notably Washington and Minnesota, contend that ERISA makes it impossible for them to stabilize or complete their reform efforts, in large part because ERISA blocks implementation of employer mandates. In general, state officials consider ERISA to be a make or break issue for state reform, and that reform is on life support without relief from the provisions of ERISA.

Predictably, business has a different view on the role of ERISA and on the desirability of providing exemptions to states. Business representatives argue that if industry is to control health benefit costs and retain flexibility, they need uniform standards that preempt state regulation of employer plans. Multistate employers fear that exemptions from ERISA will create a patchwork quilt of state reform efforts, requiring them to deal with different systems in each state where they do business.

Currently, only Hawaii has an ERISA exemption, granted by Congress as part of that state's reform effort. While further exemptions could be granted through similar special congressional action, there is little affection for a policy based on the states' scrambling for special legislation. Some state and congressional leaders have suggested a waiver process for states on ERISA, similar to the Medicaid waiver process. Senator Daniel Patrick Moynihan has observed that "the failure to enact national reform shouldn't be allowed to prevent states from moving ahead with their own reforms. In fact, in the absence of universal coverage, you must allow state flexibility, fostered by ERISA waivers."[24] Business opposition would make this a controversial and difficult proposal, however, and success is far from certain.

The Reforming States Group, a consortium of leaders from two dozen states that have enacted reform, is pursuing another strategy. Members are meeting with business groups and congressional staff to find a compromise solution that would enhance state flexibility to implement reform while still addressing business concerns. Possible approaches include establishing stricter standards for businesses that wish to self-insure, thereby reducing the number of firms insulated from state health care reform initiatives, or narrowing the scope of ERISA exemptions sought.

The ERISA debate also sets up a conflict of values for many in Congress. Some congressmen support providing flexibility to states and shifting responsibility for public programs from the federal gov-

ernment to the states. They will be responsive when the states urge
the federal government to lead, follow, or get out of the way on health
reform. On the other hand, these same individuals might also be sym-
pathetic toward the view that it is impractical for multistate businesses
to deal with 50 different state reform systems. The danger is that no
agreement will be reached between these competing views and that
progress on state health reform will be blocked.

Waivers of federal law

Efforts underway in the states to expand eligibility and alter the way
in which care is organized and delivered often go beyond what is allowed under current federal law. In these cases, states must seek federal approval for their initiatives. Typically, this is done through a
statewide demonstration under Section 1115 of the Social Security
Act. Section 1115 permits the secretary of Health and Human Services to "waive" provisions of the Social Security Act to permit research and demonstration projects to promote program objectives.[25]
Less encompassing changes can be accomplished through Section
2175 or 2176 "program waivers," which do not require research or
full-scale evaluations, as do Section 1115 waivers. But many states are
finding that these provisions do not provide sufficient flexibility, since
they do not go far enough either to expand the categories of people
that can be covered or to mandate enrollment into managed care
plans.[26]

    In large part, Section 1115 waivers fuel state reform efforts.
Several states, including Oregon, Hawaii, Rhode Island, Kentucky,
Tennessee, Florida, Massachusetts, and South Carolina have been
granted waivers to institute eligibility, benefit, and service delivery
changes in their Medicaid programs in order to implement reform.
Proposals are pending from Ohio, Massachusetts, Missouri, Minnesota, New Hampshire, Delaware, and Illinois.

    These waivers modify eligibility standards to expand coverage,
change the standard methodology used to determine financial eligibility for Medicaid, permit mandatory enrollment of beneficiaries into
managed care plans, and eliminate disproportionate share payments
for hospitals and convert the funds into insurance for individuals. The
state reforms instituted under waiver authority include Rhode Island's and Tennessee's mandatory enrollment of Medicaid recipients
into managed care, Oregon's plan that replaced a defined set of benefits in Medicaid with coverage based on prioritized treatments and

diagnoses, and Hawaii's and Florida's efforts to extend Medicaid to low-income individuals ineligible for traditional Medicaid benefits.[27]

Three questions cloud the future of waiver-based reform: (1) How far will states go with waiver requests? (2) How flexible will the federal government be in granting waivers? and (3) How stable are the state reform systems based on waivers?

States have pushed the envelope with waiver requests, seeking broader eligibility for their programs and more matching federal funds to help pay for reform. The limits of federal tolerance for waivers that move the Medicaid program farther from its initial limits, and (in the eyes of some federal officials) raid the Treasury, have not been tested.

While most agree that the federal process for reviewing and approving waivers has been streamlined, states maintain that it is still an arduous process, replete with application requirements and the need to answer endless questions. It will be an ongoing struggle to find a balance between the flexibility to allow states to experiment and federal accountability needed to assure that state actions are "budget neutral" (do not increase total spending) and protective of the interests of public program beneficiaries.

Waivers are granted for a limited period of time, usually three to five years. Arguably, permanent policy change in the states should not rest on waivers. The issue remains of how the transition will occur from acting under waiver authority to operating ongoing state reform programs.

The future of waivers is murky in a federal environment marked by calls for increased state flexibility. The line must be drawn between which actions will require waivers and which of them the states will be able to pursue on their own, under the banner of increased state flexibility. This issue is part of the ongoing debate between the states and the federal government on their respective roles and responsibilities.

Senators Robert Graham of Florida and Mark Hatfield of Oregon—both former governors—proposed the "Health Innovation and Partnership Act" in the midst of last year's rush to cobble together a congressional compromise on health care reform. The bill would have made special provision for states to apply for and receive waivers on Medicaid, the Maternal Child Health Block Grant, the Social Services Block Grant, and the Public Health Services Act. Equally important, grant funds ($50 billion over five years) would have been made available for approved state innovation projects to help with the costs of implementing health care reform in the states.

This decentralization proposal took the position that if national reform is not on the horizon, state reform should not end with it and, in fact, failure to pass a national plan should cause the federal government to help the states as an alternative. This approach will be one strand of the ongoing health care reform debate, and its outcome will determine in large part whether state efforts will remain robust.

Recommendations for Policymakers

This chapter has had two storylines: (1) although the quality of implementation in large part determines the success of policy initiatives, it is a largely ignored element of health care reform; and (2) states have an important role to play in the drama of reform but only limited capacity to do the job, and they face substantial barriers in their implementation efforts.

In response, policymakers should:

- Make implementation a central element in evaluating proposals for health care reform, on a par with the cost of the initiative and its likely impact on access to care;
- Clarify the respective federal and state roles in reform, so that implementation responsibilities are clear and reform efforts are marked by cooperation rather than conflict—at least to the extent possible;
- Build state capacity to implement reform, through financial assistance to pay for implementation, technical assistance to share lessons learned elsewhere, and research to address open questions;
- Recognize that federal efforts to control spending in programs such as Medicaid will also impede the implementation of state-based reform, as the states retrench to cope with reduced federal revenue;
- Assess models of administering reform, so that states can make more informed decisions about how to organize and manage their reform efforts;
- Study and disseminate information on state reform efforts, to extract lessons for implementation, assess what works, and identify useful strategies and tactics;
- Build public/private partnerships to implement reform, to take advantage of the strengths of both sectors. Dramatic

changes are emerging in the health care system and this new world calls for more cooperative arrangements;

- Consider the advantages and disadvantages of immediate versus sequential implementation, to permit a rational decision on how quickly implementation should proceed; and

- Use implementation decisions to lessen the risks accompanying health care reform, and to minimize the potential impact of reform on vulnerable people—the poor, sick, and disabled—and on safety net providers, such as public hospitals.

While these proposals are obvious, mustering the will to address implementation properly has been difficult. But the health care system is still in trouble. The issues that propelled health care reform to the top of the national agenda—increasing costs and decreasing access—have not changed, and the debate will be renewed around them. As one observer put it, "Policymakers have an obligation not only to conceptualize the best policy but also to increase the chances that it will work."[28] As the United States achieves health care reform—state by state or through national efforts—too much is at stake to leave its implementation to chance.

Notes

1. R. P. Nathan, "Giving Birth to an Elephant: Implementing National Health Care Reform." (Champaign: University of Illinois, Institute of Government and Public Affairs, 6 May 1994).
2. "Whatever the Reform Plan, CBO sees Administrative Problems—from Subsidies to Penalty Taxes," *Health Care Reform Week* 23, no. 31 (8 August 1994).
3. *Health Care Reform Week* 1994.
4. General Accounting Office, *Health Care Reform—Potential Difficulties in Determining Eligibility for Low-Income People* (Washington, DC: GAO, July 1994).
5. State of Washington, *Responsibilities under Health Reform by Lead State Agencies,* (Olympia, 1993).
6. D. Altman and D. Morgan, "The Role of State and Local Government in Health," *Health Affairs* 2 (Winter 1983).
7. L. D. Brown, "Implementing Health Reform: What the States Face," in *Making Health Reform Work,* edited by J. J. DiIulio, Jr. and R. P. Nathan (Washington, DC: The Brookings Institution, 1994), 147–54.
8. R. D. Reischauer, Letter to Richard Nathan, 16 May 1994.
9. General Accounting Office (GAO), *Health Insurance Regulation: Wide*

Variation in States' Authority, Oversight, and Resources (Washington, DC: GAO, December 1993).

10. Nathan 1994.

11. J. Cosgrove, in *American Healthline* 3, no. 139 (17 October 1994).

12. J. Holahan, *An Overview of State Health Reform* (Washington, DC: The Urban Institute, April 1994).

13. The Intergovernmental Health Policy Project, "Health Care Reform: 50 State Reform Profiles" (July 1994).

14. R. J. Blendon, The Voters' Health Care Agenda for the 104th Congress and Public Understanding of the Major Entitlement Programs and the Federal Budget, *Kaiser/Harvard/KRC National Election Night Survey* (Cambridge, MA: Harvard University, November 1994).

15. D. Lipson, *Keeping the Promise? Achieving Universal Health Coverage in Six States* (Washington, DC: Alpha Center, September 1994).

16. D. Cook, in "Kaiser Family Foundation/Health Care Reform," (National Public Radio, 17 October 1994, Patricia Neyman reporting).

17. D. Helms, "Lessons from Voluntary Efforts to Expand Health Insurance Coverage and Implications for Health Care Reform," Testimony before the U.S. Senate Committee on Finance (1 February 1994).

18. B. B. Manard, et al. "Implementing Health Care Reform: Issues and Options for State Executives" (Lewin-VHI Inc., Executive Summary, September 1994).

19. Manard et al. 1994.

20. C. Brecher, "Introduction and Overview," in *Implementation Issues and National Health Care Reform,* edited by C. Brecher (Washington, DC: Josiah Macy Jr. Foundation, June 1992).

21. F. P. Chisman, in *National Health Care Reform: What Should the State Role Be?,* edited by F. P. Chisman, L. D. Brown, and P. J. Larson (Washington, DC: National Academy of Social Insurance, 31 August 1994).

22. P. A. Butler, *Roadblock to Reform: ERISA Implications for State Health Care Initiatives* (Washington, DC: National Governors' Association, 1994).

23. D. Helms, "The Robert Wood Johnson Foundation State Initiatives in Health Care Reform Program." Presented at the Grantmakers in Health Annual Washington Briefing (Washington, DC, 14 November 1994).

24. G. Anders, "Some State Health Plans May Be Stalled if Congress Fails to Pass a Bill this Fall," *Wall Street Journal* (16 September 1994).

25. S. Rosenbaum and J. Darnell, "Statewide Medicaid Demonstrations: Overview of Approved and Proposed Activities under Section 1115 of the Social Security Act" (Washington, DC: Center for Health Policy Research, The George Washington University, November 1994).

26. Alpha Center, "Medicaid Waivers Programs: Lessons for the Future or Time-Limited Experiments?" *State Initiatives in Health Care Reform* (Washington, DC: Alpha Center, May-June 1994).

27. Rosenbaum 1994.

28. J. J. DiIulio, Jr., D. F. Kettl, and R. P. Nathan. *Making Health Reform Work: Implementation, Management, and Federalism* (Washington, DC: The Brookings Institution, Center for Public Management, April 1994).

7

The Role of Quality Measurement in a Competitive Marketplace

Arnold M. Epstein

Abstract. Quality measurement is not a new idea. However, in recent years, several new trends have gained prominence: greater interest in publicly reported information on quality of care, access to care, and patient satisfaction; an increased focus on health plans and integrated systems of care rather than on institutional providers and practitioners as the unit of observation; wide adoption of the techniques of continuous quality improvement within the health care sector; increased use of clinical practice guidelines to improve care for a broad range of medical conditions; incorporation of computer technology into the clinical setting; and greater appreciation for health outcomes as a measure of quality of care.

This chapter first reviews the changes in the medical landscape that have seeded these trends and the distinction between quality assurance and quality improvement. It then focuses on public policy concerns, in particular on the emergence of publicly disseminated information about quality of care, now often called "quality report cards." The major prototypes of these reports developed to date, the responses to quality reporting by different members of the delivery system, and the major criticisms of this approach are reviewed. The chapter concludes by predicting probable developments and the strategies most likely to move health care forward in a productive direction.

Quality measurement is not a new idea.[1-5] In fact, quality assessment and quality assurance in health care date back to at least the mid-nineteenth century, when Florence Nightingale calculated and published the mortality rates of London hospitals and then used the data to suggest changes in ward configuration and sanitation that reduced mortality.[6,7] In recent years, several new trends have gained prominence: greater interest in publicly reported information on quality of care, access to care, and patient satisfaction; an increased focus on health plans and integrated systems of care rather than on institutional providers and practitioners as the unit of observation; wide adoption of the techniques of continuous quality improvement within the health care sector; increased use of clinical practice guidelines to improve care for a broad range of medical conditions; incorporation of computer technology into the clinical setting; and greater appreciation for health outcomes as a measure of quality of care.

These trends represent the wave of the future. In the coming years, they will have a dramatic impact on how providers judge the quality of their care of patients, and on how they use that information and other data on the effectiveness of medical practices to improve their performance. These trends will also affect how purchasers of health care choose among competing health plans and how individual patients select institutional providers and practitioners.

This chapter first reviews the changes in the medical landscape that have seeded these trends and the distinction between quality assurance and quality improvement. It then focuses on the emergence of publicly disseminated information on quality of care, now often called "quality report cards." The major prototypes of these reports developed to date, the responses to quality reporting by different members of the delivery system, and the major criticisms of this approach are reviewed. The chapter concludes by predicting probable developments and the strategies most likely to move health care forward in a productive direction.

Changes in the Medical Landscape

The medical landscape has recently changed in a number of important ways: increased competition, greater emphasis on measuring the outcomes of care, and evolution of the delivery system in response to greater integration of care, expanding scientific knowledge, and advances in computer technology.

Increased competition

In the past two decades and especially in the past few years, the medical marketplace has consolidated and become much more competitive. Health maintenance organizations (HMOs) have evolved and proliferated. Independent practice associations (IPAs) have expanded more rapidly than traditional staff and group models, and hybrids such as preferred provider organizations (PPOs) and point-of-service (POS) plans have emerged and spread. In 1976, 175 HMOs served approximately 6 million enrollees; HMOs now number 550 and serve approximately 51 million enrollees.[8]

Managed care organizations increasingly use financial incentives to influence physician and patient behavior. More than two-thirds of existing HMOs—encompassing more than half the HMO populations—are for-profit organizations. Further, the use of managed care for Medicaid and Medicare recipients is rapidly evolving. As of July 1995, more than 11 million Medicaid recipients were participating in some sort of managed care arrangement.[9] Recently, several states undertook commitments to cover their entire Medicaid population through managed care organizations.

Measuring the outcomes of care

Although measurement of outcomes dates back to Nightingale[10] and Codman,[11] emphasis on outcomes measurement has become more pronounced in recent years.[12–16] Part of the impetus for this change in emphasis springs from the work of researchers at Dartmouth Medical School and at RAND, who have documented substantial geographic differences in the use of medical services.[17–20] These geographic differences, which persist even after adjustment for comorbidity and severity of illness, raise troubling questions about unnecessary costs in high-use regions or suboptimal care in low-use regions. Assessment of quality, and especially of health outcomes, is the obvious first step in addressing these questions.

Greater availability of clinical and administrative databases and increased computer capability have affected our ability to measure outcomes and related indexes of quality of care. State-based rate-setting commissions and third-party payers such as the Health Care Financing Administration (HCFA) have developed administrative databases that contain both clinical and billing data. Although the clinical information available on these databases is limited, it has been used by researchers, health care providers, and others to measure outcomes such as hospitalization, readmission, mortality, and other indexes of quality of care. Widespread availability of affordable, portable computers and work stations simplifies these analyses and makes their results more easily accessible.

Recent years have seen a major expansion in the types of outcome indicators that physicians and policymakers are willing to consider as valid indicators of health. These outcomes go far beyond traditional clinical indicators of health status such as mortality, comorbid disease and complications, and the biochemical and physiologic markers that have so often been used as endpoints in clinical studies in the past. Newer indicators include a variety of indexes generally assessed by interview and self-report questionnaire: functional status, neuropsychiatric function, social function, and emotional health. Health care providers and policymakers alike now increasingly recognize that these sorts of measures, based on subjective reports from patients, can provide valuable data about health that often are not covered in other indexes. Moreover, these data can be collected as reliably as many traditional measures.

Changes in the delivery system

Expansion of the scientific database underlying clinical medicine has led to many therapeutic advances, but it has also complicated clinical care. It has become difficult for practicing physicians to determine for each disease whether each new scientific advance warrants a change in the way they care for their patients. Marked geographic variations in patterns of care, along with evidence that a substantial proportion of medical care may be unnecessary,[21] have fueled concern about quality of care and inappropriate use of resources. Clinical practice guidelines developed by experts have increasingly been used to amalgamate the accumulated evidence from clinical trials and effectiveness research and to provide practicing doctors with general recommendations for the care of their patients.

Many organizations have developed clinical practice guidelines.[22] Prominent among these organizations is the Agency for Health Care Policy and Research, which was established in 1989 with a specific legislative mandate to develop guidelines. Other Public Health Service agencies, including the National Institutes of Health, the Centers for Disease Control and Prevention, and the Food and Drug Administration, issue guidelines on specific topics relevant to their mission. More than 35 physicians' organizations and national medical specialty societies have developed some form of practice guidelines.[23]

Many managed care organizations have formulated algorithms for care based on federally developed guidelines or modifications of the guidelines. Some organizations have redesigned their delivery systems to facilitate care in conformance with guidelines and have tracked the effects of their efforts in quality improvement by measuring progress on guideline-related performance measures over time.

Finally, as in so many other fields, the impact of advances in computer technology is dramatic. In many areas of the United States, computers have been incorporated into the fabric of clinical care. In hospitals, computers facilitate physicians' orders for tests and services and provide educational prompts for cost-effective care. In the ambulatory setting, computers speedily report results of diagnostic tests carried out in distant locations. Increasingly, computers are used to bind together disparate sites in integrated service networks. More than ever before, the technology is in place for online support to give physicians and other health care providers information both on their own practice patterns and on the effectiveness of specific medical interventions.

Increasing competition, consolidation, and other changes in the delivery system have sparked demands for quality measurement and have changed the way information on quality is used. Formerly, the audience was internal; information on quality remained confidential within the health plan or institution and was used by health care providers and managers to assess performance and guide quality assurance. Now, much more than before, the audience is external. Although competition in the medical marketplace is based largely on price, purchasers have begun to demand data on quality to balance their economic concerns. Increased competition, evolution toward for-profit managed care, financial incentives encouraging physicians to reduce utilization of medical resources, and increasing enrollment of publicly supported Medicaid recipients and Medicare beneficiaries in managed care organizations have also made governmental policymakers wary of a potential deterioration in quality. Information on quality given to third-party payers provides accountability and a tool with which to detect problems in quality of care.

Information on quality is still used internally, although, as discussed next, the focus has changed. Traditional quality assurance now receives less emphasis since many health plans and institutional providers have adopted the techniques of continuous quality improvement that other industries have successfully used.

Quality Assurance and Quality Improvement

Quality assurance and quality improvement have come to represent two very different approaches to managing quality of care. These approaches have different roots and different characteristics.[24,25]

Quality assurance

Institutional quality assurance began to develop during the 1960s. Before that time, quality control had largely been the province of individual physicians, their professional organizations, and the state, which exercised its responsibility to the public interest through licensure. By the early 1960s, advances in medical science were taking place so rapidly that they had begun to affect the organization of health services.[26] The emerging variety and complexity of health care technologies made it important for different types of health care personnel—physicians, nurses, nutritionists, phlebotomists, radiologic technicians—to work together in hospitals, group practices, and other settings. Responsibility for the quality of care and its cost could no longer lie solely with individual physicians, patients, and the state.

During the 1970s, quality assurance became mandatory for hospitals[27,28] through two mechanisms. The first was accreditation by the (then) Joint Commission for the Accreditation of Hospitals (JCAH); such accreditation was virtually required for a hospital to be certified as a Medicare provider. The second mechanism consisted of the review programs administered by the Professional Standards Review Organizations (PSRO) for Medicare and Medicaid. Medical auditing of hospital care to assure adherence to quality standards was an integral component of JCAH accreditation. Originally, JCAH standards were based almost exclusively on structural aspects of patient care. Since 1978, JCAH has tried to revise these standards in ways that will impel hospitals to examine and improve their organizational and clinical performance. Hospitals are required to monitor patient care, to identify and resolve problems, and to evaluate the impact of quality assurance activities. JCAH was renamed JCAHO (Joint Commission for the Accreditation of Healthcare Organizations) in August 1987, to signal the widening of its scope.

The PSRO program used three techniques: medical care evaluation, utilization review, and profile analysis.[29-31] Medical care evaluation used prescriptive criteria to assess the process or outcomes of care

Figure 7.1   The Quality of Care Curve

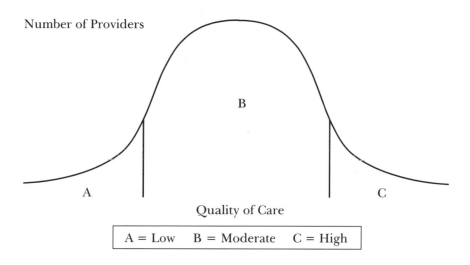

Number of Providers

B

A   C

Quality of Care

| A = Low | B = Moderate | C = High |

for particular groups of patients. Cases that failed to meet explicit criteria were subject to further implicit review by a physician. Utilization review also involved case-by-case explicit and implicit review but focused on the necessity of hospital admission and the appropriateness of length of stay. Profile analysis studied hospital claims databases to determine which hospitals and physicians had overused services and for which diagnoses and procedures.

Traditional quality assurance as exemplified by these JCAH and PSRO activities was not popular with health care providers and probably did not lead to major improvements in quality of care or to large reductions in medical costs.[32-37] Inertia within bureaucratic institutions impeded the initiatives promoted by JCAH. Hospitals often sought to comply on paper rather than in reality. Too often, physicians saw both internal and external quality review as an attack on their professional autonomy.

Critics of quality assurance see it as weak and misdirected. In particular, they are concerned about the emphasis on inspection.[38] In traditional quality assurance, inspection is used to identify outliers (see Figure 7.1: outliers are the providers represented by group A), and quality is improved by forcing those whose practice is of especially poor quality to change their behavior. No one argues that egregious behavior should be tolerated. The problem from the viewpoint of quality improvement arises when leaders *rely* on inspection to achieve improvement. Moreover, if overdone, inspection can have a downside. Critics point out that the preponderance of care is delivered by groups B and C, and that the fear inspired by inspection may drive the great mass of providers in group B to divert attention from other important activities in order to prove that they are not in group A.

Quality improvement

The theories of continuous quality improvement (CQI) or total quality management (TQM) have their philosophical and technical underpinnings in a set of managerial and statistical methods that were developed decades ago by Americans and were first applied on a broad scale in post-World War II industrial Japan.[39-47] Applications of these techniques in health care have now emerged because of shifts in the medical marketplace. Health care has become a mature industry. Prepaid groups and hospitals function increasingly as corporate health care providers, employing physicians and other health care workers and selling services competitively to patients or groups of patients who act as consumers. In this competitive atmosphere, it seems natural for health care organizations to adopt techniques for quality management that have proved successful for corporations in other industries.

At least six ideas are basic to CQI/TQM:[48-50]

- Imperfect systems and methods of work are often to blame for quality problems. Effort should be focused on system improvements that address underlying causes rather than solely on inspection for outliers and micromanagement of individual practices.

- Health care workers generally wish to provide the highest-quality care. Because the efforts of health care providers in organizations are interconnected, teamwork and cooperation must be encouraged while blame and fear are minimized.

- Because most health care is delivered by people who work in organizations, administrative structures within those organizations must provide the framework for improvement. Commitment to quality must be evident throughout the organization, from the highest levels on down.

- Quality can be continually improved through study, greater understanding of variation, experimentation with the processes of daily work, and innovation. There is no immutable ceiling to performance.

- Involvement of workers and customers is crucial to the process of improvement. Frontline workers must have the resources and statistical tools to effect meaningful change, and patients must be able to air their concerns and define their central needs.
- Improvement activities should recur in cycles and should include design of services, monitoring of consumer response, and subsequent redesign.

Use of quality measurement

Quality measurement is central to both quality assurance and quality improvement, although the focus and emphasis of measurement differ in the two approaches. In quality assurance, quality measurement has been used primarily to identify outliers (group A in Figure 7.1) and those whose performance is subpar. The ideal targets for measurement are those processes that are fully under the control of individual providers. In this situation a measurement can identify overuse, underuse, or misuse of diagnostic and therapeutic modalities. In quality improvement, measurement is used primarily to gauge overall system performance and responses to system redesign. Quality measurement also helps identify "positive outliers" (group C in Figure 7.1), who demonstrate standards of high-quality care. Although modern quality improvement does not abandon surveillance or inspection, especially in the control of serious defects, quality improvement deemphasizes these components.

Quality Report Cards

The forms of quality measurement just described will largely be used for internal purposes: to guide quality assurance and quality improvement activities within health care organizations. Although public distribution of information on quality dates back more than a century,[51,52] it has long been resisted. Only in the past decade has the health care field seen concentrated efforts to develop and disseminate information on quality indicators. As the concept has evolved, quality "report cards" have come to mean standardized reports on quality of care that are publicly released. The reports can cover health plans, institutions such as hospitals, or even individual practitioners.

The emergence of quality report cards is largely the result of increased competition in the medical marketplace, which has made large-scale purchasers of health care, most often employers, wary that health plans may stint on services to reduce price. Information on performance is seen as an aid to purchasers in seeking value in their contracting decisions and to consumers in making their health care choices. In this competitive model, consumer choice, based on quality as well as price, triggers economic forces that provide impetus for quality improvement.

One need not posit a competitive model to envision how quality report cards might be helpful. A tenet of quality improvement is that most health care providers intrinsically wish to provide the highest-quality care. Quality report cards can be educational. Publication of results across various settings can identify benchmarks for care. Studying the practices of innovative providers who deliver higher-quality care than their counterparts can yield insights that edify others. Perhaps most important, the technologies of quality measurement are fundamental to quality improvement. Widespread use of report cards is likely to speed the transport of these technologies and their use in quality improvement at the local level.

Quality report cards for hospitals

In 1987, HCFA provoked substantial controversy by releasing hospital mortality statistics on Medicare beneficiaries. HCFA originally intended to use these statistics as a screening device to identify outlier hospitals where closer quality review was warranted, not as a direct measure of quality. The data were to be considered confidential and to be used only by peer review organizations. The lay press, however, learned of the study and obtained access to the data through the Freedom of Information Act. Against HCFA's advice, the information was widely released, initiating controversy because the risk adjustments were crude. Similar data, based on improved statistical models, were released in subsequent years, although the release of these data was discontinued in 1993.

About 36 states now have some legislative mandate to examine hospitalization outcomes including mortality, length of stay, and charges, although what is done with these data varies from state to state.[53] Since 1990, three states—Pennsylvania, New York, and California—have released quality reports on hospital services. New York and Pennsylvania have both released risk-adjusted mortality rates for coronary artery bypass graft (CABG) surgery by hospital and surgeon. An excerpt from Pennsylvania's report card, released in February 1994, is included as Table 7.1.[54] Pennsylvania has released two additional Hospital Effectiveness Reports on patients in 53 diagnostic categories. These reports include the number and average severity of illness of patients admitted, the proportion of those patients over age 65, the actual and expected number of deaths, the mean length of stay, and mean charges. California has published information about the outcomes of patients who were hospitalized for myocardial infarction or who underwent back surgery.

Hospital report cards have also been developed through voluntary regional efforts. Since 1993, the Cleveland Health Quality Choice Program, a coalition of the Cleveland business community, area hospitals, and physicians has published semiannual reports that provide severity-adjusted data on mortality and length of stay, and on patient satisfaction with care.

Quality report cards for health plans

Multiple efforts have been made to develop report cards for health plans.[55] The most widely used is the Health Plan Employer Data and Information Set (HEDIS), which grew out of a partnership established in 1989 among health plans, employers, and the National Committee for Quality Assurance (NCQA). The current version, HEDIS 2.5, includes approximately 60 indicators of performance covering not only quality but also access to and satisfaction with care, membership and utilization, finance, and health plan management (Table 7.2 on pages 221 and 222).[56,57]

HEDIS has been very influential. In a recent nationally representative survey of 108 managed care plans,[58] more than 80 percent claimed to have reviewed HEDIS as a model for quality assessment. Sixty-one percent of surveyed plans reported actually measuring their performance according to at least one of the measures that HEDIS prescribes, including about three-quarters of the HMOs and one-fifth of the PPOs in the samples.

In 1993 and 1994, four health plans (Kaiser Permanente of Northern California, US Healthcare, United Healthcare, and Prudential Health Care) independently disseminated report cards on their own performance based at least in part on HEDIS 2. 0. Some of

Table 7.1 Adapted from a Report on Risk-Adjusted Mortality from Coronary Artery Bypass Graft Surgery

| Hospital, Physician Practice Group, and Surgeons | Treatment Effectiveness Measure | | | |
| | | Patients Who Died | | |
	Total Patients	Actual Number	Expected Range	Statistical Rating
Hamot Medical Center	498	24	11.7–26.1	△
D'Angelo Clinic	485	23	10.9–25.1	△
D'Angelo, George J.	161	7	2.1–10.0	△
Kish, George F.	66	5	0.3–6.0	△
Marshall, William Gene, Jr.	82	6	0.0–5.5	– '
Sardesai, Prabhaker G.	53	0	0.0–3.2	△
Tan, Wilfredo S.	123	5	1.1–8.6	△
Hanson & Associates, Inc.	13		less than 30 patients treated	
Hanson, Elbert L.	6		less than 30 patients treated	
Kerth, William J.	7		less than 30 patients treated	
Wilkes-Barre General Hospital/WVHCS	363	5	5.1–16.9	+
Cardiac Surgery Associates of Northeast Pennsylvania, PC	363	5	5.1–16.9	+
Anderson, John E.	140	1	0.1–7.5	△
Cimochowski, George E.	178	3	1.2–9.5	△
Harostock, Michael D.	45	1	0.0–3.9	△

Notes: Statistical Rating Key:
+ Fewer deaths than expected.
− More deaths than expected.
△ The number of deaths was not different than expected.
Hospitals and Physicians may have commented on this report. Copies are available upon request.
Source: Pennsylvania Health Care Cost Containment Council, 1991 data.

the report cards also included national and state standards as bench-marks. The report published by Kaiser Permanente of Northern California accorded more emphasis to measuring outcomes. For example, it included the stage at which breast cancer was diagnosed, with the rationale that this outcome indicates the effectiveness of breast cancer screening (Figure 7.2).[59]

More recently, NCQA reported results of a voluntary pilot project that rated and compared care in 21 health plans according to a subset of HEDIS 2.5. Consumer magazines in Washington, D.C. and St. Louis, Missouri have also used HEDIS to report on area health plans.

Other measures of health plan performance have also been used. In Massachusetts, 16 health plans jointly issued a report card on six quality indicators: hospital admissions for asthma; hospital readmissions for mental disorders; prenatal care during the first trimester; and rates of mammography, blood pressure screening, and cesarean section.

Response to report cards

Most of what is known about the impact of quality reports is anecdotal. Corporate purchasers have generally embraced the idea. Some large managed care organizations and HMOs have been in the forefront in developing report card measures. However, others have been more resistant. When the Federal Employee Health Benefits Program (FEHBP) tried to persuade participating health plans to comply voluntarily with a survey of member satisfaction, nearly 100 of 320 health plans providing care under the FEHBP declined,[60] citing such objections as choice of questions and size of survey sample.

Hospital administrators and health care providers were not enthusiastic about the quality reports developed early on through government mandate. A survey[61] of hospital leaders showed that they had a poor opinion of the original HCFA report card. The HCFA mortality reports, now discontinued, were a very different sort of report card from HEDIS 2.5 and were cruder than subsequent reporting efforts directed at hospitals.

The New York state experience offers insight into the response of hospitals and providers to the public release of information on quality.[62] In the initial releases of New York state data on risk-adjusted CABG mortality in 1989 and 1990, surgeon-specific rates were not included because the mean number of procedures performed by an individual surgeon was sometimes small and there was concern that

Table 7.2   Components of HEDIS 2.5

I. Quality (9 measures)
   A. Preventive Medicine
      • Childhood immunization
      • Cholesterol screening
      • Mammography screening
      • Pap smears for cervical cancer
   B. Prenatal Care
      • Low birth weight
      • Prenatal care in first trimester
   C. Acute and Chronic Disease
      • Asthma admissions/readmissions to emergency room/hospital
      • Diabetic retinal examination
   D. Mental Health and Substance Abuse
      • Ambulatory follow-up after hospital treatment of major affective disorders

II. Access and Patient Satisfaction (5 measures)
    A. Percentage of Members Age 42–64 with Plan Visit in Previous Two Years
       • Access
       • Number and percentage of primary care physicians accepting new patients
       • Provision of plan access standards for various types of visits and telephone response
    B. Member Satisfaction
       • Percentage of members who are "very satisfied" with the plan
       • Provision of plan satisfaction surveys

III. Membership and Utilization (approximately 20 measures)

- Membership: enrollment/disenrollment
- High occurrence/high cost: frequency and mean cost of five selected procedures—laminectomy, hysterectomy, coronary artery bypass grafting, angioplasty, and cardiac catheterization
- Global inpatient: medicine/surgery, maternity and newborns
- Ambulatory care: outpatient visits, emergency room visits, and ambulatory surgery
- Nonacute care: stays in nursing homes, rehabilitation facilities, hospices, transitional and respite facilities
- Maternity: total deliveries, with subdivision of vaginal births, cesarean sections, and vaginal births after cesarean section
- Newborns: well and complex newborns differentiated by length of stay
- Mental health: treatment on basis of inpatient, day/night, and outpatient locations
- Chemical dependency: treatment on basis of inpatient, day/night, and outpatient locations
- Outpatient drug utilization: mean cost and number of prescriptions per member

IV. Finance (approximately 15 measures)

- Indicators encompassing performance (income, loss rates), liquidity (cash on hard), efficiency (days in receivables), and compliance with statutory requirements (reserves)

V. Health Plan Management (approximately 15 measures)

- Indicators providing descriptive information on the provider network (board certification, turnover, compensation) and clinical management, including quality management, preventive care, case management, utilization review, and risk management

Figure 7.2   Excerpt from the Kaiser Permanente 1993 Quality Report Card

Measure	Performance	Relative Performance
Mammography Screening Rate	BENCHMARK 71.2%	No comparable benchmark
Breast Cancer Stage at Diagnosis*		
Local	BENCHMARK 63.9% 53.0%	Favorable distribution across stages
Regional	BENCHMARK 30.7% 37.0%	
Distant	BENCHMARK 4.0% 7.0%	
Breast Cancer 5-Year Survival Rate*		
Local	BENCHMARK 96.1% 92.7%	4% favorable
Regional	BENCHMARK 78.6% 71.1%	11% favorable
Distant	BENCHMARK 20.8% 17.8%	Not statistically different
Breast Cancer Mortality Rate (per 100,000 women)	BENCHMARK 29.8 28.1	Not statistically different

*Local: local stage; Regional: direct extension, regional lymph nodes, and regional lymph nodes and extension stages; Distant: distant metastasized stage.

the rates would be misleading. In 1991, the state was forced to release surgeon-specific information for 1989 through 1990 after losing a lawsuit to *Newsday* on the basis of the Freedom of Information Act. At that point the statewide leadership of practitioners of cardiology and cardiac surgery, represented by the Cardiac Advisory Committee (CAC), voted to recommend that hospitals withhold surgeons' identities (in the context of CABG mortality) from the state. Ultimately, a compromise was reached: the state and the CAC agreed that surgeon-specific data would be released only when the surgeon had performed at least 200 CABG procedures in the preceding three years.

Little is known about whether quality reports affect physicians' referral practices or patients' decisions concerning health plan, hospital, or doctor. The sparse and indirect evidence available suggests that the impact may be small. Vladeck and colleagues[63] found no change in the relative admission rates of high- and low-mortality hospitals (rated according to the HCFA data) during the second year after the original HCFA mortality reports came out. Hannan and colleagues[64] examined New York state data on CABG and likewise found no relation between changes in surgical volume across hospitals and risk-adjusted mortality rates.

Criticism of quality report cards

Quality report cards have many appealing aspects, but they also pose many problems.[65–69] When used to inform consumer choice they have been particularly controversial. Some of the following criticisms have been raised:

- Report card measures are incomplete, providing information on only a few of the many aspects of health care that are important.[70] For example, of 60 indicators of performance in HEDIS 2.5, only 9 assess quality of care (Table 7.2). Most of these nine quality indicators focus on the use of preventive services; only two focus on a health outcome (low birthweight) or a proxy for a health outcome (hospitalization for asthma).

- Risk adjustment is extremely difficult. In fact, because it is difficult, it is not included in HEDIS 2.5. Inaccurate measurements will mislead consumers, and providers may avoid caring for those who are severely ill or of lower socioeconomic status. Even when risk adjustment is included, it provides incentives for "upcoding." For example, after New York state began publicly reporting rates of risk-adjusted mortality from CABG surgery, there was a dramatic increase in the prevalence reported by hospitals of the comorbidities used in the state's risk-adjustment model.[71]

- It is difficult to assure timely presentation of data, comparable measurements across plans, and reliable calculation of indicators while minimizing expense and burden.

- Morbidity and rare but important complications of care are difficult to assess, particularly at the level of the practitioner, where small numbers hamper the evaluation of many aspects of care.

- "Statistically significant" differences in care are expected on the basis of chance alone.

- Consumers are likely to find the information provided confusing, and may make decisions based on differences that are not statistically meaningful or clinically important.

Experts are also concerned that public release of information will alienate health care providers and that the attendant publicity will have deleterious consequences. Rather than serving as an impetus for the improvement of health care through system redesign, public exposure may encourage health plans to take expedient steps to improve *measured* performance; for example, plans may recruit a different mix of patients, eliminate physicians with bad statistics, or "game" the system by focusing on components of care assessed on the report card to the detriment of other aspects of care. Critics also worry that some indicators will be incorporated into report cards without adequate scientific proof that they are truly related to quality of care. The General Accounting Office, for example, points out that HEDIS requires health plans to report the percentage of primary care physicians who are board certified, although in most studies board certification has been found to have no correlation with performance.[72]

Moving ahead with quality reporting

During the past few years, when the controversy over comprehensive health care reform was at its height, it was easy to fall under the illusion that regular dissemination of uniform quality measures would soon be national policy, *de facto* if not *de jure*. Several states initiated statewide reporting systems for hospitals. Voluntary coalitions of employers and health plans developed prototypical report cards for health plans and embarked on several rounds of pilot testing. Not only the Clinton administration's proposal for comprehensive health care reform but also its competitors' plans—legislative proposals from Congresssman Cooper from Tennessee and Senator Chafee from Rhode Island—included provisions to develop federally mandated quality report cards.

Comprehensive health care reform is now dead. With the failure of the Congress to pass legislation, the prospect of a national reporting system covering all patient groups is likely lost. Two critical factors that would have pushed the report card movement ahead are now gone: (1) large-scale infusion of federal resources into efforts to develop measures and (2) national regulation to ensure standardized reporting. How, then, should health care policymakers proceed? The following stratcgics arc proposed to move health care forward in a productive direction.

1. Stay the course: don't give up the ship. Failure of comprehensive health care reform need not preclude progress in quality reporting. The competitive environment will be an impetus for standardized quality measurement and improved measures. Health plans are besieged by employers' requests for information on quality. Standardization will reduce the burden of health plans in trying to meet multiple demands and will produce information that will allow employers to compare practice patterns across plans. Thus national and regional consortia of organizations will likely continue voluntarily to provide data based on HEDIS 2.5 or other new measures as the technology of measurement evolves.

The dramatic growth in Medicaid managed care may also propel health care forward. NCQA has recently developed Medicaid HEDIS, a version of HEDIS targeted for the Medicaid population. States that develop programs of Medicaid managed care or pursue comprehensive reform may require that health plans report Medicaid HEDIS or other standardized information on quality of care. Finally, HCFA may move forward with a report card for elderly beneficiaries cared for in HMOs, although at present such a measure would apply to only a small proportion of Medicare beneficiaries.

2. Don't overdrive the headlights. Like the airplane flown by the Wright brothers, HEDIS 2.5 is both an important achievement and a primitive instrument. Those who use this tool and its successors must be careful not to promise more than they can deliver. At present, data from consumer surveys on access to and satisfaction with care and clinical data on preventive services are available. Although these data can address a range of issues important to comsumers, quality report cards contain only limited information about broader aspects of quality. Thus, it is critical to continue work to develop the scientific basis of quality measurement.

With sufficient resources, the existing store of quality measures could be significantly expanded. Within three to five years, quality indicators for a number of common medical conditions, including coronary heart disease and low-back pain could be developed. Existing clinical practice guidelines for these conditions should facilitate the development of quality indicators.

If efforts to develop new measures continue, quality report cards can become an important aid to quality improvement. Yet even over the longer term (five to ten years), important limitations to the usefulness of this tool will likely remain. Quality report cards will never be comprehensive, and report cards by themselves will never guarantee that important aspects of the quality of care provided by health plans have not deteriorated.

3. Don't let the perfect be the enemy of the good. Quality report cards need not be perfect to be helpful. Indeed, with ever increasing price competition, their input may be critical. Imagine if health plans reported only on price and never on performance.

While quality report cards do not allow for fine distinctions among health plans, they can help identify health plans of either outstanding or seriously substandard quality. As a case in point, *Consumer Reports* is similarly imprecise. This popular magazine often rates products on a numeric scale and then categorizes them into three groups reflecting very high, medium, and very low quality. Many people nevertheless consider this publication an important aid to their decision making.

Quality report cards can be helpful even in geographic areas with a population insufficient to support health care competition. Information on practice patterns can, by itself, motivate health care providers to improve care.

4. Think strategically in quality measurement. Administrative databases, enrollee surveys, and medical records all can contribute data to assessments of quality of care. As reflected in these data, the triad of structure, process, and outcome provides an enormous menu of performance measures that could be included in report cards. From this large group, how are suitable measures best identified? Strategy in developing and choosing measures is particularly important because perfect measures of quality do not exist.

Table 7.3 lists desirable characteristics for quality indicators or groups of quality indicators used in report cards. The rationale is obvious in most cases but may require explanation in several instances. Performance on quality measures should vary widely among the health plans, hospital providers, and practitioners included in the report, and these variations should identify clinically important differences. A measure in which everyone gets a perfect score will not be helpful. The battery of measures should represent the range of services delivered by the health care organization. Any battery of measures will serve only as a biopsy of the care provided, but the sampling should be as broad as possible. When feasible, measures for health plans should be population based, reflecting the quality of care for all enrollees, not just those who seek care. Quality indicators should assess aspects of care that are important because of their high prevalence or their marked impact on morbidity, mortality, or the cost of care. Indicators should be sensitive to changes induced by the conservation of resources.

Quality indicators should be updated at appropriate intervals. Specifically, the measures should reflect changing medical knowledge; some measures should remain unchanged to allow an assessment of progress over time; and new measures should be developed and

Table 7.3   Desirable Characteristics of Quality Indicators or Groups of Quality Indicators for Use in Report Cards

---

- Reliability
- Validity, based on scientific evidence of effectiveness
- Minimal burden in data collection
- Appropriate risk adjustment
- Measures of outcome related to care under control of providers
- Reflective of aspects of care with an important impact on mortality, morbidity, and/or cost
- Sensitivity to changes induced by conservation of resources
- Variation in performance among the entities rated
- Representative of the services delivered by health care organizations
- Population-based measures for health plans when feasible
- Modifiable over time
  - Updated to reflect changing medical knowledge
  - Core measures retained to assess temporal trends
  - New quality measures developed to prevent gaming

---

added so that organizations cannot easily subvert the purpose of measurement by improving only those few aspects of care measured by the report card.

5. *The devil is in the details.* The standards in Table 7.3 are easy to understand, but many of them are difficult to meet. At least three of the criteria should be emphasized because they pose particular operational difficulties or are controversial.

Requiring that quality indicators be reliable seems like a first principle. But this is easier said than done.[73] Different data sources will be used to calculate measures in different settings. In many staff model HMOs, for example, claims data do not exist, whereas in indemnity practice complete chart data are difficult to obtain. Even among health plans that maintain claims-based payment, there is wide variability in coding, enrollment and provider updating, and quality assurance.[74]

Quality measures should be based on scientific evidence of effectiveness. The well-known method for determining appropriateness developed by investigators at RAND includes extensive review of the literature to determine effectiveness but also employs physician judgment to fill gaps where the scientific literature is lacking. This approach reflects the state-of-the-art, and use of this tool has taught us much—although it will not always work for quality report cards. Measures of appropriateness that depend largely on consensus will not be accepted readily by many clinicians across the country. The level of scientific evidence required for publicly released quality measures should be very high.

Quality measures must include appropriate risk adjustment or stratification lest misleading information is produced that inadvertently gives health plans an incentive to avoid patients who are severely ill or of low socioeconomic status. We must be content to focus on the process of care more than on its outcomes, at least until much better risk adjustment becomes possible. If quality measures are clinical, they must include sufficient detail to convince clinicians. Except for preventive services, this requirement will generally entail the abstraction of chart data for subsets of patients.

Much of the criticism of quality report cards is not based on theory or ideology. Rather, it focuses on operational issues. The success of quality report cards will depend on whether or not these sorts of technical problems are solved.

6. Make the Methods Clear. Private companies and health plans will surely continue to develop and market schemes to measure quality. These schemes may generate data that aid credentialing and improve quality. Some of the indicators of quality may even advance the science of measurement.

Unfortunately, some health plans may also release proprietary data on quality for promotional purposes, a problem that is compounded if the data are not audited or the methods are not fully specified. Specification of the measures used and auditing of the data are essential to assure large purchasers and consumers that comparisons among health plans are meaningful. Inaccurate measurement is often not intentional. For example, in a recent pilot study of HEDIS sponsored by the National Committee for Quality Assurance,[75] agreement between health plans and external auditors was greater than 95 percent for most measures of quality, but there was substantial disagreement in measuring outpatient follow-up of patients who had been hospitalized with major affective disorders. For more than 40 percent of the patients identified, the auditors found insufficient evidence in the medical record to substantiate the assertion that major affective disorder was the principal diagnosis for the hospitalization.

7. One size does not—and cannot—fit all. Promulgation of a single national report card is not necessary. Some may worry that report cards on the quality of care used by state-based and regional consortia will not yield comparable national data or identify national benchmarks, but this is a minor problem. Regionally defined quality indicators are advantageous in addressing local priorities in care. In San Francisco, for example, it may be important to assess quality of care for persons with AIDS, whereas in Florida it may be important to emphasize the availability of translation services for Spanish-speaking patients or to evaluate the appropriateness of operations that are common among the elderly. Comparative data for several sites in the same region are likely to be more compelling to providers than data from distant locations. Regional comparisons will also help consumers make informed choices.

Recently, many health plans have initiated intensive efforts to recruit specialized populations such as those covered by Medicare or Medicaid. These groups of patients have different health care needs, and performance measures to assess their quality of care should differ accordingly. Sensitive measures targeting particular groups are especially important because many managed care plans lack experience in caring for the special needs of elderly and disadvantaged populations.

Conclusion

Will quality report cards become an important component of quality assurance and quality improvement in the twenty-first century, or will they fade away? No one can be sure. It is hard to argue against providing standardized information to help purchasers and consumers make better choices and to educate providers. However, one person's standardized information is another person's bureaucracy, intrusion, provider burden, and cost.

The federal proposals for comprehensive health care reform considered in 1994 would have guaranteed the standardization of measurement and the infusion of large-scale resources to overcome the technical barriers to the implementation of existing measures. Voluntary partnerships within the private sector, federal and private foundation research support, and governmental initiatives may now bridge the gap and allow us to move ahead. Continued and determined effort is essential. If expectations and claims are appropriately metered, performance reports on quality can become a valuable tool for quality management.

Acknowledgments

This chapter was adapted in part from A. M. Epstein, "Sounding Board: Performance Reports on Quality: Prototypes, Problems, and Prospects." *New England Journal of Medicine* 333 (1995): 57–61. Copyright 1995, Massachusetts Medical Society. All rights reserved. I appreciate helpful comments on earlier drafts of this manuscript from Donald Berwick, Helen Darling, Cliff Gaus, Marion Ein Lewin, Kathy Lohr, Heather Palmer, and Lisa Simpson.

Notes

1. K. N. Lohr, ed., *Medicare: A Strategy for Quality Assurance* (Washington DC: National Academy Press, 1990).
2. K. N. Lohr and R. H. Brook, "Quality Assurance in Medicine," *American Behavioral Scientist* 27 (1984): 583–607.

3. K. N. Williams and R. H. Brook, "Quality Measurement and Assurance: A Literature Review," *Health and Medical Care Services Review* 3, no. 1 (May-June 1978): 3–15.
4. J. W. Williamson, *Improving Medical Practice and Health Care: A Bibliographic Guide to Information Management in Quality Assurance and Continuing Education* (Cambridge, MA: Ballinger, 1977).
5. R. H. Egdahl, "Foundations for Medical Care," *The New England Journal of Medicine* 288, no. 3 (1973): 491–98.
6. L. I. Iezzoni, "Risk and Outcomes," in *Risk Adjustment for Measuring Health Care Outcomes,* edited by L. I. Iezzoni (Ann Arbor, MI: Health Administration Press, 1994).
7. F. Nightingale, *Notes on Hospitals,* 3rd ed. (London: Longman, Green, Longman, Roberts and Green, 1863).
8. Group Health Association of America, *Patterns in HMO Enrollment* (Washington, DC: GHAA, June 1995).
9. Health Care Financing Administration, Office of Managed Care, *1995 Medicaid Managed Care Enrollment Report* (Washington, DC: HCFA, 1995).
10. Nightingale 1863.
11. E. A. Codman, "The Product of a Hospital," *Surgical Gynecology and Obstetrics* 18 (1914): 491–96.
12. A. S. Relman, "Assessment and Accountability: The Third Revolution in Medical Care," *The New England Journal of Medicine* 319, no. 2 (1988): 220–22.
13. D. S. O'Leary, "The Joint Commission Looks to the Future," *Journal of the American Medical Association* 258, no. 7 (1987): 951–52.
14. J. S. Roberts, J. G. Coale, and R. R. Redman, "A History of the Joint Commission on Accreditation of Hospitals," *Journal of the American Medical Association* 258, no. 7 (1987): 936–40.
15. P. M. Ellwood, "Outcomes Management: A Technology of Patient Experience," *The New England Journal of Medicine* 318, no. 23 (1988): 1549–56.
16. A. M. Epstein, "The Outcomes Movement, Its Origins, Goals and Future: Will It Get Us Where We Want to Go?" *The New England Journal of Medicine* 80, no. 7 (1990): 835–39.
17. J. G. Wennberg and A. Helsohn, "Small Area Variations in Health Care Delivery," *Science* 182 (14 December 1973): 1102–08.
18. J. E. Wennberg, J. L. Freeman, and W. J. Culp, "Are Hospital Services Rationed in New Haven or Overutilized in Boston?" *Lancet* (23 May 1987): 1185–89.
19. E. S. Fisher, J. E. Wennberg, T. A. Stukel, and S. M. Sharp, "Hospital Readmission Rates for Cohorts of Medicare Beneficiaries in Boston and New Haven," *The New England Journal of Medicine* 331, no. 15 (1994): 989–95.
20. M. R. Chassin, R. H. Brook, R. E. Park, J. Keesey, A. Fink, J. Kosecoff, K. Kahn, N. Merrick, and D. H. Solomon, "Variations in the Use of Medical and Surgical Services by the Medicare Populations," *The New England Journal of Medicine* 314, no. 5 (1986): 285–90.
21. M. R. Chassin, R. H. Brook, R. E. Park, J. Kosecoff, J. Keesey, A. Fink,

K. Kahn, N. Merrick, and D. Solomon, "Does Inappropriate Use Explain Geographic Variations in the Use of Health Care Services? A Study of These Procedures," *The New England Journal of Medicine* 258 (1987): 2533–37.

22. S. H. Woolf, "Practice Guidelines: A New Reality in Medicare: Part I. Recent Developments," *Journal of the American Medical Association* 150, no. 15 (1990): 1811–18.

23. Physician Payment Review Commission, *Annual Report to Congress, 1995* (Washington, DC: Physician Payment Review Commission, 1995).

24. Lohr 1990.

25. R. H. Palmer and M. E. Adams, "Quality Improvement/Quality Assurance Taxonomy: A Framework," in *Putting Research to Work in Quality Improvement and Quality Assurance,* edited by M. L. Grady, J. Bernstein, and S. Robinson (Washington, DC: U.S. Department of Health and Human Services), 13–37.

26. P. Starr, *The Social Transformation of American Medicine* (New York: The Free Press, 1982).

27. Lohr 1990.

28. Palmer and Adams.

29. Lohr 1990.

30. Palmer and Adams.

31. R. H. Palmer, "Considerations in Defining of Health Care," in *Striving for Quality in Health Care: An Inquiry into Policy and Practice,* edited by H. R. Palmer, A. Donabedian, and G. J. Povar (Ann Arbor, MI: Health Administration Press, 1991).

32. Lohr 1990.

33. Health Care Financing Administration, *Professional Standards Review Organization 1979 Program Evaluation, Health Care Financing Research Report.* HCFA Publication No. 03041 (Baltimore, MD: Department of Health and Human Services, May 1980).

34. General Accounting Office, *Problems with Evaluating the Cost Effectiveness of Professional Standards Review Organizations,* Publication No. (FRD)-79-52 (Washington, DC: GAO, July 1979).

35. Congressional Budget Office, *The Effect of PSROs on Health Care Costs: Current Findings and Future Evaluations* (Washington, DC: Congress of the United States, CBO, June 1979).

36. Congressional Budget Office, *The Impact of PSROs on Health Care Costs: Update of CBOs 1979 Evaluation* (Washington, DC: Congress of the United States, CBO, January 1981).

37. K. N. Lohr, *Peer Review Organizations: Quality Assurance in Medicare,* Publication No. P-7125 (Santa Monica, CA: The RAND Corporation, July 1985).

38. D. M. Berwick, "Continuous Improvement as an Ideal in Health Care." *The New England Journal of Medicine* 320, no. 1 (1989): 53–56.

39. W. A. Shewhart, "The Application of Statistics as an Aid in Maintaining Quality of a Manufactured Product," *Journal of the American Statistical Association* 20 (1925): 546–48.

40. W. A. Shewhart, *Economic Control of Quality of a Manufactured Product* (New York: D. Van Nostrand, 1931).
41. J. M. Juran, F. M. Gryna, Jr., R. S. Bingham, Jr., eds., *Quality Control Handbook* (New York: McGraw-Hill, 1979).
42. W. E. Deming, *Quality, Productivity, and Competitive Position* (Cambridge, MA: Massachusetts Institute of Technology, Center for Advanced Engineering Study, 1982).
43. W. E. Deming, *Out of the Crisis* (Cambridge, MA: Massachusetts Institute of Technology, Center for Advanced Engineering Study, 1986).
44. J. M. Juran, *Managerial Breakthrough* (New York: McGraw-Hill, 1964).
45. M. Walton, *The Deming Management Method* (New York: Dodd, Mead and Confarg, 1986).
46. D. A. Gavin, *A Note on Quality: The Views of Deming, Juran and Crosby,* Harvard Business School Note, Publication No. 9-687-011 (Cambridge, MA. Harvard College, 1981).
47. J. M. Juran, F. M. Gryna, Jr., and R. S. Bingham, Jr., *Quality Control Handbook,* 4th ed. (Manchester, MO: McGraw-Hill, 1988).
48. Lohr 1990.
49. G. D. Schiff, A. B. Bindman, and T. A. Brennan, "Better-Quality Alternative: Single Payer National Health System Reform," *Journal of the American Medical Association* 272, no. 10 (1994): 803–808.
50. D. M. Berwick, "Controlling Variation in Health Care: A Consultation with Walter Shewhart," *Medical Care* 29, no.12 (1991): 1212–25.
51. Iezzoni 1994.
52. Nightingale 1863.
53. Iezzoni 1994.
54. *A Consumer Guide to Coronary Artery Bypass Surgery, Pennsylvania Health Care Cost Containment,* Vol. II, 1991.
55. U.S. General Accounting Office. *Report Cards: A Useful Concept but Significant Issues Need to be Addressed* (Washington, DC: GAO, September 1994).
56. National Committee for Quality Assurance, Health Plan Employer Data and Information Set and User's Manual, Version 2.0.
57. *Report Card Pilot Project, Key Findings and Lessons Learned: 21 Plans' Performance Profiles* (Washington, DC: 1995 National Committee for Quality Assurance, 1995).
58. M. Gold, L. Nelson, T. Lake, et al., *What We Know and Don't Know about the Arrangements Managed Care Plans Make with Physicians,* Report to the Physician Payment Review Commission under Grant 93-GOB (Washington, DC: Mathematica Policy Research, January 1994).
59. *Kaiser Permanente, Northern California Region, Quality Report Card* (Oakland, CA: Kaiser Permanente, 1993).
60. "Shying Away from the Poll Position, Some Health Plans Resist an Effort to Find Out if the Customers Are Happy." *The Washington Post* (27 April 1994): F1.
61. D. M. Berwick and D. L. Wald, "Hospital Leaders' Opinions of the HCFA Mortality Data," *Journal of the American Medical Association* 263, no. 3 (1990): 247–49.

62. E. L. Hannan, H. Kilburn, M. Racz, E. Shields, and M. R. Chassan, "Improving the Outcomes of Coronary Artery Bypass Surgery in New York State," *Journal of the American Medical Association* 271, no. 10 (1994): 761–66.

63. B. C. Vladeck, E. T. Goodwin, L. P. Myers, and M. Sinisi, "Consumers and Hospitals: The HCFA 'Death List,'" *Health Affairs* 7 (Winter 1988): 122–25.

64. Hannan et al. 1994.

65. GAO 1994.

66. J. P. Kassirer, "The Use and Abuse of Practice Profiles," *The New England Journal of Medicine* 330, no. 9 (1994): 634–35.

67. T. S. Jost, "Health System Reform: Forward or Backward with Quality Oversight," *Journal of the American Medical Association* 271, no. 19 (1994): 1508–11.

68. B. J. McNeil, S. H. Pederson, and C. Gastonis, "Current Issues in Profiling Quality of Care," *Inquiry* 29, no. 3 (1992): 298–307.

69. Institute of Medicine, *Health Data in the Information Age: Use, Disclosure and Privacy* (Washington, DC: National Academy Press, 1994).

70. O'Leary 1987.

71. J. Green and N. Winfield, "Report Cards on Cardiac Surgeons: Assessing New York State's Approach," *The New England Journal of Medicine* 332, no. 18 (1995): 1229–32.

72. GAO 1994.

73. *Report Card Pilot Project* 1995.

74. *Report Card Pilot Project* 1995.

75. *Report Card Pilot Project* 1995.

8

The Legal Framework for Effective Competition

Robert A. Berenson, Douglas A. Hastings, and William G. Kopit

Abstract. Largely because of its indifference to spiraling costs, the professional domination model is being replaced by a market model based on competition among managed care plans and integrated delivery systems. In general, the more fully integrated previously competing providers become—for instance, by assuming financial risk together—the less legal risk is present, because of a decreased possibility of improper conspiratorial or collective behavior. Nevertheless, provider joint ventures and integrated delivery systems face a complex interaction of practical challenges and various legal and regulatory risks.

This chapter explores ways in which laws involving fraud and abuse, self-referral, private inurement, corporate practice of medicine, Medicare reimbursement policy, and antitrust enforcement affect typical integrated delivery systems.

From a legal standpoint, it might seem logical that the laws regulating health care providers would support and promote integration. A permissive legal environment to foster development of an integrated service network model assumes its development in a delivery system in which networks are at financial risk for the services provided. However, many of the laws and regulations governing integrated provider development were established at a time when joint ventures and other alliances were organizing in a predominantly fee-for-service environment and were generating significant increases in health care costs without producing demonstrable efficiencies or quality enhancements. The result is a fundamental inconsistency in government policy. The demand for collaboration by purchasers and legislatures does not necessarily cause the vast body of health care regulators to revise their concerns that many of the very collaborative activities being encouraged trigger potentially illegal acts and relationships.

In a market model, the application of federal and state antitrust laws is especially important. In 1993 and 1994, the Department of Justice and the Federal Trade Commission jointly issued "Statements of Antitrust Enforcement Policy" in a number of areas of provider uncertainty. For integrated delivery systems, the primary focus of antitrust analysis is "market power." Systems without market power (i.e., the ability to force a purchaser to do something that the purchaser would not do in a competitive market) cannot harm consumers and should be free from serious antitrust risk. Where a network may have market power, its activities may be limited only if demonstrable anticompetitive effects outweigh the benefits of the efficiencies claimed by the new arrangement. The chapter concludes that vigorous antitrust enforcement may be required to promote market competition among integrated networks of providers and the managed care plans they serve.

Competition is generally believed to be the most efficient method of resource allocation of goods and services. Indeed, in passing the Sherman and Clayton Antitrust Acts, Congress determined that competition is the preferred allocation mechanism. In most economic sectors, competition produces higher-quality goods and services at lower prices than any alternative system. Historically, however, medical care has been governed by principles based more on professional dominance than market competition.[1,2] In the professional model, the individual practitioner has a fiduciary relationship with the patient, for whom the professional makes decisions. In addition to this central "doctor-patient relationship," the professional model assumes that the profession collectively will promote and monitor high-quality standards of care, based on scientific evidence and expert opinion about best clinical process, unrelated to cost. It is also assumed that the profession will responsibly regulate itself and that it can therefore be insulated from external oversight.

In recent years, the professional model has become vulnerable to a number of social, legal, and economic developments,[3] including a societal demand for patient autonomy and empowerment; reduced deference to professional standards resulting from accumulated evidence of substantial and unexplained variation in physician practice patterns; the increased importance of institutions, particularly hospitals, that face independent liability for the actions of the professionals who practice within their walls; and the proliferation of nonphysician professionals ready to challenge the dominant role of physicians in self-regulating professional activities.

Most important, because of its indifference to spiraling costs, the professional dominance model has become unaffordable.[4] The health care system is undergoing rapid transformation, with the corporate practice of medicine often replacing professional practice. Under such a reorganization, it is logical to defer to well-established, market principles that have worked reasonably well in other sectors.

Nevertheless, until recently, health care markets in this country have worked perversely, if at all. The existence of third-party payment creates a "moral hazard," in which consumers demand more services than they would if they were paying for those services themselves. Moreover, insurers often compete by avoiding rather than managing risk, and providers duplicate expensive facilities, equipment, and services rather than increasing output and reducing price.

Additionally, the difficulty in defining the product being offered—are purchasers buying a single hospital stay, a physician encounter, a surgical procedure, health care, improved health status, or all of the above?—combined with the lack of meaningful information upon which to make informed choices and the lack of time and expertise to use appropriately the available information, all contribute to the inefficiencies inherent in health service competition.

This is not to say, however, that meaningful competition—including meaningful price competition—is not possible within health care markets. Increasingly, people can and do choose between competing health plans with different delivery systems (or at least different network arrangements). With or without legislative health care reform, competition among competing health plans, with their affiliated integrated health care delivery systems, carries the promise of improving the operation of health care markets. These integrated delivery systems, which typically offer both physician and hospital services as well as ancillary services, increasingly are the linchpin of managed care arrangements, and the core of almost all "managed competition" proposals for health care reform. Indeed, the development of integrated delivery systems and their links to health care financing arrangements—health plans—serves as the most obvious way, by far, to develop meaningful competition in health care markets in the 1990s. As Alain Enthoven, one of the most visible advocates of "managed competition" wrote recently,[5] "Some say that competition has failed. I say that competition has not yet been tried."

A commitment to competition as a guiding principle must focus primarily on antitrust concepts and the enforcement of federal antitrust laws. Antitrust law provides the only coherent conceptual framework for assessing the impact of conduct on consumer welfare, defined as increased output and quality at lower prices. (Generally, conduct that reduces consumer welfare is condemned under the anti-trust laws, while conduct that increases consumer welfare, or is indifferent to it, remains permissible.) Nevertheless, focusing exclusively on the antitrust laws and their enforcement fails to acknowledge other legal considerations that dramatically affect the nature of competition in health care markets. For example, almost everyone acknowledges that competition between and among health plans cannot be truly effective as long as risk selection, rather than risk management, predominates,[6] or as long as different forms of integrated delivery systems face vastly different forms of regulation and reserve requirements. Similarly, many argue that restrictive "fraud and abuse" requirements that limit the ability of a system to direct patients in return for payment for services can adversely affect the operation of integrated systems, as can "any willing provider" laws and "patient protection" statutes that impose regulatory, rather than market, restrictions on the ability of systems and health plans to freely select their providers.

Of course, it will not be possible to establish competing systems or networks in every geographic area of the country. Thus, according to one study, approximately 30 percent of the population live in areas that would not support more than one full-service provider network.[7] In such areas it may not be possible to create effective competition among hospitals, or among certain subspecialists. Moreover, there may be insufficient numbers of primary care physicians to create effective competition in that market as well. In such situations, an explicit recognition of provider collaboration functioning in a noncompetitive, regulatory environment may be desirable. Nevertheless, in a legal environment that presumes that competition is the guiding principle for resource allocation, the critical question remains: What kind of effective competition is possible among health plans, and among the networks of providers that deliver care on behalf of those health plans, through integrated delivery systems.[8]

Integrated Delivery Systems: A Taxonomy

The concept of "integrated delivery systems" appeared to explode on the health care scene in the early 1990s. Still, the strategic, structural, and legal issues that relate to integrated delivery systems are not new and, indeed, have been in circulation for a number of years. What is new is the urgency with which the development of these new systems is viewed.

At least four separate categories of integration are currently taking place simultaneously and at a rapid rate throughout the United
States: (1) hospital collaborations and affiliations, (2) physician practice integration, (3) physician-hospital integration, and (4) provider-
payer integration. Particular health care providers often are involved
in two or three of these different types of integration at the same time.
For example, a hospital may at one time consider collaborating with
other hospitals, developing a physician-hospital organization (PHO)
or a hospital-affiliated medical group, and discussing a joint venture
with a health maintenance organization (HMO)—all as part of a combined response to the changing marketplace.

The Legal Environment for Integration

Why are so many health care providers engaged in the development
of integrated delivery systems?

From a *strategic* standpoint, providers are seeking the following:
to be owners, or at least voting participants, in the health care delivery
systems of the future, not simply vendors in someone else's system
(or, worse, left out entirely); to maintain and increase their competi-
tiveness and attractiveness to payers; to increase their negotiating
strength with payers; to increase the future value of their facilities
and/or medical practices; to strengthen their primary care referral
channels; and to position physicians and hospitals as a unified entity
seeking to achieve common goals.

From an *economic* standpoint, providers are seeking to reduce
their costs and create economies of scale, to gain access to capital for
expansion, to secure their financial viability, and to increase their
efficiency and profitability. From a *service* standpoint, providers are
seeking to maintain and enhance their quality and centers of excellence, to gain freedom from the administrative hassles of current payment and utilization management systems, and to improve their
information systems to respond better to purchaser needs. From a
legal standpoint, providers are seeking to integrate in order to reduce
their legal exposure, at least on certain key issues.

When individuals or entities act alone (essentially the status quo
under fee-for-service medicine prior to the 1980s), the issues of con-
spiracy, inurement, self-referrals, or kickbacks do not tend to arise.
However, the typical initial response to collaborative activity is some
sort of agreement to cooperate or collaborate on certain matters. The

parties are learning to work together and are not prepared to give up the autonomy that full integration limits. However, simple agreements frequently involve the greatest degree of legal risk because of the possibility that the agreement will be viewed as a restraint of trade or the basis for an inappropriate exchange of benefits.

When parties move further into integration through a joint venture, where there is true assumption of risk and the potential of reward but on a limited basis, the legal risk moderates somewhat, but certainly is still present. For example, much of the concern raised by the Office of the Inspector General (OIG) of the Department of Health and Human Services under the anti-kickback laws has had to do with joint ventures. Moreover, joint ventures under the antitrust law are often subject to scrutiny. Finally, the Internal Revenue Service (IRS) joint venture guidelines place a burden on the tax-exempt participant to protect its exempt status in order to discourage private parties from participation in such enterprises. When integration becomes complete and formerly independent individuals or entities become part of one organization, the legal risk is generally reduced significantly since there is only a single actor and a decreased possibility for improper conspiratorial or collective behavior. Nevertheless, the creation of the integrated organization can itself create antitrust problems.

Integration of the Financing and Delivery of Health Care

Physicians and hospitals have responded to both public and private pressures to integrate by adopting a variety of collaborative organizational structures. Among these organizational responses are the following, listed in order from the less integrated to the more integrated approaches:

- Independent practice association (IPA)
- Provider network
- Management services organization (MSO)
- "Group practice without walls" (GPWW)
- Physician-hospital organization (PHO)
- Medical foundation
- Hospital-affiliated medical group

- Multispecialty group practice

- Fully integrated delivery system, with insurance and/or HMO license

Strategically, a critical factor in choosing the appropriate organizational response is proper assessment of the stage of managed care penetration into the relevant marketplace. Among the strategic risks involved in developing an integrated delivery system are creating the particular organization too early, before the market or the payers are ready to use it; picking the wrong partners; investing significant funds before a return will be possible; and entering risk arrangements with inadequate information systems to manage the risk.

On the other hand, significant risks are associated with not developing an integrated delivery system, such as being left out when other providers develop integrated approaches; being unable to attract new physicians because no supportive structure is in place; and being unprepared when a major reform initiative, predicated on integrated systems being in place, is made by a key purchaser. From a strategic standpoint, understanding the strengths, weaknesses, and uses of the various approaches on the integration continuum is critical to responding effectively to market changes.

The particular integration category or context is important not only in making good strategic decisions but also in recognizing the applicable legal issues. For example, antitrust issues are likely to arise in hospital collaboration discussions but are less likely to be of concern in some joint venture discussions between providers and payers. On the other hand, fraud and abuse issues are likely to be of concern in physician-hospital integration development, but not an issue in hospital collaboration.

Physician integration

Physicians throughout the United States are actively assessing the implications of health care reform for their practices and are considering options for new delivery structures. The expectation of primary care–oriented, managed care–driven, capitated payment systems has created particular concern among specialists regarding future referral patterns. Primary care physicians are in demand, and changes in traditional primary care–specialist relationships are likely. At the same time, the ongoing expansion of enforcement activity in the fraud and abuse and self-referral areas, and the lack of complete clarity in antitrust enforcement, create legal concerns related to the various physician strategies.

Among the strategies being pursued by physicians are the development of IPAs and other physician contracting organizations and networks, physician-owned MSOs, primary care groups, specialist groups, multispecialty groups, hospital affiliations, and managed care company affiliations. IPAs and other contracting organizations have been in place for a long time, particularly as contracting vehicles for physician participation in HMOs. They provide the advantage of being low-cost structures, implemented relatively easily, that can move quickly into managed care contracting. Participating physicians give up relatively little autonomy. Among the disadvantages: organizations of this nature are generally not well integrated from a practice management and patient care standpoint and, for this reason as well, are subject to significantly greater scrutiny and concern from a legal standpoint, particularly in the antitrust arena.

MSOs provide a certain amount of linkage through varying degrees of centralized practice management and, in most cases, also engage in centralized managed care contract negotiations. Where there is significant centralization of management services, MSOs arguably are a step toward greater integration, although physician participants remain in the groups they were in before development of the MSO. The MSO itself does not create new physician employment relationships. An issue for physician MSOs is where to find capital, and thus hospitals, managed care companies, or independent MSOs, such as PhyCor and Caremark, often become partners in or owners of the MSO venture.

"Medical groups without walls"[9] has become a much-used term, and such organizations are looked upon with disfavor by some health care regulators,[10] who are concerned about the degree of integration represented by groups without walls. Such concerns are at the heart of the debate on what kinds of organizations should qualify as "true groups" for the intragroup referral exception under Stark II (see further on for a discussion of the Stark laws) and for other single-entity protections under the antitrust and fraud and abuse laws. The principal concern of regulators is that the multisite nature of such groups, allowing physicians for the most part to stay in their own offices, inevitably reduces the degree of possible integration. In the extreme, where a group without walls is merely a contractual management relationship among independent physicians who operate essentially as before the "group" formed, single-entity protections are unlikely to be available. On the other hand, where formerly independent physicians merge their practice assets, become employees of the new group, and otherwise operate as members of a single administrative and clinical entity, such protections are likely to apply.

Fully integrated multispecialty medical groups potentially offer the advantage of "one-stop shopping" to purchasers of care, at least for the physician component of a delivery system. Such groups also clearly should gain the legal benefits previously discussed as "true groups," subject to ongoing regulatory developments.

Where physician organizations of any nature engage in risk-based contracting, whether through capitation payments, withholds, or other forms of risk-shifting to providers, their legal position also is significantly improved. Both the antitrust enforcement agencies and the OIG have indicated that risk assumption is "a good fact" in assessing the legality of physician organizations on the theory that physicians "at risk" do not have the kind of financial incentives to engage in behavior of concern to regulators. Table 8.1 presents an overview of the strategic and legal issues affecting various forms of physician integration.

Physician-hospital integration

Hospitals also are aggressively looking at options in order to survive and prosper in the rapidly changing health care environment. Like specialist physicians, hospitals are concerned about their referral base; all hospitals, in some form or another, are looking at their physician relations as a critical element of their overall strategy. Among the options being considered by hospitals are multiple hospital contracting networks, PHOs, MSOs, primary care physician linkage, multispecialty group affiliations, and managed care company affiliations. Physicians are looking to integrate with hospitals as well, in order, among other reasons, to obtain capital and to create more attractive and competitive delivery systems.

Physician-hospital integration efforts have resulted nationally in various collaborative models or approaches that are increasingly widespread. The models vary with regard to the degree of integration between the parties and the strategic and legal issues presented. Table 8.2 displays several of the key strategic and legal issues associated with the various approaches to physician-hospital integration.

The following scenario illustrates how legal considerations can affect physician-hospital integration efforts. A tax-exempt hospital or health system is seeking to facilitate the joining of two prominent primary care medical groups in the community and to link them to the

Table 8.1 Legal Risks of Physician Integration Options

Strategic and Legal Issues	IPA	Group Practice Without Walls	Physician MSO	Multispecialty Group Practice
Political feasibility	A	A	B	C
Long-term security	C	B	B	A
Degree of integration	C	B	B	A
Fraud and abuse	B	C	B	A
Self-referral	B	C	B	A
Antitrust	C	B	B	A
Corporate practice	A	A	B	A
Medicare reimbursement	A	C	B	A
Licensure/Certificate of need	B	A	B	A

A = More likely to succeed/Less legal risk.
B = Mixed success/Moderate legal risk.
C = Less likely to succeed/More legal risk.

Table 8.2 Legal Risks of Physician-Hospital Structural Options

Strategic and Legal Issues	Practice Enhancements/ Services	Managed Care PHO	MSO	Foundation Model	Direct Hospital Employment	Affiliated Medical Group
Political feasibility	A	B	B	B	C	C
Long-term security	C	B	B	B	B	A
Degree of integration	C	B	B	B	B	A
Fraud and abuse	C	B	C	B	A	A
Private inurement	C	B	C	B	A	A
Self-referral	C	B	B	A	A	A
Antitrust	A	C	B	A	A	A
Corporate practice	A	A	A	A	C	C
Medicare reimbursement	A	A	B	C	A	C
Licensure/Certificate of need	A	C	A	A	A	B

A = More likely to succeed/Less legal risk.
B = Mixed success/Moderate legal risk.
C = Less likely to succeed/More legal risk.

hospital through some kind of acquisition and employment arrangement. Such linkage would provide a strong basis for the new health system—physicians and hospitals—to provide more effective and efficient care under capitated systems and to offer more to purchasers of care. Along with the basic legal need to create a corporate structure and contractual documents that are effective and fair to the parties, the hospitals and physicians will have to address the following questions:

1. Will the corporate practice of medicine rules in their state allow for direct employment of physicians by a corporate component of the health care system? If no such direct employment is allowed, the protection of the employment safe harbor to the anti-kickback law is not available.

2. Will the new hospital-affiliated medical group or physician organization be able to obtain tax-exempt status, if desired? Under current IRS policy, only 20 percent of the governing body of the medical group could be composed of employed physicians.

3. Could such a hospital-dominated organization be treated as freestanding for Medicare reimbursement purposes? If not, total reimbursement may be reduced.

4. How can the hospital purchase the practices and fund the new physician organization without jeopardizing its own tax-exempt status or running afoul of fraud and abuse or Stark law requirements, especially regarding the acquisition aspect of the transaction? This is especially a problem if insurance companies, for-profit hospitals, or other medical groups also bid to acquire these practices—all of which can offer some incentives to the physicians not available to the tax-exempt hospital.

5. Will the new group qualify as a group under the Stark exception for group practices? If not, loss of ancillary revenues may be fatal to the transaction.

Provider-payer integration

Health care providers and health care payers are increasingly discussing integration. Virtually all health care reform proposals, excluding single-payer approaches, both at the state and federal levels, envision an important role for health plans, Accountable Health Plans (AHPs), or other similarly titled entities. Such health plans, like HMOs

Figure 8.1   Components of Integrated Delivery Systems

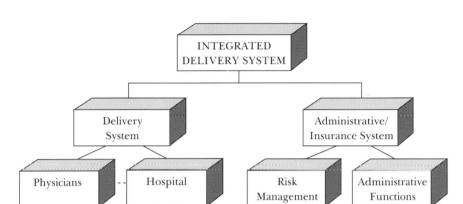

today, include both a clinical and administrative component, as depicted in Figure 8.1. Moreover, the various reform proposals, as well as enacted legislation at the state level, leave regulation of risk-bearing entities to the traditional regulators—state departments of insurance and health. Given the emphasis on capitation and other provider risk-sharing arrangements, providers and payers are naturally looking to collaborate, engage in joint ventures, and combine in various ways to become successful AHPs of the future.

Yet such collaborations are fraught with complexities, just as physician-hospital collaborations are. Nevertheless, such integrated joint ventures, health plans, and systems have formed and are forming at a rapid pace because of the intense demand for the combined expertise of the participants. Insurance laws and state insurance regulators vary in their approach to regulation of providers "at risk." This appropriately is the subject of a longer analysis. Suffice it to say here that, while in some cases individual providers are allowed to take risk without regulation in their individual capacities for their own services, new business organizations, such as PHOs, generally cannot take "insurance" risk without a license.

The exception to this rule in some states is capitation arrangements with HMOs, where the PHO operates like a traditional IPA, but assumes risk for hospital services in addition to the physician services that an IPA would be at risk for. However, even this exception is under review in many states. When PHOs, or other similar organizations or networks, desire to enter risk arrangements directly with employers, states typically will require licensure. An array of licensure avoidance approaches (sometimes called "HMO look-alikes") have evolved, wherein PHOs seek to structure capitation or other arrangements that shift risk to providers without the PHO itself becoming subject to such risk (i.e., by contracting to have the payments flow directly from the payer to the provider and/or structuring the payment to the PHO as an administrative fee).

The influence of legal issues on integration efforts in this context is demonstrated by the following example. A newly formed PHO is attempting to enter a direct contracting arrangement with a large self-insured employer in the community. Assume that the arrangement would be cost-efficient, would allow a reasonable range of choice of providers, and would otherwise satisfy the needs of the purchaser of health care services in this case. Along with developing the contractual relationship between them, the parties would have to address the following legal questions:

1. Have any antitrust problems arisen based on the size of the PHO's provider panel, or the methodology used in developing the PHO's fee schedule, or in any exclusivity provisions that may be agreed to between the PHO and its providers? Both providers involved and the contracting purchaser stand to be negatively affected by an antitrust challenge to the arrangement, at least through delay, even if the challenge is successfully defended.

2. Will there be any financial risk-sharing arrangements between the employer and the PHO, particularly any global capitation of the PHO, that could trigger state insurance licensure requirements for the PHO? Obtaining a license on the front end is costly and time-consuming. However, being forced to "cease and desist" and possibly being fined for operating without a license is worse.

3. Do any applicable state "any willing provider" laws, utilization review licensure laws, or other state laws or regulations affect the PHO, even if it does not accept financial risk? Again, fighting rearguard legal actions against disgruntled providers or state agencies is a costly diversion to an integrated delivery system trying to succeed in a competitive environment.

Legal Constraints to Integration

From a legal standpoint, it might seem logical that the laws regulating health care providers would support and promote integration. However, in large part the opposite is true. Much of the legal enforcement stems from the general distrust of providers that grew in the late 1980s. Among other factors, such distrust was based on media coverage and research studies suggesting that collaborative business relationships between and among physicians, hospitals, laboratories, durable medical equipment companies, home health services vendors, and other types of health care providers were largely improper and resulted in significant increases in health care costs without producing demonstrable efficiencies or quality enhancements.[11]

For example, the Medicare and Medicaid anti-kickback statute, which prohibits the payment of or receipt of remuneration in exchange for the referral of Medicare or Medicaid items and services, is aimed at curbing (1) overutilization; (2) inappropriate steering of patients to less convenient, more expensive, or lower-quality providers; and (3) competitive disadvantage to those who do not pay kickbacks. This statute is appropriate and relevant in a largely fee-for-service environment in which the payer, such as Medicare, is at financial risk for the utilization of those submitting bills to it.

The situation is turned on its head in a competitive environment in which the providers are at risk for the services provided, whether directly or through contractual relationships with at-risk providers. In such circumstances, overutilization is no longer beneficial to the involved providers, who now have incentives to reduce utilization and to refer to providers able to function under the altered incentive structure. In short, the overutilization concerns underlying the kickback prohibitions would not exist were the providers substantially "at risk." However, different "fraud and abuse" concerns (e.g., systematic underutilization of services) would arise if providers were at risk.

Similarly, antitrust enforcement has focused on preventing otherwise independent physicians (i.e., competitors) from collectively acting to force insurance companies and health plans to raise their prices in a fee-for-service environment when the physicians are not at risk. When physicians assume significant, collective financial risk in a formal business relationship, their association to negotiate with health plans on fees would no longer raise similar antitrust concerns, owing to the efficiencies produced. However, other antitrust concerns are raised when integrated physician organizations form (see further on for a discussion of the application of antitrust laws to provider networks.)

In short, a permissive legal environment to foster the development of an integrated service network model assumes its development in a delivery system in which networks are at financial risk for the services provided. However, many of the laws and regulations governing integrated provider development were established at a time when joint ventures and other provider alliances were being organized in a predominantly fee-for-service environment.

As a result, there is a fundamental inconsistency in government policy on health care. The demand for collaboration by purchasers and legislatures does not necessarily cause the vast body of health care regulators to revise their concerns that many of the very collaborative activities being encouraged trigger potentially illegal, even criminal, acts and relationships. An important question is whether these policy inconsistencies reflect a transition problem as the system changes from one in which providers are independent, non-risk-bearing participants in a heavily regulated system to one in which providers are formally aligned in risk-bearing entities functioning in a competitive market. In a transition over five to ten years, transition rules and interpretations could be designed to foster integration efforts, even at some cost in the short run.

A fundamental difficulty arises if, instead of a transition, the dual environments are intended to function side by side for the foreseeable future, that is, fee-for-service Medicare and Medicaid programs continuing while the private sector moves aggressively to managed care based around at-risk, provider-based service networks.[12] Functioning in a dual system, providers will surely face conflicting pressures on how to organize and provide clinical services to the variously affected populations they serve. Similarly, providers can be placed in a very difficult legal situation, having to confront legal barriers designed to interfere with the very integration that certain public policy is seeking to foster. While fully integrated and risk-bearing systems do indeed benefit from important legal protections, the process of "integrating" is fraught with legal concerns.

A lengthy list of legal issues exists, all of which create obstacles to effective integration. Among these are IRS rulings regarding private inurement and physician-hospital relations, Medicare reimbursement policies and rules, OIG initiatives under the Medicare anti-kickback law, the passage of federal and state self-referral laws, state insurance laws, state corporate practice of medicine restrictions, and, to some extent, enforcement at the federal and state levels of the antitrust laws. A brief description of each of these legal considerations follows.

Tax-exempt organization law

Concerns regarding IRS enforcement of private inurement proscriptions have inhibited strategic integration activities between hospitals and physicians. Currently, the tax status of each separate legal entity is determined independently of other organizations with which it is affiliated. Thus, physicians and physician owned businesses will participate in joint ventures with nonprofit hospitals, which receive tax-exempt status under Section 501(c)(3) as "charitable" organizations if they meet a community benefit standard.

An effective integration strategy dictates that the providers of health care services collaborate to develop bundled services for the public. However, IRS rulings and interpretations relegate the hospital participant that seeks to preserve its 501(c)(3) status to a controlling role, thereby potentially alienating physician participants. The IRS's position that no more than 20 percent of the board of a tax-exempt medical foundation can be composed of participating physicians is a significant governance problem for many integrated delivery systems currently forming.

Recent IRS positions relating to PHOs and MSOs further detail IRS concerns in this regard.[13] The IRS takes the position that a physician is an insider for purposes of an inurement analysis. For example, in *General Counsel Memorandum 39670* (October 14, 1987), the IRS provided that all persons performing services for an organization have a personal and private interest in it, and therefore possess the requisite relationship to support a finding of private inurement. Recently, the IRS reiterated this position in the Hospital Audit Guidelines.[14]

As a result, a tax-exempt hospital participant may refrain from creative financial compensation arrangements with physicians or a physician group because of the possible characterization of any payment to the physicians under these arrangements as giving rise to private inurement.[15] In *General Counsel Memorandum 39862* (November 21, 1991), the IRS provided that a joint venture must be reviewed to determine whether it serves a charitable purpose; whether and how participation by the exempt entity furthers its exempt purposes; and whether the arrangement permits the exempt entity to act exclusively in furtherance of its exempt purposes. Critics argue that this preoccupation with the status of the exempt joint venture partner fails to recognize the true sharing of risk among the partners and limits the rewards that the physician participants may enjoy.[16]

Medicare Reimbursement

The complexities of the Medicare reimbursement system greatly affect integrated delivery system (IDS) structures. Because hospitals and physicians are reimbursed differently, combining physicians and hospitals into one organization may negatively offset total compensation. Moreover, both Medicare and private payers have detailed rules regarding the granting of provider numbers that may create difficulties in billing for new organizations combining formerly independent physicians. Depending on the structure and arrangements, integration could reduce total reimbursement. Reimbursement rules also must be examined to ensure that all ancillary services are provided "incident to" a physician's services. The inability of an IDS to bill for ancillaries can place it at a competitive financial disadvantage or render it dysfunctional.

Medicare fraud and abuse

Current interpretation of the Medicare anti-kickback law is that if even one purpose of a transaction between a hospital and a physician in a position to refer to the hospitals is to induce such referrals, the transaction may be criminal.[17] This can create a severe chilling effect on a range of potentially legitimate and necessary transactions. Safe harbors, promulgated in 1991 and 1993, afford only limited protection. Moreover, in addition to issuance of the safe harbors, the OIG has issued various fraud alerts identifying areas of concern.

Of particular importance to provider integration are the Fraud Alert on joint venture activities, issued in 1989, and the OIG Special Fraud Alert on Hospital Incentives to Physicians for hospitals' physician recruitment and retention activities, issued in 1992. The joint venture Fraud Alert identified as suspect numerous arrangements that might well be part of a physician-hospital integration plan, and the recruitment Fraud Alert raised doubt as to many common hospital recruitment and retention activities. Moreover, the OIG, as well as the IRS, has issued stern warnings regarding the payment for "goodwill," a key component of many physician acquisition transactions.[18]

Stark law

Until recently, federal self-referral prohibitions were limited to financial interests in clinical laboratories (Stark I).[19] In the Omnibus Budget Reconciliation Act of 1993 (OBRA 1993), Congress expanded the list to ten additional designated health services (Stark II). Since the enactment of Stark I, many states have enacted physician self-referral prohibitions as well.[20] Such laws essentially prohibit joint physician-hospital ownership of health care facilities and group practices and severely limit other joint venture possibilities. They also affect providers differently; for example, the exception for physician ownership of hospitals gives for-profit hospitals an advantage in creating equity incentives for hospitals.

Insurance regulation

State insurance laws affect integration significantly in a variety of ways. Laws governing the taking of insurance risk and the managing of health care services may require the integration of provider networks to obtain various licenses before operating. State laws differ significantly in this regard, creating multistate licensure difficulties. The capital and reserve requirements under some statutes are prohibitive for small networks. "Any willing provider" laws potentially may hamper or completely foil the integrated delivery system's credentialing and utilization management plans by requiring the system to include all applicant providers in managed care panels and/or subjecting health plans to litigation when they seek to limit the size of their panels. Other state insurance laws prohibit the use of "gatekeeper" physicians to control referrals, limit the benefit differential available for services obtained from a preferred rather than a nonpreferred provider, and/or require payment for nonemergency out-of-plan services. All of these types of so-called anti-managed care laws, which differ in their presence and effect throughout the states, create a patchwork quilt of compliance requirements for integrated delivery systems.

Corporate practice of medicine

State corporate practice of medicine laws, in effect in several states, including California, can severely restrict integration options by making it illegal for any corporate entity (other than a professional corporation owned solely by physicians), including nonprofit hospitals or health systems, from employing physicians. Corporate practice doctrines typically prohibit two approaches to organizing care delivery: (a) employment of physicians by general business corporations and (b) ownership by nonphysicians of shares in professional medical corporations.

Such laws thus greatly reduce the options available to physicians, hospitals, and managed care companies because physicians may not be allowed to become full participants in an IDS. To get around corporate practice restrictions, complex arrangements must be structured as substitutes for direct employment or shared equity. Such arrangements often generate increased legal and administrative expense and may prevent physicians from raising capital from nonphysicians because nonphysicians may not even be passive investors in a professional medical corporation.

Antitrust law

The most important antitrust law is the Sherman Antitrust Act. Section 1 of the Sherman Act[21] prohibits "conspiracies" that unreasonably restrain competition. Section 2 prohibits "monopolization" and "conspiracies to monopolize."[22] In addition, Section 7 of the Clayton Act[23] prohibits mergers, acquisitions, and joint ventures that likely will substantially lessen competition.[24] Through these laws Congress has mandated that, unless otherwise specified, resources be allocated by the competitive process rather than by regulation.

The federal antitrust laws are enforced by the Antitrust Division of the Department of Justice and the Federal Trade Commission. The collective activity of competitors within a joint venture or integrated network normally will be analyzed by the enforcement agencies under the rule of reason, in which the procompetitive benefits of the venture are balanced against its actual or potential anticompetitive effects. Clearly, it is the impact and enforcement of antitrust law that represent at the same time both the greatest potential benefactor and the most significant threat to the development of meaningful competition among competing health plans and integrated delivery systems. Although some systems may be fully integrated into a single legal entity, through acquisition or merger, most will be created through contractual agreements. Yet, even such contractual relations may create the potential for efficiencies, and should be considered legitimate joint ventures absent an overriding anticompetitive purpose or effect.[25] Moreover, when a state in its sovereign capacity, usually through legislation, articulates and affirmatively expresses an intent to displace competition with regulation in a particular field and actively supervises collective activity delegated to private parties, those regulatory actions are immune from the antitrust laws.[26]

Of course, many different antitrust claims may be brought against integrated systems under both Section 1 and Section 2 of the Sherman Act, and, in certain circumstances, under Section 3 and Section 7 of the Clayton Act. Nevertheless, in each case, the task is to identify the relevant market, which may vary depending on the nature of the claim, and then determine whether the network has market power within that market. If the system does not have market power, such a finding should conclude the analysis, at least for any system that carries with it the potential for efficiencies. On the other hand, if the network does have market power, the analysis should next turn to the nature and extent of the efficiencies claimed, and the anticompetitive effects, if any.

Some arrangements offer no potential for efficiencies at all. These "naked restraints" should be proscribed. For example, there is no reason to permit providers to fix the fee-for-service prices they will charge to one or more health plans, particularly if the providers have sufficient market power to have an adverse impact on price. Similarly, there is no reason to permit providers to make agreements that prevent health plans from competing in a particular market, or to band together with one health plan to prevent other health plans from entering a market. Nor should health plans be permitted to agree among themselves regarding the markets they will or will not enter.

Still, even legitimate collaboration relating to network development can be problematic under the antitrust laws because it involves joint activity between previously competing institutions and individuals. Indeed, the central focus of the federal antitrust laws is to treat as suspect any agreements between previously competing firms that reduce, or may reduce, competition between these firms. However, existing health care markets—with their overcapacity and perverse incentives—demonstrate that the existence of more providers is not always synonymous with more effective competition. More hospitals and hospital beds are often correlated with unnecessary duplication of plant, equipment, and services, and more specialists often mean too many specialty services.

Because of the perception that the antitrust laws may be impeding the development of useful collaborative efforts between otherwise competing providers, 19 states[27] have enacted statutes designed to provide immunity from state and federal antitrust laws for collaborative efforts that meet certain regulatory requirements imposed by the state. While the terms of these statutes differ considerably, they all intend to take advantage of the so-called "state action" immunity doctrine. This doctrine provides that activities undertaken by private parties pursuant to an affirmative state policy, and which are actively supervised by the state, are exempt from the operation of the federal antitrust laws. Although the trend toward state immunity statutes is generally well intentioned, it may be misguided.

Some of the statutes enacted by the states do not have the

requisite amount of active state oversight to create the immunity, and as a result, collaborative arrangements submitting to the regulatory requirements may be under the mistaken impression that their activities are immune from the federal antitrust laws when they are not. Given the treble damage and attorney fee requirements of the antitrust laws, the mistake could be costly. This risk is compounded by the fact that many states have neither the inclination, the expertise, nor the staff to effectively administer the statutes that have been enacted. As a result, some statutes have never become operational at all, and even when they have, it is much more likely that the degree of regulatory oversight will be considered inadequate by the courts.

On September 15, 1993, the Department of Justice and the Federal Trade Commission jointly issued "Statements of Antitrust Enforcement Policy" in six health care areas.[28] In developing these policy statements the agencies appeared to recognize for the first time that uncertainty in health antitrust enforcement may be a significant problem. As the document itself acknowledges, "[T]hese policy statements are designed to provide education and instruction to the health care community in a time of tremendous change, and to resolve, as completely as possible, the problem of antitrust uncertainty that some have said may deter mergers or joint ventures that would lower health care costs."[29]

There was much that the initial policy statements did not cover. Perhaps most fundamentally, they did not address the development of integrated health care systems. Effective antitrust policy must signal which of these network arrangements are permissible and which are objectionable and, as a consequence, likely to be challenged. To a considerable extent this deficiency was remedied by the revisions to the initial policy statements that were published on September 27, 1994. These revised policy statements, for the first time, contained a statement of "Analytical Principles Relating to Multiprovider Networks" designed to inform the public of the principles the antitrust agencies would utilize in evaluating the legitimacy of integrated systems. Not surprisingly, the revised policy statements are not complete, nor could they be, given the rapid changes that are taking place in health care markets, and the agencies admitted "insufficient experience in analyzing these emerging and evolving types of health care delivery systems."[30] Nevertheless, the revised statements do represent a significant addition to the body of knowledge available in evaluating the legitimacy of integrated systems under the antitrust laws.

The Importance of Market Power

The primary focus of the analysis of integrated systems should be market power, as the policy statements recognize. Systems without market power, by definition, cannot harm consumers. Market power is simply the ability "to force a purchaser to do something that he would not do in a competitive market."[31] Where market choices are sufficient to prevent the system from developing market power, the development and operation of the integrated system should remain free from serious antitrust risk.

Even though competitors may be harmed by the operation of the system, the antitrust laws provide no remedy for such harm unless the conduct causes consumers to suffer higher prices or lower quality or output.[32] In order to be able to cause such effects on consumers, the parties whose conduct is being challenged must have significant market power in the properly defined relevant market.[33]

In some cases, a party's market share of the relevant market can be used as a surrogate for market power.[34,35] Market share is simply a party's percentage of the total input or output in the relevant market. The relevant market has two components: a relevant product or products and a corresponding geographic market.[36]

Even where a network may have market power, the existence and/or operation of the network may be permissible if there is a legitimate efficiency basis for the challenged conduct, unless demonstrable anticompetitive effects outweigh the benefits of the efficiencies claimed. Mere increases in market share, or decreases in the number of competitors or the number of independent pricing options available, should not be a sufficient basis to challenge the formation or operation of a network, as long as the efficiencies outweigh the anticompetitive effects. As the revised Statements of Enforcement Policy emphasize, "the greater the network's likely anticompetitive effects, the greater must be the network's likely efficiencies."[37]

Mergers

While the 1994 policy statements did not attempt to alter the 1993 statement regarding hospital mergers, the antitrust enforcement agencies did explicitly acknowledge for the first time that an analysis of market concentration does little to predict which hospital mergers are likely to create anticompetitive consequences. Specifically, the

1994 policy statements admit that the "agencies often have concluded that an investigated hospital merger will not result in a substantial lessening of competition in situations where market concentration might otherwise raise an inference of anticompetitive effects."[38] Indeed, a recent study emphasizes the point that mergers not challenged by the antitrust enforcement agencies create market concentration (shares) significantly in excess of the standards established by the government's merger guidelines.[39] Thus, antitrust enforcement policy regarding hospital mergers appears to have a somewhat random quality about it, with little meaningful guidance regarding identification of the mergers that will be challenged and which of them will not.[40] As one recent commentator has stated, "If we examine these data, we see how difficult it would be to predict whether a given merger would be challenged. The unpredictability of enforcement decisions should occasion soul-searching by the staffs of the enforcement agencies."[41]

At the same time, neither the 1993 nor 1994 policy statements address other forms of acquisitions and mergers in the health care industry, including the growing consolidation of physician practices. Guidance is needed with respect to these issues as well.

Joint pricing

The antitrust rules governing joint pricing proposals by provider-controlled integrated systems or networks have never been entirely clear, but the revised Statements of Enforcement Policy go only part of the way toward solving the problem. Specifically, the revised Statements of Enforcement Policy specifically mention only two ways of demonstrating economic integration—capitation and withholds—although there are many others, as the statement itself acknowledges, without providing guidance. Recently, the FTC, responding to criticism that the policy statements on permitted joint pricing are unduly restrictive, requested comments on whether forms of integration not based on capitation and similar risk-sharing arrangements are likely to produce efficiencies and, therefore, should trigger rule of reason analysis.[42]

To be sure, some so-called integrated systems involve very little service and/or payment integration and, as a consequence, offer very little potential for the creation of real efficiencies or "new products." Indeed, many appear to be little more than window dressing—a simple rearranging of the deck chairs on the *Titanic*. Nevertheless, even these networks may have value as transitional organizations, as long as their real effect is not to stymie more far-reaching integration. On the other hand, if the revised Statements of Enforcement Policy merely inhibit the development of garden variety PHOs, with their fee-for-service pricing arrangements, it is unlikely that the market will mourn their loss.

It should be recognized, however, that joint pricing proposals, by themselves, do not involve any exercise of market power. To the extent that a health plan or other purchaser (or potential purchaser) objects to a joint pricing proposal, the health plan or purchaser has the option of dealing independently with the network's participants. Where the system or network does not attempt to exercise market power in either the physician or hospital services market, it is difficult to see how health plans or consumers are harmed.

Of course, where the system or network participants do have market power in either the physician or hospital services market, the risk of consumer harm can be significant, particularly where the network utilizes exclusive arrangements with providers. Nevertheless, it may be that in the absence of the arrangement certain products would not be available to all. Thus, joint pricing arrangements can be legitimate ancillary restraints essential to the offering of a new product.

On the other hand, there is little utility in permitting arrangements that would simply allow competing providers in a market to jointly offer fee-for-service prices, unless the organization also provides some potential for efficiencies.[43] Moreover, if the pricing proposal also involves the operation of explicit, or implicit, exclusive arrangements—i.e., the joint proposal offered by the network represents the only opportunity to obtain the services of the network participants—then the danger to health plans and consumers is substantially greater.

Exclusive agreements

An agreement that prevents the providers from selling their services except through the system, or network, may foreclose other health plans from purchasing the services of the contracting providers if the contract between the network and the health plan also prevents the network from offering services to other health plans.[44] Where the foreclosure is significant, competition can be restrained, as the revised Statements of Enforcement Policy correctly note. In contrast, agreements that require a health plan to contract exclusively with a network for services (commonly known as a "requirements" contract) only foreclose other systems or networks of providers from contracting for services with the health plan. Unless the system has market power in the hospital or physician markets, a requirements contract alone is unlikely to create anticompetitive effects unless accompanied by an output contract.

Of course, a determination of the minimum number of providers needed by category for the operation of a viable competing system is critical to any foreclosure analysis. Thus, an exclusive arrangement that encumbers all the primary care physicians, or all the physicians available in a particular specialty, for instance, obstetrics or cardiology, will effectively foreclose competition in the market, although other types of physicians are available. However, an exclusive arrangement that only forecloses the supply of nonessential services (e.g., plastic surgery or durable medical equipment) would not significantly foreclose competition, because these services are not essential to the formation and operation of a competing system or network.

Exclusions from integrated systems

Providers excluded from systems often bring claims for violations of Section 1 of the Sherman Act, asserting that the network is engaging in an illegal boycott.[45] For the most part, these claims have been unsuccessful because the plaintiff has been unable to establish the existence of market power or anticompetitive effects.[46] The revised Statements of Enforcement Policy accurately state the general rule: "The focus of the analysis is not on whether a particular provider has been harmed by the exclusion, but rather whether the exclusion reduces competition among providers in the market and thereby harms consumers. Therefore, exclusion may present competitive concerns if providers are unable to compete effectively without access to the network, and competition is thereby harmed. The agencies also recognize, however, that there may be procompetitive reasons associated with the exclusion, such as the provider's competence or willingness and ability to meet the network's cost-containment goals."[47]

"Most Favored Nation" clauses

Unfortunately, the new policy statements do not specifically address the use of "Most Favored Nation" (MFN) clauses in contracts between health plans and providers. MFNs are contractual devices imposed by health plans (or insisted on by groups of providers) that require the providers to charge the health plan imposing the MFN no more than the lowest price charged to any other health plan. MFN clauses have been the object of substantial criticism because they may discourage and inhibit both health plans and providers from seeking to make more attractive arrangements under certain circumstances. Indeed, such arrangements also can facilitate the formation of provider cartels. Specifically, if the health plan imposing the MFN is a dominant purchaser of providers' services, then providers subject to the MFN clause may have economic incentives to discontinue or limit their discounting arrangements and to raise their price levels. As a result, competing health plans and, consequently, consumers end up paying higher prices.

Tying contracts

Another type of arrangement that did not receive, but perhaps merited, specific discussion in the revised Statements of Enforcement Policy is so-called tying contracts. An agreement between providers of medical services in different relevant product markets may constitute an impermissible "tying contract" under Section 1 of the Sherman Act if the services sold are separate products, the seller has market power in at least one market, and the buyer is required to buy the package of services. Thus, if a hospital with market power in a hospital services market uses its PHO to jointly market its services exclusively with certain physicians with staff privileges at that hospital, health plans could be required to use the services of the physicians, and, as a consequence, the conduct would be analyzed as a "tying contract." Nevertheless, there are several important considerations that must be weighed in determining whether the arrangement should be considered impermissible. For example, it must be clear that the hospital services and physician services are clearly distinguishable products for purposes of antitrust scrutiny. Where the services are sold jointly at a single price (e.g., a capitation or a global fee), then it is arguable that the sale involves a single product. On the other hand, if both are sold separately on a fee-for-service basis, even at a discount, then the services are likely to be considered separate products. Where market power forces health plans to purchase combinations of hospital and physician services that they do not want, the antitrust laws can, and will, prohibit the market distortion.

Conclusion

It is time to initiate a concerted critical campaign to make U.S. health care markets safe for competition among integrated networks of providers and the managed care plans that they serve. Through vigorous, but thoughtful, antitrust enforcement, and the elimination of the legislative and regulatory barriers that inhibit effective competition between health plans and their provider networks, much can be done to achieve that goal now, when market forces themselves are straining to achieve that result. Secure in the knowledge that it is indeed easier to ride a horse in the direction in which it is going, those who develop and implement public policy should make the effort to do so.

Notes

1. J. F. Blumstein, "Health Care Reform and Competing Visions of Medical Care: Antitrust and State Provider Cooperation Legislation," *Cornell Law Review* 79 (September 1994): 1459–1506.
2. R. A. Berenson, "Do Physicians Recognize Their Own Best Interests?" *Health Affairs* 13, no. 2 (Spring 1994): 185–93.
3. Blumstein 1994.
4. Berenson 1994.
5. A. Enthoven, "Why Managed Care Has Failed to Contain Health Costs," *Health Affairs* 12, no. 4 (Fall 1993): 28.
6. S. Jones, D. M. Cohodes, and B. Scheil, "The Risks of Ignoring Insurance Risk Management," *Health Affairs* 13, no. 2 (Spring 1994): 108–22.
7. R. Kronick, D. Goodman, and J. Wennburg, "The Market Place Health Care Reform: The Demographic Limitations of Managed Competition," *The New England Journal of Medicine* 328 (14 January 1993): 148–52.
8. Interestingly, not all proponents of integrated delivery systems (IDSs) accept the importance of competition as a guiding principle. Just as there is a policy disagreement over whether regulation or competition should be the primary mechanism for determining how health care services should be allocated, proponents of IDSs disagree over the importance of competition in limiting their size and scope. Indeed, important proponents of integration argue that the economies of scale, managerial reach, and political clout that produce the most efficient delivery systems are most easily promoted when the service organization is broadly integrated both horizontally and vertically and achieves the kind of market power that antitrust enforcers would likely label excessive. G. L. McManis, "The Industry Shake-Up in Anticipation of Health Care Reform," Paper presented at the 14th Annual Montgomery Dorsey Symposium, 14–16 July 1994. The very market consolidation that some applaud for eliminating

excess is decried by others for leading to potentially nonresponsive oligopolies. See M. V. Pauly, "Market Power, Monopsony, and Health Insurance Markets," *Journal of Health Economics* 7, no. 2 (1988): 111–128; see also R. Feldman, "The Welfare Economics of a Health Plan Merger," *Journal of Regulatory Economics* 6, no. 1 (1994): 67–86.

9. A typical "group without walls" is composed of physicians at multiple sites who are shareholders and/or employees of a corporation, thereby creating a health care delivery network. Typically, the physicians centralize overhead but retain ownership of individual practice assets. The physicians continue to do their own billings and collections, pay their own rent, and purchase their own office supplies. Group collections are credited and expenditures are debited to individual practice accounts at both the practice level and central organizational level. Other groups without walls feature multiple practice sites, but have a more centralized salary-oriented compensation system for physicians, all of whom are employees of the group.

10. D. McCarty Thornton, chief counsel of the OIG, has been quoted as saying that such groups are "shams" and should not be allowed to operate.

11. J. M. Mitchell and J. H. Sunshine, "Consequences of Physicians' Ownership of Health Care Facilities—Joint Ventures in Radiation Therapy," *The New England Journal of Medicine* 327, no. 21 (1992): 1497–1501.

12. A number of states are using Section 1115 waivers to expand coverage of the uninsured while controlling costs through expanded enrollment of Medicaid patients into HMOs. For many years, Medicare beneficiaries have had the option of joining HMOs, but in 1995 more than 90 percent of Medicare beneficiaries remain in the traditional, fee-for-service Medicare program. See chapter 8, "Medicare Risk Program Policy," in Physician Payment Review Commission, *Annual Report to Congress.* (Washington, DC: Government Printing Office, 1995.

13. See C. P. Kaiser, P. D. Hanvey, and T. J. Sullivan, "Integrated Delivery Systems and Joint Venture Dissolution Update," in 1995 IRS Exempt Organization Continuing Professional Education Technical Instruction Program.

14. Hospital Audit Guidelines at § 333. 2(2). See also, *General Counsel Memorandum 39498* (24 April 1986).

15. The IRS also has been active in cautioning hospitals on its concerns regarding the recruitment and retention of physicians. See IRS Closing Agreement with Herman Hospital, released 14 October 1994, and IRS Announcement 95-25, containing Proposed Revenue Rule on Tax Consequences of Physician Recruitment Incentives Provided by Hospitals Exempt Under Section 501(c)(3), issued 15 March 1995.

16. See also Audit Guidelines at § 333. 4(2).

17. C. Valiant, *Legal Issues in Health Care Fraud and Abuse: Navigating the Uncertainties* (National Health Lawyers Association, 1994).

18. See letter from D. McCarty Thornton to T. J. Sullivan, dated 22 December 1992, reported in *BNA Tax Reporter* (24 February 1993).

19. See Section 1877 of the Social Security Act, 42 U.S.C. § 1395nn.
20. See, e.g., Illinois 225 ILSC 47115(c)(1993); Md. Code Ann., Health Occ. § 1-301(G) (1993).
21. 15 U.S.C. § 1.
22. 15 U.S.C. § 2.
23. 15 U.S.C. § 18.
24. The Federal Trade Commission Act (15 U.S.C. § 45) generally prohibits the same conduct as the Sherman and Clayton Acts.
25. *Rothery Storage & Van Co. v. Atlas Van Lines, Inc.*, 792 F. 2d 210 (D.C. Cir. 1986), *cert. denied*, 479 U.S. 1033 (1987).
26. *FTC v. Ticor Title Ins. Co.*, 112 S. Ct. 2169, 2176 (1992).
27. R. M. Langer, "The Relationship Between the State Action Immunity Doctrine and State Provider Collaboration Statutes," paper presented at the National Health Lawyers Association Conference on Antitrust in the Health Care Field (1995).
28. The six health care areas covered by the policy were (1) hospital mergers, (2) hospital joint ventures involving high-technology and other expensive medical equipment, (3) physicians' provision of information to purchasers of health care services, (4) hospital participation in exchanges in price and cost information, (5) joint purchasing arrangements among health care providers, and (6) physician network joint ventures. The document creates "safety zones" in each of the six areas. In addition, for the first time the antitrust enforcement agencies have committed to responding to any requests for more specific guidance by providing advisory opinions within 90 days, so long as the request for guidance relates to one of the six areas covered by the Policy Statements, except for mergers outside the safety zone.
29. Initial Policy Statements at 1.
30. Revised Policy Statements at 9.
31. *Eastman Kodak Co. v. Image Technical Servs., Inc.*, 112 S. Ct. 2072, 2080 (1992) (citing *Jefferson Parish Hosp. v. Hyde*, 466 U.S. 2, 14 (1984).
32. *NCAA v. Board of Regents*, 468 U.S. 85, 106-08 (1984); *Jefferson Parish Hosp. v. Hyde*, 466 U.S. 2, 31 n.52 (1984).
33. NCAA, 468 U.S. at 110; *see also Capital Imaging Assocs. v. Mohawk Valley Medical Assocs.*, 996 F.2d 537 (2d Cir.), *cert. denied*, 114 S. Ct. 388 (1993).
34. Eastman Kodak, 112 S. Ct. at 2081.
35. However, other factors are also considered in determining a party's market power, including "the strength of competition, probable development of the industry, the barriers to entry, the nature of the anticompetitive conduct, and elasticity of consumer demand." *Barr Labs., Inc. v. Abbott Labs.*, 978 F.2d 98, 112 (3d Cir. 1992).
36. *Tampa Elec. Co. v. Nashville Coal Co.*, 365 U.S. 320, 327 (1961); *see* 1992 DOJ/FTC Merger Guidelines § 1, 4 Trade Reg. Rep. (CCH) ¶13,104, at 20,571 (1992).
37. Revised Statements of Enforcement Policy at 103.
38. 1994 Policy Statement at 13,14.
39. G. J. Bazzoli, D. Marks, R. J. Arnould, and L. M. Manhein, "Federal

Antitrust Merger Enforcement Standards: A Good Fit for the Hospital Industry?" *Journal of Health Politics, Policy and Law* 20, no. 1 (Spring 1995): 137–69.

40. Bazzoli et al. 1995.

41. N. Zwanziger, "The Need for an Antitrust Policy for Health Care Industry in Transition," *Journal of Health Politics, Policy and Law* 20, no. 1 (Spring 1995): 171–73.

42. M. D. Whitener, Deputy Director, Federal Trade Commission, "Antitrust, Medicare Reform, and Health Care Competition." Prepared remarks presented before the American Enterprise Institute for Public Policy Research, Washington, DC (5 December 1995): 15–17.

43. As a technical matter, organizations making such joint offerings can be classified as sham joint ventures.

44. Plans should not "prevent or make impracticable the formation of other plans that would otherwise be likely to enter the market." *FTC Statement of Enforcement on Physician Agreements to Control Medical Prepayment Plans,* 46 Federal Register 48,982, 48,991 (5 Oct. 1981); letter from A. Lerner, Assistant Director, FTC Bureau of Competition, to G. Frimet, Attorney, Frimet, Bellamy, Gilchrist & Lites (22 Mar. 1984): 4.

45. *Capital Imaging,* 996 F.2d 537.

46. *Capital Imaging,* 996 F.2d 537; *Hassan v. Independent Practice Assocs.,* 698 F. Supp. 679 (E.C. Mich, 1988); *Williamson v. Sacred Heart Hosp.,* No. 89-30084-RV, 1993 WL 543002 (N.D. Fla. 28 May 1993); but see Hahn v. Oregon Physicians' Serv., 868 F.2d 1022 (9th Cir. 1988), *cert. denied,* 493 U.S. 846 (1989).

47. *Revised Statements of Enforcement Policy* at 103.

9

The Changing Environment for Technological Innovation in Health Care

Clifford S. Goodman and Annetine C. Gelijns

Abstract. A distinguishing feature of American health care is its emphasis on advanced technology. Yet today's changing health care environment is overhauling the engine of technological innovation. The rate and direction of technological innovation are affected by a complex of supply- and demand-side factors, including biomedical research, education, patent law, regulation, health care payment, tort law, and more. Some distinguishing features of technological innovation in health care are now at increased risk. Regulatory requirements and rising payment hurdles are especially challenging to small technology companies. Closer management of health care delivery and payment, particularly the standardization that may derive from practice guidelines and clamping down on payment for investigational technologies, curtails opportunities for innovation. Levels and distribution of biomedical research funding in government and industry are changing. Financial constraints are limiting the traditional roles of academic health centers in fostering innovation. Despite notable steps in recent years to lower regulatory barriers and speed approvals, especially for products for life-threatening conditions, the Food and Drug Administration is under great pressure from Congress, industry, and patients to do more.

Technology gatekeeping is shifting from hundreds of thousands of physicians acting on behalf of their patients to fewer, yet more powerful, managed care organizations and health care networks. Beyond its direct effects on adoption, payment, and use of technologies, the extraordinary buying leverage of these large providers is cutting technology profit margins and heightening competition among technology companies. It is contributing to unprecedented restructuring of the pharmaceutical and medical device industries, leading to unprecedented alliances with generic product companies, health care providers, utilization review companies, and other agents. These industry changes are already having considerable effects on investment patterns and the development, adoption, and use of new technologies.

Until recently, new technologies that offered the prospect for health benefit, however marginal or unproven, were paid for with little or no regard to cost. Technical wizardry alone no longer carries the day in health care. Today's health care market increasingly demands what other markets do—measurable improvements in benefits at acceptable costs—and innovators have begun to respond accordingly. Even so, certain key venues for health care innovation are at risk.

For the past 50 years, whether the goals of U.S. health care have been to eradicate disease, build hospitals, care for the elderly, care for the poor, contain costs, or expand coverage to the uninsured, technological innovation has been presumed. Although it has been cited for two decades as culpable, in varying degrees, for burgeoning health care costs,[1] new technology marches on as the standard bearer for U.S. health care.

Strong commitment to technological advancement, a key feature of modern medicine, is embedded in American institutions devoted to innovation, including federal biomedical research agencies, academic health centers, industry, and private foundations.[2] The perseverance, good fortune, and occasional celebrity associated with innovation are embraced in the American character. Yankee ingenuity, building a better mousetrap, and garage invention are no better exemplified than in small, high-risk biotechnology firms. Confidence in innovation has been as constant as the mantras of "miracle drug" and "cure for cancer" that have infused biomedical research since World War II. Public demand for cutting-edge health care technology is fueled by television news bytes, clips from *USA Today*, and scoops off the Internet.

The rate and direction of technological innovation in health care are affected by supply-side and demand-side forces within and beyond the health care sector. These derive from an evolving and complex mix of policies for biomedical research, education, intellectual property, regulation, entitlements, employee benefits, health care payment, tort law, investment, taxes, subsidies, public works, and trade.

Historically, the following principal factors have contributed to a high rate of technological innovation: steeply increasing funding for biomedical research and medical education, national hospital construction programs, fee-for-service insurance coverage for expanding benefit plans, government entitlement health programs (principally Medicare and Medicaid), and a growing and aging population. Technology adoption decisions have usually been made by physicians with strong professional motivation to use new technologies. Competition for physicians, patients, and prestige has stimulated hospitals to acquire new technologies. Investment in innovation has had favorable returns, contributing to the emergence of strong health care product industries. Until recently, the benefit-cost equation has been largely one-sided: new technologies offering the prospect for health benefit, however marginal or unproven, have been covered with little or no regard to cost.

Many of these same factors have affected the direction of technological innovation. In particular, they have funneled the mainstream of the health care economy into hospital-based care. This has helped to steer innovation more toward acute, curative care, somewhat to the detriment of prevention, primary care, and rehabilitation. The role of academic health centers in innovation has been particularly strengthened, fueling development and adoption of leading-edge technologies and the commensurate training of an expanding cadre of specialists and subspecialists. Payment rates have generally rewarded physicians more generously for device-based medical and surgical procedures used in diagnosis and treatment than for more "cognitive" services such as taking a medical history or counseling a patient.

The environment for technological innovation in health care is undergoing significant change. Today, the dominant influence on its rate and direction is the restructured industry of health care delivery organizations. The proportion of Americans covered by some form of managed care is two-thirds and is rising, including nearly 60 million HMO enrollees.[3] Hospitals and medical groups are merging into large chains and other integrated health care delivery systems, the largest of which account for millions of patients each. In this market, the technology gatekeepers are fewer, yet highly powerful, prudent buyers. The sweeping 1990s restructuring of American health care is changing the incentives for innovation, adding risk and uncertainty to key sectors of technological development.

The Nature of Innovation

The popular model of innovation is linear and unidirectional: basic biomedical research to applied research to targeted development to manufacturing and marketing to adoption of a finished product. Many health care innovations do proceed along the model course; indeed, regulatory benchmarks for drugs and certain devices are consistent with it. Yet, the linear model does not depict the interaction, iteration, market pull, and other factors that characterize technological innovation in health care or other fields.[4,5] Technological innovation in health care depends on advances in such fields as materials science, engineering, molecular biology, computer science, management, and telecommunications. Many health care technologies are adaptations from other fields, for example, lasers, ultrasound, magnetic resonance spectroscopy, and computing. Among the many technologies that were developed with the interdisciplinary work of clinicians and physicists, engineers, and other scientists are medical lasers, cardiac pacemakers, cochlear implants, endoscopy, catheters, and cardiac imaging.[6–9]

Another flaw of the unidirectional linear model of innovation is the neat distinction assumed between R&D and adoption into practice. Many health care technologies are not perfected when first adopted. Indeed, clinical practice can disclose shortcomings and potential that could not have been revealed earlier. Clinical adoption is often just the beginning of an iterative process of feedback from users, redesign, use, and more feedback. This process has characterized incremental innovation in such technologies as lung transplantation, oral contraceptives, antibiotics, artificial joints, and percutaneous transluminal coronary angioplasty (PTCA).

With technological diversification, improving technique, and better patient outcomes, physicians are more likely to experiment with and eventually routinely use technologies in alternative ways. For many drugs, entirely new applications have arisen apart from their original uses (e.g., aspirin for antithrombosis, thalidomide for lepra and graft-versus-host disease, and fluoxetine [Prozac] for obsessive-compulsive disorder). Beyond their original uses in ophthalmology and dermatology, lasers are used in gynecology, gastroenterology, oncology, thoracic surgery, and other specialties.[10]

The linear model is primarily a supply-side depiction of the fruits of research; it does not describe how the rate and direction of innovation are affected by demand-side forces.[11] Traditionally, the main mediators of technology demand were hundreds of thousands of individual physicians acting on behalf of their patients. Today, buying power is increasingly concentrated in a much smaller number of managed care organizations and health care networks, shifting the forces influencing adoption, payment, and use of technologies. These changes affect demand for new technology, the return on investment in innovation, and patterns of investment in biomedical R&D.

Federal Support for R&D

Total U.S. funding for biomedical R&D was $32.9 billion in 1994. Of this, the federal government accounted for about $12.3 billion (37.5 percent); state and local governments accounted for about $2.2 billion (6.7 percent); and the private sector accounted for about $18.4 billion, including $17.1 billion by industry (52 percent) and $1.3 billion by private nonprofit sources (3.9 percent) such as foundations and universities. Academic health centers also subsidize biomedical research with patient care funds (derived largely from government and private sector third-party payers) estimated to be on the order of $850 million.[12,13]

Since the end of World War II, federal biomedical research funding has increased—first sharply, then steadily. From 1950 through 1965, appropriations for the National Institutes of Health (NIH), the main federal agency for biomedical research, increased 18 percent per year in real dollars. In recent years, federal biomedical research funding has increased at real rates exceeding inflation. From 1984 to 1994, federal biomedical R&D spending increased from $6.1 billion to $12.3 billion in current dollars, or 27 percent in constant dollars. As noted below, the private sector, particularly the pharmaceutical industry, has more than matched growth in federal spending for biomedical research. From 1984 to 1994, the proportion of total national biomedical research spending accounted for by the federal government decreased from 50 percent to 37 percent. Recently, Congress has considered spending freezes and cuts that, if sustained, would amount to significant real decreases in federal R&D spending.

Although most federally supported biomedical R&D is for basic research on health and disease, the government does provide substantial support for research targeted to the development of new health care technologies. In 1988, NIH and other Public Health Service (PHS) research organizations spent approximately $650 million for preclinical and clinical pharmaceutical R&D.[14] Federal spending for medical device–related R&D was about $422 million in 1992.[15]

In addition to direct, budgeted support for biomedical R&D, the federal government provides considerable indirect support for biomedical R&D in other ways. These include support for education and training of researchers, information dissemination of government-supported research, tax credits and tax deductions for industry R&D, technology transfer policies, orphan technology policies, and Medicare and Medicaid payments for patient care in clinical trials.[16,17] The government also supports research to assess the benefits, risks, and costs of medical technologies through such agencies as the Food and Drug Administration (FDA), NIH, Agency for Health Care Policy and Research, Centers for Disease Control and Prevention (CDC), Department of Veterans Affairs, and Congressional Office of Technology Assessment (for which funding was discontinued in 1995).

The Pharmaceutical Industry

The pharmaceutical industry is multinational, highly research-intensive, and among the world's most profitable industries. Since World War II, drug companies' high return on investment has led to continued increases in R&D spending and a steady stream of successful products. In 1996, combined domestic sales and sales abroad of Pharmaceutical Research and Manufacturers of America (PhRMA) member companies were estimated to be $96.6 billion.[18] U.S. spending on drugs has increased steadily in absolute terms and in relation to national health expenditures. For the decade 1981–1991, prescription drug spending increased from 4.4 percent to 6.4 percent of total national health expenditures.[19] The U.S. pharmaceutical industry has sustained real growth (corrected for inflation) of about 2 percent per year since 1988.[20] Leading drug therapies command annual sales in the hundreds of millions of dollars; top selling brand name drugs exceed $1 billion in annual sales.[21]

Pharmaceutical R&D spending

Since 1970, U.S. pharmaceutical industry R&D spending has doubled every five years, reaching an estimated $15.8 billion in 1996.[22] In 1996, R&D spending by the industry was an estimated 19.0 percent of sales (Table 9.1), three times the level of the next highest industry (medical devices). The pharmaceutical industry's considerable R&D investment reflects (1) a lengthy and expensive process of product development and evaluation requiring substantial clinical trials, (2) patent protection, and (3) largely unfettered pricing, until recently, for approved products.

Drug development is long, costly, and uncertain. The average time from discovery of a prospective new drug until marketing

Table 9.1   Research and Development, Sales, and R&D as a Percentage of U.S. Sales for Member Companies of the Pharmaceutical Research and Manufacturers of America, 1980–1996

Year	Domestic U.S. R&D ($ mil.)	R&D Abroad ($ mil.)	Total R&D ($ mil.)	Domestic U.S. Sales ($ mil.)	U.S. Exports ($ mil.)	Sales Abroad ($ mil.)	Domestic U.S. R&D as % of Sales + Exports
1980	1,544.1	427.5	1,976.7	11,997.6	1,219.3	10,515.4	11.7%
1981	1,866.2	469.1	2,339.5	12,872.0	1,393.8	10,658.3	13.1
1982	2,265.6	505.0	2,773.7	14,986.9	1,446.3	10,667.4	13.8
1983	2,663.1	546.3	3,217.6	17,095.0	1,335.7	10,411.2	14.4
1984	2,976.4	596.4	3,578.8	19,403.1	1,340.8	10,450.9	14.3
1985	3,370.7	698.9	4,077.6	21,153.5	1,556.9	10,872.3	14.8
1986	3,870.9	865.1	4,740.1	24,106.8	2,044.2	13,030.5	14.8
1987	4,503.2	998.1	5,502.2	26,566.1	2,013.3	15,068.4	15.8
1988	5,228.7	1,303.6	6,537.5	29,324.6	2,696.2	17,649.3	16.3
1989	6,019.3	1,308.6	7,330.0	33,321.6	3,145.8	16,817.9	16.5
1990	6,800.1	1,617.4	8,420.3	39,229.3	3,420.6	19,838.3	15.9
1991	7,928.6	1,776.8	9,705.4	45,264.1	3,523.5	22,231.1	16.2
1992	9,309.1	2,155.8	11,467.9	49,901.8	4,042.7	25,744.2	17.3
1993	10,473.0	2,262.9	12,740.0	52,911.3	3,982.7	26,467.3	18.4
1994	11,101.6	2,347.8	13,449.4	55,996.2	3,606.1	26,870.7	18.6
1995*	11,845.4	2,529.4	14,374.8	58,046.5	3,968.0	29,567.1	19.1
1996*	12,858.4	2,898.6	15,757.0	63,149.9	4,485.6	33,424.0	19.0

Note: Domestic U.S. R&D includes expenditures within the United States by all PhRMA member companies. R&D abroad includes expenditures by U.S.-owned companies outside the United States. Domestic U.S. sales include sales within the United States by all PhRMA member companies. Sales abroad include sales by U.S.-owned companies outside the United States.

*Estimates

approval by the FDA is about 12 years, comprising an average of 3.5 years for preclinical testing, 6 years for the three phases of clinical trials, and 2.5 years for FDA review and approval.[23,24] This expensive, lengthy process cuts into the time during which a company has market exclusivity, and raises the risk of investing in R&D.

After-tax expenditures for R&D per successful new drug are on the order of $200 million or more.[25] Nearly 30 percent of pharmaceutical industry R&D spending is for premarketing clinical trials and postmarketing clinical evaluation.[26] Spending hardly ensures success. According to industry estimates, of every 5,000 compounds that undergo preclinical testing, 5 enter clinical trials, and 1 receives market approval by the FDA.[27] The total number of new drugs that are introduced annually in the United States by the combined efforts of the industry is roughly 20 to 30, only a third of which become financial leaders.

Biotechnology industry

The term "biotechnology" embraces the evolving group of biological technologies and research tools for divulging and manipulating the molecular mechanisms underlying disease and other biological processes. Among these technologies are recombinant DNA technology ("gene splicing"), monoclonal antibodies, and cell fusion techniques.[28] Biotechnology is used to synthesize drugs, vaccines, and diagnostic products.[29]

Launched in the late 1970s, the biotechnology ("biotech") industry is in its adolescence. The U.S.-based biotech industry consists of more than 1,200 companies, with an average of fewer than 80 employees each. The industry had sales of about $8 billion in 1994, and R&D spending equaled 80 percent of sales.[30] Most biotech companies are not profitable; half have cash reserves of two years or less. Most biotech companies depend on venture capital, sales of stock, and collaborations with large pharmaceutical companies. Biotech R&D is not the sole province of the small, young companies. More than one-third of the current R&D projects undertaken by the major pharmaceutical companies involve biotech processes.[31]

Despite some breakthrough products, the overall progress and profitability of the biotech industry have fallen short of earlier, unrealistic expectations. Highlighted by several widely publicized failures, and coupled with the prospect of federal health care reform in the early 1990s, these disappointments depressed the public market for biotech firms.[32] Even so, large pharmaceutical companies have taken considerable, selective interest in these firms. In 1994 and 1995, there were substantial increases in investments, acquisitions, marketing agreements, and other alliances involving large pharmaceutical companies and biotech firms.[33] With increased in-house biotech activity and collaborations with biotech firms, the pharmaceutical industry is evolving toward a "biopharmaceutical" industry.[34]

Innovations shaped by incentives

Economic incentives, patient demographics, cultural factors, and legal considerations are among the many factors that drive pharmaceutical innovation in particular directions. Medicare coverage for an expanding aged population has provided incentives to develop drugs for chronic diseases that are common among the elderly. Certainly, there are advantages to investing in R&D for drugs that will be taken every day to manage patients' chronic conditions for the rest of their lives. Less attractive is investing in development of vaccines or contraceptives, which require lengthy testing in largely healthy populations in which adverse events are likely to lead to legal action.

Many drugs, patented though they may be, do not represent truly novel treatments. These "me-too" drugs are slight molecular variants with the same mechanism of action as existing drugs, offering little or no discernible clinical differences. Among the highest-selling drugs are multiple versions of H–2 antagonists (for treating ulcers); angiotensin-converting enzyme (ACE) inhibitors, calcium channel blockers, and beta-blockers (for hypertension and other cardiovascular disorders); HMG-CoA reductase inhibitors (cholesterol-lowering drugs); and many similar antibiotics. Concentration of R&D investment in areas such as these reflects companies' judgments that me-too drugs can be profitable in large chronic disease markets.

Patent protection

Although a patent from the U.S. government confers market exclusivity for up to 17 years, the portion of this time during which a drug is on the market is shortened by the time taken to fulfill FDA premarketing regulatory requirements. (Market exclusivity is imperfect for many patented drugs that can be substituted for by similar yet distinct me-too drugs.) The Drug Price Competition and Patent Term Restoration Act of 1984 enables companies to recoup as much as five years of protection to compensate for time taken to secure FDA approval. In turn, the act facilitates the introduction of generic drugs soon after expiration of their original patented counterparts. Whereas companies averaged approximately 10 years of effective patent life prior to the act, protection runs for about 13 or 14 years today.[35]

Companies seek to maximize their revenue streams during the limited time of a drug's market exclusivity. A recent federal report observed: "On a scale ranging between a perfect monopoly and perfect competition, the pharmaceutical industry can probably best be described as imperfectly competitive; firms have some power to raise prices and generate excess profits."[36] However, as described below, drug pricing is experiencing new cost-containment pressure that may affect the level and distribution of R&D spending.

The Medical Device Industry

Medical devices are a heterogeneous group of products, ranging from disposable surgical gloves to diagnostic kits to positron emission tomography (PET) scanners. Some 1,700 different types of medical devices are manufactured by more than 11,000 device manufacturers (domestic and foreign) registered with the FDA.[37,38]

Until World War II, the medical device industry was very small relative to modern standards. Wartime investment in R&D stimulated many advances in science and engineering, such as radar, ultrasound, and new materials, that would benefit the development of medical devices and stimulate growth in the industry. Along with other health care technologies, the market for devices expanded rapidly with boosts from the Medicare and Medicaid programs and increasingly generous insurance benefits.

Medical device innovation is often characterized by small steps rather than breakthroughs. Frequent incremental changes—and designer ingenuity for circumventing patent protection—mean short product lives for many devices, ranging from a few months to a few years. This is exemplified in the highly competitive market for balloon-tipped catheter systems used in PTCA. Since being introduced in humans in 1977, their guidance mechanisms, catheters, balloon materials and profiles, and other components have undergone continuous modification and diversification.[39]

The U.S. medical device industry was a $42 billion industry[40] in 1994; production grew about 9 percent annually from 1988 to 1993. In recent years, certain sectors of this industry have been among the fastest growing in the United States (Table 9.2). In 1993, 23 percent of U.S. production of medical devices was exported, and the United States accounted for 52 percent of global output.[41]

Table 9.2 Value of Product Shipments, Medical Device Industry, by Standard Industry Classifications

SIC Classification	Prod. Ship. 1994* ($ mil.)	Percent Change 1989–1994 (Constant 1987 $)					
		1988–89	1989–90	1990–91	1991–92†	1992–93†	1993–94*
3841 Surgical and Medical Instruments	13,550	4.9	11.1	4.7	5.2	6.8	7.1
3842 Surgical Appliances and Supplies	16,466	2.8	4.5	7.3	9.0	9.3	9.7
3843 Dental Equipment and Supplies	1,652	−1.8	6.3	16.8	1.6	2.0	3.5
3844 X-ray Apparatus and Tubes	2,655	−0.2	13.9	14.2	5.8	5.0	5.0
3845 Electromedical Equipment	5,637	15.0	2.5	7.2	2.7	0.2	0.2
3851 Ophthalmic Goods	2,085	3.7	10.6	−0.4	1.0	1.5	2.0
Total	42,045						

*Forecast.
†Estimate.

Source: U.S. Department of Commerce, 1994.

Although the total market for medical devices is large, the markets for most types of devices are small. Of the U.S. markets for each of the FDA's 1,700 device types, more than 70 percent are valued at less than $50 million per year, and only about 50 are worth $200 million or more.[42] Small device markets, and the many small companies that serve them, are quite susceptible to changes in health care, particularly regarding regulation and third-party payment.[43] In 1993, 88 percent of medical device firms had fewer than 100 employees, 10 percent had 100–499 employees, and 2 percent had 500 or more employees.[44]

R&D commitment for the medical device industry

Small and large companies tend to play different roles in medical device innovation. Start-up firms have been disproportionately responsible for the innovation and early development of truly novel devices, including angioplasty catheters, artificial joints, cardiac support devices, diagnostic ultrasound, and vascular grafts. Large firms tend to pursue incremental improvements, for example, by refining or building on current product lines for familiar markets, and getting products over regulatory and payment hurdles.[45–47]

On average, U.S. medical device companies spent 6.8 percent of sales on R&D in 1993, increasing steadily from 6.2 percent in 1988. (The all-industry 1993 average was 3.8 percent.) However, the average figure for R&D spending in the medical device industry belies considerable variation in R&D commitment depending on company size and product types. In 1993, small companies (less than $5 million in sales) spent 127.2 percent of their sales on R&D (reflecting new companies' start-up R&D investment before sales are established), compared with 23.2 percent for medium-sized companies ($5–20 million in sales), 9.7 percent for large companies ($20–100 million in sales), and 5.7 percent for very large companies (more than $100 million in sales).[48] The viability of the smaller R&D–intensive firms, which are disproportionately responsible for innovation, are particularly susceptible to market shifts and policy changes.

Venture Capital and Other Support for Small Companies

Venture capital funding is critical to the success of many small medical device and biotech companies. With innovative, yet unproven ideas and few assets, these small firms need capital to develop prototypes, conduct testing, redesign as needed, gain regulatory and payment approval, and continue to move their products toward the market. For venture capital to work, investors must perceive that assuming the financial risk of an innovation is worth the potential for significant return. Venture capital firms use their industry acumen regarding technological potential, markets, management, and other factors to select promising companies and raise financing from institutional and private investors to support their development.[49]

In U.S. industry overall, venture capital funding levels fell from $7.7 billion in 1988 to $5.4 billion in 1993. The medical device industry fared well from 1988 through 1992, increasing from approximately $300 million in 1988 (3.9 percent of total U.S. venture capital funding that year) to $434 million in 1992 (7.6 percent of the total); however, this fell to $283 million in 1994 (5.3 percent of the total). The number of medical technology companies receiving venture capital financing remained relatively stable during this period, so that the average dollar volume of financing per company increased from $2.4 million in 1988 to $3.3 million in 1993.[50]

This leveling off of the number of companies receiving venture funding may reflect narrower selection criteria on the part of investors. In addition, the mixed success of early biotech products has discouraged some investors. Caution may be shifting investments from riskier "seed capital" (first-round financing for concept or product development) toward later financing rounds that occur after innovations have demonstrated some progress, and toward companies that are already part of investors' portfolios and whose products have passed FDA hurdles.[51,52]

Smaller companies may also be adversely affected by the stock performance of larger, publicly traded health care product companies. Cost containment, prospects for health reform, and product liability actions helped to push down the stock prices of many of these companies in the early 1990s.[53] For venture capitalists, the return on investment typically occurs when a start-up company goes public or is sold to a larger company. If the market for companies in an industry is in decline, venture capitalists perceive less return on their investments there, and take their venture money elsewhere.

Many small medical device and biotech companies ultimately collaborate with larger corporate partners through marketing agreements, sale of minority shares, joint ventures, mergers, or acquisitions. Larger companies offer steady funding, opportunities for technological synergy, manufacturing capability, marketing, distribution channels, and field service. Larger companies more often have the experience and capacity to conduct clinical trials and take on regulatory and payment hurdles. Brand name recognition of large companies conveys credibility to stockholders and consumers. Collaboration with small R&D–intensive firms enables large firms to convert some fixed R&D costs to variable costs, bolster product lines, and diversify risk.[54,55] Beyond the high-risk strategy of investing in a few new molecules with therapeutic potential, large pharmaceutical companies are increasingly attracted to biotech companies that have broadly enabling technologies (e.g., gene databases and "combinatorial chemistry," automated synthesis of large libraries of compounds that are screened on automated machines for activity against molecular target sites).[56] Some of the innovative capacity of small companies may be lost if they must align themselves earlier with larger firms.

FDA Regulation of Drugs and Devices

Among numerous federal and state laws controlling drugs and medical devices, the federal Food, Drug, and Cosmetic (FD&C) Act has the greatest influence. The FDA, charged with implementing this body of law and regulation, has gradually grown in importance since the inception of the Act in 1938. FDA regulations provide the major organizing framework for the development, testing, and market entry of new drugs and devices. This framework affects the structure of the pharmaceutical and medical device industries, the cost and pace of innovation, and the types of products on the market.

FDA regulation of new drugs

For drugs, FDA involvement begins when a sponsor seeks to investigate a drug in humans. Two centers in the FDA are primarily responsible for reviewing drug applications: the Center for Drug Evaluation and Research (CDER) and the Center for Biologics Evaluation and Research (CBER).[57]

The FDA has a two-part process for premarketing drug evaluation: (1) the investigational new drug application (IND) and (2) the new drug approval application (NDA) process for products reviewed by CDER (or the product license application [PLA] and the establishment license application [ELA] for products reviewed by CBER). For an IND, a drug sponsor provides detailed information about the clinical research plans, details of manufacturing processes, and results of laboratory and animal tests to date. Once an IND is allowed, sponsors typically proceed with a three-phase clinical trial process.[58] Following completion of clinical trials under the approved IND, a sponsor may file an NDA, which is a request for FDA permission to market the drug. An NDA may comprise 30 volumes totaling 100,000 or more pages.[59]

The FD&C Act allows considerable latitude for interpretation of safety and effectiveness in determining the acceptable risk-benefit ratio for a marketing approval decision. Premarketing requirements have become increasingly detailed over time with increased public expectations for drug safety and higher standards for scientific rigor of drug evaluations.[60]

Premarketing clinical studies cannot provide a complete picture of a drug's potential benefits or adverse effects. Identification of delayed or rare adverse effects of drugs would require lengthy testing of many thousands of patients. Valuable information on the nature and extent of a new drug's benefits and adverse effects for its approved indications may emerge only after its diffusion into the diverse environment of general use. Industry and, to some extent, the FDA conduct postmarketing studies of drugs that address some of the needs left unfilled by premarketing studies, although the volume of postmarketing data is far less than that for premarketing data. The frequency of FDA's requests for postmarketing studies of approved drugs has increased significantly in recent years, particularly for studies of drug interactions.

Although the FDA closely regulates the introduction and labeling of new drugs for approved indications, it does not regulate the use of legally marketed drugs for other indications. Such "off-label" use, which is common in medicine,[61] poses risks as well as opportunities for innovative applications. Although companies can reapply to FDA for approval to market drugs for additional indications, many do not because the cost and time involved outweigh the expected increase in revenues for new labeling. Recent closer inspection of prescriptions and cost-containment efforts by payers may be limiting payment for off-label uses.[62]

Changes to expedite new drug approvals

Since the late 1970s, but mostly since 1985, the FDA has undertaken actions to expedite the premarket testing and review of new drugs, particularly those for treating persons with serious or life-threatening diseases. Among these actions, the FDA has:

- issued guidelines and points-to-consider for sponsors involved in the drug testing and approval process;

- revised IND and NDA regulations to simplify and clarify aspects of application forms, established time limits for industry and agency action (not always adhered to), and provided opportunities for direct communication between drug sponsors and the agency at certain junctures of the clinical research period;

- established new drug review priority schemes to speed review of important therapies so that they might reach the market sooner;

- allowed drug sponsors to submit computerized new drug applications (NDAs, PLA/ELAs, and others) intended to streamline FDA reviews;

- issued regulations that expedite the clinical testing process for drugs to treat life-threatening and severely debilitating illnesses;[63]

- established the Treatment IND program and parallel track program that provide access to investigational drugs for otherwise untreatable conditions for patients who cannot enroll in the main clinical trials required by the FDA;[64] and

- broadened its acceptance of applicable foreign data from studies conducted in accordance with FDA requirements.

Congress also has moved to expedite drug approval. The purpose of the Prescription Drug User Fee Act of 1992 is to accelerate drug approvals, provide additional funds for the FDA reviewers to meet an expanding workload, and provide industry with a more predictable and efficient review process. This law, which will be reviewed when it expires after five years, requires drug sponsors to pay user fees to support FDA review of new drug applications.

Approval times for new drugs

The average time required for FDA review of new drugs, that is, new molecular entities (NMEs), dropped from 39.1 months in 1984 to 19.2 months in 1995, a decrease of 50 percent (Table 9.3). For the 28 NMEs approved in 1995, the median approval time was 15.9 months.

Table 9.3 Number of New Drugs (Molecular Entities) and Mean Approval Times, by FDA Center for Drug Evaluation and Research, 1984–1995

	1984	1985	1986	1987	1988	1989	1990	1991	1992	1993	1994	1995
Number of new drugs approved	22	30	20	21	20	23	23	30	26	25	22	28
Mean approval time for new drugs (months)	39.1	31.9	34.1	32.4	31.3	32.5	27.7	30.3	29.9	26.5	19.7	19.2

Source: U.S. Food and Drug Administration.

For the 23 NMEs for which NDAs were submitted since the start of the user fee program, median approval time was 15.0 months. Of those 23, the median review time for the seven that were designated "priority" applications (for drugs expected to have important new therapeutic value) was just 5.7 months.[65]

Reductions in approval times over the past decade are due to a variety of factors, including growing familiarity of the industry and the agency with the drug approval process and effects of some of the FDA initiatives noted earlier. Given the length of drug R&D pipelines, most of these FDA initiatives are too recent to have made significant impacts on the overall length of the R&D process. In general, however, they should expedite the review process and decrease uncertainty in it.

FDA regulation of medical devices

FDA regulation of medical devices is based primarily on two factors: (1) levels of device risk and (2) availability of devices, or their "substantially equivalent" predecessors, as of the enactment of the Medical Device Amendments of 1976. The FDA uses a three-tier classification of devices according to risk. For Class I devices (e.g., elastic bandages and tongue depressors), which are the least regulated, manufacturers are required to comply with "general controls."[66] Class II devices (e.g., x-ray devices, contact lenses, and powered wheelchairs) are required to meet additional special controls, including performance standards, postmarketing surveillance, and patient registries. Class III devices (e.g., cardiac assist devices, laser angioplasty tools, and infant radiant warmers), encompassing less than 10 percent of device types, are subject to the most extensive regulation. For these, the FDA can require approval of a Premarket Approval application (PMA) submitted by the device sponsor that demonstrates the clinical safety and effectiveness of a device.

The approval process for a device depends on whether it was on the market before or after the 1976 amendments. Devices are separated into two categories: pre-amendment devices or post-amendment devices. Manufacturers are allowed to continue marketing all pre-amendment devices, except that the FDA can call for and approve a PMA for Class III devices in order to permit continued marketing. If and when the FDA calls for and requires approval of a PMA for a pre-amendment Class III device in order to continue marketing, its substantially equivalent counterparts will also require

PMA approval. Post-amendment devices are of two basic types: those found to be "substantially equivalent" to pre-amendment devices and those that are not. For substantially equivalent devices, the FDA requires clearance of a "510(k)" premarket notification application[67] prior to marketing. Devices that are not substantially equivalent represent significant changes from existing devices and are automatically placed in Class III.[68]

In practice, there are two main routes to the market for a new device. If a device sponsor can establish substantial equivalence with a 510(k) application, then premarket notification is all that is required. If not, then a sponsor must submit a PMA and have it approved by the FDA before the device can go on the market. In order to conduct clinical studies that may be required for a PMA and some 510(k)s, a device sponsor must apply for an Investigational Device Exemption (IDE) from the FDA that allows an unapproved device to be used for investigational purposes. Device makers' decisions about new product development must often consider the trade-offs between the quicker and simpler 510(k) process for substantially equivalent devices and the more rigorous, time-consuming, and costly IDE/PMA process for truly novel devices.

Changes in device regulation

Whereas recent efforts are geared toward expediting the premarketing evaluation of drugs, the trend for devices may be in the opposite direction. Widely publicized reports during the 1980s about adverse events involving a range of devices (e.g., certain heart valves, pacemaker leads, ventilators, patient chair lifts, and medical software) raised public concerns about the adequacy of device regulation. These concerns provided impetus to enactment of the Safe Medical Devices Act (SMDA) of 1990, which increases both premarketing and postmarketing regulatory oversight of devices. The SMDA

- allows the FDA to require more clinical data for 510(k) premarket notification applications;
- doubles the time to 180 days for the FDA to respond to 510(k)s before a device can be marketed;
- requires the FDA to affirm that a device is substantially equivalent before it may be marketed (where formerly a device could be marketed if the FDA did not respond after 90 days);
- requires postmarketing surveillance of high-risk devices;
- requires manufacturers to track patients who receive certain

high-risk products (e.g., permanently implanted devices and certain life-supporting devices); and

- requires health facilities and device distributors to report information indicating that a device may have caused or contributed to a death or serious injury.

In 1992, the FDA formed the Committee for Clinical Review, which examined a sample of PMA applications and section 510(k) notifications. The committee discerned "certain patterns of deficiencies" in the design, conduct, and analysis of the clinical trials that diminish FDA's ability to make adequate judgments regarding the safety and effectiveness of many devices. The committee's report argued for more emphasis on advances in clinical trial design and more rigorous statistical analysis.[69]

Together, the provisions of the SMDA, the work by the Committee for Clinical Review, and related indications that the FDA seeks to increase data requirements for device regulation should encourage higher-quality device evaluations and provide more useful information about adverse events. However, these trends do raise hurdles for device innovation, and increase uncertainties associated with such innovation.

Device applications and approvals

In general, the rate of introduction of truly novel medical devices slowed in recent years. Approval times rose significantly for PMAs and 510(k)s, then dropped in 1995 as shown in Table 9.4. Data on PMA and 510(k) applications and approvals provide only indirect indicators of the level of innovation activity, and relate nothing about the quality of particular devices. The apparent stagnation in PMA submissions and approvals derives in part from the increased time and expense of data collection by sponsors and sponsors' expectations that lengthy reviews may further erode return on investment. Delays alone would only appear as temporary decreases in submissions; longer-term drops in submissions would indicate decisions not to pursue the types of novel devices that require approval via the PMA route. The stable-to-upward trend in 510(k) submissions may reflect a willingness by firms to pursue incremental device improvements. However, closer FDA scrutiny and requests for additional data could contribute to a slowdown in 510(k) approvals.

In 1993, the FDA received approval for a significant enlargement of the Center for Devices and Radiological Health (CDRH) product review staff. The increase in 510(k) approvals from 1993 to

Table 9.4 FDA Original Premarket Approval (PMA) Applications and 510(k) Premarket Notifications, Fiscal Years 1988–1995

	1988	1989	1990	1991	1992	1993	1994	1995
PMAs								
Received	96	84	79	75	65	40	43	39
Approved	46	56	47	27	12	24	26	27
Average days for approval*								
FDA	262	247	302	335	236	547	649	606
Total	337	348	415	633	310	799	823	773
510(k)s								
Received	5,536	7,022	5,831	5,770	6,509	6,288	6,434	6,056
Approved	4,432	4,867	4,748	4,294	3,776	4,007	5,498	5,594
Average days for approval								
FDA†	64	66	78	81	102	162	184	137
Total‡	78	82	98	102	126	195	216	178

*The average elapsed time includes all increments of time a PMA was under review, including all the increments of time it was under review by FDA and all increments of time it was on hold, during which it was being worked on by the manufacturer. Thus, the average elapsed time is the average time taken to obtain approval of a PMA from the time it was filed until it received final approval.

†FDA average review time includes all increments of time FDA reviewed a 510(k) so long as the 510(k) document number did not change, which occurs rarely.

‡Includes all time from receipt to final decision; that is, it does not exclude time while a submission is on hold pending receipt of additional information.

Source: Health Care Technology Institute, 1995; U.S. Food and Drug Administration.

1995 may be attributable to these staff increases and other recent CDRH management initiatives. However, these gains could be offset by the time and resources needed to answer increased requirements for clinical data.

The device industry differs from the drug industry in ways that may affect its ability to innovate in the current regulatory environment. The large companies in the pharmaceutical industry have had since the early 1960s to adapt to largely consistent, though steadily evolving, FDA regulations that apply to what are primarily chemical and biological substances. In contrast, the device industry has had since only the late 1970s to adapt to a diversified, evolving body of regulation that applies to everything from gauze to gamma cameras, and whose implementation has been inconsistent and delayed. This can be especially daunting to the many small companies that have limited reserves of funding, regulatory experience, and expertise in managing clinical trials.

Effects of Hospital and Physician Supply

As noted earlier, policies for hospital construction, medical education, and the prominent role of academic health centers have affected the rate and direction of innovation. The number and distribution of hospitals have been key determinants of technology use. Consolidation of the hospital sector in wide-ranging mergers and vertical integration of providers into large networks are increasing the buying leverage of health care providers, leading to some reduction in demand for capital equipment, and shifting demand to technologies that can be used in outpatient settings.

Strong relationships exist between the use of technology and the number of physicians per population, as well as the patterns of medical specialization in a country.[70,71] The training, values, and interests of specialties and subspecialties affect the use of medical technology; generalists, for example, use less technology than specialists for similar conditions.[72] On average, the United States trains twice as many specialists as other industrialized nations; nearly 80 percent of all U.S. physicians are specialists, as compared with 20 to 40 percent elsewhere.

Medical specialization and rivalry

Medical specialization is closely linked to the development and diffusion of new technologies. Specialists conducting research in academic health centers have played key roles in the development and adoption of innovations. Specialties and subspecialties have burgeoned around new medical technologies, such as gastroenterology (endoscopy), interventional cardiology (PTCA and other catheter-based technologies), and nuclear medicine (radiopharmaceuticals, Anger gamma camera). Interspecialty rivalry and competition for patients can stimulate innovation. A powerful factor in the evolution of treating gall bladder disease was competition involving surgeons (advancing conventional and laparoscopic cholecystectomy), gastroenterologists (gallstone-dissolving drugs), and radiologists (lithotripsy).[73]

The federal government, state governments, and medical schools have undertaken efforts to encourage more students to become generalists. In principle, policies that provide incentives for primary care physicians, such as modifying student admission criteria, curriculum redesign, greater funding for training, improving their payment relative to specialists, and encouraging enrollment in group practices, would lead to reductions in the use of certain technologies.[74,75] Given the lead time involved in training physicians, shifting the specialty mix will not have immediate effects on technological change, but in the long run both hospital and physician supply policies should affect the rate and direction of technological change.

Coverage and Reimbursement

An important consideration for the development and marketing of innovations is the outlook for third-party payment by regional Medicare carriers, state Medicaid programs, Blue Cross and Blue Shield plans, private insurers, and managed care organizations. Each payer poses two main hurdles: coverage (whether to pay) and reimbursement (how much to pay). Differences among payers, changes in payment policies, and inconsistencies in policy implementation add to the uncertainties of innovation and delay the availability of, and access to, certain technologies. The great payment leverage of managed care organizations and other large providers is having dramatic effects on the market for technologies and will affect patterns of innovation.

Medicare and PPS

Medicare coverage policy derives from Section 1862 of Title XVIII of the Social Security Act, which excludes payment for items or services that are "not reasonable and necessary." Medicare has operated without regulations to clarify Section 1862, which has been interpreted traditionally as not interfering with medical practice or beneficiaries' free choice. This has given Medicare contractors considerable latitude in coverage determinations. In 1989, the Health Care Financing Administration (HCFA) proposed a rule to clarify the meaning of "reasonable and necessary" that added the criterion of cost-effectiveness to coverage determinations. The rule was still pending in 1996.

Medicare's prospective payment system (PPS) for inpatient hospital services has affected technological innovation directly and indirectly. Overall, it has put downward pressure on inpatient health care costs and has encouraged migration of care to the outpatient setting. Hospital adoption of new technologies has been influenced by whether use of a technology amounts to a net gain or loss in revenue based on its assigned diagnosis-related group (DRG), or whether the technology merits a revision in DRG payment or even its own DRG. The market has been accommodating to technologies that could be adapted for outpatient use and receive more generous payment (e.g., cataract surgery, breast biopsies and lesion removals, colonoscopy and sigmoidoscopy, and lithotripsy).

Prior to 1991, expenses related to capital plant and equipment were still reimbursed on a retrospective cost basis. Thus, despite PPS pressure to reduce other costs, hospitals retained incentives to continue to acquire expensive equipment. The shift toward incorporating capital equipment costs into DRGs makes hospitals more wary of expensive equipment acquisitions. For some technologies, such as MRI scanners, the lack of an add-on payment in the inpatient PPS payment helped to encourage the proliferation of freestanding outpatient MRI facilities, where MRI is eligible for the more generous charge-based payments.[76]

Coding, reimbursement, and diffusion

Innovation is sensitive to the level of reimbursement provided for new interventions. Medicare PPS initially assigned PTCA, a minimally invasive procedure, to a surgical DRG that provided a much higher level of reimbursement than the cost of the procedure itself. This stimulated rapid adoption of PTCA, the establishment of interventional cardiology as a new subspecialty, and a multitude of spinoff innovations. The diffusion of laparoscopic cholecystectomy was boosted by its expeditious acceptance by payers who recognized the financial impact of shorter hospital stays and paid for the procedure as if it were a conventional gallbladder removal operation. Payers later recognized that per-case savings on laparoscopic cholecystectomy are well overmatched by the aggregate costs of its wider use, including patients who would not have received the conventional surgery. Diffusion and further development of cochlear implants have been slowed by their status as DRG-losers. For the device, which costs about $16,000, and related hospital services, Medicare PPS pays about $9,000.

Managed care and medical technology

Perhaps the most dramatic changes affecting health care technologies are the aggressive cost-containment strategies being taken by managed care organizations, large health care networks, state Medicaid programs, the Department of Veterans Affairs, and other large providers. Increasing buying leverage can decrease profit margins for drug and device makers, decrease demand for and increase standardization of equipment and supplies, and bring volume discounts for technologies ranging from routine laboratory and radiology services to costly specialty procedures.

Pharmaceuticals are particularly affected by cost-containment measures of large providers, which include contracting with outside firms to manage pharmaceutical benefits, setting up formularies that restrict the choice of prescription drugs, requiring physicians to prescribe generics where available, and aggressive negotiation for price discounts. In many managed care organizations today, pharmacy and therapeutics (P&T) committees, which are made up mostly or entirely of physicians, vote on which drugs to add to formularies (or to designate as "preferred") based on their review of information on prices, effectiveness, side effects, dosages, and patient compliance. Physicians are increasingly requested to provide justification for prescribing brand name drugs that are not on formularies. Provider organizations with actively managed formularies[77] could account for 50 percent of prescription drug sales by 1999.[78]

Providers increasingly contract with group purchasing organizations (GPOs) that amass buying leverage representing multiple organizations. Virtually all of the 7,400 U.S. hospitals are members of one or more GPOs. The 50 largest GPOs serve 90 percent of U.S. hospitals.[79–81]

Drug companies are responding to buying leverage in a variety of ways. They are having to provide significant discounts, particularly in therapeutic classes where two or more brand name drugs are competing for market share.[82] The nature and focus of drug marketing are shifting from individual physicians to P&T committees, formulary chiefs, and health plan managers. Cognizant of providers' greater demand for evidence demonstrating clinical benefits and cost-effectiveness, and seeking footholds for new drugs, some drug companies provide financial support to providers for data collection in conjunction with the use of these drugs in their patient populations.

Cost-conscious purchasing is affecting clinical procedures and medical devices. Managed care organizations are negotiating discounts with surgicenters and hospitals for lumpectomies, cataract operations, coronary artery bypass graft surgeries (CABGs), and other high-volume procedures. Renowned medical centers are offering price discounts of 30 to 60 percent on low-volume, high-cost transplantations and follow-up treatment.[83] Increasing use of selective contracting is concentrating sophisticated medical interventions in a smaller number of institutions. In view of the volume-outcome relationships that exist for many complex procedures, such contracting may improve the efficiency as well as the quality of care. Selective contracting may also reduce the market for expensive capital equipment. By limiting their purchases of orthopedic implants, pacemakers, balloon catheters, sutures, and other devices and supplies to one or few suppliers, large providers not only secure volume discounts but gain greater familiarity and proficiency with these products.[84] This may also contribute to product standardization.

Consolidation of both the supply of medical technologies from health product companies and the demand of large provider organizations makes for bigger transactions that can impede market entry for smaller firms. A small company that has developed a new catheter or endoscopic instrument does not have the distribution channels of large companies that can also offer multiple, discounted product lines to large providers. Unless the small company has a truly novel product that offers a new standard of care, or unless it is acquired by a larger company, its product will have more difficulty breaking into the market. The buying power, organization, and communication channels of large health care systems can serve technologies that can demonstrate their cost-effectiveness. Once convinced of a technology's value, these "innovation carriers" can speed its diffusion throughout their networks.[85]

Guidelines and standardization

In order to ensure the appropriateness, cost-effectiveness, and efficiency of care, managed care organizations and other providers are implementing clinical practice guidelines, utilization management, and clinical pathways. Despite the advantages of these managerial tools, they may tend to standardize care and restrict innovation. In ensuring more systematic (and, in principle, evidence-based) guidance for clinical decisions and reducing outlier behavior by providers, these strategies may also reduce opportunities for innovative variations in clinical practice, including the use of new technologies or the application of existing technologies for new indications. On the other hand, such managerial approaches as continuous quality improvement and total quality management, benchmarking, and "best practices" can encourage clinicians, managers, scientists, and engineers to identify, try, and implement innovative products and processes for use in health care.

Payment for investigational technologies

In principle, most government and private sector third-party payers cover only those procedures that meet such criteria as "standard and accepted practice," "reasonable and necessary," and "medically necessary." Most payers explicitly exclude coverage for procedures that are "experimental" or "investigational," although there are exceptions. For example, Medicare may cover an investigational technology and/or associated hospital costs if the patient admission is not solely for clinical research purposes.[86]

Despite official policies, and in addition to allowable exceptions, payers have traditionally paid for many investigational procedures. This has occurred due to variation in interpretation of payment criteria (including judicial decisions), ambiguous coding, practical difficulties of screening for and investigating improper payment claims, and lack of concern (relative to current standards) for cost containment. This support has provided a means for many new technologies to enter the clinical mainstream. In many instances, it has enabled investigators to refine these technologies, honing clinicians' skills in applying them and, in the context of well-designed clinical trials, providing useful data on their safety and effectiveness. In other instances, especially in the absence of rigorous recorded data, this support has helped to confer acceptance of ineffective or harmful technologies.

With greater cost-containment pressure, payers are more careful about distinguishing between standard procedures and those that may be marginal, ineffective, or unproven, including investigational procedures.[87] (Clinical practice guidelines are helping to make these distinctions.) The unwillingness of payers to pay for investigational procedures does curtail support for determining their clinical value and may delay or preclude market entry of some worthy technologies. In the absence of payment, the financial risk of clinical trials of investigational technologies shifts to their sponsors. Hospital managers are less willing to pay for the use of these technologies if reimbursement is uncertain. Greater scrutiny of payment for investigational procedures may have considerable impact at academic health centers, where many innovations in clinical procedures have been developed. The possibility of legal consequences in connection with billing for investigational technologies is also discouraging their use.[88]

Various alternatives exist to help support the cost of promising investigational procedures, including handling coverage questions on a case-by-case basis, listing coverage criteria and specific exclusions (updated periodically) for such procedures in insurance policies, and offering optional riders to insurance policies. Of increasing interest to payers are forms of provisional coverage in which payers cover the routine care costs associated with an investigational procedure, or the full costs of the investigational procedure and associated routine care, provided that the procedure is conducted in the protocol of a clinical trial.[89] Provisional coverage that generates valid data on safety, effectiveness, and cost-effectiveness can support innovation, enable early access to promising new technologies for the most needy patients, and provide the basis for definitive coverage decisions.[90-92]

Payers do have reason for carefully considering decisions to refuse coverage of potentially life-saving investigational technologies. Given the ambiguity of what constitutes "reasonable" or "medically necessary" practice, payers have been successfully sued in substantial amounts for not paying for investigational procedures that may have offered the only hope to critically ill patients.[93]

Payment planning

Innovators can adapt to payment policies that influence technological use. Payment may depend on where a technology is used (e.g., in hospitals, physician offices, long-term care facilities, or patients' homes) and by whom it may be applied (e.g., physicians, other clinicians, or patients). Payment also may depend on whether or not a new technology is clinically linked to another that is covered, or whether a technology will be "bundled" in a DRG or will be paid for separately.

A product sponsor's decision to pursue an innovation may be affected by whether the payment code to which the technology will be assigned will make it a reimbursement winner or loser for providers. Where payment levels do not cover the cost for technologies that sponsors consider to be quality-enhancing, sponsors may have to decide whether or not to take on the effort required to justify new coding, which may entail additional clinical trials. Thus, "payment planning" is increasingly being integrated in product design, development, clinical evaluation, and marketing.[94]

The Role of Academic Health Centers

Academic health centers have been disproportionately responsible for the development, adoption, and evaluation of new technologies, as well as the training of specialists and subspecialists in the use of these technologies. These centers have provided the setting for advanced clinical care in which considerable incremental innovations occur. Further, their faculties have advised industry, government, payers, and providers concerning R&D, adoption, and evaluation of health care technologies. Together, these activities depended heavily on cross-subsidies from third-party payers willing to pay higher prices for care delivered at academic health centers and the continued increases in federal support for biomedical R&D.[95]

In recent years, cross-subsidies from patient revenues in academic health centers have been eroding in the face of competition from other providers and greater scrutiny by payers regarding reimbursement levels and restrictions on paying for investigative technologies. In the meantime, federal research funding has leveled off. In addition, the recent demise of federal health care reform diminished prospects for designated federal support for clinical research and medical education. Academic health centers are adapting in various ways. Closest to innovation itself, many universities are forming licensing and research collaborations with industry.[96–98] With the continued growth of private sector R&D funding relative to NIH funding for biomedical research, and competition from privately supported clinical research organizations, many academic health centers are centralizing and improving the efficiency of their clinical research operations in order to secure clinical trial contracts from pharmaceutical companies and other vendors.[99]

Product Liability

The proliferation of product liability suits in the past two decades has led to increased legal uncertainty for innovators and has had distinct effects on certain product lines. The threat of legal action has slowed, and in some instances has virtually halted development of certain contraceptives,[100,101] vaccines,[102,103] and prosthetic heart valves.[104] In the United States, uncertainty about product liability is exacerbated by the lack of uniformity among state jurisdictions, each of which develops its own liability laws.

Concerns about legal action in the medical product industries derive not only from the size of jury awards, including sizable punitive damages, but from the potential long reach of lawsuits. Under "strict liability," judgments can impose liability even in the absence of fault on the part of manufacturers. U.S. legal precedent permits an individual who has suffered harm from a product to sue all participants involved in the manufacture and sale of the product, including its components or materials.[105,106] Product liability's far-reaching effects on industry and innovation are exemplified in the current "biomaterials crisis" in which large chemical companies have curtailed or halted sales of essential synthetic materials to medical device companies after injured patients sued not only the device companies but the suppliers of materials used in those devices.[107–109] In addition to the phasing out of certain existing devices, the development, marketing, and use of new devices that use these materials may be eliminated or slowed. In 1996, Congress was considering tort reforms that would limit product liability, with some particular provisions for health care products and biomaterials.[110,111]

One way in which concerns about product liability and malpractice have stimulated development of medical technology and have added to health care costs is the increased demand for tests and monitors (e.g., for use in childbirth and anesthesia) that provide clinicians more information about patient vital signs and other health indicators.[112] The biomaterials crisis may prompt further R&D into more focused development and appropriate use of biomaterials for medical purposes.

Technological Evaluation

Health care organizations that make technology-related decisions, including regulators, clinicians, managed care organizations, hospital networks, payers, and others, are increasing the demand for technological evaluation. They seek better evidence about the relative value of new technologies compared with their alternatives, including matters of safety, effectiveness, cost-effectiveness, and other technological attributes and impacts. In addition to their clinical research capacities, health product companies (particularly major pharmaceutical firms) are establishing units on pharmacoeconomics, technology assessment, clinical effectiveness, and the like. These units are charged with collecting and analyzing data to help demonstrate how their companies' technologies improve health outcomes, quality of life, and cost-effectiveness.

The demand for data on patient outcomes is increasing the size, complexity, and cost of clinical trials. In particular, the endpoints of such studies are expanding from the traditional measures of mortality and morbidity to include health-related quality of life[113,114] and cost-effectiveness. The identification of surrogate markers for disease states and therapeutic responses may offer some efficiencies in clinical evaluation, especially in chronic degenerative diseases.[115] Similarly, implementation of "large, simple clinical trials"[116] and use of newer statistical methods such as meta-analysis[117,118] may improve efficiency of data collection and analysis. Nevertheless, clinical evaluation remains the most expensive and time-consuming segment of the R&D process.

Some Impacts on Technological Innovation

Effects on pharmaceutical innovation

The main factors affecting pharmaceutical innovation are those that place downward pressure on drug prices. This pressure comes particularly from concentration of buying power in cost-conscious and increasingly well-informed managed care organizations and other large purchasers. In this environment, new drugs that offer only marginal benefits over existing drugs in a therapeutic class are subject to severe price competition. Win-or-lose, and often delayed, formulary decisions add to the market uncertainty for new drugs. Along with pricing pressure, increased brand-name and generic competition limit the life cycles of drugs. Overall, these factors curtail the return-on-investment of drug R&D.

Companies must continually replenish their product lines in order to survive. For the large pharmaceutical companies, this is done with continued investment in R&D and through other, less traditional means. Many companies are seeking to establish more dependable revenue streams through mergers and diversification. The pharmaceutical industry is consolidating in an unprecedented fashion, including more than a dozen major mergers and acquisitions in the last few years. Among these, large research-based firms have merged with or acquired other large research-based firms, generic drug companies, and biotech firms.[119] This is in addition to various new marketing alliances, licensing pacts, and other collaborations. More broadly based companies that can "bundle" drugs into diverse portfolios can offer package deals to large providers and get more of their products on managed care formularies.

Many pharmaceutical companies are hedging their bets by extending their business from selling drugs to managing pharmaceutical care. Among these strategies, some large companies are acquiring or collaborating with pharmacy benefits management (PBM) companies[120] and drug utilization review (DUR) companies, providing capitated drug benefits to large managed care organizations, and providing care for patients in managed care organizations with particular diseases such as arthritis, asthma, diabetes, and gastric ulcers. Collaborations with health care providers and organizations that manage drug and other health care benefits raise concerns about conflicts of interest.[121,122]

How the magnitude of pharmaceutical R&D will change depends on a variety of interrelated factors. For the pharmaceutical industry in particular, any short-term changes in these factors tend to be dampened by the decade-or-longer product development pipelines. After double-digit percentage increases in most of the previous 25 years, pharmaceutical sales increases tailed off beginning in 1992, although they continued to outpace inflation. Pharmaceutical R&D spending increased even faster than sales during the last 25 years, although its rate of increase also began to tail off in the early 1990s. Even so, it stayed well ahead of inflation (see Table 9.1). R&D as a percentage of sales has increased every year since 1990, reaching an estimated 19.9 percent of sales in 1995. Mergers of large pharmaceutical firms will diminish some overlapping R&D efforts but may also provide opportunities for new R&D ventures. A flattening of R&D investment is possible, although current anecdotal evidence indicates continued R&D commitment among leading companies.[123,124]

Little is known about the efficiency of pharmaceutical R&D. It may be that a leveling off in R&D spending would result in little or no change in the yield of new drugs or their net effects on societal health and quality of life. To date, there is only anecdotal evidence for such changes. The longstanding steady increases in pharmaceutical

R&D notwithstanding, the number of new drugs approved by the FDA during 1984–1993 fluctuated between 20 to 30 (25 in 1993). Of course, the number of approved drugs per year is a crude indicator of R&D output; it is affected by factors other than R&D input and does not relate the health impact of new drugs. Consolidation of R&D operations among merged firms and continued advances in drug discovery and design processes are two factors that could contribute to greater R&D efficiency.

The changing terrain of health care also can be expected to affect the direction of pharmaceutical R&D. The new market for drugs is increasingly price competitive and less tolerant of paying premium prices for marginal benefits. A new drug with a launch price high enough to recoup R&D spending may end up a commercial failure if it offers only marginal benefits over existing drugs in its therapeutic class, especially if a low-priced generic in its class is, or soon will be, available.[125] Investment in agents that may be only marginally more effective than existing alternatives would appear to be discouraged, particularly when makers of the pioneer drug in a class are willing to resort to deep discounting to retain market share.

Some redirection of R&D spending could offer greater net benefits to societal health. Investing in R&D for me-too drugs offers limited returns given the brand-name and generic drug competition in their respective treatment classes. Further, it provides little if any measurable impact on population health outcomes. Investing in truly novel drugs and their "fast-followers" (second generation drugs with better therapeutic profiles or easier means of administration) may have better payoffs. This holds, in particular, if these drugs can provide alternatives to more costly interventions (e.g., drug substitution for radical prostatectomy) or to long-term care (e.g., for Alzheimer's disease, Parkinson's disease, and other debilitating neurological disorders). The overall effect may be to thin the pack of companies pursuing new drugs in each therapeutic class, with more companies specializing in certain lines of R&D.[126]

Effects on medical device innovation

The main factors affecting medical device innovation are trends in the FDA regulatory process, particularly increased data requirements, lengthy approval times, and perceived lack of clarity in implementing regulatory policies; increased buying leverage of large providers; uncertain and restrictive third-party payment policies, particularly for use of investigative devices; and product liability concerns. Together, these factors increase the length, expense, and risk of medical device innovation.

This is a challenging environment for small companies developing new medical devices, particularly those devices intended for small markets. Uncertainty about regulatory and payment decisions makes venture capital funding more difficult to obtain. In order to survive, more small companies may seek alignment with large companies sooner. However, the large companies are increasingly selective about such acquisitions, being particularly wary about business risks associated with certain types of medical devices. Upon acquisition, innovations are more likely to be brought under the control of general management, and product development may be more attuned to the larger companies' product lines and their market perceptions. The net effect may be that some truly novel innovations will face delay or insufficient start-up support.

Whether for PMA or 510(k) devices, prospects of longer lead times and greater expense pose disincentives for investing in medical devices. How the FDA will interpret the requirement for more clinical data for 510(k)s is not clear. Prior to the SMDA, the FDA requested clinical data for about 5 percent of all 510(k) notifications; since then, the rate has increased to 15 percent. The diversity of devices submitted under 510(k)s suggests that different types of studies are appropriate. Until the FDA makes this explicit, or establishes a stable pattern of data requirements, device developers will face uncertainty regarding the investment of time and expense for device approval.[127]

Barriers and uncertainty for medical device innovation affect large companies as well as small ones. In recent years, certain pharmaceutical companies, chemical companies, and others have divested themselves of their medical device businesses. In addition to the ones affected by the biomaterials crisis described earlier, notable examples are American Cyanamid, Squibb (prior to its merger with Bristol Meyers), Eli Lilly, and Syntex.[128] The current environment has prompted some prominent device companies (e.g., Medtronic, a leader in cardiac pacemakers, defibrillators, and other implantable devices) to move management, manufacturing, clinical trials, or other aspects of their business to other countries.[129–131]

There is evidence that downward payment pressure can stimulate cost-reducing device innovation. The considerable and unexpected national expense of the End-Stage Renal Disease (ESRD) program, enacted in the Social Security Amendments of 1972, prompted the federal government to decrease reimbursement for ESRD services. In this instance, the industry responded with cost-reducing, quality-enhancing technological changes. However, further reductions in reimbursement, coupled with reduced sales volume resulting from reusable products and elimination of support for dialysis research, may be restricting further technical improvements.[132]

Cost-containment efforts also are affecting expensive capital equipment. Manufacturers of lithotripters have replaced the expensive x-ray system and short-lived electrode configurations embedded in the original lithotripter with less costly alternatives. In the MRI market, where growth in number of units sold has passed its peak, demand has shifted from the larger, more powerful 1.5 tesla (a measure of the magnetic field density) magnet systems to the smaller, less powerful 1.0 and 0.5 tesla magnet systems. This trend is boosted by technological advances that are improving the images coming from MRIs with smaller magnetic fields.

In surgical laparoscopy, economic considerations are influencing the direction of technological change and the adoption rates, for instance, the preference for less expensive electrocautery tools over lasers[133] and more careful comparison of reusable versus disposable instruments.[134,135]

For managed care organizations seeking to reduce expensive treatment costs, more preventive care and earlier screening could stimulate demand for technologies that enable more rapid and accurate diagnoses. As managed care organizations contract with large laboratories for their diagnostic testing, the demand may increase for high-volume, rapid through-point analyzers.[136] As is the case for pioneer drugs, new medical devices that have few or no substitutes, e.g., implantable defibrillators, are insulated from growing price competition.[137]

Interviews with device manufacturers indicate that they are reducing development of technologies that do not have clear-cut clinical or economic advantages.[138] For technologies that have high unit costs or high short-term costs (e.g., artificial organs) compared with alternatives, sponsors must demonstrate longer-term (e.g., over patients' lifetimes) savings and/or significant increases in health outcomes. This may also entail arduous efforts to pursue changes in reimbursement coding and payment levels.

Conclusion

In the current health care environment, certain important incentives for innovation persist. These include patent protection, the great prevalence of chronic diseases, the absence of decisive treatments for widespread and life-threatening diseases, the sheer magnitude of the health care market, an aging population, potential for expanded health care coverage, and new market potential for U.S. technologies in countries with improving national economies. Underpinning these incentives for innovation is a substantial and influential infrastructure for R&D in many sectors of science and engineering, and particularly for biomedicine. Although the years of nearly exponential growth are past, the great federal investment in biomedical R&D is, for now, keeping pace with inflation. Private sector R&D spending maintains strong growth.

Despite its fundamentally sound foundation, technology innovation in health care faces the following significant challenges:

- Purchasing leverage of managed care organizations and other large health care providers and payers;

- FDA regulatory requirements, particularly lengthy product approval times and increasing, yet uncertain, data requirements;

- Ambiguous and restrictive coverage and reimbursement policies of third-party payers, particularly for investigative technologies;

- Greater emphasis on demonstrating measurable improvements in health care outcomes and cost-effectiveness;

- Wider use of clinical practice guidelines, utilization review, clinical pathways, and other strategies for standardizing care for particular patient health problems; and

- Potential for costly product liability actions.

As a group, these challenges (1) raise the costs of getting a product from concept to market and keeping it there, (2) place downward pressure on revenues, (3) increase uncertainty for investment in innovation, and (4) restrict opportunities for continued innovation in clinical practice. Particularly at risk from these challenges are three niches of innovation: small medical device and biotechnology firms, academic health centers, and the investigational margin of clinical practice.

For policymakers concerned about encouraging and sustaining innovation, the most useful overarching strategy would be to reduce uncertainty in the policies and procedures that mediate innovation.

This would reduce the risk of investing in innovation, enabling more informed choices about which technologies to pursue and providing more predictable paths to the market. Payers must make transparent the criteria and procedures used to make coverage and reimbursement decisions. Further, they must support more explicit transition of investigational technologies to covered technologies, including provisional coverage of promising investigational technologies in exchange for data from clinical trials with approved protocols.

The FDA must continue its efforts to increase the efficiency of new product reviews. The prospect of long product development and approval times, and unforeseen costs for meeting additional requirements for clinical data, discourage investment in innovation, particularly for novel medical devices. The FDA must carefully consider what it means, and what is practical to expect, regarding improved clinical data requirements for the highly heterogeneous universe of medical devices. Then it must make these requirements transparent and implement them consistently.

The threat of legal action for adverse events in connection with health care technologies can gut small technology companies and be sufficiently troublesome to larger ones that they pull out of health care product lines, to real public detriment. To be sure, the losses to society of innovations that are delayed or never realized owing to legal uncertainties are less palpable than adverse events experienced by specific people. Yet, unfulfilled innovations do affect certain known groups of patients. To the extent that tort reforms can guard public safety with strong sanctions against truly negligent parties and provide legal protection for those not responsible for adverse events (e.g., owing to faulty design, improper use, or other contributing improper roles), more people can benefit from promising innovations sooner.

Policymakers must monitor the well-being of small technology firms. Some will be squeezed out of the market as regulatory and payment hurdles rise; others will be acquired by larger firms sooner than may be optimal for spawning valuable innovations. To preserve the inventiveness of small firms, government should extend early and responsive guidance on regulatory processes, reinvent small business support programs, and consider ways to enhance incentives for investing in small firms.

Academic health centers are beginning to adapt to diminished cross-subsidies from patient care revenues, less bountiful federal research support, and competition from other providers. Their important roles in innovation could be strengthened by targeted government support for clinical research and education (e.g., training of primary care physicians) and by making them preferred clinical sites for coverage of investigational procedures.

While it is possible that R&D investment could flatten and, in turn, affect the rate of innovation, this has not occurred to date. Sustained decreases in real federal R&D spending would slow the pace of scientific progress and, ultimately, the stream of innovation.

The changes in the direction of innovation appear to be mostly socially beneficial. Persistent anecdotal evidence suggests that the development of quality-improving and cost-reducing technologies now have become explicit R&D targets. Still, in this era of seeking more efficient resource allocation, it is helpful to remind government and private sector funders of R&D that breakthroughs in health care technology often derive from wide-ranging and unanticipated advances throughout science and engineering. Increasing emphasis on targeted investment in R&D for currently valued technological ends is likely to be suboptimal in the long run.

The evolution of medical technologies can be a convoluted, discontinuous process. It is not possible to know, *ex ante*, whether a particular incremental improvement is a marginal, clinically insignificant end unto itself, or is the penultimate advance to the next generation of products or to an entirely different and highly beneficial application. This argues for keeping regulatory and payment doors cracked open to allow pursuit of lines of incremental change in the direction of grander ones, as well as broader or alternative applications of technologies.

The changing health care market places a premium on collecting and synthesizing evidence regarding the safety, effectiveness, cost-effectiveness, and other attributes of technologies, strengthening the knowledge base for their adoption and appropriate use for specific patient needs. This includes continued evaluation of technologies after their adoption into clinical practice. With their large patient populations and increasingly sophisticated computerized patient data systems, large health care provider organizations have considerable potential to support and evaluate technological innovation. Indeed, this is consistent with the self-interest of health care providers that intend to pursue high-quality, economical health care.

Technical wizardry alone no longer carries the day in health care. What is axiomatic for innovation in other industries—improve quality at acceptable costs—is relatively new to health care. Providers are far less willing than they once were to ring bells or blow whistles that cannot produce demonstrable, cost-effective (if not cost-reducing) improvements in health outcomes. Although innovators are responding with agility and resourcefulness in the revamped health care climate, it does pose tangible risks to environments for innovation. With greater insight into the nature of innovation, policymakers can encourage and sustain the development of socially beneficial technologies.

Acknowledgment

Annetine C. Gelijns gratefully acknowledges support from the Robert Wood Johnson Foundation Investigator Awards in Health Policy Research (Grant No. 23489).

Notes

1. Controversy exists concerning the limitations of analyses of technology's contribution to health care costs. Some approaches generalize from case studies of certain types or classes of technologies. Others break down overall health care cost increases by subtracting estimates of the contribution of other factors (population growth, general inflation, medical care price inflation in excess of general inflation, etc.), leaving a "residual" cost increase that is attributed to technology. See S. H. Altman and R. Blendon, eds., *Medical Technology: The Culprit Behind Health Care Costs?* (Hyattsville, MD: National Center for Health Services Research, 1979); Health Care Technology Institute, *Decomposition of the Health Care Spending Residual* (Alexandria, VA, 1994); J. P. Newhouse, "Medical Care Costs: How Much Welfare Loss?" *Journal of Economic Perspectives* 6, no. 3 (1992): 3–21; B. A. Weisbrod, "The Health Care Quadrilemma: An Essay on Technological Change, Quality of Care and Cost Containment," *Journal of Economic Literature* 24 (1991): 523–52; and G. R. Wilensky, "Technology as Culprit and Benefactor," *Quarterly Review of Economics and Business* 30, no. 4 (1990): 45–53. Such analyses may not adequately account for all factors that contribute to cost increases; further, they inadequately distinguish cost increases due to new technologies and those due to increased use of existing technologies.
2. R. A. Rettig, "Medical Innovation Duels Cost Containment," *Health Affairs* 13, no. 3 (1994): 7–27.
3. The proportion of the U.S. population covered by managed care depends on the definition used for managed care. Combined enrollment in HMOs and preferred provider organizations (PPOs), including point-of-service (POS) plans, accounted for an estimated 41 percent of the U.S. population in 1995. Managed care indemnity plans, which use

varying forms and degrees of managed care, accounted for an additional estimated 40 percent of the population in 1995. See Group Health Association of America (GHAA), *1994 HMO Performance Report* (Washington, DC, 1994); and J. A. Meyer, I. A. Tillmann, N. S. Bagby, S. Silow-Carroll, A. L. Dodson, and J. B. Garrett, *The Evolution of Managed Care: A Comparative Regional Analysis* (Washington, DC: New Directions for Policy, 1994).

4. S. J. Kline, "Innovation Is Not a Linear Process," *Research Management* July-August (1985): 36–45.

5. A. C. Gelijns and N. Rosenberg, "The Dynamics of Technological Change in Medicine," *Health Affairs* 13, no. 3 (1994): 28–46.

6. S. S. Blume, "Cochlear Implantation: Establishing Clinical Feasibility, 1957–1982," in *Medical Innovation at the Crossroads, Vol. V. Sources of Medical Technology: Universities and Industry*, edited by N. Rosenberg, A. C. Gelijns, and H. Dawkins (Washington, DC: National Academy Press, 1995), 97–124.

7. S. N. Finkelstein, K. Neels, and G. K. Bell, "Innovation in Cardiac Imaging," in *Medical Innovation at the Crossroads, Vol. V. Sources of Medical Technology: Universities and Industry*, edited by N. Rosenberg, A. C. Gelijns, and H. Dawkins (Washington, DC: National Academy Press, 1995), 125–154.

8. A. C. Gelijns and N. Rosenberg, "From the Scalpel to the Scope: Endoscopic Innovations in Gastroenterology, Gynecology, and Surgery," in *Medical Innovation at the Crossroads, Vol. V. Sources of Medical Technology: Universities and Industry*, edited by N. Rosenberg, A. C. Gelijns, and H. Dawkins (Washington, DC: National Academy Press, 1995), 67–96.

9. J. Spetz, "Physicians and Physicists: The Interdisciplinary Introduction of the Laser to Medicine," in *Medical Innovation at the Crossroads, Volume V. Sources of Medical Technology: Universities and Industry*, edited by N. Rosenberg, A. C. Gelijns, and H. Dawkins (Washington, DC: National Academy Press, 1995), 41–66.

10. Spetz 1995.

11. P. Lotz, "Demand as a Driving Force in Medical Innovation," *International Journal of Technology Assessment in Health Care* 9, no. 2 (1993): 174–88.

12. E. C. Bond and S. Glynn, "Recent Trends in Support for Biomedical Research and Development," in *Medical Innovation at the Crossroads, Vol. V. Sources of Medical Technology: Universities and Industry*, edited by N. Rosenberg, A. C. Gelijns, and H. Dawkins (Washington, DC: National Academy Press, 1995), 15–38.

13. U.S. Department of Health and Human Services (DHHS), *NIH Data Book 1994*, Publication no. 95-1261 (Washington, DC: U.S. Government Printing Office, 1995).

14. The PHS spending includes 13 targeted programs to develop medications for such diseases and conditions as cancer, AIDS, drug abuse, contraception, and other needs. U.S. Congress, Office of Technology

Assessment, *Pharmaceutical R&D: Costs, Risks and Rewards,* Publication no. OTA-H-522 (Washington, DC: U.S. Government Printing Office, 1993).

15. C. L. Littell, "Datawatch. Innovation in Medical Technology: Reading the Indicators," *Health Affairs* 13, no. 3 (1994): 226–35.

16. C. H. Asbury, "Evolution and Current Status of the Orphan Drug Act," *International Journal of Technology Assessment in Health Care* 8, no. 4 (1992): 573–82.

17. U.S. Congress, Office of Technology Assessment (OTA), *Pharmaceutical R&D: Costs, Risks and Rewards,* Publication no. OTA-H-522 (Washington, DC: U.S. Government Printing Office, 1993).

18. According to the Department of Commerce, the estimated total value of U.S. pharmaceutical shipments (all products and services sold by firms in the U.S. pharmaceutical industry) in 1994 was $70.5 billion, and this industry had an estimated $7.2 billion in exports and a trade surplus of $500 million in 1993. U.S. Department of Commerce (DoC), *U.S. Industrial Outlook 1994* (Washington, DC: U.S. Government Printing Office, 1994); Pharmaceutical Research and Manufacturers of America (PhRMA), *Backgrounder: U.S. Pharmaceutical R&D and Sales* (Washington, DC, PhRMA, 1996).

19. According to 1988 figures, U.S. spending on pharmaceuticals, both per capita and as a percentage of health care expenditures, was lower than in Japan, the richer western European countries, and Canada. D. A. Rublee and M. Schneider, "International Health Spending: Comparisons with the OECD," *Health Affairs* 10, no. 3 (Summer 1991): 189–98.

20. U.S. DoC 1994.

21. Glaxo's ulcer drug Zantac (ranitidine) was the industry leader in 1995 with $3.1 billion in sales.

22. R&D figures are for expenditures within the United States by all PhRMA member companies plus expenditures abroad by U.S.–owned PhRMA member companies. PhRMA includes more than 100 companies that produce brand-name drugs, representing more than 90 percent of U.S. drug sales.

23. D. E. Wierenga and C. R. Eaton, "The Drug Development and Approval Process," in *New Drug Approvals in 1993,* no. 13 (Washington, DC: Pharmaceutical Manufacturers Association, 1994).

24. The law requires the FDA to complete its review of an NDA within 180 days; this does not include time when the agency is awaiting additional information from the sponsor. Each NDA amendment allows the agency to extend its review time by an additional 180 days, and most NDAs require at least one amendment. Even so, actual FDA review time exceeds the legal allowances in some instances. In the view of many company staff and clinical researchers, FDA staff use the "application not complete" notice to manage their workloads (U.S. OTA 1993).

25. For each new drug that reached the market during the 1980s, the full after-tax R&D expenditures (i.e., full R&D expenditures averaged over the number of successful drugs), compounded to their value on the day

of market approval, was roughly $194 million (1990 dollars) (U.S. OTA 1993). Given the length of the new drug pipeline and the changes in factors affecting R&D costs since the development of drugs that were approved in the 1980s, it is difficult to estimate R&D costs for drugs currently under development.

26. Pharmaceutical Manufacturers Association (PMA), *Trends in U.S. Pharmaceutical Sales and R&D* (Washington, DC, 1993).

27. Wierenga 1994.

28. E. Broshy, "The Contribution of Pharmaceutical Companies: What's at Stake for America. Executive Summary from a Report Prepared by the Boston Consulting Group," *Annals of the New York Academy of Sciences* 729 (1994): 111–26.

29. Of the approximately 800 publicly disclosed biotech products, about 150 are in clinical trials, and only about 30 have been approved to date by the FDA. Examples of approved therapies are erythropoietin (developed by Amgen) for anemia associated with renal failure, AIDS, and cancer; tissue-plasminogen activator (Genentech) for myocardial infarction and pulmonary embolism; beta interferon (Chiron) for multiple sclerosis; factor VIII (Genentech, Genetics Institute) for hemophilia; and human growth hormone (Genentech). Most approved biotechnology products are marketed through large pharmaceutical companies.

30. L. Read and K. B. Lee, Jr., "Health Care Innovation: Progress Report and Focus on Biotechnology," *Health Affairs* 13, no. 3 (Fall 1994): 215–25.

31. Broshy 1994.

32. U. Gupta, "Now or Never: Can the Biotech Companies Deliver?" *The Wall Street Journal* (20 May 1994): R12.

33. R. T. King, Jr., "Pharmaceutical Giants Are Eagerly Shopping Biotech Bargain Bin," *The Wall Street Journal* (11 April 1995): A1, A14.

34. Broshy 1994.

35. M. R. Pollard, "Pharmaceutical Innovation in the United States: Factors Affecting Future Performance," *International Journal of Technology Assessment in Health Care* 9, no. 2 (1993): 167–73.

36. U.S. Congress, Congressional Budget Office, *How Health Care Reform Affects Pharmaceutical Research and Development* (Washington, DC: CBO, 1994).

37. Health Care Technology Institute, *1995 Reference Guide for the Health Care Technology Industry* (Alexandria, VA: HCTI 1995).

38. The widely adopted Universal Medical Device Nomenclature System developed by ECRI uses nearly 5,000 device categories for which there are tens of thousands of trade names. ECRI, *1995 Health Devices Sourcebook* (Plymouth Meeting, PA: ECRI, 1995).

39. C. Goodman, *The Role of Percutaneous Transluminal Coronary Angioplasty in Coronary Revascularization: Evidence, Assessment, and Policy* (Stockholm: Swedish Council on Technology Assessment in Health Care, 1992).

40. Industry data that reference the U.S. Department of Commerce are

based on its definition of the medical device industry that includes the following Standard Industry Classification (SIC) codes. SIC 3841: surgical and medical instruments; SIC 2842: surgical appliances and supplies; SIC 3843: dental equipment and supplies; SIC 3844: x-ray apparatus and tubes; SIC 3845: electromedical equipment; and SIC 3851: ophthalmic goods. In contrast, The Health Care Technology Institute (HCTI) definition of the "medical technology industry" includes a similar set of SIC codes, except that it includes SIC 2835: in vitro and in vivo diagnostic substances; and excludes SIC 3851. Applying DoC data to this definition, value of product shipments for the industry was projected to be $45.4 billion in 1994, including $10.5 billion in exports and a continued growing international trade surplus of $5.2 billion. U.S. Department of Commerce (DoC), *U.S. Industrial Outlook 1994* (Washington, DC: U.S. Government Printing Office, 1994).

41. DoC 1994.
42. S. Shapiro, "How Do Venture Capitalists Evaluate Medical Devices and How Are These Investment Decisions Changing?" Paper delivered at Fourth Annual Meeting of the American Institute of Medical and Biological Engineering (Washington, DC, 13 March 1995).
43. Gelijns and Rosenberg 1994.
44. HCTI 1995.
45. HCTI 1995.
46. E. B. Roberts, "Technological Innovation and Medical Devices," in *New Medical Devices: Invention, Development, and Use,* edited by K. B. Ekelman, (Washington, DC: National Academy Press, 1988), 35–47.
47. A. A. Romeo, "Private Investment in Medical Device Innovation," in *New Medical Devices: Invention, Development, and Use* edited by K. B. Ekelman (Washington, DC: National Academy Press, 1988), 62–72.
48. HCTI 1995.
49. Health Care Technology Institute (HCTI), *Trends in Venture Capital Funding for the Medical Device Industry* (Alexandria, VA: HCTI, 1994).
50. Littell 1994.
51. HCTI 1995.
52. Littell 1994.
53. F. Flaherty, "Health Care Prognosis: Cost Cuts Will Count," *New York Times* (21 May 1994): 35.
54. Broshy 1994.
55. R. Langreth, "Biotech Companies Abandon Go-It-Alone Approach," *Wall Street Journal* (21 November 1995): B4.
56. R. Langreth. "New Technique for Discovering Medicines Takes Hold," *Wall Street Journal* (11 September 1995): B3.
57. CDER is responsible for chemical pharmaceuticals, antibiotics, generic and over-the-counter drugs, and most hormones and enzymes. CBER is responsible for viruses, therapeutic serums, toxins, vaccines, and other substances used in prevention or treatment; blood and blood products; diagnostic reagents that use biotechnology-derived products; and other substances.

58. Phase I trials, typically involving 20–80 healthy volunteers, test a drug's safety, dosage range, bioavailability (absorption, distribution, and excretion), and metabolic action. Phase II trials, involving 100–300 patients with the target disease, evaluate efficacy and identify shorter-term adverse reactions. Phase III trials, involving 1,000–3,000 patients, provide verifying data on efficacy and some longer-term adverse reactions.

59. OTA 1993.

60. A. C. Gelijns and S. O. Thier, "Medical Technology Development: An Introduction to the Innovation-Evaluation Nexus," in *Medical Innovation at the Crossroads, Vol. I: Modern Methods of Clinical Investigation*, edited by A. C. Gelijns (Washington, DC: National Academy Press, 1990), 1–15.

61. According to a large survey of oncologists, about a third of cancer chemotherapy prescriptions are off-label, and more than half of all cancer patients receive at least one off-label prescription in their drug regimen. T. Laetz and G. Silberman, "Reimbursement Policies Constrain the Practice of Oncology," *Journal of the American Medical Association* 266, no. 21 (1991): 2996–99.

62. OTA 1993.

63. These "Subpart E" regulations involve close cooperation of drug sponsors and the FDA in planning to condense the traditional three-phase clinical testing process so that full phase III trials may be unnecessary or may be conducted following market approval.

64. FDA's Treatment Investigational New Drug (IND) program, established in 1987, allows earlier access to investigational drugs for patients with otherwise untreatable conditions (e.g., AIDS and certain cancers) who are not enrolled in clinical trials. In 1992, the FDA and National Institute of Allergy and Infectious Diseases agreed to expand access beyond the bounds set by the 1987 Treatment IND regulations. This parallel track program allows patients who are not enrolled in the main "scientific" clinical trials of investigational drugs to take part in concurrent studies that have more flexible patient entry criteria and are less rigorously monitored.

65. U.S. Food and Drug Administration (FDA), "FDA 1995 Approvals Show Continued Decline in Review Times" (Rockville, MD: FDA, 1996).

66. General controls, which also apply to Class II and III devices, pertain to, for instance, registration, premarket notification, labeling, reporting of adverse experiences, and good manufacturing practices.

67. The "510(k)" refers to the section in the 1976 Medical Device Amendments that requires a manufacturer of a substantially equivalent device to notify the FDA of its intention to market the device.

68. Manufacturers can petition for reclassification.

69. R. Temple, *Final Report of the Committee for Clinical Review* (Rockville, MD: U.S. Food and Drug Administration, 1993).

70. J. P. Bunker, "Surgical Manpower. A Comparison of Operations and Surgeons in the United States and in England and Wales," *The New England Journal of Medicine* 282, no. 3 (1970): 135–44.

71. J. E. Wennberg, D. C. Goodman, R. F. Nease, and R. B. Keller, "Finding Equilibrium in U.S. Physician Supply," *Health Affairs* 12, no. 2 (1993): 89–103.

72. J. L. Fleg, P. C. Hinton, E. G. Lakatta, F. I. Marcus, T. W. Smith, H. C. Strauss, and M. A. Hlatky, "Physician Utilization of Laboratory Procedures to Monitor Outpatients with Congestive Heart Failure," *Archives of Internal Medicine* 149, no. 2 (1989): 393–96.

73. Gelijns and Rosenberg 1994.

74. D. A. Kindig and D. Libby, "How Will Graduate Medical Education Reform Affect Specialties and Geographic Areas?" *Journal of the American Medical Association* 272, no. 1 (1994): 37–42.

75. C. J. Martini, J. J. Veloski, B. Barzansky, G. Xu, and S. K. Fields, "Medical School and Student Characteristics That Influence Choosing a Generalist Career," *Journal of the American Medical Association* 272, no. 9 (1994): 661–68.

76. K. A. Buto, "Decisionmaking in the Health Care Financing Administration," in *Medical Innovation at the Crossroads, Vol. IV: Adopting New Medical Technology,* edited by A. C. Gelijns and H. V. Dawkins (Washington, DC: National Academy Press, 1994), 87–95.

77. "Actively managed" formularies work from short lists of acceptable drugs that favor generics and intervene when physicians prescribe unlisted drugs.

78. A. M. McGahan, "Focus on Pharmaceuticals: Industry Structure and Competitive Advantage," *Harvard Business Review* (November-December 1994): 115–24.

79. HCTI 1995.

80. L. Scott, "Buying Groups Seek Compliance," *Modern Healthcare* 24, no. 39 (1994): 52–54, 56–62.

81. F. W. Telling, "Managed Care and Pharmaceutical Innovation," in *Medical Innovation at the Crossroads, Vol. III: Technology and Health Care in an Era of Limits,* edited by A. C. Gelijns (Washington, DC: National Academy Press, 1992), 201–217.

82. M. Waldholz, "Specter of Regulation Sets Off Price War," *Wall Street Journal* (25 September 1992), A4.

83. G. Anders, "On Sale Now at Your HMO: Organ Transplants," *Wall Street Journal* (17 January 1995), B1, B5.

84. ECRI, "Case Study: How One Hospital Trimmed Technology Costs and Cut Hospital Stays for Bypass and Joint Replacement," *Health Technology Trends* 6, no. 11 (1994): 4–5.

85. M. M. McKinney, A. D. Kaluzny, and H. S. Zuckerman, "Paths and Pacemakers: Innovation Diffusion Networks in Multihospital Systems and Alliances," *Health Care Management Review* 16, no. 1 (1991): 17–23.

86. Medicaid coverage decisions are decided by each state. Some states do not cover investigational drugs under any circumstances; others provide payment under specific circumstances. As is the case for Medicare, with inconsistent coverage policy interpretations and claims screening,

it is likely that Medicaid is paying for some investigational technologies and associated patient care costs.

87. S. Turner, "The Impact of Health Care Reform on Reimbursement for Investigational Drug Therapy," *Cancer Investigation* 11, no. 1 (1993): 68–69.

88. The Department of Health and Human Services was continuing an investigation involving more than 100 hospitals concerning possible improper billing of Medicare for cardiac arrhythmia ablation and other investigational cardiac procedures. L. Scott, "HHS Probe Stirs Device Controversy," *Modern Healthcare* 24, no. 28 (1994b): 51.

89. In late 1995, HCFA issued a rule allowing certain devices with FDA-approved IDE protocols and certain related services to be covered by Medicare. Covered investigational devices are limited to new generations of products already commercially available (e.g., cardiac pacemakers) and not "novel, first-of-a-kind devices" that have never been commercially availbale (e.g., artificial livers). "Medicare Program: Criteria and Proceduresu for Extending Coverage to Certain Devices and Related Services," *Federal Register* 60, no. 181 (1995): 48417–25.

90. M. A. Friedman and M. S. McCabe, "Assigning Care Costs Associated with Therapeutic Oncology Research: A Modest Proposal," *Journal of the National Cancer Institute* 84, no. 10 (1992): 760–63.

91. W. T. McGivney, "Proposal for Assuring Technology Competency and Leadership in Medicine," *Journal of the National Cancer Institute* 84, no. 10 (1992): 742–44.

92. L. N. Newcomer, "Defining Experimental Therapy—A Third-Party Payer's Dilemma," *The New England Journal of Medicine* 323, no. 24 (1990): 1702–4.

93. In 1994, the large California HMO, HealthNet, reached a settlement to pay between $5 million and $10 million to the family of a patient with breast cancer for whom it had denied an autologous bone marrow transplantation, an investigative procedure. The settlement came after the HMO requested a new trial based on the complaint that an earlier jury award of $89.1 million in punitive and compensatory damages was excessive. P. J. Kenkel, "HMO Settles Out of Court; Investors Appear Relieved," *Modern Healthcare* 24, no. 15 (1994): 4; A. Lewis, A. Delaney, and J. Erban, "Health Plan Ordered to Pay High Penalty," *Journal of Health Care Benefits* 3, no. 5 (1994): 32–36.

94. W. I. Roe, "How Reimbursement Planning Can Make—Or Break— Your New Product," *Medical Marketing & Media* 27, no. 7 (1992): 36–40.

95. G. Anderson, E. Steinberg, and R. Heyssel, "The Pivotal Role of the Academic Health Center," *Health Affairs* 13, no. 3 (1994): 146–58.

96. S. H. Atkinson, "University-Affiliated Venture Capital Funds," *Health Affairs* 13, no. 3 (1994): 159–75.

97. D. Blumenthal, "Growing Pains for New Academic Industry Relationships," *Health Affairs* 13, no. 3 (1994): 176–93.

98. Bond and Glynn 1995.

99. B. Japsen, "Academic Centers Vie for Research Dollars," *Modern Healthcare* 24, no. 37 (1994): 72, 74.

100. A. C. Gelijns, and C. O. Pannenborg, "The Development of Contraceptive Technology: Case Studies of Incentives and Disincentives to Innovation," *International Journal of Technology Assessment in Health Care* 9 (2 (1993): 210–32.

101. T. Randall, "United States Loses Lead in Contraceptive Choices, R&D; Changes in Tort Liability, FDA Review Urged," *Journal of the American Medical Association* 268, no. 2 (1992): 178–79.

102. Institute of Medicine (IOM). *Vaccine Supply and Innovation* (Washington, DC: National Academy Press, 1985).

103. J. C. Petricciani, V. P. Grachev, P. P. Sizaret, and P. J. Regan, "Vaccines: Obstacles and Opportunities from Discovery to Use," *Reviews of Infectious Diseases* 11 suppl. 3 (1989): S524–29.

104. R. B. Karp, and M. E. Sand, "Mechanical Prostheses: Old and New," *Cardiovascular Clinics* 23 (1993): 235–53.

105. H. C. Black, *Black's Law Dictionary*. 5th ed. (St. Paul, MN: West, 1979).

106. S. B. Foote, "The Impact of Public Policy on Medical Device Innovation: A Case of Polyintervention," in *Medical Innovation at the Crossroads, Vol. II: The Changing Economics of Medical Technology*, edited by A. C. Gelijns and E. A. Halm (Washington, DC: National Academy Press, 1991), 69–88.

107. B. J. Feder, "Implant Industry Is Facing Cutback by Top Suppliers," *New York Times* (25 April 1994): A1, D3.

108. J. D. Hill, "An Impending Crisis Involving Biomaterials," *Annals of Thoracic Surgery* 58, no. 6 (1994): 1571.

109. Large chemical companies such as Du Pont, Dow Chemical, Dow Corning, and Hoechst Celanese have supplied teflon, dacron, silicone rubbers, and other synthetic materials to medical device companies. Among a wide variety of medical applications, these materials are used in such life-sustaining devices as cardiac valves, vascular grafts, cardiac pacemakers, and hydrocephalus shunts. Of the total volume of these synthetic materials produced by chemical companies, the amount sold for use in medical devices is usually financially insignificant. For materials suppliers, the financial risk of legal action can far outweigh the revenue from sales of these materials to medical device companies. Therefore, some chemical companies have halted or restricted their supply of these materials to medical device companies. R. R. Cook, M. C. Harrison, and R. R. LeVier, "The Breast Implant Controversy," *Arthritis and Rheumatism* 37, no. 2 (1994): 153–57; R. F. Service, "Liability Concerns Threaten Medical Implant Research," *Science* 266, no. 5186 (1994): 726–27.

110. American College of Physicians, "Beyond MICRA: New Ideas for Liability Reform," *Annals of Internal Medicine* 122, no. 6 (1995): 466–73.

111. B. I. Truitt, "Injured Consumers and the FDA: Should Federal Preemption Protect Medical Device Manufacturers under a Quasi-Governmental Immunity?" *Journal of Legal Medicine* 15, no. 1 (1994): 155–84.

112. A. Kahn, "The Dynamics of Medical Device Innovation: An Innovator's Perspective," in *Medical Innovation at the Crossroads, Vol. II: The Changing*

Economics of Medical Technology, edited by A. C. Gelijns and E. A. Halm (Washington, DC: National Academy Press, 1991), 89–95.

113. T. M. Gill and A. R. Feinstein, "A Critical Appraisal of the Quality of Quality-of-Life Measurements," *Journal of the American Medical Association* 272, no. 8 (1994): 619–26.

114. G. H. Guyatt, D. H. Feeny, and D. L. Patrick, "Measuring Health-Related Quality of Life," *Annals of Internal Medicine* 118, no. 8 (1993): 622–29.

115. Laubach, G. D. and A. C. Gelijns, "Medical Innovation at the Cross-roads," *Issues in Science and Technology* 11, no. 3 (1995): 33–40.

116. R. Peto, R. Collins, and R. Gray, "Large-Scale Randomized Evidence: Large, Simple Trials and Overviews of Trials." *Annals of the New York Academy of Sciences* 703, (1993): 314–40.

117. T. C. Chalmers and J. Lau, "Meta-Analytic Stimulus for Changes in Clinical Trials," *Statistical Methods in Medical Research* 2, no. 2 (1993): 161–72.

118. T. D. Cook, H. Cooper, D. S. Cordray, H. Hartmann, L. V. Hedges, R. L. Light, T. A. Louis, and F. Mosteller, *Meta-Analysis for Explanation: A Casebook* (New York: Russell Sage Foundation, 1992).

119. G. D. Laubach, "Perspectives on Industrial R&D Management," in *Medical Innovation at the Crossroads, Vol. V. Sources of Medical Technology: Universities and Industry,* edited by N. Rosenberg, A. C. Gelijns, and H. Dawkins. 209–18. Washington, DC: National Academy Press, 1995.

120. Notable examples are Merck & Company and Medco Containment Services, SmithKline Beecham and Diversified Pharmaceutical Services, and Eli Lilly and McKesson's PCS Health Systems.

121. McGahan 1994.

122. S. B. Soumerai and H. L. Lipson, "Computer-Based Drug-Utilization Review: Risk, Benefit, or Boondoggle?" *The New England Journal of Medicine* 332, no. 24 (1995): 1641–45.

123. M. Freudenheim, "Pfizer Will Raise Spending on Drug Research by 20%," *New York Times* (17 March 1995): D5.

124. E. Tanouye, "Merck's Chairman Stresses Developing Prescription Drugs," *Wall Street Journal* (26 April 1995): B6.

125. For example, in late 1992, SmithKline Beecham announced that it would stop internal basic research for new ulcer drugs, even though its own Tagamet remained the second-leading seller in that lucrative market. This came as generic versions of Tagamet and other H-2 antagonists were lining up to enter the market.

126. OTA 1993.

127. R. A. Merrill, "Regulation of Drugs and Devices; an Evolution," *Health Affairs* 13, no. 3 (1994): 47–69.

128. The Wilkerson Group, Inc., *Forces Reshaping the Performance and Contribution of the U.S. Medical Devices Industry* (New York: The Wilkerson Group, 1995).

129. Association for the Advancement of Medical Instrumentation (AAMI), "EMBS Conference Symposium Highlights Threats to Device Innovation," *Medical Device Research Report* 1, no. 6 (1994): 2–3.

130. Association for the Advancement of Medical Instrumentation (AAMI), "Shape of Federal Regulation Highlighted at Cardiovascular Conference," *Medical Device Research Report* 2, no. 1 (1995): 2–3.
131. HCTI 1994, *Trends*.
132. R. A. Rettig and N. G. Levinsky, eds., *Kidney Failure and the Federal Government* (Washington, DC: National Academy Press, 1991).
133. Y. Nowzaradan and J. P. Barnes, Jr., "Current Techniques in Laparoscopic Appendectomy," *Surgical Laparoscopy and Endoscopy* 3, no. 6 (1993): 470–76.
134. K. N. Apelgren, M. L. Blank, C. A. Slomski, and N. S. Hadjis, "Reusable Instruments are More Cost-Effective Than Disposable Instruments for Laparoscopic Cholecystectomy," *Surgical Endoscopy* 8, no. 1 (1994): 32–34.
135. K. S. Weatherly, and S. W. Young, "Reusable Laparoscopic Instrument System: An Analysis of Quality and Cost Issues," *Journal of Laparoendoscopic Surgery* 4, no. 2 (1994): 135–41.
136. P. Lotz, "Managed Care and Its Impact on the Diagnostic Industry," *InVivo* October (1992): 8–12.
137. Flaherty 1994.
138. HCTI 1995.

10

The Special Health Care Needs of the Elderly

Marilyn Moon

Abstract. Interest in Medicare, the government's second largest social program after Social Security, reached a new high in 1995, not as part of health care reform, but as a vehicle for deficit reduction and because of a desire by Congress to restructure the program to encourage enhanced choice for beneficiaries and greater use of managed care. Medicaid, a major payer of long-term care and financer of coverage for low-income elderly, also is slated to undergo major restructuring in the next few years. As Congress and the nation debate the future of these key programs for older Americans, a number of critical issues deserve attention.

Medicare's costs are very high—but not necessarily unreasonable in the face of the demands on health care services for this part of the population. And even with these high costs, a number of important gaps in coverage remain a problem for seniors. Deductibles and copayments are also high— especially for hospital and skilled nursing services. But pressure for change may well lead to higher, not lower, cost-sharing requirements. Medicare remains a largely fee-for-service program at a time when the national health care system is shifting increasingly to a managed care environment. Moving Medicare in that direction is one likely option for change. While it is desirable to have Medicare move in concert with the rest of the system, a number of issues stand in the way of an effortless move to managed care for the elderly. Moreover, coordination of long-term and acute care services may be even more challenging in such an environment.

Medicaid covers long-term care services for older Americans, but only for those who have depleted most of their assets and income. Even when people do become eligible, Medicaid covers primarily institutional care. But little is likely to change this picture in the next few years, and private efforts through expansion of long-term care insurance will likely provide only a partial solution.

Interest in Medicare, the government's second largest social program after Social Security, reached a new high in 1995, not as part of health care reform, but as a vehicle for deficit reduction and because of a desire by Congress to restructure the program to encourage enhanced choice for beneficiaries and greater use of managed care. Medicaid, a major payer of long-term care and financer of coverage for low-income elderly, is also slated to undergo major restructuring. As Congress and the nation debate the future of these key programs for older Americans, a number of critical issues deserve attention.

The United States Congress established the Medicare and Medicaid programs in 1965. Both were targeted in large part to the needs of elderly persons. Over time, Medicare in particular became one of the most popular federal programs, achieving nearly universal coverage for acute care needs. Yet despite the existence of this popular government program, out-of-pocket spending for health care by older Americans remains high, outstripping spending levels for younger persons. Medicare pays less than half of acute care costs and largely excludes long-term care services, which are covered, albeit inadequately, by Medicaid.

After discussions in 1994 of some expansions in coverage for the elderly, the political debate has suddenly taken a 180-degree turn. Not only is there no longer any discussion of expansion, but (as of this writing) legislation to be enacted in 1996 will likely make major reductions in the rate of growth allowed under these programs. Such new legislation will not alter the facts surrounding the need for services, however. Indeed, if spending on Medicare and Medicaid is severely limited in the future, the problems that surround the health care needs of the elderly will not simply disappear: they will worsen, instead, over time.

In terms of acute care, it is neither feasible nor desirable to insulate the treatment of the elderly from changes occurring in the rest of the system. Changes underway that are altering the environment of health care delivery for other populations will naturally spill over onto Medicare. For example, if younger families are actively encouraged—or compelled—to enter managed care programs, this will inevitably affect older Americans as well. Further, if most of the health care system is organized into formal networks of providers of care, a fee-for-service system only for older Americans will not be viable. It is not desirable to create two separate health care systems, one for the old and disabled, and one for the young. Thus, some of the changes likely to be proposed under Medicare would probably occur under any circumstances; the more important issue is the rate of that change and whether it can achieve the reductions in spending growth expected of it.

Finally, the size of the Medicare program—and spending on the elderly generally—relative to the rest of the health care system means that what happens to Medicare will also affect the overall health care system. For example, Medicare payments account for 28 percent of hospital spending and 20 percent of spending on physician services.[1] Thus, Medicare has the potential to exert enormous leverage on the system, although calls for decentralization of Medicare may serve to reduce this leverage, eliminating the federal government's ability to limit growth in the costs of care.

Insurance Protection and the Lack of It for Seniors

Medicare was established by legislation in 1965 as Title XVIII of the Social Security Act and first went into effect on July 1, 1966. The overriding goal of the program was to provide mainstream acute care for persons over the age of 65—a group that had been underserved by the health care system, largely because many older persons could not afford insurance. Further, insurance coverage as part of retirement benefits was relatively rare, and insurance companies were reluctant to offer coverage to older persons even when they could afford it.[2] Thus, even in the 1960s, risk selection was an issue.

Medicare has contributed substantially to the well-being of America's oldest and most disabled citizens. In many ways the program has changed little since its passage. It is the largest payer for acute health care services in the United States, providing the major source of insurance for the elderly and disabled. Medicare is divided into two parts. Hospital Insurance (Part A) covers hospital, skilled nursing, and home care services, and is funded by payroll tax contributions of workers. Supplementary Medical Insurance (Part B) covers physician services, and other ambulatory care is funded by a combination of general revenues and premium contributions from beneficiaries.

Because Medicare leaves a number of gaps in coverage, a market for private supplemental insurance—often referred to as Medigap—has grown up around Medicare. About three out of four seniors have some form of private supplemental insurance, either purchased privately or offered as part of a retirement benefits package.[3] Retiree health insurance is at least partially subsidized by employers, reducing the costs that beneficiaries must pay. This type of supplemental insurance often is more comprehensive as well, paying not only the copayments and deductibles required under Medicare but also often including additional benefits such as prescription drug coverage. Those who must pay the full costs of supplemental insurance usually pay at least $900 per year in premiums.

Low-income persons may have gaps in Medicare covered by the Medicaid program, which is targeted to those who are eligible for income support under the Supplemental Security Income program and those who have very high medical expenses that leave them with low incomes after accounting for medical costs. In addition to the standard coverage under Medicaid, the Qualified Medicare Beneficiary (QMB) program was added in 1989; under this program Medicaid pays Medicare premiums and shares costs for persons up to the poverty line who do not receive traditional Medicaid benefits.[4] And those with incomes between 100 and 120 percent of the poverty line are eligible for assistance with Part B premiums. This expansion has had considerable impact on the elderly, raising Medicaid participation in 1991 to 11.9 percent of the elderly as compared to 7.6 percent in 1987.[5]

Nonetheless, even with Medicare, Medicaid, and private insurance, persons over the age of 65 face substantial out-of-pocket expenses for acute care services. Total spending on behalf of the elderly for all acute care services was expected to average about $6,930 in 1994, of which $1,055 was paid directly by individuals. To that should be added the amount that individuals must pay in premiums for Medicare and supplemental insurance—another $1,137 on average in 1994. These burdens vary by age, income, and other characteristics.

A smaller share of elderly Americans face even larger burdens from the costs of long-term care. Currently, nearly 1.6 million older Americans reside in nursing homes and another 2.3 million severely disabled persons remain in the community.[6] For those in the community who use home health care services, for example, 1994 estimated out-of-pocket costs (not covered by Medicare) averaged about $1,620. For persons in nursing homes, expenses can overwhelm the family since costs of housing someone in a nursing home start at about $35,000 per year and can reach much higher.

Unlike acute care, there is no comprehensive public insurance to cover the costs of long-term care. The Medicaid program does provide basic support—mostly for nursing home services. But Medicaid is a welfare program, designed to protect those with low incomes and minimal assets. Thus, only when the families' resources are exhausted, or if they have none to begin with, can individuals rely on Medicaid for support. And even then, they must continue to devote substantial amounts of their incomes each year to nursing home care before Medicaid's contribution begins. Unlike insurance, which protects people against financial catastrophe, the current system provides people protection only *after* catastrophe occurs. Medicaid is not an insurance program; it is a welfare program for those who have impoverished themselves paying for health care. Even after becoming eligible, families must devote most of their incomes toward the cost of that care.

Special Concerns Regarding Health Care and the Elderly

How should these high rates of health care spending by elderly persons be interpreted? Is spending on health care out of line for the elderly as compared with the rest of the population? Average acute care spending for persons over age 65 is about 3.8 times as high as for those under age 65.[7] A number of critical factors boost the costs of acute health care spending for older persons: the higher acute and chronic care needs of older persons, demands on services at the end of life, the aging of the population, the role of technology, and the special needs of long-term care. Since the elderly disproportionately use long-term care services, the ratio would likely be even higher if these services were taken into account as well. These constraints must be considered when assessing how the elderly should be treated relative to the rest of the population.

Acute and chronic care needs

Older persons are more likely to suffer chronic and acute care illnesses than are younger persons. The incidence of problems such as heart disease, cancer, arthritis, and diabetes rise with age. Rates of disability and the share of the population reporting poor or fair health status are also positively correlated with aging.[8] International comparisons also show increasing health problems by age and, despite lengthening life expectancies, morbidity at older ages is still high.[9]

For those with multiple health limitations, treatment of any particular problem is more complicated when other health conditions must be taken into account.

The end of life

Many casual observers of the health care system suggest that controlling use of services in the last year of life may be the magic bullet for reining in the growth of health care spending. And since most of those who die each year are over the age of 65, this is particularly a problem for the Medicare program. Certainly, few statistics sound as compelling as the widely quoted statistic that 28 percent of Medicare spending is concentrated on the 5 percent of enrollees in their last year of life.[10]

But like most magic bullets for solving problems with the health care system, there is more to this story than simply excessive spending on hopeless cases. First, if technology is being used extensively in futile cases involving the very old, the share of resources devoted to health care in the last year of life should be rising as technology has expanded. Anne Scitovsky[11] pursued this question and found that high expenditures were not a new phenomenon; they even preceded the introduction of Medicare in 1965. More recently, Lubitz,[12] updating an earlier study, found that between 1976 and 1985, a period of enormous cost growth in health care, there was no increase in the share of Medicare resources going to those in the last year of life. The proportion of decedents increased slightly but the proportion of Medicare dollars fell slightly.

Further disaggregation of Medicare data also reinforce this analysis. While the fact that Medicare spending increases steadily by age seems to support claims about disproportionate spending on the very old, the data show exactly the opposite pattern for persons in their last year of life. Considerably more is spent on the 65- to 69-year-olds who die in a given year than on decedents over age 85.[13] That is, more is spent on younger Medicare beneficiaries who are more likely to recover—a result consistent with reasonable health care policy. Since life expectancy at age 65 is now about 17 years, spending on the younger old is not just cheating death for a few months, but rather treating patients with many useful years left.[14]

These findings suggest several things. Physicians do not always know that death is imminent when making health care spending decisions. And since people often die after being ill or requiring medical treatment, it is only natural to see extraordinary spending in the last year of life (as well as for those who survive major illnesses). The issue more appropriately is whether it appears that disproportionate amounts are spent on those with no chance of survival and whether that contributes substantially to the problem of the growth in health care spending. And here the evidence is much weaker. There does seem to be a drop-off in spending on the very old as compared to the young in their last year of life, suggesting that at least, on average, decisions are being made to resist heavy acute care expenditures.

The problem of excessive use of medical care by the elderly thus is likely overstated. However, Medicare does face some unique challenges in addressing the problems of assessing inappropriate care and in finding ways to manage a disproportionate number of high-cost cases.

The aging of the population

Spending on the end of life and the higher average costs of health care for the elderly are not the only reasons for the higher costs of Medicare. Medicare is a program in which the number of enrollees is growing more rapidly than the size of the rest of the population. Each year the number of enrollees is growing by about 1.4 percent,[15] and much of that growth is occurring among the very old, who have higher than average levels of expenditure. As a result, not only should Medicare spending overall be expected to grow more rapidly than health care spending for the population as a whole (because of increases in the number of Medicare beneficiaries), but growth will increase on a per capita basis as well, since the composition of the Medicare population is also changing. The share of beneficiaries with higher expenditure needs is rising compared with those with lower average expenditures.

The aging of the population probably adds only about 0.2 percentage point to the growth of Medicare spending each year relative to the rest of the population.[16] This is not a very great amount in any one year, but it means that just to keep Medicare on an even footing with the rest of the health care system, spending growth per capita likely should be higher for Medicare.

The role of technology

One of the important pressures on health care spending arises from the use of new technology, but these pressures may be disproportionately large for the Medicare population. Technology has provided new tools such as CT scans and magnetic resonance imagers (MRIs) and new procedures such as endoscopies and arthroscopies. These new testing technologies are often less invasive and hence less risky than earlier means for detecting illness. For example, subjecting older or disabled patients to exploratory surgery might not be feasible, but giving them MRIs does not carry the same risk. Thus, it is not surprising that these new tests are particularly important for high-risk Medicare patients. These tests constitute the fastest-rising categories of services under Medicare.[17]

Surgery and other technical procedures also continue to grow, while becoming increasingly more complex and expensive over time. For example, rates of coronary artery bypass graft surgery for men over the age of 65 rose from 2.6 per 1,000 in 1980 to 10.4 per 1,000 in 1989.[18] The improved success of procedures such as total hip replacement and cataract surgery mean that outcomes have improved relative to risks. Thus, higher rates of use would certainly be expected and appropriate, and the increases will disproportionately benefit older and disabled patients.

While these issues are pervasive in the overall U.S. health care system, the role of technology may thus have an even greater impact on spending for the Medicare population, helping to explain increasingly high rates of service use within this age group. The combination of an aging population and the special benefits of new technology for frail populations underscores the fact that Medicare will have difficulty in holding down its rate of growth both absolutely and relative to the rest of the population in the foreseeable future.

Challenges posed by the need for long-term care

Long-term care may represent an extremely large source of health care costs for seniors. While long-term care services used by this group are likely to be more supportive and hence less expensive than services for some of the younger disabled groups, the elderly disproportionately require such care.

Moreover, because of the inadequacy of financing of long-term care, available acute care services may be used as a substitute for long-term care. Medicare is the major insurer affected by this misuse and likely incurs higher costs because of it. For example, Medicare's home health care benefit is intended to provide rehabilitation and other medical services, but it may also serve as a long-term home care benefit. Rapid growth in home health care since regulations on eligibility were eased in 1989 may be attributable to its increasing use as a chronic care as well as an acute care benefit.[19] Pressures to use skilled nursing facility beds to meet long-term care needs also have helped raise Medicare spending, particularly since 1988. Further, when patients' long-term care needs are neglected, these needs may escalate into acute medical crises that raise the costs of care.

While improved long-term care coverage makes sense for meeting the needs of the elderly and disabled and for reducing inappropriate reliance on acute care services, its prohibitive costs have tended to limit proposals for relief in this area. But, if little expansion of long-term care occurs, the pressures to misuse Medicare will remain strong and will likely provide an upward bias in spending on this part of the program.

Is Medicare itself a source of the problem?

A number of critics of the Medicare program blame it not only for the high costs of health care for the elderly, but for aggravating health care inflation in general. The rapid growth in the program in its early years—expanding well beyond predicted spending levels—is often cited as an example of why no government programs should be trusted.

But the original goal of the legislation creating Medicare was to offer mainstream medical care to older persons, and early fears about the program were that it would not be accepted by doctors and hospitals. Thus, there was a conscious decision not to undertake cost-containment efforts initially.[20] Medicare likely did contribute to some inflation as it expanded demand for additional services, but no efforts to counteract this impact were undertaken. And when cost-containment efforts were undertaken in the 1980s, Medicare's track record improved substantially.[21] Although the rate of growth of Medicare as compared with that of the private insurance sector was lower between 1984 and 1991, an upturn in Medicare costs compared with private insurance in 1992 and 1993 is being touted as "proof" of the inadequacy of the program's cost-containing efforts (Figure 10.1).[22]

Problems and Strengths of the Medicare System

On the acute care side of the ledger, an analysis of the needs of older Americans must focus on the adequacy of Medicare, its viability as

Figure 10.1   Per Capita Growth Rates of Consistently Covered
Services, 1976–1993

Source: National Health Expenditure Data, Health Care Financing
Administration.

part of the health care system, and the special role it plays. Because
of some of the problems of seniors described earlier, it may make
sense to keep Medicare separate from the rest of the health care system, but that does not imply that Medicare should be ignored nor
that coordination with the rest of the system is unnecessary. Moreover,
pressures on Medicare both to contract the program and to expand
it must be reconciled.

Special pressures on a public program

Although relative to total health care costs Medicare performed
rather well in the 1980s, it is viewed as a runaway item in the federal
budget. The strong performance of the private sector relative to
Medicare for the past two years underscores this claim. Further, since
Medicare is funded with tax dollars in an era of anti-tax sentiment,
it is more heavily scrutinized than health expenditures paid for by

individuals or by businesses. Its absolute size and rate of growth cause Medicare to stand out from most other domestic programs.

Medicare began the 1970s as 3.5 percent of the federal budget; by 1990 it accounted for 8.6 percent. Even with the cuts of 1993, Medicare's share in 1995 will likely total more than 11 percent of the federal budget.[23] In the view of many policymakers, Medicare may be crowding out expenditures on other domestic programs or standing in the way of controlling the federal deficit, or both. Critics often argue that Americans will only accept a certain level of public spending, so if Medicare grows rapidly, it hurts other spending even if it has its own revenue source. This alone makes it a potential target for budget reduction efforts.

In addition, a second fiscal pressure faced by Medicare arises from the status of the Hospital Insurance (HI) trust fund. Current law provides a fixed source of funding for HI—and these revenues are not growing as fast as the level of spending, creating a likely future crisis when the trust funds become exhausted. So far, that day of reckoning has been postponed several times by major cost-cutting efforts and an increase in the wage base subject to taxation. Current projections indicate that exhaustion of the HI trust fund will occur in 2002.[24] Even strong supporters of the Medicare program thus face the prospect that further changes will be needed, either increasing the payroll tax rate devoted to Medicare or reexamining the generosity of the program itself.

Medicare's acute care focus

One of the major problems cited with Medicare lies in what it fails to cover. Actually, this represents a backhanded compliment to the program, since what Medicare does cover tends to be taken for granted. Older Americans receive mainstream care in hospitals and from physicians. Nonetheless, the program is faulted by some for its focus on acute care services. The most obvious omission in meeting the needs of the elderly is long-term care—social and supportive services for those with disabilities and the frailties of old age. But when the program was established, concern centered on helping older persons gain access to services surrounding acute illnesses. In fact, the original proposal for Medicare was that it cover hospital services alone (Part A). Part B was added at the last minute to also cover physician and other ambulatory care services.[25] This emphasis has meant, however, that treatment of chronic and post-acute care has been less well covered by the program. In particular, the lack of public insurance for prescription drugs remains a problem. The elderly use more prescription drugs than other population groups, but many seniors lack insurance protection for this expense.[26]

Changes that would make the coverage more responsive to the actual needs of older Americans would, of course, be very expensive. This establishes a crucial dilemma for proposals to expand health care insurance: which would be more politically palatable—improved coverage requiring substantial new tax support or providing the sickest subgroup of the population less complete protection than that provided to younger persons? Even without such expansions, it is difficult to justify major cuts in benefits offered under Medicare when many younger families enjoy richer insurance packages.

The issue of equity in treatment of the old and the young is complicated by the fact that costs of providing the same benefit package are much higher for older persons than for younger persons. Would equitable treatment require substantially more resources for the elderly as compared with the young? And if so, where should the line be drawn? The basic assumption in the financing of Medicare has traditionally been that a substantial share of the costs for such coverage must be borne by the young and not the old through the implicit subsidies that Medicare provides. Budget pressures have already begun to strongly test this assumption, and this trend will likely continue.

Cost sharing and premium structures

Medicare's requirements for premiums and cost-sharing contributions are out of sync with requirements that individuals in employer-subsidized plans face (and with the proposals of various reform plans). This also raises important equity issues and calls into question the ability of the United States to ever ensure seamless health insurance coverage. But in this case, not all of the discrepancies are to the disadvantage of seniors.

Currently, under Medicare an enrollee is required to pay a premium equal to about 25 percent of the costs of Part B.[27] When taken as part of total Medicare spending, however, that represents only about 10 percent of the overall costs of Medicare.[28] This premium contribution represents a considerably smaller share of total spending than with most private employer-subsidized plans that require families to pay about 20 or 25 percent of the costs of their premiums.[29] Thus, as part of a coordinated reform approach, premiums under

Medicare might be increased to look more like those of younger families. On the other hand, Medicare benefits are also less comprehensive than those offered to younger families, and many older Americans must pay all or a substantial share of the costs of supplemental Medigap premiums.

Over time, a variety of proposals have been made to increase premium contributions, usually as part of the annual budget reduction debates. These can be divided into across-the-board proposals and income-related options. Proposed across-the-board increases are usually quite modest—for example, raising premiums to 30 percent of Part B costs—because many of those who would be subject to this increase have relatively low incomes and would find the changes burdensome. For example, for an individual with an income of $10,000, setting the Part B premium to 30 percent would by itself consume about 5.9 percent of her income.

To raise further revenues from premiums, it is tempting to seek income-related increases, such as was contained in the Medicare Catastrophic Care legislation of 1988.[30] The challenge is to find a politically acceptable change that recognizes both the need for reducing federal outlays on Medicare and the limited ability of many seniors to take on ever-greater health care burdens. If the limits where income-related burdens begin are set high, the change will raise few new revenues. But to substantively increase revenues means charging higher premiums to middle-income families. Many of the 1994 reform proposals advocated an income-related premium, suggesting that the fears from the negative reaction to the Medicare Catastrophic legislation have waned over time and that premium changes are likely to come in some form in the near future. All of those proposals, however, would have affected only a small number of beneficiaries since they would not begin to take effect until incomes reached at least $75,000. If more dramatic moves are made to reduce Medicare's spending, the income cutoff for such premiums would likely have to be lowered considerably.

Another area where Medicare's practices are at odds with most of the rest of the health care system is the required payments that beneficiaries must make in the form of deductibles and coinsurance. When Medicare began in 1966, the deductibles for Part A and for Part B were set at nearly the same level: $40 and $50, respectively. But over time the Part A deductible has grown substantially, to $716 in 1995 as compared with just $100 for Part B. Coinsurance is assessed on all physician services, as well as on some hospital and skilled nurs-

ing facility days, but not on home health benefits or laboratory services. This combination of deductibles and coinsurance for Medicare
represents an ad hoc collection of payments with little defensible justification as points of control for the use of health care services. Thus,
it makes sense to consider reshaping this cost sharing even if the reshaping is not tied to any larger efforts to expand or contract the size
of the Medicare program. And to bring it more closely into line with
private insurance plans for younger families, much of the cost sharing
would be reduced.

The goal of cost sharing is to provide cost awareness and thus
give beneficiaries incentives to make careful use of services. But the
importance of these incentives varies by type of health care service.
For example, many analysts believe that hospital deductibles and coinsurance do little to discourage use of such services. Patients rarely
make the decision to check into a hospital on their own. Moreover,
other constraints on use of hospital care, such as preadmission screening, serve to limit inappropriate use. Medicare gives hospitals strong
incentives to release their patients as early as possible, reducing the
justification for coinsurance on very long stays. Consequently, hospital
cost sharing—which is particularly high under Medicare—could be
reduced or eliminated with no expected increase in the use of
services. In 1994, however, hospital cost sharing saved the federal
government about $6.7 billion by shifting costs onto beneficiaries (or
employers who helped pay a share of retirees' health insurance).
Eliminating or reducing it would thus be expensive.[31]

Another candidate for reductions in cost sharing is the coinsurance on skilled nursing facility services. When the program was established in 1965, the coinsurance was set at one-eighth the hospital deductible. But over time, hospital costs have risen faster than costs of
skilled nursing facility care, raising this coinsurance to an unreasonably high level. In some areas of the country coinsurance amounts for
skilled nursing facility benefits are now higher than the value of the
benefit.[32] This effectively restricts the number of days of skilled nursing facility care available to beneficiaries to about 20 days rather than
the 100 days that are on the books.

In Medicare, the most likely areas for expanding cost sharing
are in coinsurance for home health care services and on the level of
the Part B deductible. More and more enrollees exceed the Part B
deductible each year since it has not kept up with Part B spending. It
could be raised to $200 or $250 per year and still be comparable to
or lower than that often found in many private insurance plans. Fur-

ther, the reintroduction of coinsurance for home health care services might help to slow the growth in this part of the Medicare program. When the original coinsurance requirement for home health care was eliminated in 1972, use of that benefit grew rapidly, particularly on the Part A side of Medicare.[33] The problem with raising home health care coinsurance, however, is that it falls particularly heavily on the old and the frail who also tend to have lower incomes. Moreover, because persons who have home health care visits tend to receive them for an extended period of time, coinsurance can mount up very quickly for these services. For example, a 20 percent coinsurance would raise the out-of-pocket burdens on the average home health care recipient by over $1,200 if instituted in 1995.[34] A better approach would be to shift home health care to Part B where it would be subject to the premium, and limit any copayment to a smaller amount (perhaps 5 percent of costs).

Finally, totally missing from Medicare is any upper-bound limit on cost-sharing liabilities. Beneficiaries with complicated illnesses (and no Medigap protection) can end up owing tens of thousands of dollars in Medicare cost sharing. Thus, adding stop-loss protection—that is, the guarantee that above a certain threshold, the individual should not have to continue to pay out-of-pocket for Medicare-covered services—would be a valuable addition to Medicare. Again, for purposes of consistency, it makes sense to extend this to Medicare beneficiaries since stop-loss protection is routinely a part of insurance for younger families and would likely be included in any comprehensive reform package for younger families. But stop-loss protection for this age group would be very expensive to provide. In the absence of stop-loss, care should be taken not to overextend other cost-sharing increases.

Overall restructuring of Medicare cost sharing could improve the Medicare program by shifting cost sharing to those areas where the incentives might be more effective. This could be done in a relatively budget-neutral way with increases in some areas offsetting changes in others, simplifying the program and making it more consistent with insurance for the under-65 population. In addition, the QMB program could be expanded to improve protection from cost sharing for the low-income population. If cost-sharing changes overall become too expensive to provide—for example, in the case of stop-loss protections—one way to offer at least partial relief would be to expand the QMB program. At least in theory, the QMB program now provides stop-loss for those with the lowest incomes. And although participation is low,[35] about 10 to 12 percent of Medicare enrollees now potentially have this protection. It has likely helped an additional 4 to 5 percent of the elderly population hold down out-of-pocket expenses.[36] Thus, one less expensive way to provide some protection for the most vulnerable beneficiaries would be to expand the QMB program to, say, 150 percent of the poverty level (again a move consistent with low-income protections often proposed in other health care reforms) and seek ways to increase participation in it.

Gaps in payment levels between medicare and the private sector

At present, Medicare's payment levels are below the amount allowed by most private insurers.[37] Indeed, much criticism has been leveled at the current system over "cost shifting"—the process that results in some private payers helping to compensate providers for the low payment levels of Medicare (and Medicaid). This raises costs in one part of the system while lowering them elsewhere. Such changes do not truly save costs; they just shift the burdens.

Consequently, advocates of reform often call for a reduction in cost shifting. But ironically, many of the 1994 health reform proposals and the 1995 budget proposals for Medicare would have potentially *increased* cost shifting by keeping Medicare a fully separate system while cutting payments to health care providers. With continuing pressures to restrict Medicare's growth over time, the differential is still likely to be expanded in the future.

Will a changing delivery system's pressures on doctors and hospitals to provide care at lower costs help or hurt this situation? Providers who feel squeezed from all sources, but most heavily from Medicare, may see that the simplest option available to them for raising their revenues may be to favor non-Medicare patients, for whom fees are higher. Even providers who now overlook the differential may be less willing to do so as payments from all sources are squeezed in the future. If there is now a "cushion" in the generosity of private payers, its elimination through cost-containment efforts may implicitly squeeze Medicare patients as well. On the other hand, if the private sector pushes down payment levels to be nearly on a par with Medicare, it may be easier to continue price reductions in the program.

The payment differential creates a problem for Medicare when it affects patients' access to care. The impact of the differential could be felt by patients in terms of lower access to care if, for example, doctors declined to take on new Medicare patients. And the entire health care system would be affected if hospitals that serve a disproportionate share of Medicare patients were squeezed sufficiently to close their doors altogether. This suggests that lowering provider payments as a policy for holding down Medicare costs may be difficult to sustain over time.

Prospects for Major Restructuring of Medicare

The terms of the debate over the future of the Medicare program are changing dramatically. The focus has shifted from minor expansions in some areas and substantial savings in others to an emphasis on even greater reductions on Medicare spending into the future. Balancing the budget by shortly after the turn of the century has become an overriding goal for many in the Congress; the tenor of the discussion has thus shifted to considering even more radical restructuring of the program. Moreover, as the health care delivery system in the United States seems to be moving rapidly toward some form of managed care, it will be increasingly difficult—and likely undesirable—merely to bolster Medicare's fee-for-service framework.

Two types of major restructuring of Medicare are beginning to receive serious consideration: changing the way that care is delivered to rely on some form of managed care, and turning Medicare into a voucher program. While these two elements could be combined, each implies important changes for Medicare, and each has different implications. Moreover, it is possible to have one without the other. For example, Medicare beneficiaries could simply be given vouchers to purchase whatever type of insurance they wish—subject to insurers meeting certain standards. This would give beneficiaries the option of buying into an HMO, some looser form of managed care, or remaining in a traditional indemnity type plan. But managed care options could also be offered to elderly and disabled persons in which they could enroll in HMOs or similar plans, but where the plans would be certified by Medicare and overseen more directly—as is the case with the current HMO optional program.

Vouchers

Advocates of a private approach to financing health care for Medicare enrollees argue for a system of vouchers in which eligible persons would be allowed to choose their own health care plan from among an array of private options. For example, individuals might be able to opt for larger deductibles or coinsurance in return for coverage of other services such as drugs or long-term care. Since many Medicare enrollees now choose to supplement Medicare with private insurance, this approach would allow beneficiaries to combine the voucher with their own funds and buy one comprehensive plan. No longer would they have to worry about coordinating coverage between Medicare and their private supplemental plan. Moreover, persons with employer-provided supplemental coverage could remain in the health care plans they had as employees. This is the general approach advocated in the Balanced Budget Act of 1995 passed by the Congress and vetoed by President Clinton.

To the government, this option has the appeal of enabling a predictable rate of growth in the program. For example, the federal government could set the vouchers to grow at the same rate as GDP or some other factor. Since such options are usually developed to achieve major savings, the "price" of offering choice to enrollees might be a voucher set at 90 or 95 percent of the current level of government spending per enrollee. Moreover, by placing a cap on the rate of growth of the benefit, vouchers would effectively shift the risk either to the private insurer or to the enrollee, or both. If a plan was not successful in holding down costs and Medicare's contribution was fixed, the likely response would be to raise the supplemental contribution required of enrollees, effectively creating an indirect premium increase.

Figures vary on how much of a reduction in growth in the program would be sought from the vouchers. Lowering the growth rate in spending by 3 to 4 percentage points from its current projected average growth of about 10 percent per year is the goal of the budget resolution passed by Congress for the years 1996 to 2002. That means a 30 to 40 percent decline in growth—an extremely ambitious goal for any cost-containment strategy. Thus, unless private insurers could find ways to achieve such reductions, the likely consequence would be a shifting of the burden onto beneficiaries. Advocates of vouchers argue that consumer opposition to paying higher prices would force insurers to hold down costs. Opponents claim that both consumers and insurers would lack the clout to achieve such limits.

How successful is the private sector likely to be? First, private insurers will have higher administrative overhead costs than does Medicare. Insurers will have to advertise and promote their plans. They will face a smaller risk pool that may require them to make more conservative decisions regarding reserves and other protections against losses over time. These plans expect to return a profit to shareholders. All of these factors work against private companies performing better than Medicare. At least in Medicare, the government's track record at efficiently providing services is quite good, with overhead two to three times less than that in the private market.[38]

On the other hand, private insurers may be able to innovate with new, more effective cost-containment schemes. They may be able to bargain for good prices and adapt to changing circumstances more readily than the public sector can. But, as noted earlier, Medicare's payment levels are already at the low end of the scale. The real challenge will lie in whether they can truly manage the care that beneficiaries use. Finally, by combining coverage of those services that Medicare now covers with other medical care such as preventive services, drugs, and long-term care, the private sector may be able to find better ways to package and deliver services.

Regulation would be needed to require insurers to take all comers and to guard against problems of adverse selection, wherein one plan might be able to compete by choosing carefully what persons to cover. The program will most likely be problematic if it is voluntary. Further, adverse selection will be more likely if Medicare enrollees are free to supplement their vouchers to enhance coverage; insurers may find that those with the most to spend on certain types of supplemental coverage may be the best risks. For example, covering the "extras" such as private rooms and specialized nursing care may appeal to enrollees who are relatively healthy and well-off as compared with enrollees attracted to a supplemental package that mainly offers coverage of prescription drugs or those who can afford only the bare minimum package. If such schemes prevail, many Medicare enrollees who now have reasonable coverage for acute care costs, but who are the less desirable risks, will not be able to affordably obtain even a minimal level of protection.

On balance, vouchers offer less in the way of guarantees for continued protection under Medicare. They are most appealing as a way to substantially cut the federal government's contributions to the plan indirectly through erosion of the comprehensiveness of coverage that the private sector offers rather than as stated policy. The problems of making tough choices and the financial risks would be borne by beneficiaries. Further, the federal government's role in influencing the course of the national health care system would be substantially diminished. For some, this is a major advantage of such reforms. But the history of Medicare is one in which the public sector has often played a positive role as well, first insuring those largely rejected by the private sector and then leading the way in many cost-containment efforts.[39]

Capitated care options

Rather than creating vouchers that effectively put enrollees at risk, Medicare could move to a system of requiring managed care arrangements; the program would still be operated and overseen by the federal government, so that the government could continue to share some of the risks. Enrollees could be required to operate within an HMO, an independent practice association (IPA), a preferred provider organization (PPO), or some other similar entity paid to offer health care on a per capita basis. All of these organizations seek to control costs by managing the overall level of care that the patient receives, moving away from a system that pays on a fee-for-service basis, in which the more the patient uses, the more the provider makes.

In a well-managed, high-quality capitated system, the individual can receive much better continuity of care. Patient records and information can readily be shared within the organization and services will be better coordinated. Physicians have no incentives to prescribe unnecessary tests or procedures since that only adds to the costs of care. On the other hand, they also must perform good diagnostic and preventive services in order to reduce use of the big ticket items such as hospitalization. Moreover, if Medicare performs its role as a careful overseer, any propensity to skimp on care can be reduced as well. And, in such a system, payments would be made on the basis of the experience of the best providers, rather than locking into some fixed rate of growth.

Such systems can mainly save on the costs of care by reducing use of services. This reduction may lessen unnecessary care, but it can cut into important services as well. Consequently, such organizations often place an important burden on consumers to be aggressive advocates for their own care. The barriers to care that HMOs and others establish to discourage overuse may be intimidating, particularly for the very old or frail. It may be easier to establish barriers to services than to manage care carefully on a case-by-case basis. Further, the restrictions on choice implicit in such a system are viewed negatively by many.

Medicare's experience suggests that protections for consumers and careful oversight will be needed to avoid major problems and scandals that could taint reform. Medicare's experience with HMOs has certainly raised some concerns about how to expand use of managed care and its likely effectiveness in broader reform. Some HMOs have found it difficult to bring the elderly and disabled into their programs. These patients do not always behave like younger HMO patients and hence HMOs sometimes find it more difficult to hold down the costs of care. As a result, they have not always been able to cover patients adequately with the payments that Medicare makes on behalf of beneficiaries. There have been some notable crises with HMOs suddenly dropping Medicare enrollees because of such financial difficulties.[40] Those that have attracted seniors have sometimes done so selectively, seeking beneficiaries whose average costs will be lower than Medicare's per capita payment not because of better management and oversight of care but because they have selected low-risk patients. Consequently, such activities cast doubt on whether these arrangements truly save costs for the Medicare program.[41,42] Moreover, the program has had difficulty in determining a reasonable payment to make to HMOs for each enrollee—a critical factor in assuring fair competition among plans.

The promise of managed care and the pressures that will arise over time as the rest of the health care system moves in this direction make it inevitable that considerable effort must go into improving Medicare's managed care efforts. But will such a shift lower the rate of growth sufficiently to achieve the stringent limits that some have in mind for the program? Or will stronger limits that effectively place both the insurer and the beneficiary at risk be required to meet those goals? This is one of the major challenges likely to face Medicare in the foreseeable future.

Possible Improvements in Long-Term Care

Almost no one expresses satisfaction with the long-term care benefits provided by Medicaid, the primary payer of long-term care apart from individuals' own resources. Despite current public expenditures of over $60 billion on that part of Medicaid, many gaps and inequities remain. Most experts agree that further efforts to expand the availability of long-term care services are desirable, but there is little consensus on how any expansion should take place or how it would be financed.

Moreover, expansions that seemed possible in the context of broader health care reform are likely to be much less feasible in an environment in which Medicaid will more likely be contracted than expanded. Nonetheless, improvements in the public provision of long-term care will remain an important goal of those who recognize the following concerns associated with the existing Medicaid program.

Lack of home- and community-based services

One of the most commonly cited problems with long-term care is the strong emphasis on institutional benefits to the exclusion of other services. For many years, nursing home services were about all that Medicaid covered in long-term care. Program rules encouraged this emphasis in the beginning, and institutional care is a required federal benefit. Although the federal government now allows greater flexibility in services that can be offered, states have been reluctant to expand substantially into home- and community-based services.[43]

Despite rapid growth in the home- and community-based services area (over 20 percent per year since 1984), Medicaid remains primarily a nursing home program; in 1992, nearly 87 percent of all spending on long-term care went to nursing home services.[44] This problem is largely a financial one. At present, states are often reluctant to expand their Medicaid programs, recognizing that new benefits, even if cost-saving for some, are likely to add to their existing expenditures. Once people are in nursing homes, it is extremely difficult to move them back into the community. And a new home- and community-based benefit program could rapidly expand, resulting in very high expenditures unless other types of controls were put in place.

If states are relieved of some of the required benefits they now must provide under the program in exchange for lower federal contributions, some states might opt to shift more dollars from the institutional side of the program into home- and community-based services. The balance of services might improve, but perhaps to the detriment of nursing home provision for those who do not have the option of remaining in the community.

The welfare nature of Medicaid

Unlike insurance, which protects people against financial catastrophe, the current system mainly provides protection *after* catastrophe has occurred. To be eligible for Medicaid, individuals either must initially be poor or must have spent enough on acute or long-term care so that their incomes minus health care spending are low enough to qualify. Further, they must not have substantial assets.[45]

Since long-term care is so expensive, many people qualify by "spending down" either their income or their assets, or both. Even after becoming eligible, families must devote much of their income toward the cost of that care; that is, Medicaid only picks up the amounts not paid by the family or individual. In the case of a single person, this will amount to *all* income above a personal needs allowance—usually $30 per month. Moreover, the special rules for nursing home asset protections do not apply for home-based services.

The welfare aspect of long-term care leads to a number of problems. First, much of the public's dislike of Medicaid centers on the requirement that individuals impoverish themselves or at least lower substantially their standards of living in order to receive help from the government. The relaxation of requirements on couples when one spouse enters a nursing home has eased the problem, but certainly has not solved it. Particularly for older persons who have saved all their lives, the limits are often viewed as punitive. And when a spouse is left in straightened economic circumstances, it may make dependence on Medicaid more likely in the future for the surviving member of the couple.

The harsh eligibility requirements for Medicaid also create problems with compliance. In part because Medicaid spend-down requirements are viewed as unfair, organized efforts to circumvent the law have sprung up. Divestiture of assets to children or other relatives offers a means for protecting resources while becoming eligible for help from Medicaid. Such responses tap state budgets to pay for middle-income beneficiaries. Tightening restrictions on a system already viewed as unfair may not reduce costs, however.

Finally, many older persons fear having to depend upon Medicaid and seek to avoid it if possible. The stigma Americans associate with welfare operates as a powerful disincentive to obtaining care. Moreover, private-pay patients have advantages in nursing homes not usually available to Medicaid beneficiaries, resulting in a two-tier system.

Variability in programs across states

State Medicaid programs vary enormously across a number of dimensions.[46] For example, total spending on long-term care per low-income aged resident ranged from $8,460 in Connecticut to $220 in

Utah in 1992.[47] Spending on home health care varied from $2,031 in New York to $4 in California. These disparate levels of effort in part reflect differences in states' abilities to contribute to the program. But in addition, they capture the willingness of states to expend resources on these particular programs. If society believes that there should be a minimum level of protection for the costs of long-term care for those of modest means, the level of variation that now obtains makes little sense. Proposals to give states more flexibility will likely lead to even greater variability, however.

Lack of coordination with acute care

Since acute care services for the elderly mainly occur under Medicare and long-term care services are under the purview of Medicaid, there is a natural tendency for each program to seek to shift the burdens off onto the other. This is exacerbated by the fact that states must pay a substantial share of the costs of Medicaid, but none of Medicare's costs. Any well-designed program for improving long-term care ought to seek better integration or, at the very least, a reduction in the incentives for gaming that currently exist. Proposed changes that will give states more flexibility are likely to create even greater challenges to coordination of care.

Approaches to improving coverage

As recently as the mid-1980s, serious discussions of a comprehensive program of social insurance for long-term care took place. Such a program would have guaranteed access to nursing homes and to home- and community-based services for all disabled persons as needed. But the high and escalating price tags for long-term care, coupled with the enormous growth in the acute care portions of Medicare and Medicaid, moved the discussion away from such solutions to more modest initial steps. Only the most generous health care reform proposal offered in 1994—the McDermott-Wellstone bill—contained a full social insurance approach. At the other extreme, many of the proposals largely ignored long-term care (aside from some modest private insurance initiatives). The Clinton approach was to offer a new home- and community-based services program outside of Medicaid, phased in gradually over time, and some improvement in the nursing home portion of Medicaid.[48] Democratic attempts to build consensus in 1994 generally kept the basic outline of a new home- and community-based services program, but stretched out the phase-in period. But the shifts in 1995 in prospects for long-term care have clouded any discussion of expansion. Substantial cuts in Medicaid have been scheduled and the long-term care portion of the program is unlikely to be spared.

The limited home- and community-based block grant approach of the Clinton proposal now likely represents an upper bound on possible expansion of long-term care services in the public sector. Another approach would be to encourage purchase of private long-term care insurance, supplemented with modest expansions in Medicaid for those with the lowest incomes. The only proposals now under discussion would provide tax relief for those purchasing private long-term care insurance.

Thus, even if proposals to expand long-term care are again seriously debated in the next few years, it is likely that any long-term care piece will be modest, at least initially. Options likely to receive the most attention would limit both eligibility and benefits to keep the scope of any new program manageable. Some combination of strategies for limiting liability for the public side of any plan—whether a Medicaid expansion or a new program—raises similar issues.

Limits on public expansion

The first way to limit the amount spent on expanded long-term care coverage would be to rely on the welfare-based approach of Medicaid and means-test access to any program, restricting eligibility based on the financial situation of disabled persons, usually in terms of both income and assets. While this approach concentrates eligibility on those least able to pay, it may result in making persons ineligible who, while a little better off, still cannot afford the costs of long-term care. That is, if income and asset limits are low enough to substantially limit the number of disabled persons who qualify, many who need services will be excluded. Medicaid deals with this problem by establishing eligibility on the basis of income after health care spending has been subtracted. In other words, persons will ultimately get government help but only after they have "spent-down" their incomes and assets. As discussed earlier, spending-down is extremely unpopular with potential beneficiaries, in part because of its punitive character.

Moreover, the level at which these limits are set will determine how well a combined public/private approach would fill in the gaps for those with moderate incomes. If set too low, it will be unlikely that private purchase of insurance can attract most of those ineligible for the means-tested program.

A second type of limitation would be to require substantial out-of-pocket contributions by those receiving the care—often related to their incomes. Thus, eligibility could extend further up the income scale, but higher-income persons would have to contribute to the costs of care. This cuts costs directly through the sharing of expenses and may limit demand for care when recipients must pay something for it. This limitation is less burdensome than a full spend-down requirement and hence may be somewhat less subject to the gaming that often occurs under the traditional Medicaid approach. It may be possible to achieve much the same goal as means-testing but in a less demeaning fashion.

Costs may also be limited by restricting eligibility to those with severe disabilities. This may satisfy concerns of policymakers that mildly disabled persons might otherwise take advantage of homemaker and personal care services that they do not need. It is easier, too, to make a case for the needs of the severely disabled population. At the same time, however, this restriction precludes early intervention for disabled persons whose functional limitations might be reduced or eliminated. Critics of limited long-term care coverage often make the analogy to preventive services for acute care. Moreover, many of the exciting innovations in long-term care are occurring for the less severely disabled who are still able to retain considerable independence. But if severity is the strategy for limiting eligibility, the program will not be able to take advantage of these innovations.

A fourth way to reduce the costs of new coverage would be to limit benefits offered—usually by expanding just home- and community-based services, for example. While home- and community-based services are the most undeveloped part of long-term care, what people fear most are the crippling costs of institutional care. Moreover, any strategy that places arbitrary limits on ways of delivering care will likely distort choices and lead to inefficiency.

A fifth strategy would focus on controlling payments to care providers. This could be done through price controls or fee schedules for services to limit the rate of growth of payments. Moreover, allowing less formal care to be provided, thus avoiding expensive certified agencies, is another way to potentially limit provider reimbursements. Critics of this strategy claim that if payments are too restrictive, quality of care will suffer.

Finally, some proposals place fixed limits on the amount of funds allowed for the program. For example, the federal government could either give grants to states or offer a matching program with an upper bound on what the federal government is willing to contribute. Such an effort might effectively provide allowances for people to supplement coordinated acute and long-term care services under a capitated system. This is in contrast to the open-ended nature of entitlement programs that would otherwise expand automatically with eligibility and service needs. A variation on this approach is to combine broad eligibility standards with fixed appropriations. These so-called "capped entitlements" are intended to avoid the problem of expenses going up directly in response to beneficiary demand, while assuring open-ended eligibility to the disabled. If states or other entities are left to administer such a program, they must find ways to live within budgets.

Each of these options for limiting the scope of any long-term care expansion thus has advantages and disadvantages. Any program that seeks to hold down the costs of long-term care must adopt several of these strategies. If means-testing is a major strategy, it makes sense to build on the Medicaid program (or at least to take the existing Medicaid program and combine it with any newly named long-term care system).

But if means-testing is ruled out as a mechanism for limiting public liability, the other strategies could be combined to create a complementary long-term care program. This was the strategy of the Clinton proposal and the first two congressional leadership proposals. These proposals would have used all of the techniques aside from means-testing to lower costs. However, full implementation would still have meant new federal spending of about $40 billion per year. Consequently, these proposals went even further to limit the initial costs of the new long-term care benefit by phasing in the system very slowly over time. Few details were offered on how to accomplish this feat, however, suggesting that it would have been difficult to develop such a plan. Instead, the burdens of deciding how to limit spending would have fallen to the states since they would have been liable for any promised benefits beyond the "capped" federal payments. It is not clear in retrospect whether states would have been willing to gamble on such a program.

Facilitating public/private partnerships

In an effort to help expand coverage for long-term care beyond what a public expansion would offer, some might wish to encourage families and individuals to purchase long-term care insurance. Currently, about 2 million persons hold such coverage, and it is likely that more policies will be sold in the future. But what will it take to expand this line of business enough to provide serious relief? If substantial tax benefits or offering those with insurance some expedited eligibility for Medicaid as a backup are considered, new federal resources would be needed as well for this part of the effort.

A first step for making insurance a viable option would be to establish federal standards to protect consumers. These would include outlawing high-pressure marketing tactics and requiring inflation protection so that the benefits would provide protection when the services were needed. If products are to be made attractive to younger persons, some type of nonforfeiture benefit is needed to guarantee that someone who pays in for 20 years but then lapses can withdraw some portion of the payments. (Insurance companies now price insurance premiums low for those in their 40s, for example, precisely because they believe many will fail to keep their premiums current until they need the care.) Americans thus far have shown a healthy and well-founded skepticism about policies. But all of these changes would add to the costs and reduce the number of persons who would buy such coverage.

Estimates prepared for the Pepper Commission[49] indicated that only 6 percent of today's elderly population could afford such a policy without spending more than 5 percent of their income—and even then they would not be fully protected against the costs of care.[50] Many older Americans wishing to protect themselves from the costs of long-term care would have to lower their standard of living for many years in order to obtain partial protection. Rice, Thomas, and Weissert[51] also found that the insurance policies they studied failed to provide much protection against the possibility of high out-of-pocket costs from long-term care expenses. High deductibles and relatively low daily payment rates may leave policyholders vulnerable to spending down their assets even if they have insurance, for example.

Thus, private insurance, with the addition of consumer protection standards, could provide a minority of Americans some security against the financial risks of long-term care. But for the vast majority of the elderly, anyone who already has a disabling condition, and the younger population with a small but real risk of long-term care needs, the emerging market provides little prospect of protection. Major expansion of the private sector will also require new public spending or tax benefits.

Prospects for the Future

The Medicare and Medicaid programs that serve the elderly are on
the brink of major change—designed less to reform these programs
to meet the needs outlined in this chapter than to meet spending reduction targets to help in balancing the federal budget. As a consequence, the prospects for careful debate and modification of these
programs to meet the needs of older Americans are not very bright.
A number of ways do exist in which these programs, particularly
Medicare, could be scaled back—taking advantage of changes now
occurring in the private sector and asking beneficiaries to contribute
more to the costs of their care. Some of these changes could be beneficial for the elderly—increasing flexibility and choice concerning
their insurance, for example. But moving too fast or expecting too
much in cost savings will put these programs and their beneficiaries
at risk. Unfortunately, it appears that reductions will be substantial,
beginning in 1996.

One of the lessons salvaged from the 1994 debate on health care
reform is that achieving comprehensive changes in the U.S. health
care system that expand coverage will be difficult to achieve. The winning "option" in 1994 was simply to retain the status quo. The budget
imperative of the current political climate is leading to major
change—but not necessarily in ways that will be helpful either to the
elderly, or indirectly, to other health care consumers.

While national health care reform would have largely ignored
the special needs of older Americans, the effects of the new health
care environment for the end of the 1990s pose even greater challenges. Since so much of the spending on the health of the elderly
stems from public programs and the new rallying cry is to reduce such
spending, the prospects for older Americans are not encouraging.
Further, changes in Medicare raise important issues about the role
of government in health care. If many of the decisions concerning
Medicare and Medicaid are decentralized, the federal government
will forego much of its ability to influence the health care marketplace.
Indeed, a full voucher approach would eliminate the federal government as an interested party in the costs of acute care services available
to the elderly. The approach likely to emerge in 1996 will lead to further fragmentation of the system by reducing the concept of a consistent national effort to bring the health care system under control.
Such fundamental change deserves careful debate rather than precip-
itous action.

Notes

1. K. R. Levit, C. A. Cowan, H. C. Lazenby, P. A. McDonnell, A. L. Sensenig, J. M. Stiller, and D. K. Won, "National Health Spending Trends, 1960–1993," *Health Affairs* 13 (Winter 1994): 14–31.
2. K. Davis and C. Schoen, *Health and the War on Poverty: A Ten-Year Appraisal* (Washington: The Brookings Institution Press, 1978).
3. G. Chulis, F. Eppig, M. Hogan, D. Waldo, and R. Arnett, "Health Insurance and the Elderly: Data from MCBS," *Health Care Financing Review* 14 (Spring 1993): 163–81.
4. This was part of the Catastrophic Care legislation and survived the repeal of some of the other portions. Participation in the QMB program has been a problem, however, with less than 60 percent of those eligible receiving these extra protections.
5. Chulis et al. 1993.
6. Public Health Service, U.S. Department of Health and Human Services, *Health United States 1993* (Washington, DC: U.S. Government Printing Office, 1994).
7. D. Lefkowitz and A. Monheit, *Health Insurance, Use of Health Services and Health Care Expenditures,* AHCPR Pub. no. 92-0017, National Medical Expenditure Survey Research Findings 12, Agency for Health Care Policy and Research (Rockville, MD: Public Health Service, 1991).
8. Public Health Service 1994.
9. T. Miles and J. Brody, "International Aging," in *Health Data on Older Americans: United States, 1992. Vital and Health Statistics,* National Center for Health Statistics, Series 3, no. 27 (Hyattsville, MD: Public Health Service, 1993).
10. J. Lubitz and R. Prihoda, "Use and Costs of Medicare Services in the Last Two Years of Life," *Health Care Financing Review* 5 (Spring 1984): 117–31.
11. A. Scitovsky, "The High Cost of Dying: What Do the Data Show?" *Milbank Memorial Fund Quarterly* 62, no. 4 (1984): 591–608.
12. J. Lubitz, "Use and Costs of Medicare Services in the Last Year of Life, 1976 and 1985," Health Care Financing Administration, mimeo (11 May 1990).
13. Lubitz 1990.
14. U.S. Congress. House Committee on Ways and Means, *1994 Green Book: Background Material and Data on Programs Within the Jurisdiction of the Committee on Ways and Means.* U.S. House of Representatives (Washington, DC: U.S. Government Printing Office, 15 July 1994).
15. Congressional Budget Office, "The Economic and Budget Outlook: Fiscal Years 1996–2000, A Preliminary Report," mimeo (Washington, DC, 5 January 1995).
16. M. Moon and J. Mulvey, *Entitlements and the Elderly: Protecting Promises and Recognizing Realities* (Washington, DC: Urban Institute Press, forthcoming).
17. R. Berenson and J. Holahan, "Sources of Growth in Medicare Physician

Expenditures," *Journal of the American Medical Association* 267 (February 1992): 687–691.

18. National Center for Health Statistics (NCHS), *Health, United States, 1990* (Hyattsville, MD: Public Health Service, 1991).

19. G. Kenney and M. Moon, "Supply Changes in Medicare Home Health Care in the 1980s," Urban Institute Discussion Paper, 3978-05-02 (October 1993).

20. J. M. Feder, *Medicare: The Politics of Federal Hospital Insurance* (Lexington, MA: Lexington Books, 1977).

21. M. Moon, *Medicare Now and in the Future* (Washington, D.C.: Urban Institute Press, 1993).

22. M. Moon and S. Tuckerman, "Is Medicare Spending Growing Faster than Private Insurance?" Henry J. Kaiser Family Foundation, Menlo Park, CA (July 1995).

23. U.S. Congress 1994.

24. Board of Trustees, Federal Hospital Insurance Trust Fund, *1995 Annual Report of the Board of Trustees of the Hospital Insurance Trust Fund* (Washington, DC: U.S. Government Printing Office, 1995).

25. T. R. Marmor, *The Politics of Medicare* (Chicago: Aldine Publishing Company, 1970).

26. Lefkowitz and Monheit 1991.

27. Under the original legislation, this premium was set at 50 percent of the costs of physician and related services covered by Part B. After 1966, the growth in the premium was far in excess of the growth of Social Security benefits, effectively crowding out other consumption by the elderly. In 1972, the formula was decoupled from the costs of Part B and set to rise at the same rate as Social Security benefit payments—that is, it was tied to the Consumer Price Index. Because Medicare costs rose so rapidly over the next eight years, the share of Part B costs covered by the premium fell to about 25 percent of the overall costs of Part B. Thus, more of Medicare's costs were shifted to the federal government. As part of the emphasis in the early Reagan years on cutting the federal budget, the growth in the premium was again tied to a share of the costs beginning in 1981, but set at 25 percent. Since then this "temporary" change has been periodically extended and currently is in force until 1999. But between 1991 and 1995, exact dollar amounts for premiums were specified in law, and since Part B spending growth was slower than expected, the premiums have drifted higher than 25 percent. They are scheduled to return to 25 percent in 1996.

28. Moon 1993.

29. C. Sullivan, M. Miller, R. Feldman, and B. Dowd, "Employer-Sponsored Health Insurance in 1991," *Health Affairs* 11 (Winter 1992): 172–85.

30. That legislation, which was later repealed, added an income-related supplement on top of the basic premium. It was to rise gradually with income and reach a maximum of $800 per year for individuals with incomes above about $40,000 and couples with incomes above about $70,000.

31. HI Trustees 1995.
32. Moon 1993.
33. G. Kenney, "Understanding the Effects of the PPS on Medicare Home Health Use," *Inquiry* 28, no. 2 (1991): 129–39.
34. Moon and Mulvey forthcoming.
35. P. Neuman, M. Bernardin, E. Bayer, and W. Evans. *Identifying Barriers to Elderly Participation in the Qualified Medicare Beneficiary Program* (Baltimore, MD: Project HOPE Center for Health Affairs, August 1994.)
36. Moon and Mulvey forthcoming.
37. M. Miller, S. Zuckerman, and M. Gates, "How do Medicare Physician Fees Compare with Private Payers?" *Health Care Financing Review* 14 (Spring 1993): 25–39.
38. Congressional Research Service, *Health Insurance and the Uninsured: Background Data and Analysis.* Print 100-2, Senate Committee on Education and Labor. (Washington, DC: U.S. Government Printing Office, 1989), 122–23.
39. Moon 1993.
40. General Accounting Office, *Medicare: HCFA Needs to Take Stronger Actions against HMOs Violating Federal Standards.* HRD-92-11 (Washington, DC: GAO, November 1991).
41. K. Langwell and J. Hadley, "Evaluation of the Medicare Competition Demonstrations," *Health Care Financing Review* 11 (Winter 1989): 65–79.
42. R. Brown, D. Clement, J. Hill, S. Retchin, and J. Bergeron, "Do Health Maintenance Organizations Work for Medicare?" *Health Care Financing Review* 15 (Fall 1993): 7–23.
43. Personal care, which is an optional service under Medicaid, has become a major way to expand services for some states, such as New York. Several waiver programs are now in place and restrictions on them have been eased. The 1915(c) waiver programs used to be limited to those at risk of institutionalization and now can be used for certain persons with chronic conditions as well. Moreover, the 1915(d) program for the elderly no longer has to meet the budget neutrality requirements that originally restricted its use.
44. T. Coughlin, J. Holahan, and L. Ku, *Medicaid Since 1980* (Washington, DC: The Urban Institute Press, 1994).
45. The requirements are much more stringent for single individuals—whose assets must generally be less than $2,000. The Medicare Catastrophic Coverage Act relaxed the stringency of income and asset requirements for those with a spouse left in the community. In this case, the community-dwelling spouse may retain an income of at least 150 percent of the poverty line and assets of up to $60,000.
46. Moon 1994.
47. To capture a sense of spending holding the population constant, these figures divide Medicaid expenditures by the number of elderly persons with incomes below 150 percent of the federal poverty threshold in each state.
48. U.S. Congress. Senate. 1993. S. 1757, Health Security Act. November.

49. Pepper Commission (U.S. Bipartisan Commission on Comprehensive Health Care), *A Call for Action* (Washington, DC: U.S. Government Printing Office, 1990).

50. Although 5 percent does not seem to be an exorbitant amount, it would be in addition to any insurance purchased for acute care. Moreover, most analysts believe that the annual cost must be quite low, since it is a premium that must be consistently paid for many years.

51. T. Rice, K. Thomas, and W. Weissert. "The Effect of Owning Private Long-Term Care Insurance Policies on Out-of-Pocket Costs," *Health Services Research* 25 (February 1991): 907–34.

11

Managed Care for People with Disabilities: Caring for Those with the Greatest Need

Stanley S. Wallack, Helen J. Levine, Margaret
A. McManus, Harriette B. Fox,
Paul W. Newacheck, Richard G. Frank,
and Thomas G. McGuire

Abstract. Disability is discussed in terms of three categories: conditions that result from biomedical conditions and chronic, lifelong illnesses; role or social functioning difficulties that result from behavioral, developmental, or brain disorders; and conditions that limit physical functioning. The range and depth of services needed by the disabled result in higher costs of health care for this population. Because their service needs vary so widely, no single program can address all of the needs equally. Currently, no integrated public policy or program is specifically designed to serve people with disabilities. Rather, they are served by a range of programs that provide specific benefits (e.g., health, social services, and income).

Section 1 of this chapter provides an overview on extending the concept of managed care to disabled populations. Special attention is paid to the financing of health care, the delivery of care, reforming the health care system, the cost-containment potential of managed care, and the need to align care with the nature of the individual disability. In sections 2 and 3, the current status of managed care for two special populations—children and the mentally ill—is discussed in greater detail. Section 2 addresses the characteristics of chronically ill and disabled children, public and private health insurance coverage of children with disabilities, other public programs for chronically ill children, and current directions and strategic choices for managed pediatric care. Section 3 describes the mentally ill and the system of providers that currently supplies care to them, offers some conclusions regarding how managed care is changing the policy debate in mental health care, assesses the key factors affecting policy choices in managed care, and considers prospects for the future shape of managed behavioral health care.

SECTION 1: Overview

Stanley S. Wallack and Helen J. Levine Batten

Disability is usually discussed in terms of three categories. The first category comprises illnesses that result from various biomedical conditions and includes such chronic, lifelong illnesses as diabetes, asthma, hypertension, and arthritis. The second category comprises role or social functioning difficulties that result from behavioral, developmental, or brain disorders; clearly mental illnesses including schizophrenia and bipolar disorder, attention deficit disorder, and substance abuse addiction fit into the category. The third category comprises conditions that limit physical functioning, in which the disabled person needs personal assistance to carry on normal age-appropriate activities of everyday life, such as attending school and working.

Regardless of the criteria used for describing people with disabilities, the size of the disabled population is significant. Estimates using each of these categories suggest that perhaps 10–15 percent of the total U.S. population fall under the classification "disabled."[1] Obviously, these estimates are not additive, but no estimates exist on the extent to which the populations overlap, and therefore the total number of individuals that can be classified as disabled is not known. However, because of advances in medicine, the number of disabled at all ages is increasing.

The range and depth of services needed by the disabled result in higher costs of health care for this population. Even for public programs with prescribed benefits, such as Medicare and Medicaid, the per capita health care costs for the disabled population are greater; they need more care by both physicians and other professionals.

People with disabilities are less likely to be in the workforce, so they are less likely to have private insurance. Because of their disabilities, adults with a substantial work history may become eligible for Medicare. Because of higher costs, limited work history, and lower incomes, others may become eligible for Medicaid. When the numbers of individuals covered by private and public insurance programs

Table 11.1 Health Insurance Coverage among Adults Aged 18 to 64 by Chronic Physical Impairment or Serious Mental Illness

	n (1,000s)	Not Insured %	Total %	Private Only %	Public Only %	Private and Public %
		Insured				
Total Population	149,707	16.7	83.3	75.6	5.2	2.4
Population without chronic physical impairment or serious mental illness	112,562	17.1	82.9	76.9	4.1	1.9
Chronic physical impairments only	34,603	15.8	84.2	73.4*†	6.9	3.9
Serious mental illness only	1,303	9.4*	90.6	50.1*	37.0	3.6
Serious mental illness *and* chronic physical impairments	1,239	21.7	78.3	44.7*	28.2	5.3

*Significantly differed ($p > .05$) from the rest of the population.
†Significantly higher than other two study groups: serious mental illness only, serious mental illness and chronic physical impairments.
Source: 1989 National Health Interview Survey.

are combined, the level of insurance coverage for the disabled population is roughly comparable to that for the nondisabled population. However, while the most severely disabled individuals have an even greater than average likelihood of being insured (because of Medicaid), those with moderate disabilities and a combination of mental and physical disabilities are less likely to have insurance, as shown in Table 11.1[2]

Because the service needs of disabled populations vary so widely, no single program can address all of their needs. Not surprisingly, many categorical or disease-specific programs have been created. There is no public policy or program specifically designed to serve people with disabilities; rather, the approach has been to deal with the problems of the disabled from a service/program perspective, for example, by providing income protection, social services, special education, housing, and health care (both acute and long-term care). The Americans with Disability Act has increased sensitivity to how policies in the public and private sector adversely affect people with disabilities. However, sensitivity to the impacts on people with disabilities does not mean that a new, special health care program must be created or an existing one altered. Since a health care program includes both the financing and the delivery of services, it is possible that comprehensive financing mechanisms may remain intact, but that the delivery of care must be specialized. Paying special attention to the delivery of care is particularly important given the acceleration into managed care by public and private payers.

Financing Health Care for People with Disabilities

The working disabled or the disabled dependents of employed individuals are covered for the same benefits under private health insurance plans. Since health insurance is a fringe benefit provided by employers in order to maintain workers, the benefits are for acute as opposed to chronic illnesses and are linked to employment status. Those who are severely disabled and not in the labor market are likely to be covered by Medicare or Medicaid. Federal law sets medical and income parameters for defining severe disability. To be deemed eligible for the federal disability programs run by the Social Security Administration (SSA), an individual must be "unable to engage in any substantial gainful activity by reason of a medically determined physical or mental impairment expected to result in death or that has lasted, or can be expected to last, for a continuous period of at least 12 months."[3]

Two major government programs are offered. Individuals with an established work history of at least five of the past ten years are usually eligible for Social Security Disability Insurance (SSDI), which is a cash benefit and provides access to Medicare. It is typically seen as an earned entitlement. In 1993, SSDI provided average monthly benefits of $642 to 3.7 million disabled workers.[4] Supplemental Security Income (SSI) is a cash benefit program awarded to low-income persons with severe disabilities and makes Medicaid benefits available to most recipients. In 1993, 6.1 million individuals of all ages received a weekly average payment of $348. About 14 percent of persons with SSDI benefits had low enough incomes to qualify them to receive SSI benefits as well.

Distributions by sex, age, race, and diagnosis vary substantially by SSA disability program.[5] As those who receive SSDI are disabled workers and those with SSI have low incomes, these variations are not surprising. SSDI recipients are more likely to be men, older than 45, and white. In the SSI population, beneficiaries are more likely to be women, younger than 45, and nonwhite. The type of disability also varies. While mental disorders account for about a quarter of each group, physical disability diagnoses are more frequent among the SSDI population (72 percent compared to 46 percent). Although some mental retardation diagnoses are found among the SSDI population (5 percent), mental retardation/developmental disability was diagnosed for more than a quarter of the SSI population.

What is the impact of health care delivery systems for people with disabilities? Do private health insurance plans and public programs meet the needs of those covered under them or do they discriminate against them? It may well be that once individuals are covered, the programs work reasonably well. However, many groups may be left without the coverage, such as the moderately disabled, those whose disabilities are not severe enough to be covered by a public program, but who are too disabled to be steadily employed (and thus likely covered by a private insurance plan) or who have an income adequate to purchase a private policy. Policymakers must analyze the needs of each group and determine whether the needs of people with disabilities are being met and, if not, whether there is a need for specialized financing arrangements.

The Delivery of Care: Implications of Managed Care

The U.S. health care system is moving rapidly toward managed care for acute and chronic illnesses. A managed care plan restricts services to its enrolled population. While the form that managed care will take in the future is not yet known, it is clear that the unrestricted fee-for-service system will certainly become a thing of the past.

Managed care has undergone significant changes in a very short time. In general, it has moved from rationalizing utilization, to incorporating selected providers, to using capitation to ensure efficiencies and cost savings. The major policy appeal of managed care resides in its promise to ration health care services according to the needs of individuals. Under a fee-for-service system in which consumer cost sharing is used to limit service use, the level of appropriate as well as inappropriate service use is reduced when the price to the consumer is raised. For example, the RAND Health Insurance Experiment (HIE) of utilization patterns under capitated and fee-for-service payment arrangements found that hospital days were 40 percent lower in HMOs, but only 20 percent lower for appropriate hospitalizations.[6]

The savings resulting from managed care can be largely attributed to lower hospitalization rates and use of less expensive settings. Further, it appears that preferred or discounted prices have been combined with provider selection. The evolution of managed care has been driven by the private purchasers of insurance, that is, by employers. Since the disabled are a small proportion of the employed population and not a major consideration in the design of the delivery system, one must ask: How well do the contracted managed care plans serve the disabled, and are they well served regardless of whether they are privately or publicly insured? Furthermore, since so few of the current enrollees of managed care organizations are disabled, one must ask whether and how these organizations must change in order to serve the disabled adequately.

Following the demise of national health care reform, states have rapidly begun to move into managed care. Policy analysts are predicting that by the end of this century the vast majority of Medicaid recipients will be enrolled in managed care. States are starting their managed care efforts with the AFDC population and the SSI recipients who are mentally ill. Moving these publicly insured populations into managed care first is easier since HMOs and managed behavioral health care firms are already serving younger populations and the mentally ill in the private sector. The gradual phase-in of the SSI population is an important recognition of the unique challenges posed by children and adults with chronic disabling conditions.

Medicaid-funded managed care plans have shied away from forcing disabled consumers to give up specialty providers with whom they have an ongoing relationship. Some states are concerned that advocacy group opposition could derail or at least delay any attempt to incorporate disabled consumers into Medicaid managed care programs. In several states, disabled consumers have brought in their specialty providers to act as their primary care physicians.

Furthermore, there is little evidence that traditional, private-sector-oriented managed care plans, such as HMOs, fully understand the nature of chronic disability or the full scope of their service responsibilities under Medicaid.[7] Because of their recent entry into the market and the dearth of information, it is not currently possible to say whether HMOs improve access, quality, or cost-effectiveness for this population. More research is needed. It is clear, however, that HMOs can include the disabled Medicaid population and remain solvent, as has been shown in Arizona.[8]

Reforming the Health Care System for People with Disabilities

Advocates for people with disabilities, as well as other observers, have questioned whether U.S. national health care policy should be guided by the principle of treating all people equally or, instead, of treating people with different health needs differently. People with disabilities are less likely than other people to join large managed care organizations and HMOs. And when required to choose between an HMO and a primary care physician manager, they prefer the latter. The reasons for this are many: HMOs have not sought this population out, and people with disabilities are often loyal to their current providers. Thus, a most important policy decision for states as well as the federal government is whether people with disabilities should have a managed care option beyond the very large HMOs currently being constructed under the auspices of Medicare and Medicaid. A more general question is whether there are strong reasons for bringing disabled populations into traditional managed care organizations or whether the elements of managed care shown to be cost-effective should be applied to the specialized providers of the disabled.

Health care reform was the focus of recent congressional debate for two reasons: the lack of insurance coverage for about 40 million individuals, and excessive health care expenditures. The insurance status of the disabled is roughly equal to that of the general population. However, those adults with moderate physical and mental disabilities would benefit disproportionately from any expansion in insurance protection.[9] Cost containment, the other major impetus of health care reform, was to be achieved by expanding the enrollment in managed care organizations. Many proposals included the entire Medicaid population and, therefore, placed people with disabilities into managed care organizations. Risk adjustors for payment rates became critical to assure that managed care organizations would not be financially harmed if they enrolled higher-risk or costlier individuals. Since any major reform or expansion in financing will tie expansions in Medicaid eligibility to cost savings from managed care (as evidenced by recently awarded state Medicaid waivers), it is clear that attention must be given to examining ways in which managed care could be effective for various types of disabled individuals.

Containing Health Costs
Through Managed Care
For People with Disabilities

To date, managed care organizations have contained costs by certifying and recertifying the need for medical services and then providing the care in the least expensive setting. In terms of insurance risks, managed care organizations have dealt with incidence (need for) and duration (length) risks and with intensity of care as far as it relates to the location of service provision. These do not appear to be the techniques appropriate for managing the care of the disabled since these individuals need medical care on a continuing basis. Recently, managed care organizations have begun to pay more attention to managing the care of individuals, particularly those with chronic illnesses such as diabetes and asthma.

Disease-specific managed care programs are being developed both by HMOs and new disease-specific organizations. Until recently, mental health problems and substance abuse and addiction were the only illnesses that were under the control of specialty managed care companies, usually referred to as managed behavioral health care firms. In internally implementing new managed care programs for those with chronic illnesses, HMOs must assess the cost and benefits. Specialized treatment programs for illnesses must have a certain number of cases to justify the costs. This means that comprehensive programs for people with AIDS may or may not be desirable to the general managed care organization.

Whereas the financial benefits of managed care (disregarding favorable selection) have come from deciding whether an individual needed care and at what level (i.e., risk management), the benefits of managed care for people with disabilities may well rest with individualized care management. Individualized care management entails personal assessment, plans of care, and the monitoring of service provision. Individual care management has been at the core of public delivery programs that specialize in caring for people with disabilities. This suggests that the appropriate managed care organizational models for people with severe disabilities may be different from those that predominantly care for people without disabilities or for people with disabilities who are capable of maintaining a job.

Aligning Managed Care with the Nature of the Disability

Because people with disabilities have different medical and nonmedical service needs based on their disabilities, this chapter assesses the needs and managed care experiences of disabled populations. The mental health field, experienced with managed care, provides some insights into how managed care plans have both rationalized utilization and selected providers. The majority of these programs are administered under the auspices of specialized managed behavioral health care firms. However, the focus of these firms has been the employed population for whom managing the need for and duration of mental health care will have greater impact on costs than for those who are chronically disabled and unable to work.

Whereas the majority of managed behavioral health care is provided by specialized firms, the disabling conditions of childhood are handled by general HMOs, which focus on the biomedical nature of children's disabilities and tend to limit those interventions aimed at improving developmental functioning. Managed care plans have set up special programs or altered primary care arrangements for a few of the chronic conditions of children, most notably asthma and diabetes and other conditions for which hospitalizations can be avoided. Although HMOs are beginning a number of new initiatives. Still, little is known about the performance of HMOs for children with chronic conditions, particularly those with less common physical conditions and those with various developmental, behavioral, and emotional problems. It seems reasonable to assume that HMOs could serve the vast majority of children with chronic conditions well by combining preventive and primary care programs with specialty arrangements. For some children with more severe disabilities, the ability of HMOs to provide adequate care is less certain, given their current structure and their focus on reducing high-cost illness rather than on the appropriate development of children. Private and public policymakers must discuss the value derived from disease-specific service or population-based carve-outs for these children.

Very little is known about the impact of managed care for physically disabled adults. Much of the data that are available concern public programs. Although several states have programs that cover persons with physical disability through Medicaid managed care programs, few have reliable data that can be used for establishing their cost-effectiveness. States have used a variety of strategies. In addition to fully capitated managed care plans, states have usually chosen to manage care for adults with severe physical disabilities through primary care case management (PCCM) programs. PCCMs focus on individual care management. In a traditional PCCM program, a primary care provider acts as a gatekeeper for access to specialty services. In some states, PCCM providers for people with disabilities are specialty physicians who coordinate all other types of needed care. PCCM providers are often paid on a fee-for-service basis, and care management is recognized and funded through a small monthly payment.

PCCM programs that report success in treating disabled consumers are more likely than others to use specialty providers to coordinate routine care.[10] Their guiding principle is that the specialty physician acting as primary care medical provider has the basis for understanding the patient's medical needs and also has an incentive to provide efficient care. This approach also addresses the concerns of some that people with serious physical disabilities need specialty care to deal with medical complications that arise.[11,12]

Another approach has been to build managed care organizations around an established network of providers who already care for a specific severely disabled population. In this model, providers must assume some financial risk. Master and coauthors,[13] with joint funding from the Robert Wood Johnson and Pew Foundations, have worked to establish such networks in several states. However, much still remains to be learned about providing managed care to children and adults with physical disabilities. In particular, what incentives should be provided to specialty providers, whether they be PCCM programs or networks? Should they be paid on a full capitation basis? or will partial capitation or fee-for-service payments with a sharing of total savings be as effective?

Conclusion

A great deal more must be learned about the appropriate system for managed care when it comes to children and adults with physical and mental health conditions that result in disabilities. A great deal is already known about the importance of individualized care management for people with disabilities. The question is how this technique should be incorporated into managed care organizations that to date have been primarily concerned with the risk management of employed, relatively healthy individuals. Before establishing a policy in which people with disabilities are treated like all others in terms of managed care, policymakers should learn what the impact would be in terms of quality, access, and cost. Those questions have been asked and answered positively for people without disabilities. However, because of the chronic nature of their illnesses and differences in the managed care techniques needed for achieving efficiency for disabled populations, there is good reason to believe that the findings are not directly transferable to people with disabilities. Thus, separate studies and separate managed care models should be tried and evaluated.

SECTION 2: Children with Chronic and Disabling Conditions*

Margaret A. McManus, Harriette B. Fox, and Paul W. Newacheck

Growing numbers of children with chronic and disabling conditions are obtaining their health care through HMOs. According to the Group Health Association of America (GHAA), 26 percent of all HMO enrollees in 1991 were children. Based on GHAA's 1993 enrollment figures, an estimated 20 percent or 12 million American children receive their care through HMOs. The majority of these children are insured privately, but many also are enrolled in HMOs through the Medicaid program. A significant portion of children enrolled in HMOs experience chronic illness and disabilities.

Despite the size of the child population participating in HMOs, there is a paucity of recent research on the effects of managed care on children with chronic conditions. The most comprehensive source of evaluation data on children comes from the Medicaid Competition Demonstrations of the early 1980s. However, even this study inten-

*The work in this section was supported by the Annie E. Casey Foundation and the Maternal and Child Health Bureau of the U.S. Department of Health and Human Services.

tionally excluded children with disabilities. From what can be derived from the limited published literature, the strength of managed care lies in its ability to deliver routine preventive and primary care. Its weaknesses, which are a function of its financial incentives and utilization management controls, are reduced access to specialized services.[14,15]

Childhood chronic conditions are highly variable in terms of prevalence, severity, and impact on children's lives. Unlike adults, there are few prevalent childhood chronic conditions, namely asthma, allergies, and attention deficit disorder. A substantial portion of chronic childhood conditions are rare, such as spina bifida, Down syndrome, and cerebral palsy. In addition, the severity of pediatric conditions may vary over the course of childhood. Most chronic disabling conditions are mild and moderate; yet even these may require greater medical attention at certain critical periods. Moreover, disabling chronic conditions affect children at home, at school, and at play, causing family stress and limiting a child's functional capacity. The variability of chronic conditions, as well as the marked differentials in service needs and unmet needs among various groups of children with prevalent and rare chronic physical and mental illnesses, poses unique challenges for managed care.

Several questions must be considered in designing managed care arrangements appropriate for children with chronic conditions. What safeguards can be instituted? What payment policies are most appropriate for high-cost children? What level of public and private coordination could improve service delivery? What are the advantages and disadvantages of subcontracting with specialty managed care programs for certain groups of children, or alternatively with integrated child health networks to provide all children's services?

Characteristics of Chronically Ill and Disabled Children

Thirty percent of all children under age 18 are affected by some type of chronic physical condition, according to the National Health Interview Survey on Child Health.[16] The most common chronic physical conditions are respiratory allergies, frequent or repeated ear infections, asthma, eczema and skin allergies, and speech defects. A large proportion of these are mild chronic conditions, such as allergies or minor respiratory diseases, that are outgrown as children mature. National survey data also indicate that up to 20 percent of U.S. children have experienced developmental delays, learning disabilities, or emotional or behavioral problems sometime during their lifetime.[17] Specifically, 4.0 percent of children under 18 have experienced delays in growth or development, 6.5 percent have suffered from learning disabilities, and 13.4 percent have had emotional or behavioral problems. Because of differences in data collection methods, it is impossible to assess the combined prevalence of chronic physical and mental conditions among children.

Only a small proportion of children with chronic physical and mental conditions are so severely affected as to be disabled as indicated by the presence of a limitation in their usual childhood activities. These children, who numbered some 4 million nationwide in 1992, represent 6 percent of all noninstitutionalized children under age 18. The level of disability associated with chronic illness ranges from children who are limited in their ability to engage in sports or other recreational pursuits to those who are so severely limited that they are unable to attend school or to engage in ordinary play activities. Approximately 40,000 additional disabled children reside in institutional settings.

Childhood disabilities result from a variety of physical and mental conditions. Based on the most recent national survey data available, the leading causes of disability among children are respiratory system diseases, principally asthma; mental retardation; mental and nervous system disorders; and orthopedic impairments (including deformities). These four groups account for over two-thirds of all disabling childhood chronic conditions.[18] Many of these children have health problems that are severe but low in prevalence, such as cerebral palsy, sickle cell disease, and spina bifida. Most rare diseases are genetic and tend to appear at birth or in early childhood. Since 1960, the prevalence of disability among children, as reported in national surveys, has tripled due to advances in medical care, especially in newborn intensive care; extended survival of children with chronic conditions; and increased awareness brought about by improved screening and diagnosis and expansions in early intervention, special education, and disability programs.[19]

Children with disabling chronic conditions experience medical and psychosocial service needs greater than those of other children.[20-23] These health needs may include more frequent and higher-intensity use of hospital services, primary and specialty physician services, ancillary therapies, mental health services, prescription drugs,

Table 11.2   Insurance Coverage of Children under 18 Years in 1992

Insurance Status	*Children with Disabilities*		*Children without Disabilities*	
	Estimated Number	*Percent*	*Estimated Number*	*Percent*
Private Insurance Only	1,991,000	51.5	38,620,000	65.4
Public Insurance Only	1,180,000	30.6	10,730,000	18.2
Both Private and Public	142,000	3.7	1,122,000	1.9
No Insurance	550,000	14.2	8,563,000	14.5
Total	**3,863,000**	**100%**	**59,035,000**	**100%**

Note: Excludes persons with unknown insurance coverage.
Source: Original tabulations from the 1992 National Health Interview Survey.

nutritional services, home health care, durable medical equipment and supplies, assistive technologies, and case management.

Private and Public Health Insurance Coverage

According to the National Health Interview Survey, 86 percent of children with disabilities under age 18 had some form of private or public health insurance protection in 1992 (Table 11.2). However, 14 percent of children with disabilities, or an estimated 550,000 children, were without any form of health insurance during 1992.

The rate of coverage for disabled children was the same as the rate for children without disabilities. However, children with disabilities are much less likely to be insured under a private plan than children without disabilities (52 percent versus 65 percent). Private health insurance coverage of children with disabilities has eroded substantially since 1989, when as many as 62 percent of disabled children were privately insured. The decline in coverage for children with disabilities is reflective of a progressive and gradual trend toward loss of private coverage that has occurred for children generally during the past decade.[24] In addition, children with disabilities are disproportionately represented among the poor, and their parents are less likely to have jobs that provide affordable health insurance to dependents.

The discrepancy in private coverage for children with disabilities is compensated in large part by the public health insurance system, essentially Medicaid, but also including CHAMPUS. Public health insurance covered 31 percent of children with disabilities in 1992, up from 27 percent in 1989. Thus, Medicaid has played an increasingly important role in serving children with disabling chronic conditions.

Although the vast majority of children with disabilities have some form of health insurance protection, the quality of the coverage they have varies considerably. Under traditional private health insurance, the services that a child is entitled to, the amount of coverage, and the share of the bill met by the insurer differ enormously from plan to plan. Generally, private insurance offers good protection for hospital, physician, and other medical services, but the various kinds of psychological, ancillary therapy, durable medical equipment, and family support services that children with disabilities may require are as likely not to be covered as to be covered.[25,26] Moreover, even if these services are covered, the benefits may not be structured to meet developmental and chronic care needs of children. Benefits frequently are short-term and restricted to situations in which the child has experienced an injury or illness and the condition is likely to improve quickly. Moreover, some private plans contain preexisting condition exclusions that would deny coverage for any services related to the treatment of a health problem identified at the time of enrollment for a period of six months, a year, or even longer.

By contrast, Medicaid benefits for children are more comprehensive in scope and, historically, less restrictive in application.[27] Federal Medicaid law defines a broad array of medical, therapeutic, and rehabilitative services, and permits coverage of these services in homes, schools, and other community-based settings. For children up to age 21, federal law requires states to reimburse such services whenever the state determines that they are medically necessary to correct or ameliorate an identified health problem; benefit limits otherwise applicable may not apply.[28] Although states retain some discretion in implementing this mandate, children with disabilities who are covered by Medicaid are entitled to a more substantial package of mental health, home care, ancillary therapy, and other health professional services than do similar disabled children with private coverage.[29] Medicaid-enrolled children, however, may have greater difficulty finding private sector providers willing to accept the program's relatively low reimbursement rates. They may also experience new access difficulties due to the use of stricter service authorization and medical necessity criteria in managed care organizations.

Other Public Programs Serving
Chronically Ill Children

Over the past several decades a number of unique federal programs have been established to provide free or subsidized care to children with disabilities. Prominent among the federal programs are the Title V Program for Children with Special Health Care Needs operated by the Health Services and Resources Administration of the Department of Health and Human Services (DHHS), the Children's Mental Health Services Program operated by the Substance Abuse and Mental Health Administration of DHHS, and the Special Education and Early Intervention Programs operated by the Office of Special Education and Rehabilitative Services of the Department of Education.

With the exception of the Special Education Program, the budgets of these federal programs are relatively small compared with health care financing programs such as Medicaid. As a result, they generally provide only a limited range of services and meet the needs of only a small segment of the potentially eligible child population. Nonetheless, the programs are important because they offer specialized therapeutic services, often in flexible settings, with a variety of physician and other health professionals, and emphasize family support and involvement. Each of these public programs was created because existing financing and delivery systems were not adequately serving the needs of chronically ill children.

While each of these programs have notably identified vulnerable groups of children with disabling chronic conditions and have targeted health and related services that are not well insured, most are only partially able to achieve their service goals because of limited funding. Moreover, few of the programs have succeeded in working collaboratively with managed care organizations.[30] As a result, the innovations in service delivery and in infrastructure building that has been the hallmark of these federal and state programs have not been transferred to the managed care sector. Increased collaborative activity could lead to more efficient delivery of services and holds the potential for improved outcomes, both for children and payers.

Current Directions and Strategic Choices
for Managed Pediatric Care

Few broad-scale initiatives have been undertaken in the last decade to improve services to children with chronic physical and mental conditions enrolled in commercial and Medicaid HMOs. With the exception of asthma and juvenile diabetes management programs, and high-cost case management programs, plans have not made significant departures from usual managed care practices in serving children with chronic conditions. It appears that, unless immediate cost savings can be identified, innovations directed at chronically ill and disabled children are often limited.[31]

HMOs often emphasize preventive and primary care services for children. Numerous efforts are under way to promote timely use of preventive services (including immunizations), perform comprehensive risk assessments, and deliver both individual and group health education in a variety of settings. While these programs can benefit all children, they often are not tailored to children with chronic health problems.

Moreover, most HMOs have not structured their provider networks to meet the special needs of children with chronic conditions. They are composed largely of primary care providers (pediatricians, family physicians, and nurse practitioners) and include a very limited array of medical and other pediatric specialty providers. It appears that children who require specialty services are frequently seen by adult specialists so that referrals do not have to be made out of the plan network.

Even for Medicaid-insured children, who technically are entitled to a very comprehensive benefit package, HMO enrollment is likely to reduce access to certain necessary specialty services. Plans appear to be applying to these children many of the same benefit and medical necessity rules that they apply to their commercial enrollees.[32]

Nevertheless, based on a 1993 survey of large commercial HMOs with well-reputed pediatric plans, Fox and McManus[33] found that some innovative service delivery policies are being introduced. These are largely occurring in the following areas: provider referral assistance, alternative gatekeeping arrangements, multidisciplinary assessment and service planning, care coordination assistance, and integration of physical and mental health services.

In addition, some state Medicaid agencies are establishing contractual provisions aimed at protecting children with chronic conditions. In a recent review of Medicaid contracts in 24 states using HMOs, Fox and McManus found that state Medicaid agencies are beginning to experiment with specific recommendations or requirements to promote guaranteed access to perinatal centers; plan participation of pediatric specialists; multidisciplinary teams for diagnosis, evaluation, and treatment planning; family involvement in service delivery and evaluation; coordination of primary and specialty pediatric services; comprehensive case management; coordination with other public programs; and pediatric quality of care and other performance measures for a range of chronic childhood problems. In general, however, development of specific policies toward treatment of chronically ill children remains limited.

Thus, while some state Medicaid agencies may be pursuing more innovations to serve chronically ill children than commercial plans are, neither the public sector nor the private sector has experimented with new clinical service delivery models for the broad population of chronically ill children. The following section addresses several policy questions related to the care of chronically ill children. These include safeguards, payment policies for high-cost children, public and private coordination, and managed pediatric care initiatives.

Safeguards

Little is known about the impact of HMOs on children with chronic conditions; therefore, it is very important that safeguards be established to assure that these children receive appropriate services.[34] To date, the federal Health Care Financing Administration and state Medicaid agencies have adopted more safeguards and oversight mechanisms than their counterparts in the private sector.

Several state Medicaid agencies have instituted safeguards in their enrollment, benefit, and payment policies. A number of states with mandatory managed care enrollment policies have excluded certain chronically ill children from HMO enrollment. These exemptions have been primarily targeted to children who qualify for the SSI Program and the Title IV-A Adoption and Assistance Program. Other states have adopted policies limiting or eliminating a plan's obligation to deliver certain specialty services, such as mental health services or health-related special education services, while others have taken the approach of requiring plans to contract with designated specialty providers and centers of excellence, such as childrens hospitals. In addition, a few states simply require that plans coordinate with other public providers, such as the Title V Program for Children with Special Health Care Needs and the Early Intervention Program. Also, payment policies have been adopted by a large number of state Medicaid agencies to allow higher premiums for chronically ill children, stop-loss protections, and risk sharing after certain levels of incurred expenses.[35]

HMOs and employers are increasingly directing their attention to establishing improved quality of care standards and other performance measures, both as marketing tools and as a means to ensure that services are delivered in an appropriate fashion. In many cases, they also have established procedures for appeals and grievances. For children with chronic illness, the development of quality measures has been hampered by the dearth of measures to define medically necessary or clinically appropriate care for children in a way that takes account of their health and functional status. As a result, reliance on existing quality of care measures to safeguard this population is problematic, especially for children with rare but severe conditions and others with developmental, behavioral, and emotional problems.

Payment policies

As the nation moves rapidly toward managed care and insurance market reforms to limit medical underwriting and eliminate pre-existing-conditions clauses, designing accurate risk adjustment mechanisms is critical, particularly for children with chronic and disabling conditions.[36] Without adequate risk adjustment, health plans have a strong financial incentive to avoid or underserve high-cost children. Unfortunately, the field of pediatric risk adjustment is still just beginning.

A recent review of 12 state Medicaid agencies with relatively well developed capitation rate-setting programs revealed that each of these states uses some form of risk adjustment in determining its capitation rates, but that no state has adopted any risk adjustment mechanism specifically for children.[37] Comparable published reviews of risk adjustment mechanisms used in the private sector are not available. As a result, flexible adjustments and separate payment mechanisms for outliers through reinsurance funds, add-on premiums, or partial capitation fees have been adopted by state and federal policymakers.

Research on risk adjustment methodologies has focused primarily on historic utilization experience and has been limited to the elderly population. Predicting expenditures using historic utilization data compares favorably with predicting expenses based on socio-demographic characteristics, functional health status, self-reported health status, and clinical indicators. Moreover, utilization data are easily obtained for other purposes; they are reliable across plans and over time; and they do not require individual patient data collection.[38] Yet certain groups of children, those who have no prior utilization data (e.g., newborns) or those who use services in other public health or special education programs, will present problems using this approach.

One prior-use risk adjustment model that has been developed for children is the Ambulatory Care Group (ACG) case-mix system, developed at Johns Hopkins University.[39] Unlike other prior-use models based on inpatient hospital use, this system is based on diagnoses associated with ambulatory visits. Children (or adults) are placed into one of 51 ACGs based on their age, sex, and ICD-9-CM diagnosis codes incurred during a specific time period in an ambulatory setting. However, because this case-mix system applies only to ambulatory care, it has limited utility for risk adjustment of premiums that include inpatient and ambulatory care.

In developing risk adjustors for children, large data sets will be required to capture the experience of children with not only high-prevalence, low-morbidity conditions but also with low-prevalence, high-morbidity conditions. Linking Medicaid and commercial claims data with other public program claims or service data could provide a more complete utilization base from which to set appropriate capitation rates.

Public and private coordination

Numerous efforts are under way to coordinate the delivery of health, education, and social services for specific children with chronic conditions, but few initiatives have been implemented to integrate multiple funding sources to create a new comprehensive and coordinated system of health care services for all children with chronic conditions.[40,41] Nevertheless, states and localities have been successful in making more flexible use of Medicaid. Medicaid reimbursement has been obtained from health, early intervention, and special education providers to reimburse for a variety of health and social services. In contrast, private health insurance reimbursement has seldom been obtained by these public providers to reimburse services. Moreover, there have not been any efforts to test a social HMO model, similar to the one created for Medicare recipients, where acute and long-term care services and multiple funding arrangements are integrated.

Three federal programs—the Title V Program for Children with Special Health Care Needs, the Children's Mental Health Services Program, and the Early Intervention Program—have invested substantial resources in promoting and testing integrated service models and infrastructures to better serve children with chronic illness. These programs have been directed primarily at integrating services but not funding sources. The Robert Wood Johnson Foundation (RWJ) has also supported service integration models for children, as part of a mental health services program for youth and a child health initiative to remove categorical barriers to care. These latter programs have been targeted at blending both services and funding sources.

Each of these programs has adopted different administrative and policy strategies for services integration. These strategies have included collaborative activities around needs assessments, the formulation of common program goals and objectives, the development of joint eligibility and application procedures, and the integration of data systems. Case-oriented strategies for services integration have also been addressed by the three federal programs and RWJ. These strategies include case management or care coordination, individualized child and family care assessments and service planning, outcome monitoring, focus on the family, home visiting, and flexible funding in selected programs.

In recent debates on national and state health care reforms, policymakers have begun to address the question: what defines the separate roles of the public and private sectors in financing medical and other specialty pediatric services for chronically ill children? For children enrolled in Medicaid, this question is more easily addressed, since all specialty health care services essentially are covered for children through age 21. Thus, all children who qualify for Medicaid should have access to all needed Medicaid and other specialty pediatric services (whether in the physician's office, in school, or at home).

Under most private health insurance plans, however, only a limited set of children's specialty services are covered, and typically for a short period of time. In the absence of uniform and comprehensive benefits among public and private payers, families who are privately insured (and uninsured) are faced with fewer covered services and greater cost-sharing responsibilities. Since public programs, except early intervention and special education programs, are designed primarily to serve poor and near-poor families, middle-income families, even when insured, are often at a significant disadvantage.

At least three types of services have presented unique challenges for children and their private and public insurance payers. The first type are services perceived by plans to be the responsibility of a public program, particularly early intervention and special education programs. Should the HMO or the school, or both, pay for a child with attention deficit hyperactivity disorder or sensory integration problems who may require ongoing and extended periods of occupational therapy and speech therapy to manage and improve his or her health and functional status in school as well as at home?

The second type are services for which private health insurance coverage is limited in amount or duration, such as high-cost chronic or long-term care services. Who should pay for required ancillary therapies, home health, assistive technologies, and other services that exceed coverage limitations in a standard benefit plan? For example, private insurers will typically cover home health services only when they are provided in lieu of higher-cost services, such as hospitalization.

The third type are support services, such as care coordination, outreach, and family education and training. Whose responsibility is it to pay for the health professional who develops and monitors an individualized service plan and coordinates other nonplan services?

Still unexamined is whether or not coverage of these types of special services is best achieved through services integration or through laws requiring HMOs to furnish a more comprehensive package of pediatric services. In the meantime, families are faced with a very limited and confusing mix of uncoordinated services. Since no operational models exist for integrating funding streams and services for children, research and demonstrations are needed to develop them. In order to obtain a broad-based population, these models could be designed not only for Medicaid beneficiaries, but also for privately insured and uninsured children with a wide range of chronic conditions. If policymakers focused on a broader population, more opportunities would exist for early treatment and management of chronic conditions and for cost savings over the long term.

The major programs and services to be integrated are health, education, and social services. It would be useful to test how each of these programs might organize integrated services and funding if they were the lead agencies. What strengths and weaknesses lie in financing and delivering a more comprehensive health care service system if education and social services funds are pooled with private and public health insurance funds and operated by a given managed care organization? Similarly, what are the pros and cons of giving the school system or the social welfare system health funds to operate a more comprehensive health service system?

Managed pediatric care initiatives

Two types of pediatric managed care initiatives are now under development: specialty managed care plans and integrated child health networks. Neither of these approaches has been formally evaluated to determine its relative strengths or weaknesses compared with general managed care arrangements that serve chronically ill and disabled children.

The specialty pediatric managed care model, designed to serve SSI-eligible children, is an idea supported by at least one state Medicaid agency. Two of the major features of this arrangement are comprehensive case management and flexibility in crafting individualized benefit plans that best meet the needs of vulnerable children and their families. Because this specialty arrangement focuses on the highest-cost cases, those that account for a disproportionate share of hospital or institutional services, substantial savings are anticipated, as is greater continuity of home, school, and community-based care using the high-quality pediatric providers that have historically served this population. Children's hospitals and related institutions and state Title V Programs for Children with Special Needs have assumed a leadership role in designing and implementing specialty pediatric managed care arrangements.

Integrated child health networks are another new initiative in managed care for children and are being advanced primarily in the private sector. Advocated by the National Association of Children's Hospitals and the American Academy of Pediatrics, integrated child health networks are designed to meet the full continuum of children's preventive, primary, acute, subspecialty, post-acute, habilitative, rehabilitative, and long-term physical and mental health care needs. These networks are just beginning to form in a few localities, typically as physician-hospital organizations, integrating children's hospitals, community pediatricians, and other local providers. Most of these networks subcontract to general managed care plans and a few market their services directly to employers.

At present, integrated child health networks target all children in their catchment areas for enrollment, and their operations resemble those of other managed care organizations including fully capitated ones. What is unique about these integrated networks is their reliance on pediatricians as primary care providers; their access to medical specialists, ancillary therapies, and other pediatric specialty services; and their use of child-specific quality improvement efforts. None of the existing networks are linked to health-related educational and social services.

Both specialty and integrated pediatric managed care initiatives offer advantages and disadvantages over pediatric care in the general managed care sector. On the positive side, the pediatric managed care initiatives can provide a high-quality provider network trained to care for some or all children.

Families in HMOs increasingly report that when their children experience serious or persistent health problems, they are often re-ferred to a specialist in adult care or to a community hospital that may not be qualified to diagnose, refer, or manage children's chronic needs. Families would have a greater assurance that their children would be served by pediatricians and other children's health profes-sionals who specialize in the care of chronic physical and mental con-ditions if they were able to enroll in an integrated or specialty child health network. Payers could join a single integrated child health net-work and obtain all of their pediatric services rather than developing multiple subcontracting arrangements.

On the other hand, there are disadvantages in using integrated or specialty child health networks. First and most important, few of these networks exist and their experience has been limited, primarily in terms of their financial viability and competitive value. General managed care plans have both the capital and the clout. For most HMOs, the pediatric portion of their business has been considered to be relatively lucrative. In fact, if plans can manage newborns and adolescents, who use a disproportionate share of hospital and other high-cost services, and also the small proportion of children with dis-abling chronic conditions, then they generally consider that their challenges have been met. Unfortunately, in this scenario many chil-dren, particularly those with mild to moderate chronic developmental, behavioral, and emotional problems, are often not ade-quately served.

Conclusion

Far more children have chronic and disabling conditions than ever before in U.S. history. National estimates of chronic physical problems are about 30 percent and of chronic mental problems, about 20 per-cent, with substantial overlap between the two. While only 6 percent of these physical and mental conditions result in disability, of equal import are all children with chronic illness. As Drs. Hobbs, Perrin, and Ireys wrote a decade ago:

> The extent of a child's problem has only a modest relationship to the severity of a child's condition. Some children with severe disease in a physical or physiological sense will have little impairment of their ability

to participate in usual activities with healthy children. Other children with only mild physical illness find their lives greatly affected by disease.[42]

Critical to designing new and improved managed chronic care services for children is an understanding of the nature and diversity of childhood chronic conditions and their relationship to developmental delays and to behavioral, emotional, and learning problems. However, current experience in state and national health care reform and in managed care organizations reveals that most policymakers and medical directors perceive that nearly all children are healthy and that only a very small proportion require specialty services. To a large extent, it is this perception that has thwarted the identification and treatment of many chronically ill children in managed care organizations and has spurred the development of multiple public service systems to fill in the gaps.

To date, most HMOs have not opted to focus on the care of chronically ill children for some obvious reasons. A systematic review of the literature, private health insurance benefits, public service systems, service integration models, current managed care practices and innovations, payment policies, and safeguards reveal a disturbing picture. Chronically ill children have not been afforded the same measure of public and private attention and investment in health services research and delivery that adults with chronic illness have experienced. Unless new initiatives are brought forward to identify, treat, and manage chronically ill children more comprehensively when they are young, managed care organizations will inherit more difficult problems as these children become adults.

Several key policy choices must be considered in improving managed care for privately and publicly insured children with chronic conditions. Assuming that these children will increasingly be enrolled in HMO arrangements, various public policy strategies could be adopted to remedy existing problems.

- Federal tax or other laws could be used to require HMOs to furnish a more comprehensive package of pediatric benefits to address the unique needs of children with various types of chronic conditions. These services could include ancillary therapy, psychosocial, home care, and other services furnished by appropriately trained and experienced providers. It is not clear, however, whether most HMOs would want to take on these added service responsibilities or whether it would be more appropriate for public gap-filling programs to be revised and expanded. Moreover, the extent to which HMOs should be required to reimburse for insured services provided by public providers remains an issue.

- Federal laws, in tandem with private organizations, could be used to promote the development and implementation of pediatric quality of care and performance measures that reflect the special service needs and outcome objectives of children with chronic conditions. However, there is still enormous work to do in this area, and the costs associated with new data collection responsibilities for plans are very high.

- In addition, public funds could be made available to HMOs to help subsidize the care of children with costly conditions. This would eliminate, or at least minimize, the inherent financial disincentive for plans to furnish health care services that may be necessary to help a child achieve improvements in functioning but that would not result in cost offsets for the plan. The trade-offs between risk-adjusted premium supplements and risk sharing for high-cost cases should be carefully studied. State Medicaid programs have had experience with risk-sharing arrangements, but much work remains to be done to establish effective pediatric risk adjusters.

These are all issues that would have to be dealt with even if children with chronic conditions were enrolled in separate managed care arrangements. Plans serving either a general child population or only those children with disabling chronic conditions might be able to provide more comprehensive care, particularly if their exclusive child focus resulted in greater collaboration with public programs serving children and more emphasis on coordinated, multidisciplinary interventions. Yet many additional issues would have to be addressed concerning the feasibility of separate pediatric managed care arrangements.

Without more experimentation, several basic factors are unknown: the population base required for a pediatric managed care entity to survive, the degree of difficulty in attracting the necessary capital, or the chances of this type of plan competing successfully with general HMOs for medical and other child health providers. In addition, even if state Medicaid programs could be persuaded to contract directly with separate pediatric arrangements, employers, accustomed to paying a single family premium, would presumably have to be convinced of the relative merits of creating a separate child capitation rate. The viability of pediatric plans, therefore, would depend largely on their ability to subcontract to general HMOs that may be unwilling to relinquish the profits they have historically made on the pediatric population.

Finally, of course, differences in the feasibility and quality of care that might exist between pediatric plans that serve subgroups of chronically ill children and those that serve a broad child population must be studied. For a specialized plan to operate successfully, for example, the population presumably would have to be larger than that in place for a general child plan, and issues of public subsidy for care would be more urgent. Other issues, pertaining to marketing and financial solvency, are less easy to speculate about. In summary, more experimentation with careful evaluations is required to test out alternative models of managed care for children with chronic physical and mental conditions using pediatric HMO arrangements.

SECTION 3: Individuals with Severe Mental Illnesses*

Richard G. Frank and Thomas G. McGuire

Policymakers have continuously been confronted with the apparent failure of insurance markets to provide satisfactory levels of financial protection against the costs of treating mental disorders.[43] State and federal budgets have also been stressed by growth in Medicaid mental health costs.[44] Private insurance plans face the dual challenges of dealing with the strong response of mental health care utilization to the terms of coverage and the consequences of biased selection. Medicaid plans are attempting to contend with the utilization and cost control problem that is similar to that of private plans as well as being influenced by biased selection in private markets. Both public and private decision makers are turning to "managed behavioral health care" (MBHC) as a means of controlling expenditures for mental health care, rationalizing the delivery of services, and possibly expanding coverage.

Private employers have reported a number of important success

---

*The authors of this section gratefully acknowledge financial support for the research in this section from the Robert Wood Johnson Foundation, Grant # 24066; and the National Institute of Mental Health, Grant #K05-MH00832. Haiden Huskamp provided expert research assistance and helpful discussion. The authors are also grateful to Stan Wallack and the reviewer for helpful suggestions.

stories where costs have been reduced, benefits made more flexible, and delivery of care improved. Similar reports have begun to emerge from state Medicaid plans. Costly and restrictive inpatient care has apparently been reduced and community-based alternatives have been developed and used. Reports from DuPont, Dow, Federal Express and Xerox have been among the most striking; these corporations have reported cost reductions of 30–50 percent over one or two years. These firms have also increased the flexibility of the mental health benefit by eliminating certain coverage limits. At the same time, skeptics question how the savings are achieved. The possibility of undertreatment has been raised, and it is a recurring concern in applying strong financial incentives and other cost containment methods to vulnerable population groups such as individuals with severe mental illnesses.[45,46]

If MBHC programs have, in fact, developed methods of applying clinical judgments in ways that better allocate mental health treatment services than those that occur with the traditional benefit design solutions (usually limiting coverage), then the traditional cost-coverage trade-off will have changed. The implication of such a development is that, instead of targeting primarily the cost control issue, policymaking could focus on other aspects of the problem of providing coverage to individuals with mental illness. Three key decisions regarding organization and financing of MBHC care are (1) the degree of integration between public and private mental health systems, (2) the desirability of relying on specialty carve-out arrangements for managing mental health care relative to full integration with general health care, and (3) the optimal form of risk-sharing arrangements between payers and MBHC organizations. These are the three areas in which strategic choices must be made in order to broadly apply MBHC arrangements in a socially responsible fashion.

The Mentally Ill and the Health Care Services System

The mentally ill

Mental illnesses are quite prevalent and in their most severe forms create a great deal of impairment.[47,48] The 12-month prevalence of any DSM-III-R psychiatric diagnosis is estimated to be 29.5 percent of the U.S. population. This figure includes substance abuse disorders (11.3 percent had some substance abuse diagnosis) as well as psychiatric illnesses. Severe mental illnesses, defined as bipolar disorder and psychoses, were estimated by Kessler et al. (1994) to have a 12-month prevalence of 2.6 percent. A recent report by the National Advisory Mental Health Council used a broader definition of severe illness and estimated a somewhat higher level of severe mental illness in the population (3 percent). Persons with a psychiatric disorder frequently have more than one condition. Fourteen percent of the population have a lifetime history of three or more psychiatric diagnoses. These individuals account for 59 percent of the 12-month prevalence.

Psychiatric illnesses are accompanied by other undesirable circumstances. Individuals with mental illnesses are 2.2 times more likely to suffer work loss days than is the general population. Individuals with incomes of less than $20,000 in 1991 suffered from mental illnesses at 3.36 times the rate found in the segment of the population earning above $70,000. Mental illnesses are also associated with lower levels of educational attainment. For example, individuals with less than high school educations are 3.76 times more likely to have a diagnosable disorder than are individuals who complete college.

Utilization and expenditures for care

During the course of a year, 34 percent of individuals with a diagnosable mental disorder received treatment from a health care provider for their illness.[49] It is notable that 7 percent of the population with no diagnosable illness also received mental health treatment from a health care provider, so that the treated prevalence is about 15 percent per year. Individuals diagnosed with more severe conditions obtained care at roughly the same rate as the overall population of individuals with mental disorders. Approximately 33 percent of individuals with manic depression and 28 percent of those with major depression received mental health treatment from a health care provider. The implication of these data is that some segments of the population may be "overtreated" while others have inadequate access to care. MBHC is primarily oriented toward the problem of overtreatment. If the application of MBHC is to improve the delivery system, it must also contend with the problem of undertreatment.

Table 11.3 shows the distribution of spending on mental health care in the United States in 1990.[50] In 1990 it is estimated that $42.4 billion was spent on mental health services. Government sources account for 56 percent of these expenditures. The main sources of government expenditures are the Medicaid program (accounting for 19 percent of total expenditures) and direct expenditures for services by

Table 11.3   Mental Health Care Spending, 1990

	Billions $	Percent
Private insurance	18.8	44.3
Medicaid	8.1	19.1
State and local	11.7	27.6
Medicare	1.5	3.5
Other federal	2.3	5.4
Total	$42.4	100%*

*Number may not add to 100% due to rounding.

Source: R. G. Frank, T. G. McGuire, D. A. Regier, et al., "Paying for Mental Health and Substance Abuse Care." *Health Affairs* 13, no. 1 (1994): 337–42.

state and local government (28 percent of the total). The Medicare program for the elderly comprises about 3.5 percent of mental health spending. These figures can be contrasted with all personal health care spending. For this larger category, 41 percent of all spending originates from government sources, but half of this is Medicare expenditures. Spending on direct services by state and local government accounts for less than 7 percent of total expenditures.

The share of direct payments by individuals and families for mental health care is much higher than for general health care because of restrictions on mental health coverage such as higher copayments or limits on reimbursable days and outpatient visits, and because some health insurance contains no coverage for mental health care at all.[51] Another unique aspect of expenditure patterns for mental health care relates to the composition of expenditure. It is estimated that between 65 percent and 75 percent of all mental health care spending is for institutional care.[52] In addition, almost 40 percent of all expenditures on mental health care are accounted for by approximately 2 percent of the population. This indicates the concentration of spending on a few people in institutional settings. The ability to alter the composition of mental health care spending is central to the success of MBHC.

Strategic Decisions for Managed Care

The managed behavioral health care industry

The MBHC industry has experienced impressive growth during the late 1980s and early 1990s. This is evidenced by a 31 percent growth in enrollment during the period 1992–1994.[53] The industry actually consists of several distinct segments: (1) Employee Assistance Plans (EAPs) (20 million enrollees) and Integrated EAPs (6.6 million enrollees), (2) Risk-Based Networks (20.4 enrollees), (3) Non-Risk-Based Networks (14.9 million enrollees), and (4) Utilization Review Case Management or so-called managed indemnity (37 million enrollees).[54] Thus, about 82 million individuals have insurance coverage for mental health and substance abuse treatment at least partly managed by an MBHC organization (the sum of categories 2–4). In addition, 20 million individuals are potentially served by an EAP (Open Minds). A recent survey of the industry reports that there are 42 vendors offering MBHC services. Market share varies considerably across the four segments of the industry, but in general the industry is moderately concentrated. The top four firms account for 45.5 percent of all enrollees. The risk-based networks and the EAP segments have experienced the highest rates of growth during the early 1990s.

Cost control and MBHC

Among the most controversial issues in discussions of competition among insuring organizations and the role of managed care is the question of pinpointing exactly the level of savings it is reasonable to expect from adoption of managed care techniques to control utilization. Several reviews of cost saving attributable to managed care in the general health care context have appeared in the literature. Perhaps the most authoritative assessment of managed care is the report produced by the Congressional Budget Office.[55] All forms of managed care were assumed to save on average about 9 percent over unmanaged fee-for-service arrangements. This figure is a composite of various effects for various forms of managed care. Thus, the group/staff model HMO was assumed to reduce costs by about 11.6 percent relative to unmanaged fee-for-service. Independent practice association (IPA) and network model managed care, which is quite common in the MBHC field, was estimated to result in savings of 3.2 percent. Utilization review and precertification review programs, also common in MBHC, were estimated to save approximately 4 percent over unmanaged fee-for-service. Finally, preferred provider and point-of-service arrangements were estimated to save 2 percent over unmanaged fee-for-service arrangements.

The literature on specific MBHC programs is considerably less well developed than that in general health services literature. The impression in both the employer and financial communities is that the potential savings in the mental health and substance abuse area are considerably larger than in overall health care.[56,57] Hodgkin[58] has carefully reviewed the literature on the effects of utilization management. The lone study that was identified as methodologically sound showed savings in the neighborhood of 10–15 percent on total claims costs.

Research on organizationally based forms of MBHC provide clearer results. Studies by Manning and coauthors[59] and by Diehr and coauthors[60] examined mental health care expenditures in the context of group/staff and IPA or network model HMOs. The results from the randomized trial in insurance coverage done by RAND[61] examined approximately 10,000 person years of coverage. The results of that analysis showed clear differences in the pattern of ambulatory mental health care between fully insured (zero copay) fee-for-service and pre-paid health plans. For the fee-for-service population, mental health expenditure levels were 2.8 times those found for enrollees in the prepaid health plan ($69.70 versus $24.60 in 1977 dollars). It is interesting to note that enrollees in prepaid plans were more likely to see a mental health professional once in a year than were the enrollees of the free care fee-for-service plan.

The study by Diehr and coauthors[62] compared the use of outpatient mental health care in a fee-for-service plan, a staff model HMO, and an IPA prepaid plan. The population studied was state employees in Washington state. The results of the analysis showed that (1) enrollees of both the HMO and the IPA were more likely to use some mental health care than the fee-for-service population, (2) the fee-for-service population used significantly more services than either the IPA or HMO enrollees, and (3) the estimated per enrollee expenditures for each group were $23 for the fee-for-service plan, $9 for the HMO, and $8 for the IPA. It is important to note that the individuals were not randomized into health plans and therefore the results are subject to selection bias.

The CHAMPUS program experimented with an at-risk PPO during the late 1980s in the Tidewater, Virginia area. This region was known for high costs of mental health care. The demonstration showed significant savings (about 31 percent below expected costs in the absence of the program over several years), stemming largely from reduced inpatient care. In spite of the reported savings, there were clearly areas of considerable waste in expenditures and difficulties in effectively running the program.[63]

The Massachusetts Medicaid program created a carve-out plan for 375,000 enrollees in January 1992 for mental health and substance abuse services (with the exception of state hospital care). In the first year of the program, Medicaid costs were 22 percent below projections based on past experience (taking into account the higher administrative costs of running the carve-out).[64] The managed care vendor (Mental Health Management of America) achieved savings by diverting hospital admissions to outpatient care (particularly for substance abuse care), and by negotiating substantial price reductions with hospitals. Access, as measured by users per enrollee, actually grew slightly in the program's first year. It is also worth noting that to date no evidence has surfaced indicating substantial amounts of cost shifting attributable to the MBHC carve-out plan in Massachusetts. Thus, it appears that the savings reported were not primarily realized by shifting responsibility for individuals with severe mental disorders to the state-funded categorical care system.

Finally, a number of corporations have adopted MBHC arrangements and have reported substantial declines in mental health claims. Although these reports are anecdotal in character and do not take account of factors such as increased use of publicly funded services, they do offer a view that some potential for cost control is present in MBHC. Acceptance of the claims made by anecdotal corporate reports would tend to overestimate the savings that might be found from applying MBHC approaches on a wider scale. The firms most likely to hire MBHC organizations are those with a cost problem in the mental health and substance abuse area. It is therefore unlikely that the same savings could be realized if MBHC organizations were to manage mental health and substance abuse care of other health plans.

Integration and MBHC

A longstanding frustration with the delivery of mental health services is the fragmentation of services. There are discontinuities in the relationship between general health care and mental health care as well as between public and private treatment of mental disorders.[65] The distinction between health care and mental health care is often arbitrary and may be made for reasons of payment or administrative simplicity rather than being motivated by clinical concerns. Many mental health problems are first seen and subsequently treated in the general health care sector.[66–68] Care of mental illnesses in the general health care sector may be most acceptable to certain patients (due to stigma or established patterns of care) and may be more effective if comorbid physical conditions are significant clinical factors.[69] These are the reasons generally cited in support of integration of mental health and general health within health plans.

There are some significant arguments against integration of health care and mental health care. While it is true that a substantial share of mental illness is treated in the general health care sector, important questions arise concerning the quality of that care. A respected body of research exists showing that primary care clinicians often fail to recognize mental illness in their patients. For example, one study showed that nearly 50 percent of depression was not recognized in primary care.[70] Moreover, one experiment showed that, even when clinicians are informed of the presence of psychiatric problems in their patients, they often do not alter their approaches to treatment.[71] Finally, one study of depression reports that in cases in which primary care clinicians recognize illness and attempt to treat the illness they prescribe pharmacotherapies at dosages that are below the demonstrated therapeutic level.[72] For these reasons some advocates for the mentally ill tend to prefer financial and organizational arrangements that encourage referral of the mentally ill to specialized treatment programs.

The second dimension of integration relates to linkages between the public categorical financing system and other public and private insurance systems. We know of no private insurance arrangements that have been organized to span all financing systems. Several states are at various stages of integrating the Medicaid and public mental health system. Integration of public categorical systems and Medicaid begins to address one persistent and vexing problem in mental health policy, that is, the incentives for organizations not to take responsibility for the most severely ill individuals that are created by the presence of multiple competing financing systems. The financial incentives to shift clinical responsibility and costs are accentuated under financial arrangements that place a private organization at risk for gains and losses from care management. Therefore, efforts to integrate and control opportunistic use of often fuzzy system boundaries are very important for protecting the care of individuals with severe mental disorders. Efforts to integrate Medicaid and public mental health systems represent a large step toward eliminating one of the key boundary problems in mental health.

The state of Massachusetts is in the process of integrating all acute care parts of the public mental health system within their Medicaid carve-out program. While this will not completely eliminate the incentive to shift patients across delivery systems, it will set the new boundaries that are defined clinically, thereby eliminating one whole set of cost-shifting opportunities. The state of Ohio, in its Ohio Care plan, will integrate several related behavioral health care systems. These include the public mental health system, Medicaid, and substance abuse care. Long-term and acute care services will all fall under the new behavioral health carve-out system.[73] The state of Iowa has taken a somewhat different approach, in essence by creating financial incentives for the Medicaid carve-out vendor not to exploit the existing boundaries between the mental health financing systems. This is being accomplished by making the MBHC organization in Iowa (Merit Behavioral Health) financially liable for any utilization of public mental hospitals that exceeds historical norms. Each of these states takes a different tack toward dealing with incentives to shift responsibility for care that are potentially heightened under at-risk financial arrangements. The lesson to be gleaned here is that creative measures can be taken by buyers of MBHC services in the design of contracts that serve the public interest.

Carve-Out MBHC programs

Concerns over the ability of generalists to effectively deal with many mental health problems argues for specialization and delineation of clinical roles. One way in which this can be accomplished is by having a "mental health department" within an organized health plan. For example, an integrated HMO such as the Harvard Community Health Plan has a clearly identifiable specialty mental health group within the larger health plan. A more extreme form of specialization is the so-called *specialty carve-out*. A carve-out can be thought of as a distinct health plan that deals with a specialty area such as mental health and substance abuse.[74] Carve-out programs typically have budgets, provider networks, and incentive arrangements that are distinct from the larger plan.

Two main arguments are offered in support of the carve-out concept. The first, which builds on the weaknesses in primary care treatment of mental illness noted earlier, asserts that specialization is very important to the provision of high-quality mental health care. As mentioned previously, however, specialization does not necessarily imply a carve-out. There may nevertheless be important organizational problems with attempting to coordinate the activities of a specialty mental health and substance abuse program within a general health plan. A few industry attempts to accomplish such integration, outside of a limited group of staff model HMOs, have met with both financial and operational difficulties.[75] For this reason, specialization is offered as a direct argument for establishing carve-out programs.

The second argument advanced in favor of a carve-out is that general health care plans currently compete for "good" risks and will have opportunities to do so in the future. The severely mentally ill, because of the high costs of their care and other undesirable qualities, are individuals that health plans have attempted to avoid enrolling.[76] Historically, this has been accomplished via benefit design, that is, offering only limited coverage for mental health care. Under mandated benefit packages (either privately or publicly mandated) managed health care plans can control access to services, and this effectively reduces coverage.[77] This is especially the case for services aimed at treating persistent and severe forms of mental illness and substance abuse. Such services include extended hospital care, case management, and day hospital programs. A specialty mental health carve-out program usually specifies a separate contract for the management and provision of mental health and substance abuse treatment. Thus, a sub-budget is created that identifies a specific level of funding for mental health and substance abuse care. One can view this sub-budget as analogous to a benefit mandate in the indemnity insurance world. The carve-out contract sets a level of expenditure for mental health services that may constrain tendencies to undertreat individuals with mental illness.

Payment systems

The foregoing discussion of the carve-out approach raises concerns associated with the incentives for health plans to avoid the mentally ill by limiting access to services of value to severely mentally ill patients. Capitated payments to health plans strengthen the traditional incentives to minimize services for treatment of severe mental disorders. A small portion of enrollees require very expensive mental health care. Capitated health plans have an incentive to limit use of all services. They have an especially strong incentive to avoid those people who are expensive to treat. Payment arrangements for health plans can be structured, however, to reduce some of the potentially undesirable responses to capitation by MBHC organizations. Specifically, a key set of strategic decisions revolve around defining payment systems that attenuate the so-called selection problem and the related incentive to undertreat individuals with severe mental illnesses (including the shifting of responsibility for their care).

Addressing the selection problem entails aligning expected premium revenues and treatment costs for various types of individuals. If revenues and costs of treating different groups of individuals are closely aligned, there is no economic incentive to avoid a group of potential enrollees. One approach to improving the alignment of revenues and costs is to develop risk-adjusted premiums based on methods of classifying individuals accurately according to their expected future costs. A good deal of research in the general health services field is being devoted to this topic; however, little of the ongoing research focuses on mental health care. Moreover, while the existing system of risk-adjusting premiums based in part on past use has been shown to improve prediction of expenditures over what is possible using only demographic indicators, their success has been quite limited.[78,79]

At present none of these classification systems is capable of dealing adequately with setting capitated prices for mental health care in a competitive environment. Given the experience in developing a classification system to explain inpatient episode costs for prospective payment of mental health and substance abuse care, the prospects are not good for developing a classification system that adequately captures variation in costs of treating mental disorders.[80-82] Even if the selection problem was solved using such an approach, the incentive for undertreatment of a very impaired population would remain (or even increase due to the higher profit potential from the risk-adjusted premium).

A different approach to aligning revenues and expected costs takes aim at both the selection and "undertreatment" problems. Premiums (revenues) can be made to depend partly on predicted costs and partly on actual expenses. Ambulatory Care Groups (ACGs), Diagnostic Cost Groups (DCGs), and Payment Amounts for Capitated Systems (PACS) are based on past utilization but are used to make payments that are fully prospective, based on predicted costs. The portion of the payment that is prospective could be altered to levels below 100 percent with the remainder based on the incurred costs of care. Thus, a plan could receive a fixed premium for mental health care but be eligible for increased revenues if incurred costs exceeded a defined threshold. Similarly, revenues would be taken away if costs fell below a defined lower boundary. This "soft capitation" approach to paying for MBHC decreases the reliance on the classification system to align revenues and expected costs. This course would be wise, given the existing state of the art in classification of mental disorders. It also reduces the ability to profit by reducing services to vulnerable populations, thereby attenuating the undertreatment incentive of "pure" capitation. Of course, reducing incentives to undertreat also reduces incentives to contain costs. Therefore it is critical to find a payment system that mixes the prospective and retrospective components in a manner that will create incentives to economize while limiting profits stemming from undertreatment. This is a fundamental strategic decision for both public and private policymakers.

It is significant to note that a rich variety of payment systems for MBHC carve-out programs are emerging in the private sector. Most offer mixes of prospective and retrospective payment that both limit the financial risks of MBHC organizations and constrain the earnings that stem from reducing care. These payment arrangements are often quite nonlinear, making use of cost and profit targets to define payment levels; these contracts also make very little use of patient classification systems in defining payment levels.

Conclusion

Managed behavioral health care is clearly changing the terms of the debate over benefit design and organization of care. A market test of sorts reveals some key trends. Major corporate health plans and a number of state Medicaid programs are increasingly adopting MBHC carve-out programs. The carve-out approach appears to be receiving the majority of marketplace votes. As such, creation of flexible benefit arrangements within the context of tightly controlled provider networks and application of aggressive utilization review techniques appears to be an increasingly dominant form for organizing and financing mental health care. A strategic decision of the payer (insurer or Medicaid program) is the design of the "soft" capitation payment to the managed care vendor. The choice will affect the vendor's incentives regarding risk selection and provision of treatment.[83]

Carve-out programs, as mentioned, have an aspect that is akin to a mandated benefit. For this reason it is important to develop a notion of what the minimum levels of expenditure are that may result in plans offering "adequate" levels of service to contend with a wide range of mental health needs. The range of expenditures varies dramatically as does the willingness to serve the severely mentally ill. Some observers have noted that carve-out programs result in expenditure levels for mental health care that are roughly twice those found in a traditional HMO.

The original rationale for an insurance mandate was to counteract competitive forces in insurance markets that would tend to limit coverage for individuals with a chronic illness. Selection issues arise anew in the debate about mental health carve-outs and the role of competition in risk bearing. If a carve-out plan (or the wider plan of which it is a part) is in competition with other insuring organizations, specification of the carve-out expenditure target and other regulations of carve-out activity must pay attention to competitive incentives in addition to traditional moral hazard/risk trade-offs. Many private corporations have essentially contracted out their entire mental health coverage to a vendor and, in such cases, competitive issues come up with little force. In other scenarios in which national policy might be involved (such as anything like a managed competition–based policy), selection issues come to the fore, and regulation of the mental health carve-out takes on a new dimension.

Notes

1. J. D. Foley, "Sources of Health Insurance and Characteristics of the Uninsured: Analysis of the March 1992 Current Population Survey," SR-16 Issue Brief No. 133 (Washington, DC: Employee Benefit Research Institute, 1993).
2. G. Strickler, A. Tumlinson, and M. Cohen, "Insurance Status of Individuals with Serious Mental Illness and Chronic Physical Impairments," Working Paper (Waltham, MA: Institute for Health Policy, Heller Graduate School, Brandeis University, January 1995).
3. U.S. Congress. House Committee on Ways and Means, *1994 Green Book: Overview of Entitlement Programs*. U.S. House of Representatives (Washington, DC: U.S. Government Printing Office, 15 July 1994).
4. Social Security Administration (SSA), *Annual Statistical Supplement, 1994* (Washington, DC: U.S. Government Printing Office, August 1994).
5. SSA 1994.
6. W. G. Manning, A. Leibowitz, G. A. Goldberg, W. H. Rogers, and J. P. Newhouse, "A Controlled Trial Of the Effect of a Prepaid Group Practice on Use of Services," *The New England Journal of Medicine* 310, no. 23 (June 1984): 1505–10.
7. H. L. Batten, S. Bachman, M. Drainoni, G. Strickler, and K. Watson, *State*

   Experiences with Medicaid Managed Care for the SSI–Disabled Population,
   (Washington, DC: HCFA Final Report), 1995.
 8. N. McCall, C. W. Rightson, L. Paringer, and G. Trapnell, Managed Medicaid Cost Savings: The Arizona Experience. Health Policy Research Series. Discussion Paper #94-1 (January 1994).
 9. Strickler et al. 1995.
10. Batten et al. 1995.
11. A. I. Batavia, "Health Care Reform and People with Disabilities," *Health
   Affairs* 12 (Spring 1993): 40–57.
12. B. Griss, "Strategies for Adapting the Private and Public Health Insurance Systems to the Health Related Needs of Persons with Disabilities or
   Chronic Illness." *Access to Health Care* 1 (Berkeley, CA: World Institute on
   Disability), 3–4.
13. R. J. Master, C. Tobias, and R. Kronick, "Medicaid Working Group Update" (January 1995).
14. H. B. Fox and M. A. McManus, "Medicaid Managed Care Arrangements
   and Their Impact on Children and Adolescents: A Briefing Report"
   (Washington, DC: Fox Health Policy Consultants, 1992).
15. D. A. Freund and E. M. Lewit, "Managed Care for Children and Pregnant Women: Promises and Pitfalls," *The Future of Children* 3, no. 2
   (1993): 92–122.
16. P. W. Newacheck and W. Taylor, "Prevalence and Impact of Childhood
   Chronic Conditions," *American Journal of Public Health* 82, no. 3 (1992):
   364–71.
17. N. Zill and C. A. Schoenborn. "Developmental, Learning, and Emotional
   Problems: Health of Our Nation's Children, United States, 1988," *Advance Data: Vital and Health Statistics of the National Center for Health Statistics*
   190 (November 1990): 16.
18. P. W. Newacheck, "State Estimates of the Prevalence of Chronic Conditions among Children and Youth" (San Francisco: Institute for Health
   Policy Studies, University of California, 1991).
19. P. W. Newacheck, P. P. Budetti, and N. Halfon. "Trends in Activity-
   Limiting Chronic Conditions among Children," *American Journal of Public
   Health* 76, no. 2 (1986): 178–84.
20. D. Cadman, M. Boyle, P. Szatmari, and D. R. Offord. "Chronic Illness,
   Disability, and Mental and Social Well-Being: Findings of the Ontario
   Child Health Study," *Pediatrics* 79, no. 5 (1987): 805–12.
21. N. Hobbs and J. M. Perrin, eds., *Issues in the Care of Children with Chronic
   Illness* (San Francisco: Jossey-Bass Publishers, 1985).
22. P. W. Newacheck and M. A. McManus, "Financing Health Care for Disabled Children," *Pediatrics* 81, no. 3 (1988): 385–94.
23. I. B. Pless and P. Pinkerton. *Chronic Childhood Disorder: Promoting Patterns
   of Adjustment* (London: Henry Kimpton Publishers, 1975).
24. M. A. Teitelbaum, "The Health Insurance Crisis for America's Children"
   (Washington, DC: Children's Defense Fund, 1994).
25. H. B. Fox, L. B. Wicks, and P. W. Newacheck, "Health Maintenance Or-

ganizations and Children with Special Health Needs: A Suitable Match?" *American Journal of Diseases of Children* 147 (May 1993a): 546–52.

26. H. B. Fox and P. W. Newacheck, "Private Health Insurance of Chronically Ill Children," *Pediatrics* 85, no. 1 (1990): 50–57.

27. H. B. Fox, L. B. Wicks, and P. W. Newacheck, "State Medicaid Health Maintenance Organization Policies and Special Needs Children," *Health Care Financing Review* 15, no. 1 (1993b): 25–37.

28. H. B. Fox and L. B. Wicks, "State Implementation of the OBRA '89 EPSDT Amendments within Medicaid Managed Care Arrangements" (Washington, DC: Fox Health Policy Consultants, Inc., 1993b).

29. H. B. Fox, L. B. Wicks, R. W. Kelly, and A. Greaney, "An Examination of HMO Policies Affecting Children with Special Needs" (Washington, DC: Fox Health Policy Consultants, Inc., 1990).

30. H. B. Fox and L. B. Wicks, "State Efforts to Maintain a Role for Publicly Funded Providers in a Medicaid Managed Care Environment" (Washington, DC: Fox Health Policy Consultants, Inc., 1993a).

31. H. B. Fox and M. A. McManus, "Preliminary Analysis of Issues and Options in Serving Children with Chronic Conditions through Medicaid Managed Care Plans," Speech delivered at a meeting of the National Academy for State Health Policy (Portland, ME, 15 August 1994).

32. Fox and McManus 1994.

33. Fox and McManus 1994.

34. P. W. Newacheck, D. C. Hughes, J. J. Stoddard, and N. Halfon, "Children with Chronic Illness and Medicaid Managed Care," *Pediatrics* 93, no. 3 (1994): 497–500.

35. Fox and McManus 1992.

36. M. Regenstein, J. A. Meyer, H. B. Fox, M. A. McManus, T. Riley, and K. McGaughey, "Challenges for Decisionmakers: How Managed Competition Could Affect Children with Special Health Care Needs" (Portland, ME: National Academy for State Health Policy, 1994).

37. G. Andersen, "Importance of Risk Adjustors to Children and Children's Hospitals" (Baltimore, MD: The Center for Hospital Finance and Management, Johns Hopkins University, 1993).

38. Andersen 1993.

39. J. P. Weiner, B. H. Starfield, and R. N. Lieberman, "Johns Hopkins Ambulatory Care Groups (ACGs): A Case-Mix System for UR, QA, and Capitation Adjustment," *HMO Practice* 6, no. 1 (1992): 13–19.

40. A. J. Kahn and S. B. Kamerman. "Integrating Services Integration: An Overview of Initiatives, Issues and Possibilities" (New York: National Center for Children in Poverty, 1992).

41. S. D. Robison, *Putting the Pieces Together: Survey of State Systems for Children in Crisis* (Denver, CO: National Conference of State Legislatures, 1990).

42. N. Hobbs, J. M. Perrin, and H. T. Ireys. *Chronically Ill Children and Their Families* (San Francisco, CA: Jossey-Bass Publishers, 1985).

43. R. G. Frank and T. G. McGuire, "An Introduction to the Economy of

Mental Health Payment Systems," in *Mental Health Services: A Public Health Perspective,* edited by B. Levin and R. Petrilla (Oxford: Oxford University Press, 1995).

44. This problem stems in part from growth in utilization and costs of mental health care. It also is in part due to efforts by states to shift the costs of public health care onto public budgets. Perhaps the most dramatic example of such practice has been the disproportionate-share provisions of the Medicaid program that have paid for substantial parts of state mental hospital systems in certain states that have been especially astute in maximizing federal subsidies.

45. J. Hamilton and M. Galen, "A Furor over Mental Health," *Business Week* (8 August 1994): 66–69.

46. J. B. Christianson et al., "Mandatory Enrollment of Medicaid Eligible Mentally Ill in Prepaid Plans: The Minnesota Demonstration Project." *Administration and Policy in Mental Health,* 1989.

47. R. C. Kessler, K. A. McGonagle, S. Zhao, C. B. Nelsen, M. Hughes, S. Eshleman, H.-U. Wittchen, and K. S. Kendler, "Lifetime and 12-Month Prevalence of DSM III-R Psychiatric Disorders in the United States," *Archives of General Psychiatry* 51, no. 1 (1994): 8–19.

48. The data presented in this section come from the National Comorbidity Survey (NCS). The basic results on prevalence from that study are reported in Kessler et al. 1994.

49. Health care providers are defined as hospitals, outpatient clinics, office-based professionals such as physicians, nurses, psychologists, social workers and counselors, and substance abuse clinics.

50. For a detailed discussion of how these estimates were constructed, see Frank et al. 1994.

51. B. S. Arons, R. G. Frank, H. H. Goldman, T. G. McGuire, and S. Stephens, "Mental Health and Substance Abuse Coverage under National Health Reform," *Health Affairs* 13, no. 1 (1994): 192–205.

52. See, for example, T. G. McGuire, "Predicting the Cost of Mental Health Benefits," *Milbank Quarterly* 72, no. 1 (1994): 3–23.

53. M. Oss, *Open Minds,* 1994.

54. Risk-based networks make use of some financial incentives on providers; non-risk-based networks are networks that limit membership and involve contractual relationships that may adhere to managed care rules and performance standards.

55. Congressional Budget Office, *Managed Competition and its Potential to Reduce Health Spending* (Washington, DC: CBO, 1993).

56. Hamilton and Galen 1994.

57. R. Geraty, J. Bartlett, E. Hill, et al., "The Impact of Managed Behavioral Healthcare on the Costs of Psychiatric and Chemical Dependency Treatment" (American Managed Behavioral Healthcare Association, 1994).

58. D. Hodgkin, "The Impact of Private Utilization Management of Psychiatric Care: A Review of the Literature." *Journal of Mental Health Administration* 19, no. 2 (1992): 143–57.

59. W. G. Manning, K. B. Wells, and B. Benjamin, *Use of Outpatient Mental*

Health Care: Trial of a Prepaid Group Practice versus Fee for Services, RAND Report R-3277 (Bethesda, MD: National Institute of Mental Health, 1986).

60. P. Diehr, S. J. Williams, D. P. Martin, and K. Price, "Ambulatory Mental Health Services Utilization in Three Provider Plans," *Medical Care* 22, no. 1 (1984): 1–13.

61. Manning et al. 1986.

62. Diehr et al. 1984.

63. G. Coulam and J. Smith, *Evaluation of the CPA-Norfolk Demonstration: Final Report,* Department of Defense Contract MDA 907-87-C-0003 (Cambridge, MA: Abt Associates, 1990).

64. J. Callahan et al., "Evaluation of the Massachusetts Medicaid Mental Health/Substance Abuse Program" (Waltham, MA: Brandeis University, 1994).

65. There are two dimensions of the public-private distinction. One relates to the economic status of individuals, where those with insurance are generally cared for in the private sector and the medically indigent are treated by public providers. A second central issue in the public-private distinction relates to long-term versus acute care. Relatively little long-term mental health care is paid for by insurance and it is thus primarily a public responsibility.

66. D. A. Regier et al. (1993) using data from the ECA study estimate that roughly 50 percent of all mental health care is delivered by the general health sector. (See Note 68.) The NCS reports similar levels of utilization in the general health sector.

67. Kessler et al. 1994.

68. D. A. Regier, W. E. Narrow, D. S. Rae, R. W. Manderscheid, B. Z. Locke, and F. K. Goodwin, "The DeFacto U.S. Mental and Addictive Disorders Service System," *Archives of General Psychiatry* 50, no. 1 (1993): 85–94.

69. D. Mechanic, "Integrating Mental Health into a General Health Care System," *Hospital and Community Psychiatry* 45, no. 9 (1994): 893–97.

70. K. B. Wells, R. D. Hays, A. Burnam, W. Rogers, S. Greenfield, and J. E. Ware, "Detection of Depressive Disorder for Patients Receiving Prepaid or Fee-for-Service Care," *Journal of the American Medical Association* 262, no. 23 (1989): 3298–3302.

71. S. Shapiro, P. S. German, E. A. Skinner, M. VonKorff, R. W. Turner, L. E. Klein, M. L. Teidelbaum, M. Kramer, J. D. Burke, and B. J. Burns, "An Experiment to Change Detection and Management of Mental Morbidity in Primary Care," *Medical Care* 25, no. 4 (1985): 327–39.

72. M. B. Keller, G. L. Klerman, P. W. Lavori, J. A. Fawcett, W. Coryell, and J. Endicott, "Treatment Received by Depressed Patients," *Journal of the American Medical Association* 248, no. 15 (1982): 1848–56.

73. For the integration strategies being taken in Massachusetts and Ohio, a number of technical problems need to be solved vis-à-vis the method of paying vendors. Integration serves to combine the Medicaid population, which has a defined denominator population, with the categorical care system, which has no clear denominator population. Thus, making capi-

tation payments to all will be difficult, at least in the short term. Several possible solutions are possible. They include setting prospective budgets, creating pseudo denominators for the categorical population, and using a mix of budgets and capitation.

74. Other services such as disability and long-term care are dealt with in similar ways.

75. This point has been made in several interviews with individuals within and close to the MBHC industry.

76. M. Schlesinger and D. Mechanic, "Challenges for Managed Competition from Chronic Illness," *Health Affairs* 12 (1993 Supplement): 123–37.

77. Schlesinger and Mechanic 1993.

78. J. P. Newhouse, "Patients at Risk: Health Reform and Risk Adjustment," *Health Affairs* 13, no. 1 (1994): 132–46.

79. The Ambulatory Care Groups (ACGs), the Diagnostic Cost Groups (DCGs), and the Payment Amount for Capitated Systems (PACS) have all been evaluated compared to demographic predictors. These systems have only minimal mental health content. On ACGs, see J. P. Weiner, B. H. Starfield, D. M. Steinwachs, and L. M. Mumford, "Development and Application of a Population-Oriented Measure of Ambulatory Case-Mix," *Medical Care* 29, no. 5 (1991): 452–72. On DCGs, see A. Ash, F. Porelli, L. Gruenberg, E. Sawitz, and A. Beiser, "Adjusting Medicare Capitation Payments using Prior Hospitalization Data," *Health Care Financing Review* 10, no. 4 (Summer 1989): 17–30. On PACS, see G. F. Anderson, E. P. Steinberg, N. R. Powe, S. Antebi, J. Whittle, S. Horn, and R. Herbert, "Setting Payment Rates for Capitated Systems: A Comparison of Various Alternatives," *Inquiry* 27 (Fall 1990): 225–233.

80. R. G. Frank and J. R. Lave, "The Psychiatric DRGs: Are They Different?" *Medical Care* 23, no. 8 (1985).

81. T. G. McGuire, B. Dickey, G. E. Shively, and I. Strumwasser, "DRGs and Private Insurance Implications for Design of Prospective Payment Systems," *American Journal of Psychiatry* 144, no. 5 (1987): 616–20.

82. C. M. Horgan and S. Jencks, "Research on Psychiatric Classification and Payment Systems," *Medical Care* 25, no. 9 (1987): 522–36.

83. The MBHC industry is engaged in a very active debate concerning the limits of capitation for MBHC carve-out programs.

Index

List of Contributors

Helen J. Levine, Ph.D., is an Associate Research Professor at the Institute for Health Policy, the Florence Heller Graduate School, Brandeis University. She is currently principal investigator of a study sponsored by the Social Security Administration comparing the social networks of disabled applicants and nonapplicants to SSA disability programs. She was principal investigator of the 1990 Drug Services Research Survey and was co-principal investigator and project director of the 1995 Alcohol and Drug Services Study sponsored by the Substance Abuse and Mental Health Administration.

Dennis F. Beatrice is Director of Policy and Implementation Studies and Human Services Management Professor in the Institute for Health Policy at the Florence Heller Graduate School, Brandeis University. He also serves as Senior Advisor and Program Director with the Henry J. Kaiser Family Foundation. As Vice President at the Kaiser Family Foundation, he directed efforts to help set new directions in major public programs in health services. He has also overseen grantmaking at the Pew Charitable Trusts in the areas of health care policy and reform and programs for vulnerable populations.

Robert A. Berenson, M.D., F.A.C.P., is a board-certified internist in private group practice in Washington, DC. He recently worked on malpractice reform and the structure and function of accountable health plans as a member of the Clinton White House Task Force on Health Reform. He is National Program Director of the IMPACS (Improving Malpractice Prevention and Compensation Systems) program, funded by the Robert Wood Johnson Foundation, and is currently on the Health and Public Policy Committee of the American College of Physicians. In that capacity he helped write the ACP position on health care reform.

Deborah J. Chollet, Ph.D., is Associate Director of the Alpha Center in Washington, DC, where she directs a technical support team for the Robert Wood Johnson Foundation's grants to states involved in major health care financing reform. Earlier, she directed the Center for Risk Management and Insurance Research at Georgia State University where she also served as Associate Professor of Risk Management and Insurance. Dr. Chollet has also served as Executive Director of the Advisory Council on Social Security and as a Senior Researcher at the National Center for Health Services Research (DHHS).

Arnold M. Epstein, M.D., M.A., is a practicing general internist on the faculty of Harvard Medical School, where he is Professor of Medicine and Health Care Policy and Chief of the Section on Health Services and Policy Research in the Brigham and Women's Hospital. During 1993–1994, he served as Senior Policy Advisor to the White House for health care with a particular emphasis on quality management and other delivery system issues. Dr. Epstein has written extensively on issues combining elements of the social sciences and clinical medicine, including access to care for disadvantaged populations and quality of care.

Harriette B. Fox, M.S.S., is President of Fox Health Policy Consultants, specializing in the financing and delivery of maternal and child health services. She has managed federal and state projects analyzing Medicaid, private health insurance, and other financing options to support coordinated service delivery systems for children with special physical, mental health, or developmental problems. With Margaret A. McManus and Paul W. Newacheck, she codirects the Maternal and Child Health Policy Research Center, federally funded to examine state and national health care reforms affecting children with chronic illness.

Richard G. Frank, Ph.D., is a Professor in the Department of Health Care Policy at Harvard University and a Research Associate with the National Bureau of Economic Research. His primary work is in the economics of health and mental health, with an ongoing interest in the financing of health services for vulnerable populations. In 1993, he was awarded the Georgescu-Roegen prize from the Southern Economic Association for his joint work (with David Salkever) on drug pricing. Professor Frank has served as a commissioner on the Maryland Health Services Cost Review Commission and as a staff member of the President's Task Force on Health Reform.

Annetine C. Gelijns, J.D., L.L.M., Ph.D., is Director of the International Center on Health Outcomes and Innovation Research, and Assistant Professor in the Department of Surgery and School of Public Health, Columbia University. Her research focuses on the rate and direction of innovative activity in medicine, relation of technological change to health care costs, and surgical outcomes measurement. Earlier she directed the Program on Technological Innovation in Medicine at the Institute of Medicine, National Academy of Sciences. She has been a consultant to various national and international organizations.

Clifford S. Goodman, Ph.D., is a Senior Manager at the Lewin Group, a health care policy and management consulting firm in Fairfax, Virginia. His work as an international consultant has involved technology assessment methods, specific technological diagnosis and treatment, management of hypertension, biomedical engineering, medical informatics, and technical innovation. Dr. Goodman is a board member of the International Society for Technology Assessment in Health Care (ISTAHC) and of the Health Care Technology Assessment Division of the International Federation for Medical and Biological Engineering (IFMBE).

Douglas A. Hastings, a member of the American Academy of Hospital Attorneys and the American Bar Association, serves on the board of directors and executive committee of the National Health Lawyers Association where, as Program Chair of the Managed Care Law Institute, he works with physicians, hospitals, and managed care companies in establishing physician-hospital organizations, managed service organizations, managed care networks, medical groups, and other integrated health care delivery systems. Mr. Hastings speaks and publishes regularly on health care law, integrated delivery systems, and managed care.

Kathleen E. Hull, M.A., is a doctoral graduate student in the Department of Organization Behavior, J. L. Kellogg School of Management, and the Department of Sociology at Northwestern University. She previously held policy, research, and administrative positions in health care associations, including the American Hospital Association and the American College of Healthcare Executives. Her previous graduate work includes master's degrees from the University of Chicago in social service administration and the University of Michigan in English. She received her bachelor of arts degree from Princeton.

David A. Kindig, M.D., Ph.D., is Professor of Preventive Medicine and Director of the Wisconsin Network for Health Policy Research (a university-sponsored program to build a Wisconsin health services research community and to conduct policy analysis of relevance to the state) at the University of Wisconsin-Madison, School of Medicine. He is currently Chair of the federal Council of Graduate Medical Education, on the board of directors of the Association of University Programs in Health Administration (AUPHA), and on the Board of AHSR. Dr. Kindig has written extensively on both medical and health policy issues.

William G. Kopit, J.D., specializes in antitrust, managed care, and policy litigation. He is a member of the Bar in New York, the District of Columbia, the Supreme Court, and the U.S. Court of Appeals for the District of Columbia Circuit and the Federal Circuit, as well as seven circuit courts. Mr. Kopit has litigated several important recent health care cases, including two Supreme Court cases: *North Carolina v. Califano,* which upheld the constitutionality of federal health planning legislation, and *AHA v. Bowen,* the "Baby Doe" case, which invalidated government regulations involving seriously ill newborns.

Thomas G. McGuire, Ph.D., Professor of Economics at Boston University, is currently recipient of two sequential five-year Research Scientist Awards from the National Institute of Mental Health to study payment and financing of mental health services. He is also a recipient of an Investigator Award in Health Policy from the Robert Wood Johnson Foundation (joint with Richard Frank) to study reform of the organization and financing of programs in mental health and substance abuse. He received the Carl Taube Award for outstanding contributions to mental health services research from the American Public Health Association in 1991.

Margaret A. McManus, M.H.S., is President of McManus Health Policy, Inc., a Washington-based consulting firm that specializes in health care financing and delivery issues affecting children. With Harriette B. Fox and Paul W. Newacheck, she codirects the Maternal and Child Health Policy Research Center to examine state and national health care reforms affecting children with chronic illness. Ms. McManus has consulted with the American Academy of Pediatrics for the past ten years on a range of health care financing issues. She is currently focusing on ongoing studies of managed care financing and children.

Marilyn Moon, Ph.D., is a Health Economist with the Health Policy Center of the Urban Institute. Previously she served as Director of the Public Policy Institute of the American Association of Retired Persons. She has also been a Senior Analyst at the Congressional Budget Office, a consultant to the U.S. Bipartisan Commission for Comprehensive Health Care (the Pepper Commission), and an informal advisor to the Clinton campaign and health care transition team. Dr. Moon's current work focuses on health care system reform and financing. She writes an occasional column for *The Washington Post* on health care coverage issues.

Paul W. Newacheck, Dr.P.H., is Professor of Health Policy and Pediatrics at the Institute for Health Policy Studies and the Department of Pediatrics at the University of California, San Francisco. With Harriette B. Fox and Margaret A. McManus, he codirects the Maternal and Child Health Policy Research Center. His focus is on health care delivery to children with multiple needs, including chronically ill and impoverished children, and he provided related analytical assistance to national health care reform efforts. Dr. Newacheck serves on the Board on Children and Families for the Institute of Medicine.

Stephen M. Shortell, Ph.D., is the A. C. Buehler Distinguished Professor of Health Services Management and Professor of Organization Behavior in the Department of Organization Behavior at the J. L. Kellogg Graduate School of Management and the Center for Health Services and Policy Research at Northwestern University. His current research analyzes vertically integrated health systems and the impact of new approaches to quality improvement. He has received many awards for his published studies. He is a past president of AHSR and FHSR, and an elected member of the Institute of Medicine of the National Academy of Sciences.

Stanley S. Wallack, Ph.D., is Director of the Institute for Health Policy, which he founded in 1978, at Brandeis University. He is also Chairman of the Board and CEO of LifePlans, Inc., a long-term care risk management company and Chairman of the Coalition for Long Term Care Reform. Much of Dr. Wallack's research has focused on reimbursement systems and organization for acute and chronic health care. He developed the concept of the social/health maintenance organization and is currently developing Medicare voluntary volume performance standards for physician groups and a capitated program for end-stage renal dialysis patients.

About the Editors

Stuart H. Altman, Ph.D., is the Sol C. Chaikin Professor of National Health Policy at the Florence Heller Graduate School for Social Policy, Brandeis University. He is an economist with research interests primarily in the area of federal health policy. Professor Altman was dean of the Florence Heller Graduate School from 1977 until July 1993. He is currently chairman of the Prospective Payment Assessment Commission responsible for advising Congress and the Administration on the Medicare DRG Hospital Payment System and other system reforms. He is a member of the Institute of Medicine of the National Academy of Sciences, a member of the Board of Trustees of Beth Israel Hospital in Boston, and Chairman of the Board of the Institute for Health Policy at Brandeis University.

Uwe E. Reinhardt, Ph.D., is the James Madison Professor of Political Economy at Princeton University. His research interests, primarily in health economics and policy, have led to membership on several national commissions and to frequent appearances as a commentator on national health policy issues. An elected member of the Institute of Medicine of the National Academy of Sciences, he currently serves on the IOM's Committee on Technical Innovation. Professor Reinhardt is a past president of AHSR and FHSR, and is a member of numerous editorial boards. He is currently serving his third three-year appointment to the Physician Payment Review Commission established by the Congress as an advisory body on issues related to the payment of physicians.